MULTI-AGE AND MORE

MULTI-AGE AND MORE

COLLEEN POLITANO

•

ANNE DAVIES

PEGUIS PUBLISHERS
WINNIPEG • CANADA

Printed and bound in Canada by Hignell Printing Limited

94 95 96 97 98 5 4 3 2

Canadian Cataloguing in Publication Data

Politano, Colleen, 1946–

    Multi-age and more

    (Building connections)
    ISBN 1-895411-65-3

1. Nongraded schools. 2. Classroom utilization.
3. Classroom management. 4. Education – Experimental methods. I. Davies, Anne, 1955– II. Title.
III. Series.

LB1029.N6P64   1994   371.2'54   C94-920041-7

Book and Cover Design: Laura Ayers

Peguis Publishers Limited
318 McDermot Avenue
Winnipeg, Manitoba
Canada R3A 0A2

We both come from large families with a wide range of ages, interests, and abilities among the siblings, and yet our parents were able to give us what we'd wish for every child in every classroom—the feeling that each of us was special and appreciated for our unique talents and contributions. We dedicate this book to our parents, Janet and George Best and Patricia and Gwilliam Davies.

CONTENTS

FOREWORD

MAKING YOUR EIFFEL TOWER STURDIER

The first multi-age classroom I ever visited was Stephens Elementary Children's School in Columbia, Missouri. The teacher was Kittye Copeland. Kittye told the story of two adults visiting her classroom overhearing a conversation between two children:

"I think that if you move that brace back at least an inch, your Eiffel Tower will be sturdier," suggested Tara. Without hesitation, Lara takes the suggestion, which does the job. The adults observing comment, "How wonderful it is to have older children guide younger ones." Kittye smiles; you see, Tara is nine and Lara is twelve.

Along with Anne Davies, Colleen Politano, and a growing number of progressive educators like Kittye Copeland, I question the notion that education is best done "by litter." The policy of herding and keeping children together just because they happen to be nine years of age seems questionable indeed.

Anne Davies and Colleen Politano argue that multi-age classrooms personify education at its best in that they represent:

- ☞ collaborative classrooms where communities of readers and writers work together to make and share meaning regardless of age;

- ☞ noncompetitive classrooms where learning is the real focus of schooling;

- ☞ authentic learning environments, which truly respect children, their interests, and concerns.

The authors present teachers with ideas that not only help children articulate their beliefs by engaging them in activities that allow them to tap what they intuitively know, but also show how to operationalize these beliefs into classroom practice. I found their chapters on creating communities of learners and the use of physical space, materials and supplies especially helpful, probably because I am working with a group of teachers in setting up a multi-age school and these are the areas in which we are making decisions. Other readers will love their ideas on how to handle assessment, encourage multiple ways of knowing, and communicate effectively with parents.

I recently conducted a library search for materials on multi-age classrooms. Interestingly, there were few things available. Given the school restructuring movement that is afoot in the United States and Canada, as well as the current interest in multi-age classrooms, I found this surprising.

The good news, then, is that books such as *Multi-Age and More* will be in much demand. Here are two teachers who are out ahead of the pack. They have not only embraced the idea, but figured out how to make it work in their classrooms.

I asked the kids in Kittye Copeland's classroom what they saw as the benefits of being in a multi-age classroom. Here are some of their responses:

It gives me real reasons to read to other children.

You don't have to worry about what you play with. I'm eleven but still love toy cars, so I have an excuse when I'm helping the little kids.

The bigger kids give me more grown-up words when they help me revise my stories.

A foreword is supposed to set things in historical context. This is why I see the Eiffel Tower story as a metaphor for what this book is all about. Multi-age grouping is not just a fad. It is a way of making the whole educational tower sturdier. Like this book, multi-age classrooms allow us to worry about new things and give us real reasons to forge educationally ahead.

Jerome Harste
1994

ACKNOWLEDGMENTS

Special thanks to Annalee Greenberg, our editor at Peguis, Caren Cameron, Marilyn Chapman, Marlene Dergousoff, and Leon Politano, our good friends and colleagues whose inspiration, additions, and subtractions helped us refine our manuscript. Many people enriched this book by contributing samples or ideas as well as by sharing their stories. We have tried to acknowledge them appropriately in the text. It is through such connections that we can all build the kinds of classrooms that make living and learning both joyous and worthwhile.

We are grateful to the members of the Wishart and Tsolum Elementary school staffs who created the kind of community that allowed us to be learners. In particular, we want to express our appreciation to Jennifer Davidson and Marina Mahabir, our teaching partners, whose willingness to share their ideas and support us while we tried out ours shaped the experiences we share in this book.

INTRODUCTION

As our world becomes more diverse socially, culturally, and economically, there are growing expectations that the individual's differences and rights be recognized, respected, and responded to in positive ways—from wheelchair accessibility to legislation regarding non-discriminatory hiring practices to the ever-increasing numbers of women in the workplace.

As we come to value the diversity in our general population more, there are growing expectations—both moral and legal—that this be mirrored by and in our schools. As educators, our task is to find ways to value, respect, and respond to the diversity that occurs among students in classrooms, leading to more effective, exciting, and enabling learning environments for students and teachers.

The traditional structure of grades assumes that students are more similar than different, that curriculum can be packaged into discrete chunks, and that each chunk is substantively different. In responding to diversity we have come to realize that the structure of grades may be countering our efforts to meet the range of educational needs among children. It is important, therefore, that we seek new structures that will assist us in planning for children's unique talents and abilities.

WHO IS THIS BOOK FOR?

Multi-Age and More is for teachers who are trying to make sense of the many changes taking place in education today. There are many ways that multi-age classes enhance learning for students. This book can serve as a starting point for (1) teachers who are considering teaching in a multi-age classroom for the first time; (2) teachers in single-age classrooms who are striving to meet the challenges of a wide range of skills, abilities, and interests among students; and (3) those who have been teaching in multi-age classrooms and want to expand their repertoire of strategies for developing and working with a wide range of students.

This book includes

- ☞ effective ways to plan and organize for multi-age classes
- ☞ ways for students to represent their thinking and show what they know

- ☛ successful classroom strategies for making assessment and evaluation an integral part of learning and teaching
- ☛ ideas practicing teachers have used to organize time and space
- ☛ possibilities for meeting diverse needs of students in terms of physical space, materials, and supplies
- ☛ strategies for organizing curriculum experiences to ensure successful learning and teaching
- ☛ ideas for designing instruction to meet the needs of students
- ☛ ways to work successfully with others—parents, colleagues, and school administrators

In this book we share many ideas that have worked for us in our multi-age classrooms. We invite you to take only the ideas and thoughts that make sense for you and your students. We encourage those of you just beginning multi-age teaching to trust yourselves and keep those parts of your practice that work—with slight modifications they will work in a multi-age classroom just as well. To make your experiences more positive and to provide support and confirmation for those many things you already do successfully, we share some of ours. There are many right ways to teach and learn. This book is an invitation to recognize the expert within each of us.

ARTICULATING OUR BELIEFS

WHAT IS A MULTI-AGE CLASS?

We define a multi-age class as a class composed of children of different ages intentionally grouped for learning. Multi-age classes are more than just a way of organizing, however. They are a reflection of our understanding of how children learn and of how teachers can provide effective learning environments.

We create multi-age classes because we know that this structure supports the task of schooling, encouraging children to fulfil their potential as active, independent, self-regulating individuals. Teachers in multi-age classes, supported by an understanding of research in the areas of learning theory and child development, apply their knowledge of the curriculum to ensure that each child's learning is supported by and is supportive of others.

WHY HAVE MULTI-AGE CLASSES?

Multi-age classes give each child an opportunity to associate and work with others on the basis of skills, abilities, interests, personality, and age. Multi-age classrooms provide children with greater opportunities for a wider range of relationships and social experiences and therefore promote development of their social skills and cooperative behaviors. The varied levels of social and emotional development found among children of different ages mean they can be both supported by and supportive of one another.

When the age range among a group of children is increased so is the range of development. Children begin to see themselves and others more realistically as they come to appreciate the diversity of talents, skills, and abilities of their classmates. This leads children to use more appropriate and varied criteria than just age as a basis for building relationships and learning from one another.

Multi-age classes take the focus off meeting the needs of a group of children and instead challenge the teacher to meet the needs of individual learners.

Multi-age classes are sometimes called family groupings. Just as a family gains strength from the range of talents and interests of its members, the multi-age class is enriched by the diversity of the class members.

Multi-age classes encourage intentionally diverse communities of learners in which differences in individual strengths, needs, and learning styles complement rather than divide. Multi-age classes are more likely to reflect the range of social situations in which individuals will find themselves throughout their lifetime.

Multi-age classes increase a school's ability to place each child in the most positive learning environment possible because of an increased range of possible classroom organizations. Having multi-age classes does not mean that single-age classes are no longer an option at the school level. Schools meet the greatest range of student needs when they offer choices to students, parents, and teachers.

Why would a multi-age class be the choice for you?

WHAT DO WE BELIEVE ABOUT LEARNING AND LEARNERS?

When teachers describe their successes, the same words and phrases come up again and again. When classroom experiences are successful, they say, their children are

- building on what they already know
- feeling good about themselves and their work
- making some choices
- showing what they know in different ways
- feeling a sense of accomplishment
- working together and by themselves
- knowing that what they say is valued by their teachers and their classmates
- finding out that they can learn from others and that others can learn from them
- learning that they have something to offer others
- seeing teachers as learners
- having fun learning
- excited about sharing what they are doing with others
- talking about what they are doing and how they are doing it

Current research describing how children learn parallels teachers' descriptions of successful learning experiences. Based on what teachers are saying about their successes and what the researchers are reporting about their findings, effective learning takes place when students

- 👉 want to learn and need to learn
- 👉 realize what they have learned
- 👉 enjoy what they are doing
- 👉 can relate what they are doing to their total experience
- 👉 are able to take risks
- 👉 feel a sense of support
- 👉 talk about their new knowledge with others
- 👉 feel good about themselves
- 👉 have opportunities to work with others
- 👉 get to make some decisions
- 👉 have a chance to touch, smell, see, hear, feel, think

These views about learning apply, whether talking about children learning to read or write, learning math, learning science, or learning about their world. Learning is not dependent upon age or what is being learned—learners are learners are learners.

All teachers have beliefs about learners and learning. When teachers can articulate their beliefs clearly, they are able to screen every element of their practice by asking whether or not their practices are in alignment with their beliefs.

DO MULTI-AGE CLASSES PROMOTE LEARNING?

Yes. The major purpose of multi-age classes is to promote learning. Multi-age classes provide many opportunities for learning that is relevant, connected, fun, and purposeful, allows choice, and makes connections with the world in which our students live. The range of ages offers depth and texture; the learning has more spark and energy. Multi-age classes work best when we consider all the needs of our children and let the differences among us invite new learning.

All multi-age classes benefit from the diversity of experiences, abilities, and interests contributed by the members, benefits compounded by the increased range of ages. Unlike same-age classes, where children view their successes by how well they compare to their age mates, multi-age classes provide environments that focus on personal progress, not comparisons.

Relevance is important because all people learn when it has meaning for them.

Learning becomes relevant when it is based on children's interests, needs, and abilities. Learning increases in relevance when children are involved in tasks that have purpose beyond the classroom or have a clear understanding of why they are being asked to do a particular activity.

Connections are important because learning is more lasting and significant when we can integrate what we are learning with what we already know.

Identifying and inviting connections between children and topics, between children and children, between classes and classes, between the school and the community, between old knowledge and new knowledge, and between process and content, increase the opportunities for learning. The shared experience of constructing knowledge gives learners opportunities not only to connect with each other but to connect their own knowledge in ways that are lasting and meaningful for them. The greater the range of ages in a multi-age class, the greater the possibilities for these connections.

Fun is essential. When learning is joyful, people think of it with pleasure and want to learn more and more.

Feeling a sense of accomplishment, realizing that you discovered something you didn't know before, and finding out that you can learn from others and others can learn from you can be fun. Having a shared purpose and learning from each other is joyful. Multi-age classrooms stimulate conversations that lead to more learning. Effective learning communities are broad-based. The fun of learning comes easily to children in a multi-age class; as the pressure for sameness is removed, the possibilities for creativity multiply.

We learn when we know there is a real purpose to what we are doing.

In multi-age classrooms teachers and students work together to increase the purposefulness of learning. We increase the connections to real audiences for our writing and our reading, and we design real ways to help in our classroom, school, and community. Our diversity means we have differing talents, skills, and ideas. Learners in multi-age classrooms find themselves reaching out to make their learning more meaningful.

Choice allows for ownership because it respects the uniqueness of each individual.

Choice is a powerful motivator for learners. A range of learners of different ages and different interests encourages teachers to have a common focus while allowing each student to build upon his or her strengths, interests, and experiences. Side-by-side learning extends ideas about what can be learned and how it can be learned. In a multi-age classroom we know we have diversity and we plan for it.

Integration of ages and interests is natural. Multi-age classes offer us a way to erase the lines that schools have created between and among people.

The school is one of the few places that separates people on the basis of narrow age divisions. The multi-age classroom is a more authentic environment in which to learn, similar to the workplace or the home. Learning is easier when we see what form it might take and how it might be accomplished: our ability to learn is enhanced when we see the larger context for what is being learned. For example, watching a younger classmate solve a puzzle helps us appreciate how much we know; watching a mathematically gifted classmate solve a problem might help us figure out how to do it another time.

What do you believe about learning and learners?

HOW DO WE BEGIN?

As teachers of multi-age classes we face many of the same challenges all teachers face. One of these is figuring out how to put together all the pieces to make a strong and coherent program for our students. As teachers we have thousands of bits and pieces and may feel overwhelmed by the choices we face. Making sense of these choices requires that we have a picture of where we want to go, the pieces needed to create that picture, and a clear sense of how we want to get there—a vision, knowledge of curriculum expectations, and a set of beliefs to guide our decision making.

As we come to know and understand the research about learning, and articulate our beliefs, we decide on those pieces we keep and those we discard. We also decide how we will interact with others as we progress towards our goals. Building our vision or "big picture" means considering our ultimate goals for our students. Think of the vision as a puzzle. The big picture is the lid of the puzzle box. Our vision of what we want our classrooms to be is the big picture that guides our decision making. The lid shows us where the pieces go and the progress we are making. Without the lid it is hard to know where to put the pieces, tough to know what works together and what doesn't work, and impossible to know when we're close to reaching our goal.

Teachers work with many "pieces" as they design instructional programs and environments for children—curriculum expectations and developmental needs; materials and resources; furniture arrangement and use of physical space; and assessment and evaluation strategies. Just as puzzle-builders have many different ways to successfully build a puzzle, teachers have many successful ways to approach their teaching. There is no one right way. Rather, our challenge is to create a strong and coherent program.

Once you have determined your big picture and your beliefs, it is up to you to build the puzzle your way. In the following chapters we have set out some of the bigger pieces. You can read the chapters in any order—this is not a linear process. It is up to you to select those ideas that make sense for you and your students. There are many right ways to meet the needs of students in multi-age classrooms. We encourage you to adapt and change our suggestions to fit your situation.

The following ideas are activities designed for use with parents. Whether you use these for parents or not we strongly recommend that you think these through for yourself. These activities will help you be clear about your beliefs before you start your planning.

Articulating Our Beliefs:

Articulating Our Beliefs: BUILDING A SHARED VISION

We think it is important to clarify the kind of person we—parents and teachers—want our education process to develop. One strategy is to have parents engage in the activity, Think of a Person.

Think of a Person

Have participants group themselves around tables (five to seven per table). Provide notepaper, pens, and name tags. An overhead projector, blank transparencies, and transparency pens are also needed. Then proceed as follows:

> Agenda 7:30-9:00 p.m.
>
> Introductions
> Task - Building A Shared Vision
> * characteristics of a respected & admired 'elder'
> * individual notes
> * group record
> * share
> * what's similar? what's different?
> Summary / Conclusion
> Coffee, tea & treats

Agenda for parent evening

1. Have all participants think about a person who is respected and admired. Think about why. Ask: "What characteristics of that person do you respect and admire? Jot down a personal list of characteristics."

2. Within each group, have each person read and talk about his or her list and then, as a group, compile a list of characteristics.

3. Have each group contribute one characteristic until all the characteristics have been recorded. (Use an overhead transparency and projector to record their responses.) Encourage participants to ask questions if any characteristics need clarification.

List of characteristics

4. When all the characteristics have been shared, explain that many groups have participated in similar activities. Some jurisdictions have published statements of the kind of person they want their education system to help develop and create. In British Columbia, Canada, the Ministry of Education has formulated a statement called, "The Educated Citizen,"

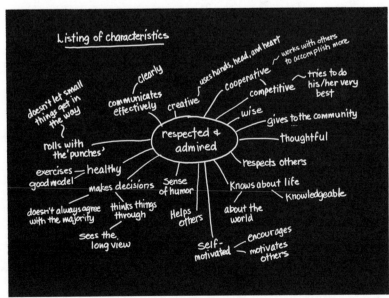

The Educated Citizen

Educated citizens are
- thoughtful; able to learn and think critically, and to communicate information from a broad knowledge base
- creative, flexible, self-motivated, and possessing a positive self-image
- capable of making independent decisions
- skilled and able to contribute to society generally, including the world of work
- productive, able to gain satisfaction through achievement, and to strive for physical well-being
- cooperative, principled, and respectful of others regardless of differences
- aware of the rights and prepared to exercise the responsibilities of an individual within the family, the community, Canada, and the world

(reprinted by permission of the Ministry of Education, British Columbia, Canada)

which is based on similar discussions held throughout their jurisdiction.[1]

5. Ask participants to compare and discuss the lists—similarities, differences, surprises—and any questions they might have.

6. Some effective ways to conclude are by noting that we share many of the same aspirations for our children, or by inviting parents to talk with each other about what they want for their children as learners.

What characteristics do you want to encourage in your students?

In this time of educational change, many jurisdictions and various professional organizations have produced videos that illustrate the evolution of schools and schooling. Select one that is appropriate for your area. As a follow-up to the evening you may invite parents to view a short video that both clarifies and supports this view of the learner. Explain to the parents that building a shared understanding will inform your planning and help you determine the design of classroom activities.

---

1. Terry Johnson, Norma Mickelson, Allison Preece, Robert Anthony, and Susan Smith, Faculty of Education, University of Victoria, B.C., use a similar exercise to identify the characteristics of a successful learner. Their book, *The Tiger's Kiss: Assessment and Evaluation in the Classroom* (in press), is an excellent source of ideas to simplify yet enhance evaluation practices.

Articulating Our Beliefs: FOCUSING ON CHARACTERISTICS OF LEARNING

This strategy helps parents—and teachers—clarify how people learn successfully.[2]

Agenda for parent evening

> Learning and Learners
> Agenda
>
> Welcome! Introductions!
> Think of a Time
> Think, Talk, Listen, Record, Share
> Supporting Learning
> Summary

Think of a Time

Have participants group themselves around tables (five to seven per table). Provide notepaper, pens, and name tags. An overhead projector, blank transparencies, and transparency pens are also needed. Then proceed as follows:

1. Have all participants think about a time when they successfully learned something outside of school. Have them make some personal notes describing what they learned. Ask questions such as: "Why did you learn it? Did you choose to learn it? Did someone suggest you learn it? Where did you learn it? How did you learn it? Was anyone with you? How long did it take? Did you make any mistakes? How did you feel?" (Prepare a transparency to help parents recall the questions.)

2. Within each group, have each person talk about his or her experiences and then, as a group, compile a list describing the learning.

Think of a Time

> 1) Think of a time when you successfully learned something
>
> Think about:
> What was it you learned?
> Why did you choose to learn it?
> How did you learn it?
> What made it possible for you to learn it?
> Who was with you?
> How long did it take?
> How did you feel?
>
> 2) Make some personal notes about your experience
>
> 3) Form groups of 5-7 and describe your learning one by one
>
> 4) Record words and phrases that describe the experiences

2. Adapted from Think of a Time, a strategy presented by F. Brownlie, S. Close, and L. Wingren in *Tomorrow's Classroom Today*. (This book is full of many excellent ideas to use with any class.)

3. Have someone from each group contribute one or two words to describe the learning needs of the group members until all the descriptions have been recorded. (Use the overhead to record their contributions. We suggest you group similar ones together as you record.) Encourage participants to ask questions if any responses need clarification.

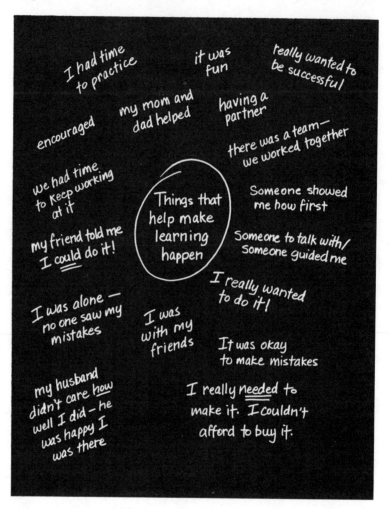

Characteristics of learning

4. When all the characteristics have been shared, explain that a great deal of research has been conducted over the last twenty years focusing on how people—and children specifically— learn. This research has powerful implications for how we work with children to ensure successful learning takes place in school.

What We Know About Children as Learners

- Children need self-esteem to develop their individual potential. The way they feel about themselves is related to their ability to learn (Bruner 1960). The classroom climate and nature of school work contribute directly to the way children feel about themselves.

- Children strive to make sense of their world based on what they have already learned, experienced, and constructed (Donaldson 1978, Piaget 1977, Wells 1986).

- The prime need of all learners is to make meaning of their experiences (Caine and Caine 1991).

- Educators have now moved beyond thinking that learning is rote memorization (Cambourne 1988).

- Children learn through the process of play. It is a natural universal learning activity of children and adults. It plays a significant role in a child's development and learning and must be incorporated on a daily basis in the primary years…alongside project work and systematic instruction (Katz and Chard 1991).

- Children are naturally curious. From the time they are born, children want to know and to act or interact (Clay 1991).

- Children learn through collaboration with others. Social, emotional, and intellectual development is fostered through interaction with others. All significant development and learning occurs in the context of social interaction (Vygotsky 1978, Wells 1986).

- Children develop many ways of understanding the world. We now recognize that they are using many different kinds of intelligences as they describe what and how they think, feel, or do. As we come to understand more about human potential we realize the need to provide a variety of opportunities for people to represent what they "know" in order to gain a richer view of learning (Gardner 1985).

- Children acquire, develop, and express their understandings through the use of language—written and oral language develop concurrently (Bissex 1980, Lemke 1989).

- Children learn best in an environment that encourages risk taking and from their mistakes (Goodman 1986, Smith 1974).

- Children gain knowledge by creating relationships. Children pursue learning in a holistic way without restrictions imposed by subject area boundaries (Caine and Caine 1991).

(From *Supporting Learning*, B.C. Ministry of Education)

Read "What We Know About Children as Learners" (above) aloud and explain that teachers have begun to use this and other similar lists as a guide for their own work. Explain that some questions teachers ask as they plan for successful learning are:

☞ What do I want for these children? What do their parents want? What is my vision?

- What do I know about the way children develop and learn in this age range?
- What are the state/provincial curriculum expectations?
- What kind of daily and yearly plans do I need to make to promote learning?
- How will I involve my students in planning and creating a supportive learning environment?
- What do I need to learn about my students so I can be responsive to their emerging learning needs?
- How can I help my students understand and appreciate their learning so that together we can inform their parents about their accomplishments, efforts, needs, and goals?
- How can I use this information to continually refine and improve my plans?
- How can I ensure that parents know their children are learning "the basics," as well as such "learning-how-to-learn" skills as problem solving, question forming, and thinking strategies?

5. Ask participants to discuss their lists—similarities, differences, surprises—and any questions they might have.

6. Ask if there are any comments participants would like to share with the group.

7. Invite participants to stay for coffee, tea, or juice. You may want to show them a video of their children learning or a display of students' work; have them observe a presentation by students demonstrating some aspect of their learning; or invite them to view a brief video that both clarifies and supports this information we now know about learners.

SUMMARY

In this chapter we have defined multi-age classrooms and written about their advantages. We have also talked about learning and learners, how multi-age classes promote learning, and provided two activities that we've used effectively with parents to help them understand our view of learners and learning. The questions we use to focus our attention on the important issues are:

- What kind of people do we want to encourage our children to become?
- What do we believe about learners and learning?

☛ How can we help children become lifelong learners—active, independent, and self-regulating individuals?

☛ How can we keep our eyes on the big picture (our vision) while making instructional decisions? What are the beliefs that guide our decision making?

In chapter 2 we address the practical issues of taking our beliefs about learners and learning and use them to plan for a term, a week, and a day in a multi-age classroom.

What are the conditions you need for learning?

Are these the same for your friends?

PLANNING FOR DIVERSITY

Curriculum planning for single-age classrooms used to be done on the assumption that everyone learned at the same rate. The school system sorted students who were different into special programs, institutions, or right out of school. Today this practice is being questioned in schools as it is in the larger society.

Multi-age classrooms, by their very nature, defy this illusion of "sameness." Yet teachers in multi-age classrooms, like all teachers, have curricular responsibilities. When we examined elementary

curriculum documents for single-age classes from many jurisdictions, we consistently noted two similarities and two differences from grade to grade. The similarities are: (1) children are expected to develop positive attitudes towards learning and (2) children demonstrate ever-increasing levels of expertise in basic skill and processes—reading, writing, developing mathematical understanding, thinking, and representing. The differences we noted are: (1) expectations regarding performance levels of skills and processes changed over time and (2) so did specific arbitrary content requirements (knowledge and information) for each grade level.

Our challenge is to move past the differences among curriculum requirements and students, and towards the development of curricular plans that are responsive to children's learning needs. Many educators and parents have asked: "How do you teach more than one grade at the same time?" We tell them we use our understandings about learners and learning and curriculum essentials to create environments that invite each child to succeed.

When we think of the planning process we followed in our early years of teaching, we have memories of sitting down with a tower of curriculum guides and objectives and asking

- ☛ What curriculum needs to be covered?
- ☛ How can I space it out over the year to make sure I get through it all?

- What techniques am I going to use to manage my students and my classroom?
- How do I keep everyone going at the same rate? What can I do to help the students who are behind keep up and what do I do with those who surge ahead?

As report cards approached and we prepared to tell parents where their child stood, we searched for tests that would tell us how much the children had learned.

Now, when we consider the way we plan, we have a new set of questions. These questions make planning more effective for us and our students. Realizing that our task is to work with parents within the expectations of society to help prepare children for their future, each of us begins the planning process by asking

- What do I want for these children? What do their parents want? What is my vision?
- What do I know about the way children develop and learn in this age range?
- What are the state/provincial curriculum expectations?
- What kind of daily and yearly plans do I need to make to promote learning?
- How will I involve my students in planning and creating a supportive learning environment?
- What do I need to learn about my students so I can respond to their emerging learning needs?
- How can I help my students understand and appreciate their learning so that together we can inform their parents about their accomplishments, efforts, needs, and goals?
- How can I use this information to continually refine and improve my plans?

We used to plan by starting with the curriculum; now we plan by starting with the children. We view each new class through the lenses of our vision, our knowledge of learners and learning, and the curriculum expectations. We build learning structures that support learners' ongoing growth and development. We plan for learners' successes by creating environments that help children develop positive attitudes and by designing activities so all children have the opportunity to refine and extend their repertoire of skills and processes and build their knowledge base.

The following ideas are strategies that we have used successfully. Please use those that will assist you and modify them to ensure they work for you and your students in your situation.

Planning for Diversity:

Planning for Diversity: IDENTIFYING CURRICULUM ELEMENTS

Students, parents, and our colleagues need to be assured that curriculum expectations are considered as we plan for our students' learning experiences.

The stack of curriculum documents for any single grade can be intimidating; for a multi-age classroom it can be overwhelming. Identifying the common curriculum elements is one strategy we have found useful. Its purpose is to reduce the curriculum documents to their simplest form so we can make sense of them and be confident that our planning is complete and thorough.

1. Collect the curriculum documents. Identify the key information (specific skills, processes, knowledge, attitudes) relating to each grade and copy those pages.

2. Decide the order in which you will examine the documents.

3. Gather the materials you will need: scissors, tape, glue stick, highlighters, large sheets of blank paper. Ask a good friend or colleague to help you. (We have used this activity with groups of teachers, entire school staffs, as well as individually.)

4. Assign a different highlighter color for each subject and another color for each grade (e.g., language arts, yellow; math, green; science, blue; Grade X, orange stripe; Grade XX, black stripe; Grade XXX, dark blue stripe). Decide which subject you are going to begin with and tuck the other curriculum expectations away.[1] (There are lots of different ways to sort—by subject, by concept, by theme. Choose the way that makes the most sense for you.)

5. Color code each grade level by running stripes down the page. Read through the documents grade by grade highlighting those expectations that are repeated in each year.

You can repeat this for all curriculum areas if you wish but probably one or two subjects will be enough to show overlap.

6. Take one set of documents, cut out every item that is repeated in the other grades, and glue these to a large sheet labeled *Common Curriculum Elements.*

7. Take the remaining items for each grade (sorted by colored stripes) and put on separate sheets labeled for each grade (e.g., Isolated Elements, Grade X; Isolated Elements, Grade XX; Isolated Elements, Grade XXX).

---

1. Marion Boyd, Sid Halls, Solweig Williams, and Howard Shultz, colleagues at Brooklyn Elementary, concentrated on Language Arts, see page 21.

8.   Repeat for every subject area until done. Examine your work. Look for repetition across curriculum documents as well as across grade expectations. Our experience has shown us that, for example, science and math as well as language arts and social studies have similar expectations, especially in terms of processes such as problem solving and research-skill development. Once you've identified all possible overlap, put the sheets aside. Clean up—we'll use the information on these sheets later!

Identifying curriculum elements: example

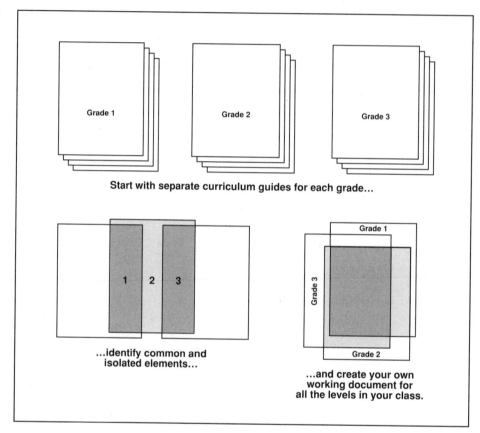

Start with separate curriculum guides for each grade...

...identify common and isolated elements...

...and create your own working document for all the levels in your class.

9.   Congratulate yourself—and your colleagues! This information will stand you in good stead for a long time because subject-area curriculum documents are expensive to produce and are not often revised.

In our experience there are three parts to every set of curriculum expectations—attitudes, skills and processes, and knowledge.[2] Curriculum expectations, when viewed in this way, are more similar than different. As teachers we have experienced the increasing diver-

2. See British Columbia's *Primary Program* or Nebraska/Iowa's *Growing and Learning in the Heartland.*

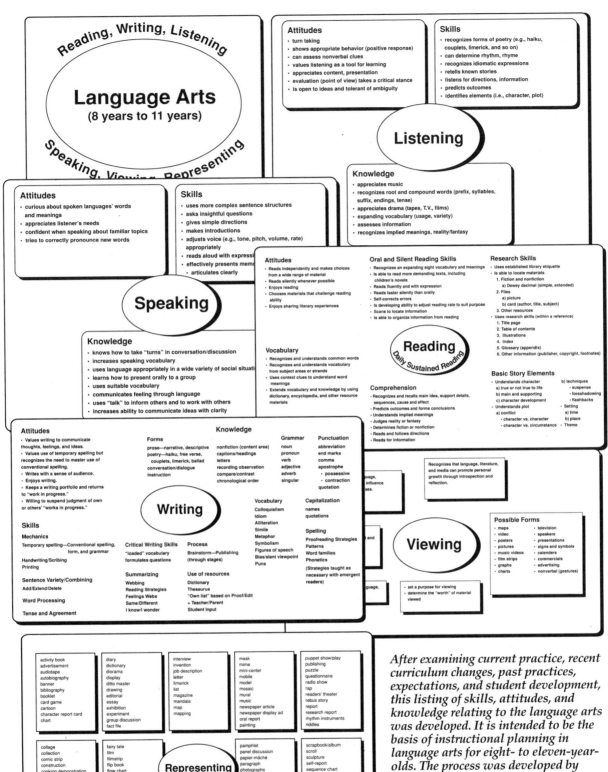

Language Arts (8 years to 11 years)
Reading, Writing, Listening
Speaking, Viewing, Representing

Listening

Attitudes
- turn taking
- shows appropriate behavior (positive response)
- can assess nonverbal clues
- values listening as a tool for learning
- appreciates content, presentation
- evaluation (point of view) takes a critical stance
- is open to ideas and tolerant of ambiguity

Skills
- recognizes forms of poetry (e.g., haiku, couplets, limerick, and so on)
- can determine rhythm, rhyme
- recognizes idiomatic expressions
- retells known stories
- listens for directions, information
- predicts outcomes
- identifies elements (i.e., character, plot)

Knowledge
- appreciates music
- recognizes root and compound words (prefix, syllables, suffix, endings, tense)
- appreciates drama (tapes, T.V., films)
- expanding vocabulary (usage, variety)
- assesses information
- recognizes implied meanings, reality/fantasy

Speaking

Attitudes
- curious about spoken languages' words and meanings
- appreciates listener's needs
- confident when speaking about familiar topics
- tries to correctly pronounce new words

Skills
- uses more complex sentence structures
- asks insightful questions
- gives simple directions
- makes introductions
- adjusts voice (e.g., tone, pitch, volume, rate) appropriately
- reads aloud with express[ion]
- effectively presents mem[o]
- articulates clearly

Knowledge
- knows how to take "turns" in conversation/discussion
- increases speaking vocabulary
- uses language appropriately in a wide variety of social situati[ons]
- learns how to present orally to a group
- uses suitable vocabulary
- communicates feeling through language
- uses "talk" to inform others and to work with others
- increases ability to communicate ideas with clarity

Reading
Daily Sustained Reading

Attitudes
- Reads independently and makes choices from a wide range of material
- Reads silently whenever possible
- Enjoys reading
- Chooses materials that challenge reading ability
- Enjoys sharing literary experiences

Oral and Silent Reading Skills
- Recognizes an expanding sight vocabulary and meanings
- Is able to read more demanding texts, including children's novels
- Reads fluently and with expression
- Reads faster silently than orally
- Self-corrects errors
- Is developing ability to adjust reading rate to suit purpose
- Scans to locate information
- Is able to organize information from reading

Vocabulary
- Recognizes and understands common words
- Recognizes and understands vocabulary from subject areas or strands
- Uses context clues to understand word meanings
- Extends vocabulary and knowledge by using dictionary, encyclopedia, and other resource materials

Comprehension
- Recognizes and recalls main idea, support details, sequences, cause and effect
- Predicts outcomes and forms conclusions
- Understands implied meanings
- Judges reality or fantasy
- Determines fiction or nonfiction
- Reads and follows directions
- Reads for information

Research Skills
- Uses established library etiquette
- Is able to locate materials
  1. Fiction and nonfiction
     a) Dewey decimal (simple, extended)
  2. Files
     a) picture
     b) card (author, title, subject)
  3. Other resources
- Uses research skills (within a reference)
  1. Title page
  2. Table of contents
  3. Illustrations
  4. Index
  5. Glossary (appendix)
  6. Other information (publisher, copyright, footnotes)

Basic Story Elements
- Understands character
  a) true or not true to life
  b) main and supporting
  c) character development
- Understands plot
  a) conflict
     · character vs. character
     · character vs. circumstance
- b) techniques
  · suspense
  · foreshadowing
  · flashbacks
- Setting
  a) time
  b) place
- Theme

Writing

Attitudes
- Values writing to communicate thoughts, feelings, and ideas.
- Values use of temporary spelling but recognizes the need to master use of conventional spelling.
- Writes with a sense of audience.
- Enjoys writing.
- Keeps a writing portfolio and returns to "work in progress."
- Willing to suspend judgment of own or others' "works in progress."

Skills

Mechanics
Temporary spelling—Conventional spelling, form, and grammar
Handwriting/Scribing
Printing
Sentence Variety/Combining
Add/Extend/Delete
Word Processing
Tense and Agreement

Knowledge

Forms
prose—narrative, descriptive
poetry—haiku, free verse, couplets, limerick, ballad
conversation/dialogue
instruction

nonfiction (content area)
captions/headings
letters
recording observation
compare/contrast
chronological order

Critical Writing Skills
"loaded" vocabulary
formulates questions

Process
Brainstorm—Publishing (through stages)

Summarizing
Webbing
Reading Strategies
Feelings Webs
Same/Different
I know/I wonder

Use of resources
Dictionary
Thesaurus
"Own list" based on Proof/Edit
+ Teacher/Parent
Student Input

Grammar
noun
pronoun
verb
adjective
adverb
singular

Punctuation
abbreviation
end marks
comma
apostrophe
· possessive
· contraction
quotation

Vocabulary
Colloquialism
Idiom
Alliteration
Simile
Metaphor
Symbolism
Figures of speech
Bias/slant viewpoint
Puns

Capitalization
names
quotations

Spelling
Proofreading Strategies
Patterns
Word families
Phonetics
(Strategies taught as necessary with emergent readers)

Viewing

Recognizes that language, literature, and media can promote personal growth through introspection and reflection.

- set a purpose for viewing
- determine the "worth" of material viewed

Possible Forms
- maps
- video
- posters
- pictures
- music videos
- film strips
- graphs
- charts
- television
- speakers
- presentations
- signs and symbols
- calenders
- commercials
- advertising
- nonverbal (gestures)

Representing
Uses a Variety of Forms to Communicate Meaning

activity book
advertisement
audiotape
autobiography
banner
bibliography
booklet
card game
cartoon
character report card
chart

diary
dictionary
diorama
display
ditto master
drawing
editorial
essay
exhibition
experiment
group discussion
fact file

interview
invention
job description
letter
limerick
list
magazine
mandala
map
mapping

mask
mime
mini-center
mobile
model
mosaic
mural
music
newspaper article
newspaper display ad
oral report
painting

puppet show/play
publishing
puzzle
questionnaire
radio show
rap
readers' theater
rebus story
report
research report
rhythm instruments
riddles

collage
collection
comic strip
construction
cooking demonstration
court trial
crossword
debate
demonstration
diagram

fairy tale
film
filmstrip
flip book
flow chart
folk/native dance
game
game board
graph
illustration
interpretive dance

pamphlet
panel discussion
papier-mâché
paragraph
photographs
picture
play
poem
poster
project cube

scrapbook/album
scroll
sculpture
self-report
sequence chart
skit
slidetape
song
sociogram
tableau
video snippets

After examining current practice, recent curriculum changes, past practices, expectations, and student development, this listing of skills, attitudes, and knowledge relating to the language arts was developed. It is intended to be the basis of instructional planning in language arts for eight- to eleven-year-olds. The process was developed by Marion Boyd, Sid Halls, Solweig Williams, Howard Shultz, and Anne Davies as part of S.U.C.C.E.S.S. Project '93, Brooklyn Elementary.

sity among our children and been challenged to consider our vision for students, define our knowledge of learners and learning, and make sense of the stacks of curriculum expectations.

We used to think that every grade's curriculum was separate and unique.

Now we know that knowledge, skills, attitudes, and processes, which develop as we learn, are recursive in nature—we return again and again becoming more "expert" as the years advance.

While we have not viewed *your* curriculum, likely the bulk of your "common elements" are attitudes and skills and processes outlined in the documents. These occur because we learn a little bit of just about everything during our early years and then we spend the rest of our time (in and out of school) getting better and better. Researchers in the area of language acquisition usually refer to this as continuous "successive approximations"—getting better and better at what we do—otherwise known as learning. Those items that usually end up on the grade-by-grade sheets tend to be specific, arbitrary content requirements—decisions usually based on a combination of past practices and current research theories in the various disciplines. This list varies depending on where and by whom your curriculum was written—usually a portion is adjusted to better meet the needs of children in a particular area. (We used to think that the writers of curriculum documents had access to some special font of knowledge—they don't. They are people like us— and like us they sometimes make mistakes.)

When we take time to clarify the curriculum for parents and administrators we benefit from "setting up our thinking" so that our planning is comprehensive and responsive. We then use our intimate knowledge of the curriculum to tentatively plan our year. The process we have described is a necessity for beginners, but in reality the majority of this "curricular knowing" resides in the heads of experienced teachers.

Planning for Diversity: SETTING UP THE TERM

Once we know the common denominators we can plan with confidence, fulfilling our professional responsibilities by balancing the needs of children with the expectations of the curriculum. Sometimes we plan by thinking through each subject area, sometimes by considering the knowledge, skills, and attitudes that weave themselves through every subject area, or by considering the significant goals or outcomes we are working towards.

Use your curriculum common elements and your children's needs, interests, and abilities as your guides. There are many planning frames to assist you in your thinking—select the one that makes sense for you.

Planning frame

Reproducible master in appendix A

Term __1__ September – November

Theme Building A Community / Canada

	Language Arts/Drama/Art/Computers	Maths/Computers	Social Studies/Science	Physical Ed.
Attitudes	· trust/confidence with new classmates · enjoy listening to novels read aloud · confidence in own abilities · team-work / co-presenting · build home/school work & study habits · build daily reading habit	· able to self-assess & plan personal math program · able to work with classmates to create & solve problems and practice together	· able to be positive member of self-selected team and teacher-selected team	· safety · trust in others · willingness to take risks · team work
Skills/ Processes	· speech writing · organizing campaigns /platforms · reading practice — silent & oral, fiction & non-fiction · ways to respond to reading materials · listening to news (radio) · reading newspapers · research report — strategies, writing formats, note taking, organizing, proof reading · daily journal writing · using word processing programs & printers in computer lab · skill practice based on class/student assessments	Topics – addition subtraction multiplication {over time division geometry Continuous problem solving	Community · seeing value of each classmate — lots of work building connections · overnight camp experience (Sept.) · leadership / teamwork · purpose and function of community	· equipment use · team work · soccer volleyball }indoor/ basketball }outdoor
Knowledge	· class favorites · Canadian authors } fiction — Canadian artists · Science fiction · CD ROM Research / Card Catalog · Research – books – newspapers – brochures } non-fiction – campaign speeches	Beginning- developing- extending · computer skills practice · daily mini-lessons based on assessment results · cooperative teams- guided practice of specific skills · students working independently/partners on selected activities	Canada · maps · capitals, provinces, territories · federal vs. provincial · election – party – leaders – voting process	· rules · ball handling · fouls

What kinds of planning strategies work for you and your students?

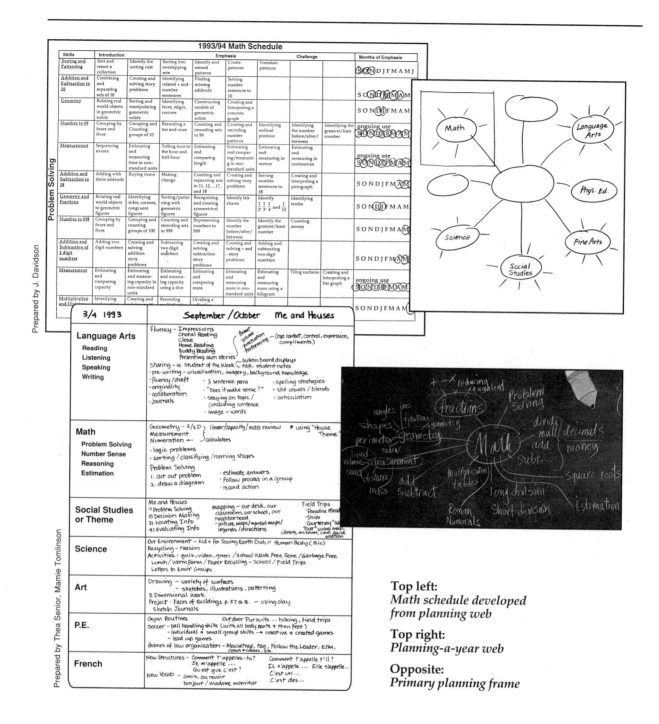

Top left:
Math schedule developed from planning web

Top right:
Planning-a-year web

Opposite:
Primary planning frame

 Planning for Diversity: SHAPING THE WEEK

The timetable you develop will depend on the decisions you and students make about the use of time and the scheduling considerations unique to your school. Our goal is to establish blocks of time that have sufficient length to allow children to become engrossed in projects and activities. Blocks of time also provide teachers with more time to observe and interact with students.

In some situations it is necessary to renegotiate traditional time arrangements (for example, when children in the class have special assistance or specific subjects such as music, which may be taught on a grade-by-grade basis). Although there are always exceptions, we try to keep our class together as a family and invite specialists (such as the music teacher) to join us in our classroom.

We're not going to talk you through every minute of every day; however, we have provided some examples of timetables (this page) we've found to be particularly effective.

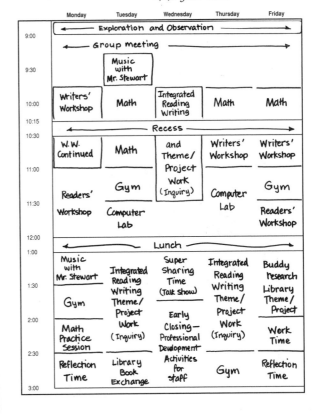

Primary timetable for 6,7,8 year olds

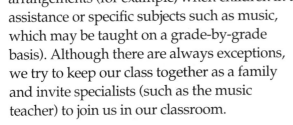

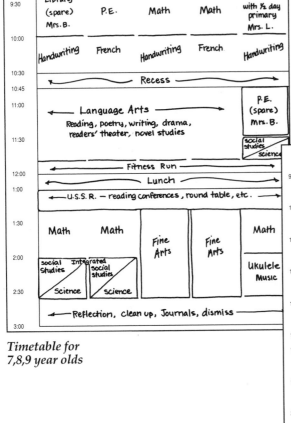

Timetable for 7,8,9 year olds

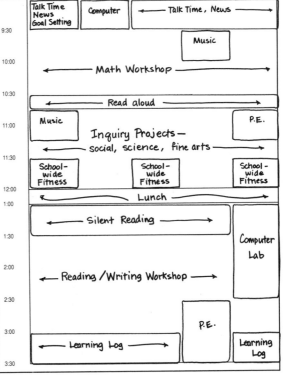

Timetable for 10,11,12 year olds

Planning for Diversity: **POSTING THE AGENDA**

Posting the daily agenda on a chalkboard or chart paper lets students know what is planned for each day. As the day progresses checking the agenda gives the class a sense of what is being accomplished and what adjustments need to be made. Children soon learn that they can make suggestions and figure out ways to accommodate time and activity conflicts.

For a change of pace we sometimes determine with the children what needs to be accomplished on a particular morning or afternoon and ask them to plan and record their personal agendas. This is an excellent practical experience in scheduling their own time. We've learned we can facilitate success by stopping hourly to ask students to conduct personal "progress checks."

The following activities, which we use to shape our day, help us work with—not against—the diversity that exists in every classroom.

Agenda
Exploration—Try the new magnifying glasses
Group Meeting—News, Mystery Message, cops, Number of the Day, Poem
Math—mini-lesson, measurement, use of standard measuring tapes
Recess
Math Activities (con't)
Reading and Writers' Workshop—Readers' Club, work on biographies
Lunch
Storytime—sharing and sing-along
Computer Lab
Project/Theme Work—sign up if you need a conference
Reflection—1 proud moment / 1 next step
Safe Trip Home

Agenda   93-09-23
Talk Time
Daily Edit
Math Puzzler
News—9:00 a.m.
 - Keep notes, be prepared to talk about one item
 - Find countries on world map, outline and color
Mathematics
Mini-Lesson—Finding patterns Practice session
Music
Read-aloud—The Phantom Toll Booth
Fitness
Silent Reading & Readers' Response
Mini-Lesson & Activity
Learning Logs
Closure

Planning for Diversity: **EXPLORATION AND OBSERVATION**

Beginning the morning with an exploration time, inviting children to choose from a variety of activity areas in the classroom (see chapter 4 for activity areas), has many benefits. Children look forward to coming to school and are rarely late. Starting the day with something they like gives them positive feelings that set them up to be successful throughout the day. Working together during exploration time gives the children and teachers a safe relaxed environment that helps develop the collaborative relationships crucial to a well-functioning group. This time also affords teachers the opportunity to observe and interact with the children.

Start with only a few choices. Develop agreements with the children about use, care, and storage of materials, and provide easy-to-care for activities such as reading, writing, math play, games, puzzles, drawing, painting, and science observations. Introduce new activities on an ongoing basis.

 Planning for Diversity: **TALK TIME**

For teachers who do not wish to start the day with exploration time, a ten-minute Talk Time has the value of setting the tone for the day and helping students feel ready to work. Children have the opportunity to meet with a partner or in small groups to talk. Children may also use this time to read or figure out a daily math or logic puzzle challenge.

 Planning for Diversity: **GROUP MEETING TIME**

Group Meeting Time (about thirty minutes) is a forum for sharing information and teaching specific skills and concepts. There are many possible combinations of activities for this time—one basic is a review of the daily agenda. Reviewing the agenda of events planned for the day lets children know what to expect, prepare for, and look forward to. Some teachers record the time by each item as a way of giving the students more specific information, and experience in reading time.

The following activities are possibilities for making Group Meeting Time a successful teaching and learning time.

Mystery Message

A daily cloze procedure provides an ideal opportunity for children in primary classrooms to talk about how language works. Ensuring the message contains information that is important for the class is the key to capturing children's interest.

Picture a group of children and their teacher gathered so that everyone can see the mystery message displayed on a chalkboard, chart, or on a screen by an overhead projector. So that children of varying abilities can all benefit from this activity the teacher has written the message to invite response from all participants. As the children volunteer suggestions for the standard spellings of the following sentence, the teacher or one of the children fills in the missing letters:

Th_ __oor i_ _he gy_ _s be___
w_x_d s_ _e w_ll n__d t_
d_ __r p__a __ute
ac_iv_ti__ __tsid_.

This activity provides daily opportunity to talk about the patterns and inconsistencies of English spelling. Its enjoyment value is demonstrated when children begin to write messages to parents, teachers, and each other using the cloze form.

The missing elements can be changed depending on the language elements the teacher wishes to emphasize. With young children begin by omitting initial consonants and long vowels. With older children word endings and tricky vowel combinations can stimulate discussion about the intricacies of the English language. In a multi-age class we provide a range of possibilities so that the same message challenges all the children.

C.O.P.S./Daily Edit

An extension of Mystery Message is C.O.P.S.—Capitals, Omissions, Punctuation, and Spelling. Complicating the mystery message by also including errors and omissions in these key language structures would overwhelm younger children. For their benefit we do two separate activities.

Imagine the children have just finished Mystery Message. The C.O.P.S. message is printed (this can also be done on an overhead projector). So that children of varying ages and abilities can all participate, the teacher has included a range of editing challenges:

toda wee r havin A
visidor two tak aboud
Mexico has ben their

To start the process the teacher and children try to read the message aloud. Children then suggest corrections until the message is in standard form.

Older children, able to deal with many more language challenges similtaneously, may be ready to have Mystery Message and C.O.P.S. combined: We call this Daily Edit.

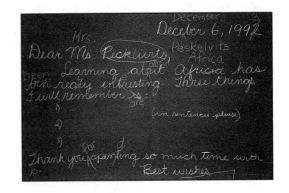

Imagine. Our older students arrive, talk about their plans for the day, check the agenda for the day, and begin their opening learning activities—one of which is Daily Edit. They "solve" the daily edit as they write it correctly in their notebooks:

Good morning, I am relly plesed two notise that youre africain progects our well on there way to Bein competed? Mrs. P. will be comin these after noon to show us slides abut botswana! She has spoken to me abut how inpressed she is with youre questions and obnious intrest in africia.

Later in the morning everyone turns to their corrected version of the daily edit and the teacher leads a group edit where students, in turn, are asked to point out errors and the correct form. Later, as students become more experienced, they take turns leading the correction process.

Number of the Day

Students particularly enjoy the challenge of seeing how many questions they can create whose solutions equal the number of the day's date. You may choose to determine the functions (addition, subtraction, multiplication, and division) to be included; other days the students might choose. We usually let the students choose. You might expect that more sophisticated responses will come from older children—we've found that a love of numbers and a gift for mathematics are not age-related. This activity can be extended by asking students: "Where do you find this number in the real world?"

Pause for a Poem

Poetry reading only takes minutes in the day but yields excellent results in children who enjoy listening to, reading, and writing poetry. The daily poem might be chosen to match a season, theme, local event, or simply because someone (teacher or student) thinks it might appeal to the class. (After a week or two of daily poetry pauses, children often start writing their own poems.) You can initiate this activity by providing a collection of books that *invites* children to pursue poetry.[3]

Planning for Diversity: SING-ALONG

One challenge for teachers in primary multi-age classes is finding songs that appeal to both younger and older children. We have solved this problem by establishing children's choice time. Class members take turns choosing a selection from favorite records and familiar songs. These choices are recorded and sometimes graphed.

In addition to providing another mathematics experience, it gives children an opportunity to reach agreement in a peaceful manner, taking into consideration different needs and perspectives.

Favorite songs for sing-along

---

3. Georgia Heard's *For the Good of the Earth and the Sun* is an excellent source of ways to inspire writing poetry.

Planning for Diversity: **TRANSITIONS**

The key to smooth transitions is setting clear expectations about what children need to do during transition times and following breaks in the day. One strategy we learned from our colleague Linda Silverthorne is to introduce a math activity before recess. Asking children to get right back into the activity following recess reduces wait time and increases productive activity; they are eager to resume because they already *know* how to get started. Two other examples of effective transitions are personal reading time after a lunch break and requesting children upon their return from an out-of-class activity to get their writing folder and read through it in anticipation of writers' workshop.

SUMMARY

In this chapter we have outlined possibilities for planning and shaping the day—from the big vision, to planning a term, a week, and a day, as well as outlining activities that are "classroom classics." The questions we use to guide our decision making are:

- ☞ Is the range of activities sufficient to appeal to different ages, interests, learning styles, and rates?
- ☞ Are there times when we are together as a large group, in small groups, and working individually?
- ☞ Have I planned times for mini-lessons and guided practice?
- ☞ Is there a comfortable working rhythm to each day? Is anything interfering with student learning?
- ☞ Is there a balance between active and quiet learning times?
- ☞ What times do I have to observe students at work?

In the next chapter we focus on building the positive relationships and expectations that support our learning goals.

What favorite strategies and routines do you use to support diversity in your classroom?

CREATING A COMMUNITY OF LEARNERS

While all well-functioning classes can become communities of learners, the advantage of multi-age grouping is that the emphasis is on learners rather than on grade requirements. This shift in focus provides teachers of multi-age classes with an opportunity to focus on learners and their learning rather than on whether or not the grade requirements have been met at a particular point in time. This change

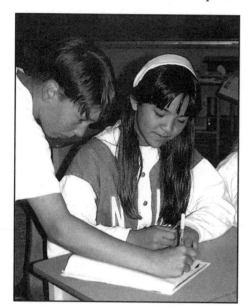

in emphasis—from covering the curriculum to supporting each learner—helps avoid problems that may arise by asking children to do things that are beyond their current developmental levels, or risking boredom in students who are ready to move on.

Acknowledging diversity in every group of children and planning for ways to work with it rather than against it allow us to enhance all students' learning. Students and their learning become the driving force behind our teaching. We create a community that sees "difference" as an asset. As teachers we look for ways to make differences work to our advantage by ensuring they lead to more and better learning for everyone.

The ideas in this section exemplify some ways that we, as teachers, can set the tone and create with students a learning community. There are three steps to creating a community of learners: (1) get a class, (2) acknowledge the range of ages, interests, and abilities of the students, and (3) build strong relationships among the individuals in that class. In this chapter we describe ideas ranging from a school-wide process for establishing classes to setting expectations, appreciating differences among children, building a group identity, and spotlighting strengths.

Creating a Community of Learners:

Setting up multi-age classes requires a little more planning than assigning children to grades. Caren Cameron, Basil Boardman, and Jennifer Davidson, as well as other teachers in Sooke School District, developed a process to establish the possible class combinations:

- ☞ Determine how many children of each age will be in each class.
- ☞ Provide enough unifix cubes to give each age a different color (e.g., five-year-olds, blue; six-year-olds, red; seven-year-olds, green).
- ☞ Use local guidelines to determine how many teachers (classrooms) are being allotted to your school.
- ☞ Decide what class groupings you would like to establish (e.g., two- or three-year spread).
- ☞ Use the unifix cubes to see age combinations that are practical in your school.

You now have graphic demonstrations of possible class configurations. Decide if these situations match children's needs (e.g., having at least six same-age children in each class) or teacher preference (e.g., some teachers feel comfortable with a two-year spread while others seek a wider range of ages).

Next:

- ☞ Take a blank sheet of chart paper and, for each class, note the number of children and their ages.
- ☞ Put the name of each student on a colored strip that corresponds to age, and give each teacher a Post-it glue stick so the strips can be moved.
- ☞ Have each teacher place the students that will be continuing with them (we are not referring to retention or failure; rather those children that will stay for two or more years with the same teacher).
- ☞ When all the children have a tentative placement have teachers and administrators work together to make sure each class has a fair balance of boys and girls, interests, and abilities.
- ☞ Look at each class and move children's name strips if needed to create the best possible placement for each child.

In the traditional single-age classroom, where children are assumed to have the same abilities and interests, students are given a lesson or demonstration and then all are expected to respond in the same way.

How then, you might ask, can children of different ages and abilities in a multi-age classroom all do the same activity? When someone asked our colleague Daphne McNaughton that question, she clarified the situation by using the example of a group of friends who go to the same movie: we all experience it differently. Some like it, some don't. Our responses may vary from telling others, reading the book the movie was based on, to the professional viewers who are paid to publicly share their responses.

In the real world our response has a personal and/or practical function. The functions of response in school are often assessment or practice of skills. We want to know what students learned, felt about a shared experience, or we want to provide opportunities for more practical use of the skills and processes of communication.

Because one task of the school is to help students build their communication skills and increase ways they represent what they know, asking them to share their responses is valid. The problem occurs when we expect all students to respond in the same way at the same time. Those who do not respond in the expected way at the expected time are assessed as having a "problem."

A key to understanding multi-age classes is to get beyond the expectation that everyone needs to do the same thing at the same time in the same way. Inviting children of various ages to listen to a speaker, watch a class demonstration, film or video, and respond in a variety of ways increases the number of students who are able to demonstrate their learning and build upon it.

To create a community of learners, we must increase the possibilities for students of various ages and abilities to respond to their experiences. Chapter 6 (on Representing) provides practical examples of turning this concept into classroom reality.

Creating a Community of Learners: **SANITY SAVERS**

Sometimes it will feel like your multi-age class is not working. What may be happening has little to do with multi-age grouping and a lot to do with routines that are causing, not solving, problems.

When you work with a multi-age class you have to find ways to ensure each child becomes a considerate and responsible class member. Watch that younger children are not seen as helpless or held back from doing tasks because of their age. Make sure older children participate but are not burdened by expectations of taking care of the younger children. Like all well-functioning classrooms, multi-age classes work best when there are routines that facilitate an equal sharing of rights and responsibilities.

Consider these five sanity savers.

① Children need to use the bathroom when they decide but, for safety, teachers need to know where they are. Try these:

· wipe-off slate so that children can sign out when they need to leave.

· give each child a clothes peg with his or her name. When the child leaves the room the clothes peg is moved to designated spot

② 20-30 children in a cloakroom area invite disaster. Try this:
· give each child a number for the year and send children according to even/odd multiples— numbers to match numbers on coat hooks

③ A group of activities children can do as soon as they enter the room allows teachers time to deal with the unexpected occurrences and parent requests
Try:
· morning exploration
· logic puzzles
· reading routines
· jigsaw puzzles
· "What's next!" on chalkboard with activities detailed

When things aren't going well check to see if it is because of the location of furniture, materials, supplies, or transition routines.
Try *Instant Replay!* p. 37
Try *Asking Students.* p. 85

⑤ Getting materials and books.
· Containers of materials strategically located around the room save needless trips and confusion.
· A rotating system of equipment monitors.

④ Lining up can become a listening and thinking activity if children are invited by birth month, number in family, number of letters in name, buttons on shirts, colors on clothing, first and/or last initials, and so on.
Consider that pairs of students make a more manageable line.

Sanity savers

What are your favorite sanity savers?

Creating a Community of Learners: INSTANT REPLAY

A picture (video) is worth a thousand words. Instead of *telling* students when their behavior is inappropriate, *show* them. Have them watch themselves on video, then guide them to identify helpful behaviors. There is no need to talk about the negative ones—they're obvious! Here's a sure-fire recipe to increase the positive behaviors! Try this during classroom cleanup.

1. Set up a video camera.

2. Record what's going on.

3. Show the class the video.

4. Ask: "What's working? What could we be doing better?" (Set guidelines for what can be discussed; for example, actions, not individuals.)

5. Repeat the process in two to five days and as a group focus on what is working now and what could have been done better.

Creating a Community of Learners: SHARED RESPONSIBILITY AND INDIVIDUAL ACCOUNTABILITY

Clear expectations for behaviors by everyone help maintain a positive classroom community. When children help establish the expectations, they understand and are more likely to act responsibly within the agreed upon limits. Use the following strategy in a class of older students to collaboratively set expectations:

1. Explain to students that communities that work well together have agreed upon ways to get things done, get along with one another, and take care of one another. Sometimes the rules are so well understood they don't need to be written down.

2. Arrange the students in groups of four. Ask the groups to think about how they would like to be treated by the teacher and by one another. Record their ideas for guidelines of behavior on a sheet of paper. Common ideas we have observed are being respectful of others, being helpful, working quietly, and listening to others.

3. Have a member of each group share one idea. Proceed around the groups until all ideas have been shared. Post each group's ideas and have everyone think about the ideas.

4. When you are ready to revisit the guidelines (in a couple of hours or the next day), remind students of their earlier discussion. Have them meet in their groups and list the three most important ideas they, as a group, would like as classroom expectations.

5. Have one member of each group report the three ideas. Record all ideas on an overhead transparency, grouping similar ones. Share with the students the ideas you think are important and add them to the list.

6. Have the members of each group talk among themselves about the ideas that have been generated. Have each group make a list it thinks everyone in the class will agree upon.

7. As a class, discuss the ideas and clarify any problems. Then ask the groups to work towards a class consensus. As facilitator, look for common ground among group suggestions. Inform the students they are presumed to be in agreement unless they indicate disagreement. Class consensus is achieved when students agree that they either, at best, enthusiastically agree or, at worst, can live with the expectations recorded. (Our preference is to avoid voting because it forces individuals to pick sides and tends to divide communities into winners and losers.)

Once the ideas have been agreed upon, have groups create reference charts of preferred behaviors and what they look and sound like. Display these in the classroom.

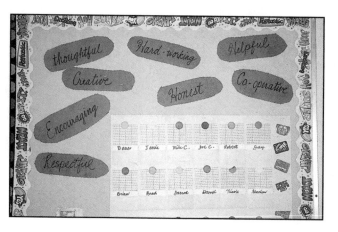

These expectations are gradually woven into the fabric of classroom interactions as you: (1) ask students to consider their actions in light of agreed upon expectations; (2) use the "looks like" and "sounds like" lists as tools for reflection; or (3) ask students to monitor their own behavior during classroom activities.

Part of developing a community of learners is having everyone take responsibility for their actions. Students and teachers establish and reinforce the expectations. This process lets teachers build a safety net within which their students are able to make positive decisions and become individually accountable for their actions.

Creating a Community of Learners: GETTING TO KNOW EACH OTHER

It is important for people in every group to get to know one another, particularly in a multi-age class, so that stereotyping by age can be avoided or overcome. Every teacher has a repertoire of ways to help classmates get to know one another. One of our favorites includes beginning the year with a "Getting To Know You" theme.

The web below shows some possibilities of activities that help us learn about one another. The more we learn about the things we have in common the less we focus on our differences. The more we know that we share with others the more likely we are to feel safe and able to take risks. We repeat these activities and find new ones throughout the year as we continue to thoughtfully build a powerful learning environment.

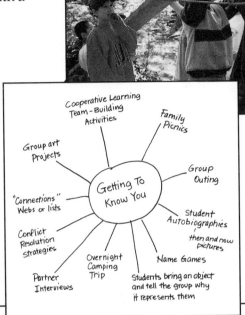

"Getting to Know You" web

Connections web

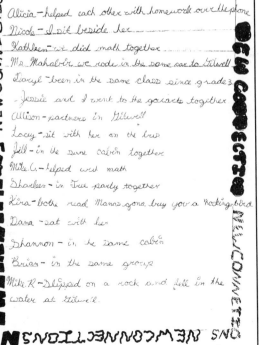

Connections list

*Creating a **Community** of Learners:* **TALENT SPOTLIGHT**

Many of the talents children demonstrate outside school have less to do with age than with experience and opportunity. Highlighting these talents helps everyone see beyond age and towards the contribution each child can make. One way to turn the spotlight on individual strengths is to have a talent week.

- ☞ Invite students to decide on a talent they are willing to share.
- ☞ Provide a sign-up sheet and a note to parents (or have students write their own note).

Talent Spotlight Sign-Up

Date	Name	Name
M 13th	Willow - ballet	Shawn - Taekwon Do
T 14th	Rady - ice hockey	Laurie - oil painting
W 15th	Sara - piano	Mrs. Davidson - cross-stitch
Th 16th	Kimberly - auto mechanics	Chondeh - chess
F 17th	Rachel - figure skating	Taylor masks
M 20th	Lindsey - clarinet	Sterling modeling
T 21st	Thea - swimming	Sammy - computer
W 22nd	Anna - gardening	Jerome - dogs
Th 23rd	Davinder - sewing	Han - cribbage
F 24th	Field Trip ———————————————→	
M 27th	Amy - synchronized swimming	Klaus - fishing
T 28th	Steven - soccer	George - horses
W 29th	Luke pencil drawing	Janet - X country running
Th 30th	Paul - Magic	Liam - poem

- ☞ Set aside time for Spotlight so that several children can perform or tell about a skill they have.
- ☞ Encourage other students to ask questions and make positive comments.

To extend this activity a colleague, Julie Wilmot, has developed an Expert Lesson process. When a student reports on his or her area of expertise, all the other students take notes during the presentation and talk or write about what they learned from their classmates. Talent Spotlight can also be used to invite parents to share their talents.

Creating a Community of Learners: "WE" POSTERS

Building a sense of community means spotlighting similarities as well as talents to establish shared interests and abilities.

☛ As a class, we brainstorm to discover shared interests and abilities. All suggestions are recorded.

☛ In partners or small groups, children choose a topic and make a poster to illustrate it.

☛ Posters are set up around the classroom. Children have time to sign the posters that pertain to them and their interests.[1]

"We" posters

We like the Blue Jays!!	We have dogs !!	We ride bikes to School
Rebecca Luke	Sheena	A.J.
Leon Elijah	Ross	Dallas
Randy Paul	Mac	Basil
Scott Ret	Jolene	Rochelle
Joy Caren	Lori Sue	Linda

Creating a Community of Learners: CLASS MEETINGS

While group meetings are teaching and sharing times, class meetings, as described in many texts and programs on classroom management, help overcome the practice of putting the "oldest in charge" and are used to develop positive, productive relationships among students. The structure of the meeting allows everyone to express opinions and ideas. To set up class meetings:

1. Announce when and where the meeting is to be held, explaining that all who attend may discuss anything about the class that they need to talk about.

---

1. We adapted this activity from the "We" Banners activity presented in a cooperative learning workshop by Laurie Robertson of Kagan and Associates.

2. Provide a space on the chalkboard or on chart paper for children to record topics they wish to discuss.

3. Decide on a chairperson.

4. Arrange the chairs in a circle so everyone can be seen and heard.

5. Call the meeting to order. During the meeting have the student chairperson name the first topic, give everyone an opportunity to comment (this is not a debate), and ask for ideas for solutions. Each topic should be discussed until the students agree upon a plan and decide the action they will take.

6. To conclude the meeting, have the chairperson review the agenda, invite comments on how the meeting went, set the date for the next meeting, and remind everyone to list topics as they arise for the next meeting.

 ### Creating a Community of Learners: FAMILY PICNIC

Planning an informal activity early in the year that involves the students' families helps to create a comfortable climate between parents and the teacher. Such an activity gives the teacher the opportunity to informally talk about the child's experiences in a

multi-age class and sets the tone for ongoing communication. One such event is a family picnic held in a local park. Other ways to build a comfortable climate and let parents see multi-age classes in action are:

☛ Invite parents to join the class for lunch at school.
☛ Invite parents and their children to join you and your family for a swim at a local pool.
☛ Hold typical year-end events like beach trips, camping trips, outdoor games and sports days in the first month of school.

SUMMARY

In this chapter we have described some ways that help us make a group of individuals into a supportive learning community. We make our selections and decisions about the types of activities we use by asking ourselves the following questions:

- ☛ Is the class a workable group? Does it have a range of ages and abilities, and a mixture of perspectives?
- ☛ How will the routines we've selected facilitate rather than interfere with building positive relationships?
- ☛ How are we sharing decision making with children?
- ☛ What things are we doing to help children learn about and appreciate one another's talents?
- ☛ What processes do we have for solving problems?
- ☛ How are we involving our students' families?

The following chapter contains a wealth of suggestions for practical, functional ways to organize space and materials to facilitate learning.

What are some possibilities for creating a community with your class?

Using Physical Space, Materials, and Supplies

A multi-age class needs the same things other classes need—a space in which to learn and materials with which to work. Any differences may lie in how the space is arranged and how materials are used. Decisions about space and materials are motivated by the teacher's desire to help the students acquire skills in working cooperatively and becoming independent learners.

We, as educators, all dream of huge classrooms with lots of natural light, unlimited storage space, carpeted and wet areas, as well as numerous electrical outlets. In reality the classrooms we get range from our ideal to our worst nightmare. We have to do the best we can with what we have.

No one but you can plan your classroom. First, the available space, furniture, and learning resources and materials need to be assessed. And, throughout the year, as you and your children work together, it will need to be rearranged to meet emerging needs. Regardless of the space allotted or the ages of your students, however, consider the following needs when you are setting up:

☞ **A space for everyone to store their belongings.** This might be a desk, a plastic bin, cubby hole, or locker.

☞ **Enough space for everyone to work.** This does not mean a desk for everyone or any permanent space. There is an ongoing debate about the value of children having their own personal space in the class—a desk versus flexible spaces that can be used at different times for different things. We prefer flexible spaces.

☞ **A group meeting place.** Younger children seem happy with a large carpeted area while older children tend to prefer desks and chairs, or to lounge on cushions, beanbag chairs, and sofas.

☞ **Storage space and containers for materials.** Rectangular containers allow for better use of space and help keep storage shelves tidy. Shelves on casters are easy to move when you want to create functional working spaces and storage for paper and art materials.

☛ **Storage space for different-sized books, magazines, and charts.** Not only does our ideal classroom have plenty of shelves for books of different sizes, magazines, and charts, but it has comfortable seating for reading and relaxing. Books can also be stored in plastic bins, boxes, or baskets. You can mount rows of chalkboard ledges on the walls under chalkboards to create more display space for books.

☛ **A variety of working spaces and places.** Create smaller working spaces by using furniture that can be easily moved such as shelves, couches, and chairs. Consider having all furniture put on casters.

Just as library collections are built over time so too are classroom collections. Make your wish list and build towards it. Appeal to colleagues and parents for donations. Over time you will shape and reshape your classroom to better meet your needs and the needs of your students.

Once basic requirements have been considered, you may find it useful to organize the classroom into activity and storage areas. There are many possibilities. Some teachers choose to have several areas, others select a few, while still others rotate materials in and out of the classroom depending on their students' learning needs and the space available. The decision to have a particular set of learning materials has to do with increasing the learning possibilities. Consider involving your students in planning and choosing activities and materials that support and further their learning.

One way to make materials accessible is to arrange them according to their use. Some people call these collections "centers" but because of the many interpretations of this label we prefer to talk about "activity areas." These areas give us a way to organize our regular classroom "stuff" plus the things we've added to encourage more active, hands-on learning for children. These areas or centers hold no special qualities of their own. They are simply places to store things until they are brought to life by children and teachers posing thoughtful questions and challenges and interacting with one another.

As you read through this chapter, you may think it would take a classroom the size of a gym to contain all the activity areas we mention. Certainly, most classrooms do not have enough space for all the things described. One time we made a large sign for each area, then realized that several activity areas were so compact they were hidden by the signs themselves! Some areas, for example the listening area, do not require a lot of space. You have to decide which activity areas and materials will be most beneficial to your students at any particular time. They will, by their choices, let you know which activity areas meet their needs. Some people may think that setting up activity areas in the classroom is for younger children—in our experience such an organization is equally beneficial for older children.

Using Physical Space, Materials, and Supplies:

Can you think of a friend/colleague who will help you assess the space, materials, and equipment you have?

Using Physical Space, Materials, and Supplies: **READING AREA**

An ideal reading area has storage for a wide selection of books (fiction and nonfiction), reference materials (atlas, dictionary, globes, maps, thesaurus, set of encyclopedia), magazines, and charts, as well as comfortable seating (couches, chairs, cushions, oversize bean-bags). Although we don't use class sets of anthologies or readers, multiple copies of some books are useful. Space to attractively display books helps to draw children into the collection. A container for holding reading response journals can be placed on the shelf so that children get into the habit of recording their reading selections. Lap tables make writing more inviting.

 Using Physical Space, Materials, and Supplies: **WRITING AND DRAWING AREA**

Locating a writing and drawing center near the reading area gives children access to reference materials and a quiet environment. The basics of a writing and drawing area are a selection of paper (lined, unlined, various sizes and colors), mini-chalkboards, pens, pencils, chalk, and a recycling bin. This area can include a table or group of desks. The materials can be stored in the area and used where the children choose to write or draw. Date stamps can be attached with strings to shelves or tables to help children and teachers get into the habit of dating all their work.

Using Physical Space, Materials, and Supplies:
TAKE APART/DECONSTRUCTION AREA

The only cost involved in setting up this area may be in buying tools such as screwdrivers, small hammers, and pliers. We have found we could gather most of these through donations. Things to take apart—

telephones, radios, toasters, watches, and clocks—are easily obtained. Have children wear safety goggles when they are working in this area and review safety procedures with them. This center has as much appeal and learning value for older children as for younger children.

Using Physical Space, Materials, and Supplies:
WOODWORKING AREA

Some teachers are fortunate enough to have classrooms equipped with a workbench, vise, safety goggles, and accompanying tools that provide children with opportunities to build projects with wood. These teachers consider themselves even more fortunate if the equipment is located in an area that has easy access to outdoor space. Lumber may be available through donation, and safety rules need to be emphasized.

Using Physical Space, Materials, and Supplies:
MATHEMATICS AREA

As we involve children in enjoyable mathematics activities, they develop a love of mathematics. This becomes obvious as they seek out opportunities to play games and use materials introduced during

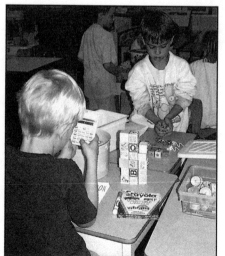

math lessons. Having math materials and manipulatives available for children provides opportunities for practice and play, which leads to a deeper and richer understanding of mathematical concepts. Basic materials include dice, unit blocks, pattern blocks, calculators, and materials for classification. Professional organizations, books, catalogs, and colleagues are helpful in identifying additional materials.

Providing materials for every classroom can be expensive. To lower costs one solution is to create math carts that hold a cataloged set of materials. These can be borrowed on a rotating basis. The materials might include geometric solids, a range of equipment used for measurement, sophisticated building materials, tangrams, and puzzles.

Using Physical Space, Materials, and Supplies: MUSIC AREA

Locating a music area adjacent to the listening center lets children listen to tapes and records of their choice. As records become less available many classrooms are acquiring CD players. Musical instruments available on short- or long-term loan to the classroom let children explore sound and experiment with making their own music. In schools where sufficient computer technology is available children can create their own compositions and have them replayed and recorded as sheet music. Those of you lucky enough to have music specialists to consult with may discover additional and exciting possibilities.

Using Physical Space, Materials, and Supplies: ARTS AND CRAFTS AREA

An area where art materials (e.g., variety of papers, crayons, markers, pens, brushes, charcoal, Plasticine, oil pastels, glue, scissors, and fabric scraps) are readily available gives children a place to experiment with different media and extends their capabilities through self-directed projects. Agreeing on or establishing a place to dry, display, and store creations saves everybody a lot of grief. Portable clothes drying racks and clotheslines strung below chalkboards are effective options.

Collecting wonderful junk not only contributes to recycling but provides many children with powerful media to represent their ideas. Cardboard boxes, paper tubes, plastic packaging can be transformed into computers, spaceships, motorcycles, and sailboats. Although the budget for masking tape may triple, the cost is worth it as the skills that children develop and refine through construction show them the possibilities for expressing their ideas in three dimensional forms. Having writing and drawing materials available encourages designing, planning, and labeling.

Using Physical Space, Materials, and Supplies: BLOCKS AND CONSTRUCTION AREA

The large wooden and foam blocks found in many primary classrooms are ideal but expensive. Some teachers have been able to get high-school woodworking classes to sand and finish lumber scraps. Others have created blocks by pushing open ends of milk cartons into each other. You may know of other creative alternatives. Smaller construction materials (such as Lego, Construx, Googolplex) can be used as effectively in all classrooms by all ages. More complex building materials (such as Lego Technic), designed to encourage older children to explore advanced scientific and mathematical relationships, allow for the construction of structures with moving parts—some advanced projects include computer technology such as robotics. Having writing materials available encourages children to label their creations or plan and refine their designs.

Using Physical Space, Materials, and Supplies: EASEL PAINTING AREA

Students of all ages benefit from the opportunity to express their ideas through large-scale painting. If your classroom is not equipped with an easel or does not have space for one, a bulletin board can be converted by attaching a ledge with holes cut to hold paint containers. Two hints: (1) dish detergent added to liquid tempera helps it to adhere to all surfaces and makes it more washable and (2) trimming the handles of long-handled paintbrushes reduces the number of classroom accidents.

Using Physical Space, Materials, and Supplies: SAND TABLE AND WATER TABLE AREA

Sand[1] and water tables as well as containers, molds, and measuring equipment are basic to many primary classrooms. We are beginning to value the possibilities these pieces of equipment have in helping older children to understand mathematical and scientific concepts (observation, classification, measurement, and inference). A practical way of responding to the cost of this equipment is to share between classrooms.

---

1. We prefer to use sand rather than rice, wheat, or beans because of our concern about the message that is delivered when children play in food while other children in our world may not have enough to eat.

Using Physical Space, Materials, and Supplies: LISTENING AREA

This area provides not only a good learning space to listen to music or read along with books on tape but also a place of relative quiet in a busy classroom. A record, CD or tape player, and a listening post with headphones are basic equipment. Supplement commercial books and recording sets by taping daily read-aloud sessions. Besides providing enjoyment the listening area gives emergent and struggling readers access to interesting and relevant stories and information. Local public libraries have many books on tape.

Using Physical Space, Materials, and Supplies: ASSESSMENT AREA

As ongoing assessment becomes an integral part of our daily routine, we must establish places to hold collections of children's works-in-progress. Shirt boxes, pizza boxes, magazine files, plastic bins, and shopping bags can provide personalized storage. Having storage bags available is one way to encourage students to take work-in-progress home to share with family members. The assessment area needs to be easily and constantly accessible to students and they have to be given time on a regular basis so they can decide what work they want to save in their files or portfolios. Tying a date stamp in a prominent location will assist students in developing the habit of dating their work.

Using Physical Space, Materials, and Supplies: GAMES AND PUZZLES AREA

When students use games and puzzles they learn how to identify the strategic and cooperative skills they need. By being involved in their own learning, children value their own play more and, in turn, help parents understand the value of games in the classroom. Games and puzzles that appeal to the range of ages and interests of everyone in your class need to be provided. A newsletter appeal for quality used items usually nets a beginning collection. (Any incomplete contributions are well used in the arts and crafts area.) Students' use of games and puzzles is enhanced if you involve them in identifying the strategic and cooperative skills they need to use during play.

Using Physical Space, Materials, and Supplies: COMPUTER AREA

Many classrooms are now equipped with computers. These can be used in conjunction with the writing center or, depending on the range of software available, with any number of activity choices. A timer and agreement on length of time individuals or groups may remain at the equipment facilitates classroom harmony.

Using Physical Space, Materials, and Supplies: DRAMATIC PLAY AREA

Dramatic play centers have evolved from the house center found in many kindergartens. Teachers who observe children selecting materials to complement themes comment that the children's play reveals their understanding of curricular concepts. Older children make effective use of a "prop box" to dramatize stories, readers' theater scripts, and historical events.

Using Physical Space, Materials, and Supplies: PUPPET PLAY AREA

Commercial or student-made puppets encourage children to express themselves through the safety of taking on a character. Puppets provide effective ways for students to retell and demonstrate their understanding of stories and situations. Inexpensive, easy-to-store puppet theaters can be made by hanging fabric across doorways or chart stands.

Using Physical Space, Materials, and Supplies: SCIENCE AND NATURE AREA

This area contains an ongoing collection of items that can range from a snake's skin to abandoned birds' nests to things like magnifying glasses, microscopes, weight scales, measuring devices, and tracing paper (and other things useful for examining/studying the collection). Have paper and writing materials available to encourage students to record their observations.

Using Physical Space, Materials, and Supplies: CHILDREN'S CHOICE AREA

Have children bring in their own collections for display or have them set up activities that other children can try. For example, one child might bring a rock collection, guidebook, and magnifying glass while another might teach others how to make paper baskets. (Make a list of contents so that all the pieces get safely home again.)

Using Physical Space, Materials, and Supplies: GROUP MEETING AREA

Many primary classes have a carpeted area set aside for meetings; in intermediate classrooms students may sit in their work areas. Regardless of the seating arrangements, choose a focus area where the daily agenda and other important materials are posted. Read-aloud materials and charts for classroom routines such as attendance and lunch count are kept here.

Teachers need ready access to equipment such as an overhead projector, video camera and tripod, VCR, and monitor. To make space for activity areas, many teachers have traded their oversize desks in for a "teacher center"—a shelf, a storage cupboard, or a small table that takes the place of the traditional desk.

Using Physical Space, Materials, and Supplies: GOING GREEN

Making the three *R*s—reduce, reuse, and recycle—part of the classroom routine has many benefits. We become more thoughtful about and make a practical contribution to environmental awareness. As well, students are given more choice in and responsibility for tasks. Some things that work for us are

- using small chalkboards rather than paper for writing, math practice, and line drawing

- having children create their own comment sheets using the backs of paper from the recycling bin
- encouraging students to write their own frames on recycled paper instead of giving them precopied sheets. (Beyond the cost of the paper, every copied sheet costs money and uses chemicals!)
- storing copies of readers' theater scripts in the library for classes to borrow when needed instead of having copies produced for each class

SUMMARY

Our goal in this chapter has been to demonstrate ways to use resources and turn any classroom space into a dynamic learning environment. To evaluate the way we have set up our classroom we ask ourselves the following questions:

- What do I need to consider to make this a safe place for all of us?
- Have I created a variety of work spaces that appeal to people with different interests and learning needs?
- How do the traffic patterns lend themselves to harmonious movement?
- How have I invited children and colleagues to make suggestions about the design of the classroom or be partners in its construction?

In the chapters that follow we present the activities and structures we have found to be effective in facilitating instructional planning and promoting student learning.

How can you close the gap between what you have and what you want to have?

RETHINKING INSTRUCTION

The questions people usually ask are, "What do you do when you've got children who are barely able to write their name and others who are able to do anything and everything? How do you do it? How do you handle the range?"

Our answer: We expand our notion of instruction. We reconsider and revisit our instructional strategies/processes to ensure they allow the widest possible range of response. If we think about any curriculum area as being something we do with a particular set of materials in a particular way at a particular time, we are unable to respond to a wide range of abilities, interests, and needs.

All instruction has two facets—learning *about* the curriculum or subject area and learning *through* the curriculum or subject area. For example, we learn *how* to read different kinds of materials and we learn *when* we read different kinds of materials. As teachers we provide opportunities for children to learn about the curriculum through mini-lessons, demonstrations, modeling, and activities. We help students learn through curriculum when we provide opportunities to construct knowledge and use skills and processes by, for example, conversing, thinking, writing, talking, reading, constructing, computing, creating, building, and experimenting.

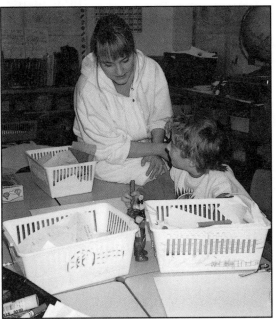

When we think about any curriculum area and when we consider the range of abilities, interests, and needs among our group of children we can find ourselves in the midst of chaos. As educators we have selected from teaching strategies that have been effective in the past and we have developed some additional open-ended processes that provide order for us and our students. They work because they provide choice, personal connections, and purposeful learning. They work because they acknowledge that children

- ☞ need to work both alone and with others
- ☞ learn in different ways and at different rates
- ☞ learn by actively participating in their own learning

The ideas in this section are examples of the ways students engage in learning about their world, and how, as readers, writers, mathematicians, scientists, thinkers, learners, and doers of all kinds, they learn. Please select those ideas that make sense for you and your students. Use these ideas as starting points for refining strategies you currently use as well as new strategies you and your students might invent. Please notice the routines facilitate learning—and provide time for teachers to observe and plan.

Rethinking Instruction:

Rethinking Instruction: READERS' CLUB—THEIRS AND MINE!

Readers' Club is an activity that engages children of all ages and abilities in reading. Its purposes are to:

- engage children in reading
- get children talking about books
- support children reading aloud
- focus children's attention on what good readers do when they read
- give the teacher time to listen to and assess each student's reading
- model the giving of specific compliments

Hold Readers' Club daily until the children are ready to move on to another reading activity such as Nine Ps (see page 59) or Triple Choice (see page 60).

Before beginning Readers' Club develop the routine of having the children select books from the library or a classroom collection to use for independent reading. This is known by many names—USSR, SSR, DEAR, SYNIB—and is a quiet, independent reading time. Encourage children to read with partners or in small groups as long as their reading does not disturb others.

When the children are comfortable with this routine, introduce Readers' Club by talking about the reasons why they need to share their reading.

Have the children pick one day per week when they will share something they are reading. Provide a sign-up sheet and have them each choose their day to come to Readers' Club.

Have the four to six children who have signed up for Readers' Club select a book or part of a book that they can read to the group. Then, meet at a central location in the classroom, while the other children read independently or in quiet partnerships.

For the first several meetings guide the process by asking:

- Who would like to read first?
- What did you choose?
- Why did you make this choice?
- Can you read your book or selection for us?

Have a notebook or file cards set up with each child's name on a separate sheet or card. Enter the date, title of selection, and comments about the child's reading in the notebook. Use these notes to glean information on what specific reading strategies might be useful to teach to the whole class or small groups of students.

When each child is finished reading ask the Readers' Club group, "Who has compliments for _____?" (See page 88, chapter 7 for more on the concept of compliments.) Initially compliments tend to be general: "She did a good job." Ask questions such as, "What made it good?" or "Can you describe what she did well?" to elicit more specific compliments.

Once the children have given each other compliments, model compliments that are even more specific ("You really used expression with that!"). These in turn help children to identify the strategies good readers use.

At the conclusion of Readers' Club invite the children to compliment group members and the many students who had been reading on their own. Give the class another five minutes to read while you talk with other children about their reading, and make individual comments about their helpful behavior. Note who is signed up for the next day's Readers' Club session.

Two or three times a week, spend five to ten minutes with the whole group for a mini-lesson or group reading before or after the Readers' Club session. This is an opportunity for you to teach a specific concept such as using punctuation to guide reading.

Readers' Club, held every day for approximately thirty to forty minutes, includes the following routine:

- ☞ All children are reading.
- ☞ Children who are signed up for Readers' Club meet with the teacher to share a selection, listen to others, and give compliments.
- ☞ Teacher circulates to talk with children who have been reading on their own (having most of the class reading while club members share enables the teacher to concentrate on the club members).

Marilyn Chapman, a colleague of ours who introduced us to this activity, found that having children bring books by other authors one week (Readers' Club) and their own writing the next week (Writers' Club) provided real reading practice, and also helped children make connections between what published authors did in their writings and what they did in their own.

Readers' Club works as effectively for young children who might be selecting familiar big books or pattern books as for older readers who may be focusing on highlights from chapter books or nonfiction selections. Students may also choose to read from their own writing. Many teachers say that if they read poetry to the class, children begin to choose poems for their Readers' Club selections on a regular basis.

Readers' Club becomes a favorite reading routine for children and teachers. Once the routines are established the children can run the club meetings. This will give you opportunities to make notes about individual progress and reading behaviors. Remember—you can shape the basic format to meet the needs of your class.

Rethinking Instruction: NINE Ps READING

Nine Ps Reading is designed to help all readers—whether beginning, developing, or independent—extend their reading abilities. The process is as follows:

1. **Partners:** The teacher chooses a partner for each child.

2. **Pick:** Each child picks something to read.

3. **Plan:** The children decide where to sit, how much each person will read, and in what order they will read.

4. **Practice:** The child most comfortable with the task reads his selection first, receives a compliment from his partner, and then reads his partner's selection. Following this the partner reads her selection and is complimented by her partner.

5. **Polish:** After each child has had a chance to read, the children get together, pick a short selection to polish, and then read it to the whole group.

6. **Politeness please:** Before the partner presents, the teacher asks if there is anything they want from the group while they are presenting. Typical comments include "If you have anything in your hands put it down please" or "Please look at us when we present."

7. **Present:** All students gather to share their polished selections. The children arrange chairs in a circle so that everyone can be seen and heard. Each child or group of children is given the chance to present a short selection.

8. **Praise:** Each presenter is invited to choose one person to give them a compliment for their performance. A child's ability to recognize good reading strategies becomes apparent in the kind of compliment he or she gives the presenter.

9. **Put books away:** Give children sufficient time to put books away. Have bins or shelves available so that children can store the books with care.

At the conclusion of Nine *P*s Reading, have the children make comments about favorite reading materials and what they have learned from others in their group.

Rethinking Instruction: TRIPLE CHOICE READING

To emphasize the range of reading choices available and to accommodate different levels of readers, we developed another reading routine for primary children: Triple Choice. All children choose to join one of three groups:

- ☞ **Big book buddies** (for emergent readers) read familiar big books together.
- ☞ **Picture book partners** (everyone) read picture books together.
- ☞ **Chapter chatterers** (for those who can manage this material with fluency) meet in groups of two to four to read passages from chapter books and talk with one another about what they have read.

Divide the room into three zones. Have big book buddies meet in an area large enough for four or five children to read big books at an easel, chalkboard, or on the floor. Have chapter chatterers and picture book partners meet in the other two areas.

While each of the three groups is working, move around and join each group for a time to observe or lend support. Near the conclusion of Triple Choice time, invite one person from each group to tell the rest of the class what their group did.

Children who have had experience with Readers' Club or Nine *P*s Reading are familiar with the responsibilities of being part of a group of readers. In Triple Choice Reading children know they can be part of any group they select and that any group they select will provide valuable reading practice. This way of sharing also helps children identify books they want to read.

A variation of Triple Choice is Magazine Mixers, Nonfiction Fanciers, or Realistic Readers.

Children, like adults, eventually experience information overload. Collecting information from a variety of sources and then making sense of it is an ongoing, lifelong challenge. In this reading experience the task is to gather as much information about a single topic from as many different sources as possible. The starting point is always something of interest to the children—a question that they, and you, wish to pursue.

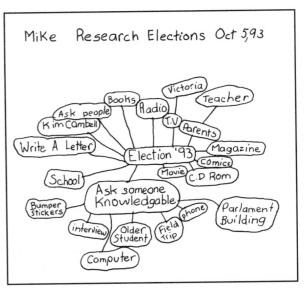

Information roundup web

1. Identify a common interest of everyone in the classroom or ask a burning question to which everyone wants to know the answer.

2. Web or chart all that everyone knows or thinks they know about the topic.

3. Identify all the possible sources of information about the topic.

4. Begin to collect the information sources—books, filmstrips, family stories, magazines, CD-ROM databases, videos, and so on.

5. Find a place to store the collected materials—provide separate places for stories, quotations, pictures, posters.

6. Identify the different ways that learning can be represented. Consider: dioramas, word webs, picture mosaics, key phrases, readers' theater presentations, poetry, and journal writing.

7. Discuss and determine how students are going to work with the information. The class may choose to work together as one large group, contributing to a vast collection of commonly held information; as several small groups focusing on gathering and sharing information for presentation; or as individuals working side by side with others on personal projects.

8. Collect, read, talk, read, share, read, collect, read, talk, read, share, read, collect, read, talk, read, share, read until the topic has been exhausted.

9. Conclude the activity by reviewing where information can be found, what kinds of information were useful, ways to keep the information, and ways to display information. Finally, reflect on what has been learned individually, as a group, as readers, and as learners.

Rethinking Instruction: MIX, MATCH, COMPARE, AND CONTRAST FORMS

As readers gain fluency, we provide additional reading challenges. One such challenge is to discover the kinds of things to be learned through a single form of writing, such as newspapers, diaries, historical novels, encyclopedias, and text of various kinds. A companion challenge is to write in these different forms.

While children have encountered all kinds of texts and have developed a working familiarity with a variety of forms through their daily reading and ongoing research projects, they need to become aware of what they know and learn how to use their knowledge effectively.

Older students have experience reading for a variety of purposes. They need to learn to use different text structures to gain meaning. They need to understand that words and pictures only give part of the message and that authors use other ways, such as charts, figures, metaphors, and text arrangement, to communicate.

Students acquire some of this knowledge through mini-lessons and reading. They also learn through writing when they write like an author in a particular form or genre. They learn when they analyze the texts themselves. The following strategy helps students analyze how authors of different kinds of text convey meaning.

1. Select a form of writing, such as a diary, newspaper article, or poem.

2. Record what you know about that form of writing.

3. Gather lots of samples of that form of writing.

4. Read, read, talk, talk, read, read, talk, talk—in small groups and as a large group. Explore—as a class, as a group, and as individuals—the different ways authors present information to the reader.

5. Record what is being learned on large charts. Formulate hypotheses and look for examples to illustrate the different things different types of writers do depending on the form of writing they do. Prepare charts for each form to use as a class resource.

With older students unfamiliar with examining different kinds of text in this way, have them spend a couple of weeks in intense study, and plan to return later in the year, form new groups, and update the charts.

While this exercise focuses mainly on the *form* of different types of writing, and the purposes served by those forms of writing, it can also be used to explore the different *genres* of writing, such as science fiction, mysteries, and fairy tales. This will focus more on *content* issues; that is, fairy tales usually start with "once upon a time," contain an evil stepmother, queen, or witch, use the number three or seven (three brothers, seven dwarfs), and so on.

Rethinking Instruction: WRITING MATTERS

Writing is one of the easiest instructional adjustments to make in a multi-age classroom. To create a community of learners who use writing in a variety of forms and for specific purposes, however, you must understand the stages children work through as they move towards fluent independent writing and accept each writer at his or her own developmental level.

To help younger children accept and appreciate the writing process, spend time talking with your students about how they learned to walk, talk, eat, swim, ride bikes, and then connect this discussion to their progress as writers. Writing samples collected from previous students are useful for helping children—and their parents— see how writing progresses.

Assure the children that their ideas are important. All learners, moving through stages and expressing themselves in standard written form, achieve over time. By striving for quality, all writers can improve their writing. Developing simple habits such as rereading their writing and rewriting when necessary (as appropriate for their age and abilities) helps children refine and increase their skills as writers. As one child said: "When you are just starting to write you write all the letters you can; when you have written lots and lots you make your writing look more like in books."

All children, regardless of age, must be given the following if they are to develop confidence and power as writers:

Time: Set aside specific times to give children opportunities to work on their writing. The times that work for us are Writers' Workshop, Reading-Writing Connections, and any other occasion when writing serves a purpose.

Choice: Inviting children to choose topics that interest them and select the appropriate form gives them a sense of commitment and ownership to writing activities. Leon Politano recalls a lesson on paragraph structure with his mixed-age class to which one student responded: "I'll do it to show I can but right now I think better in poetry." Leon responded: "That's great! Write stanzas."

Supportive environment: Creating a climate that shows all efforts are valued gives writers a safe place to develop and refine their abilities. Establish guidelines that make peer editing and presentation sessions positive influences on writing. For example, we use "two stars and a wish" (the writer always receives two positive comments before any suggestions may be offered).

Demonstrations: A five- to ten-minute mini-lesson at the beginning of Writers' Workshop helps provide children with information they might use in their writing. The sources for these lessons are your observations from the children's work. Typical topics for mini-lessons include looking at a piece of published writing and discussing what made it successful, searching for powerful words, or rehearsing the writing process by doing a read-aloud and group edit for a piece of work.

Teachers who write with or in front of the class on a regular basis or read their own writing aloud, report the ongoing chat that accompanies their writing is an effective way to let children see the process in action. Practical situations, such as composing a letter to parents to tell them about an upcoming trip, are ideal ways to involve the class and demonstrate the writing process in action. For example:

1. Ask students: "What do we need to tell your parents about our upcoming trip?" Write their responses on the chalkboard, using a web or list. As a group, decide on an order and priority of the ideas.

2. Compose the first draft in front of the class. This exercise gives you a real reason to talk about standard letter format.

3. As a group, reread the draft. This step reveals to the students the power of read-alouds as a way of matching intent with what was actually written.

4. Have a student do a final draft, then photocopy and send it home with the students.

Daily demonstrations during group meetings help children focus on significant surface features in writing.

Framework: Once children understand that each person is at a different stage of development in writing then we use the framework of viewing writing as a process of

- ☛ collecting ideas
- ☛ writing a first draft
- ☛ revising, proofreading, and editing
- ☛ publishing selected works

This framework for writing provides children with a way of becoming better writers—it is not a lock-step program to be applied to each occasion of writing but rather a way to approach every writing task.

Rethinking Instruction: **MANAGING MATH**

Managing mathematics in a multi-age classroom is similar to planning for a single-age class. We ask ourselves:

- ☛ What experiences do I need to provide (for example, measurement, geometry, numbers)?
- ☛ What do my students know? What can they do? Am I meeting my students' needs?
- ☛ How can I "open up" activities to meet the needs of children with varying understandings and skills? For example, give younger children one die and older children two or three dice. Instruct them to "roll and record." The younger children get practice rolling one die and recording the corresponding digit; the older ones get practice adding or multiplying the numbers on two dice.

Our colleague Jennifer Davidson taught us a simple way to design activities that meet the needs of children at differing levels of mathematical understanding. She asks, "What could this activity look like for beginners, for those with developing understanding, and for children who are ready for challenges?" Each jurisdiction has its own documents outlining curricular requirements. The National Council of Teachers of Mathematics has published guidelines for planning comprehensive mathematics experiences for children.

Stage	Concept:
Beginning	Explores with pattern blocks Creates simple patterns
Developing	Creates and repeats more elaborate patterns. Works with partners to record and recreate patterns.
Extending	Uses tangram shapes and cards to create complex patterns.

Concept grid

We have found it useful to organize math time into three sections: the mini-lesson, guided practice, and independent practice.

During mini-lesson time, talk about what learners need to do to gain knowledge and achieve skill with a particular concept, for example, subtraction with regrouping. Provide guided practice with the concept and then encourage students to work at activities appropriate for their current level of understanding. Because assessment is an integral part of classroom activity, both you and your students need to be aware of what they know and what they need to be doing to learn more. Such information guides students to practice at their own level and refines and extends their understanding.

Use the same concept grid in an intermediate classroom to design appropriate mathematics instruction and activity choices for ten-, eleven-, and twelve-year-olds. Students select appropriate activities given their developing skill with a particular concept. Regardless of the activity chosen students receive practice with the concept being currently focused upon.

Leon Politano has extended this concept with seven-, eight-, and nine-year-olds. After the mini-lesson and guided practice students work on their personal mathematics plan (P.M.P.). Students are responsible for designing the amount and kind of practice required to prepare them for the post-test to be given on that concept. After the mini-lesson and guided practice students get to work, calling upon their teacher when necessary.

Math lesson plan

Tuesday, October 5, 1993

Mathematics: Concept— Addition + Subtraction

    Mini-Lesson— Subtraction with Regrouping

      Guided Practice— Three questions – check with a partner

        Independent Practice— Children choose from a range of options

      Beginning   Developing   Extending

Activity	Activity	Activity	Activity
Round-table Math	Sharpen Your Skills	Partner Math	Puzzles, Problems, and Challenges
(Meet me at the round-table for a group working/learning session.)	(Select questions from p. 31-78 and use a calculator to check your accuracy.)	(Find a partner, get a timer, create your questions and see how speedy you can be!)	(Select a puzzle, problem or challenge; work alone or with a partner.)

Student's Concluding Reflection:
During this mathematics class we practiced ___ subtraction and addition ___ I completed ___

Reproducible master in appendix A

> Mathematics
> Test results
>
> 1. Post-test Addition and subtraction
>
> The only thing I got wrong was
> I forgot to look at the signs.
>
> In my other test I got a very poor
> mark too. I am going to practice questions like
> this :
>
> 5)945   8)1624   128   41)7674
>   x 26

Post-test

Rethinking Instruction: GYM FOR ALL

Some teachers have concerns about planning physical activities for the younger children in a multi-age classroom. Two ways to facilitate appropriate activities for children of all ages are:

Centers: Establish safety criteria for using equipment in the gym. Make sure all students know and understand the rules and regulations before you allow them access to the equipment set out in several centers around the gym.

Zones: Divide the gym into three clearly marked zones. For example, create a space for indoor hockey; another space for activities that use small equipment (such as scooter boards, scoops, and ropes); and a third area for ball activities such as indoor soccer.

Rethinking Instruction: INTEGRATING TO INCREASE CONNECTIONS

We prefer to integrate topics that have been traditionally categorized as science and social studies. Involving children in formulating research questions, doing research, and presenting what they know to others not only builds on their fascination with the world and how it works but also provides them with practical applications for their basic skills. Of course, children will have focused time to develop reading, writing, and mathematics skills. These skills are reinforced and extended through inquiry as children work on integrated projects or themes.

Begin by identifying students' interests and finding a focus that is broad enough to encompass many individual areas of interest. When there are state or provincial requirements for covering particular topics, share this information with the students and invite their suggestions for meeting these requirements.

Traditionally, teachers often had to *drag* students through the curriculum. The simple act of giving children a voice in how and when topics are to be covered creates energy that *propels* them into each subject.

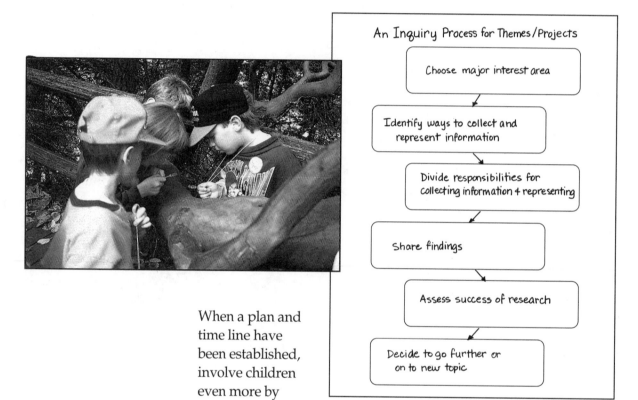

An inquiry process for themes/projects

When a plan and time line have been established, involve children even more by having them build connections between the way they investigate the interest area, topic, subject, or issue and the other instructional activities that are part of their daily classroom life. The chart that follows is an example of the connections a class of six-, seven-, and eight-year-olds made between curriculum areas and their study of rocks.

Integrating learning around themes (the processes we described in *Making Themes Work*) provides us with ways to

- ☛ identify and build on students' interests
- ☛ use relevant topics to extend the curriculum
- ☛ foster development of knowledge, skills, and attitudes

- ☛ give students opportunities to represent and share their learning
- ☛ encourage students to use reflection and self-assessment to refine their work

SUMMARY

In this chapter we have provided you with some examples of ways to extend the curriculum so that your students can be supported in their learning. The common thread throughout is rethinking instruction so that curriculum is beneficial to learners of different ages, abilities, and interests. The questions we use to guide our decisions about how we design instruction are

- ☛ What experiences do I need to plan for (curriculum requirements)?
- ☛ What do my students know? What can they do? What are their interests?
- ☛ How can I broaden activities to meet the needs of children with varying understandings and skills?
- ☛ What have I done to provide challenges?
- ☛ Have I provided children with ways to learn about the curriculum as well as given them opportunities to use processes and strategies?

Topic: Rocks	
Reading	read books, magazines, posters, charts, about rocks
Writing	Make descriptions of rocks, label rocks
Speaking	Tell the class what was found
Listening	Invite a person from the rock shop to talk to us. Watch a film on volcanoes
Representing	Make web, poster, chart to show different kinds of rocks.
Math	· Weigh · Measure · Sort rocks by shape, size, color, type · Count rocks in our collection
Science	· Collect rocks · Match rocks we find to rock sample chart in library · Go to the Rock Shop to find out more information
Social Studies	Find out how people use rocks: · houses · sign posts · artwork
Fine Arts	· Make pebble pictures · Paint rocks · Look at native rock paintings · Compare colors (+ texture) of rocks

Connecting interests to the curriculum

You cannot determine how successful instruction has been until students show what they have learned. The following chapter focuses on how you can provide opportunities for children of different ages and stages to represent what they know in a variety of ways.

Remind yourself of your favorite personal and professional resources.

Is it time to revisit them?

6

REPRESENTING OUR LEARNING

Traditionally, students showed what they knew or felt in written form. Students who did not master this form quickly or easily were often viewed as "slow learners." Today, we realize that these "slow learners" might know or understand a topic but may not yet have the skills to present that knowledge in the expected form.

Howard Gardner's work (1985) on multiple intelligences shows that there are more ways to view and show intelligence than through the traditional tests used in schools. By creating arenas that allow individuals to display their strengths we, as one child said, "Let more kids be smart!"

The confidence in one's self and one's abilities that comes from working in an area of strength carries over and helps students develop and refine their abilities and skills in all areas.

Encouraging children in multi-age classes to represent their thinking in a variety of ways has the added benefit of breaking down the stereotypical notion that older children are more capable and, therefore, will always help younger children. Watching children paint reveals that talent has little to do with age. When students can express their learning in different ways, individual strengths can be highlighted and used to support further learning. Encouraging the development of various ways to represent learning helps students see each other's potential and sets the stage for combining the various abilities found in the class for collaborative efforts.

Some of the different ways of representing are[1]

activity book	fairy tale	panel discussion
advertisement	film	papier-mâché
audiotape	filmstrip	paragraph
autobiography	flip book	photographs
banner	flow chart	picture
bibliography	folk/native dance	play
booklet	game	poem
card game	game board	poster
cartoon	graph	project cube
character report cards	illustration	puppet show/play
chart	interpretive dance	publishing
collage	interview	puzzle
collection	invention	questionnaire
comic strip	job description	radio show
construction	letter	rap
cooking demonstration	limerick	rebus story
court trial	list	report
crossword	magazine	research report
debate	map	rhythm instruments
demonstration	mapping	riddles
diagram	mask	role drama
diary	mime	scrapbook/album
dictionary	mini-center	scroll
diorama	mobile	sculpture
display	model	self-report
ditto master	mosaic	sequence chart
drawing	mural	skit
editorial	music	slidetape
essay	newspaper article	song
exhibition	newspaper display ad	sociogram
experiment	oral report	tableau
group discussion	painting	video snippets
fact file	pamphlet	

---

1. *Thinking in the Classroom*, Vol. I & II. Ministry of Education, Victoria: British Columbia, 1991.

Representing Our Learning:

Representing Our Learning: THE REPRESENTING PROCESS

The representing process is the way people refine and present their ideas to others.[1] Different people use different ways of representing (see list, page 71). Applying the stages of the writing process to the representing process helps teachers and students see representation as a tool to aid their expression. Leon Politano found that this structure helped his eight-, nine-, and ten-year-olds develop and refine their representations.

1. **Pre-representing:** Gather ideas by talking, webbing, listing, and questioning.

2. **Drafting:** Express your ideas. Play with different materials and forms. Make the first draft of your creation/representation.

3. **Editing:** Look at what has been made. Does it express what you are trying to say? Do you need to gather more ideas? Should you reconsider the form you have selected?

4. **Proofing:** Are there details that you need to refine? Is it finely crafted? Does it require a title?

5. **Presenting:** What form is best suited for showing this work? Who should the audience be?

Just as Harste, Burke, and Short (*Creating Classrooms for Authors*) view authoring as a cycle, representing can also be viewed as an ongoing, cyclical process.

Once children understand that each person is at a different stage of development in representing ideas then the representing framework is a process of

- ☞ collecting ideas
- ☞ creating a draft of the representation

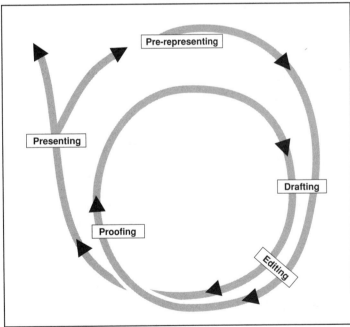

The representing process

---

1. This view of representing as a process is based on the work of Elliot Eisner.

- revising, proofing, and editing as appropriate
- presenting selected works

This framework provides children with an effective way to represent ideas. It is not a lock-step program to be applied to each occasion; rather, it is a way to approach the task of communicating ideas.

Representing Our Learning: REPERTOIRE OF REPRESENTING

Helping students build a repertoire of ways to represent their thinking begins with identifying all the ways they can express their ideas. The process outlined here is one way to get started.

1. Read a selection to the students.

2. Ask students how they can let others know what they learned, what they think, or what they recall about the story. Depending on the story, ask a question: "If you were an artist how would you show what you know?" or "If you were a scientist how might you show what you've learned?" or "If you were a cook how might you show what you learned?" or "If you were a builder how would you show what you know?" or "If you were at home what might you do to show what you learned?" List their responses. Acknowledge the range of ways we use to show what we know, think, feel, and can do.

3. Ask students which ideas could be realized with the materials available in the classroom and which would need materials not presently available.

4. Ask students to work with a group or a partner. Have them decide how they would like to respond to the selection and what materials they need.

5. Provide time for students to work on their representations.

6. Have the groups share their work with the class or with small groups. Invite class members to provide specific compliments.

7. Give students time to talk or write about the process, what they learned, and what they might try next. Keep a list posted in the class of different ways people have represented ideas.

8. Repeat the process until students are comfortable expressing and representing themselves in a variety of ways. (This is a lifelong undertaking!)

9. Have children set up a simple record-keeping system to keep track of what forms of representing they use. Watch for patterns and encourage children to experience a wide range.

Representing Our Learning: TALK SHOW

Show and Tell was developed to provide children with reasons to use language. Unfortunately, a daily succession of children introducing their possessions quickly leads to boredom.

The activity Talk Show alleviates this. When done with small groups, it offers a way for children to refine their speaking skills and holds their interest. Do the following:

1. Assign one student to the role of host. Assign another student to the role of guest. Let the remaining students be the audience.

2. Have the host introduce the guest. The guest then tells one or two things about the topic or item being discussed.

3. Have audience members ask the guest questions relevant to the topic. Repeat this for several guests. Several talk shows can occur simultaneously.

You can also use this process to review information or stories. For example, the guest may be a scientist who has come to talk about habits of migrating birds or a fictional character from a story the students are reading.

Representing Our Learning: ONE TOPIC MANY WAYS

A topic that holds general interest for most class members has great potential for illustrating the multitude of ways people can view topics, solve problems, and represent their learning.

1. Suggest a topic or recent event in which students have shown great interest.

2. Review the topic. Make a list on the chalkboard of the various ways the topic can be represented.

3. Have students sign up (in singles, pairs, or groups) for their choice of media or way to represent the topic.

4. When students have had sufficient time to work on their projects organize a group meeting so that they can present their work and explain why they chose the way they did to represent.

5. Ask other students to suggest reasons why the forms of representation chosen were effective.

6. Repeat the process so that the students gain experiences by selecting different forms of representing for different ideas.

Representing Our Learning: **STUDENT-DESIGNED BULLETIN BOARDS**

Involving students in designing displays on bulletin boards gives them real-life opportunities to use their representational skills and gives teachers more time for other tasks such as observing and recording student activities. This can become a year-long project.

1. Divide the class into multi-age groups (mixed ages mean more possible ideas).

2. Stipulate which bulletin boards are available.

3. Set up a schedule and sign-up system so students know when it will be their turn.

4. Provide necessary materials and time for production.

5. Have each student make a sign with his or her name written on the bottom. Attach a large envelope to each sign. Provide sheets asking for positive comments about the projects. Have students fill in the sheets and put in envelopes.

 Representing Our Learning: **PERSONAL BULLETIN BOARDS**

Helping children assume responsibility for bulletin board displays has several benefits. Teachers can devote more time to professional reading or other pursuits once the decorating is done. Children gain a greater sense of ownership for their classroom environment, express their creativity, and have real and purposeful work to do in the classroom. For example, the number of students in the class and the amount of bulletin board space available are the components of a practical math experience as the space is divided into equal sections for each students.

We start our students off with a label card and their photo. For the rest of the year each child must keep his or her space filled with a piece of current work. Use other bulletin boards for group murals related to class themes or projects.

Representing Our Learning: RESPONDING TO READING

Students can respond to what they have read by answering questions or writing their opinions. However, a steady diet of these two ways to respond can turn children off reading. Responses made in a variety of ways maintain enthusiasm and deepen understanding of what has been read. Resources such as *Literacy Through Literature* and *Bringing It All Together* by Johnson and Louis, and well as *Creating Classrooms for Authors* by Harste, Burke, and Short show how responses can be made using sociograms, retellings, posters, story maps, letter writing, literacy countdown, chapter summaries, and so on.

Ways to Respond	
Retelling	☐
Sociogram	☐
Letter to Author	☐
Poster	☐
Story Map	☐
Literacy Countdown	☐
Chapter Summary	☐

As a group, use one book and introduce one type of response at a time. This technique allows children to support one another as they work together to learn. When the students have a bank of strategies to choose from, have them work individually or in partners, using books that vary in topics and levels of difficulty:

1. Choose a book.

2. Look at the list of ways to respond.

3. Choose one way, do it, and record your response or how you responded in your reading response journal.

Teachers need to ensure that children respond to literature in different ways. One way to do this is by having students record on a bar graph the kinds of literature response they choose to do. They will quickly see what they are using most, and what forms they haven't yet tried.

Representing Our Learning: **FOCUS ON THE ARTS**

Students become comfortable with different ways of representing when we increase their opportunities to immerse themselves in different art forms. The following is one strategy that has proven successful:

- ☞ Choose an artist.
- ☞ Display a brief biography of the artist and pictures of the artist's work.
- ☞ Provide art materials and ask students to replicate one of the selected pictures.

We have found these pictures, when displayed together, look incredible and are a tribute to the artist. Replication of an artist's work helps students understand some of the techniques the artist used to achieve his or her representation. This strategy increases students' appreciation of the artist and of different representational techniques. Another version of this activity is In the Style of…. Ask students to select an artist and replicate a favorite work or do their own choice of image using a particular technique (e.g., Seurat—pointillism).

 Representing Our Learning: **INVESTIGATE CAREERS**

When students understand how people outside of school represent their thinking they appreciate the breadth of skills, talents, and interests that exist in the world, and they are made aware of the range of possibilities for representation. The range of ways people work is paralleled by a range of ways people represent their work.

Careers	Ways of Representing
Graphic artists	· graphic design · cartoons · computer imaging · laser disk · art collection
Park Warden	· elevation maps · lists
Electrician	· wiring diagrams · building codes
Pilot	· navigation signs · flight plans · flying logs

In this project students collect samples of peoples' work and make lists of careers that correspond to specific ways of representing.

Representing Our Learning: TIMELY TALKING

We know that talking is more than just telling what we know—talking helps us refine and extend our knowledge. The more opportunities children have to talk about their learning, the more likely they are to retain what they have learned. Two ways to connect talking and learning are Thirty Second Speech and Sentence Frames.

Thirty Second Speech

When students have been working on an interest area or have been pursuing a topic, a quick way to help children summarize their learning is to put them into pairs with the following directions:

"You have thirty seconds to tell everything you know about [*topic*]. When you finish, your partner will tell you two important things you stated. We will do this again so you each have a turn."

When students gain skill and confidence with thirty second speeches, extend these to one minute.

Sentence Frames

Sentence frames

Another way to help students focus their talk about a subject is to give them sentence frames. Frames such as Three, Two, One, Talk; And Then; Once There Was (below and right) provide effective ways to help children organize their thoughts and recall events.

Once there was a __boy__
who __cried wolf__
and __everyone hurried to help him__
at last __he learned a lesson when the wolf really came and he yelled and no one believed him.__

At first __we bought the aquarium__
Then __we had to set it up__
Next __we had to let the water sit for 2 days__
Finally __we got our fish!__

Three things I can tell you about __our trip to landfill__ are
__there is a net to keep birds out__
__they don't take cardboard__
__it didn't smell too bad__

Two things I like are
__watching the machines__
__riding on the bus__

One thing I'll always remember is __they dug up a lettuce wrapped in a twenty-year-old newspaper. The lettuce was still green!__

Representing Our Learning: **WHO? WHAT? WHERE?**

A simple way to encourage writing and stimulate talk is to put out a large sheet of paper with questions written at the top. During Talk Time or Exploration children record the answers to the questions on the sheet; they then read their responses at Group Meeting Time. Later, post this sheet as an instant mural writing sample.

Some sample questions are:

- ☛ Where did you go this weekend?
- ☛ Who could bring information about rocks?
- ☛ Where could we get things for our take-apart center?

SUMMARY

In this chapter we have described some alternatives to traditional written representations. There is an old saying that the richest person is the one with the most possibilities. Students today need choices and experiences in deciding the most suitable way to represent their knowledge and ideas.

When we assess whether or not we are doing everything we can to expand our students' power of representation, we ask ourselves:

- ☛ What models and demonstrations of various representations have we provided?
- ☛ What materials need to be gathered?
- ☛ What opportunities are available for students to share their representations?
- ☛ How do we show that all forms of representation are valued?
- ☛ What are we doing to help parents and the public understand the value of representation in a variety of forms?

How can you and your students extend the ways learning is represented in your classroom?

Once we have created space and a community where a diverse group of individuals can learn together, our next most important task is to determine ways to appreciate and assess their learning.

ACCOUNTING FOR LEARNING: ASSESSMENT, EVALUATION, AND REPORTING

When teachers think about assessment and evaluation in multi-age classes one of their first comments is, "With all the children at different ages and stages, there isn't a single test I can give them to find out what they know." Agreed—there isn't a single test. There are, however, many different ways for teachers to find out about their students' strengths, achievements, abilities, and future learning needs. The value in multi-age classes is in the learning that takes place—accounting for the learning means looking for assessment and evaluation strategies that provide for a range of abilities, stages of development, and levels of understanding. As teachers our task is to select and use evaluation processes that enhance children's learning.

The scientific basis that underlies our assessment and evaluation perspective arises from the processes used by anthropologists, sociologists, and ethnographers —social scientists who work with humans. Our perspective is adapted from the work of Lincoln and Guba (1981) and others who have detailed methods and considerations in naturalistic inquiry. The fundamental principles are: (1) observations must be made in context and over time and (2) data must be collected from at least three different sources (conversations, observations of process, and observation of product). This varied data gives us a balanced view of learners and their learning.

For multi-age classes we look for assessment activities that, like our curriculum, allow for and invite a range of responses. When children demonstrate their learning in different ways we have a wide range of possibilities for evaluating and assessing children of various ages. The ideas in this section focus on students and their learning, students sharing their learning with parents, and students and teachers reporting to parents about learning.

There are many books and ideas on authentic assessment and evaluation. Many teachers have developed their own successful ways of organizing and recording what is taking place in the classroom. The ideas included in this section are examples of assessment activities that are particularly effective for use in multi-age classes. For more ideas that you can easily adapt to multi-age classes, see *Together Is Better: Collaborative Assessment, Evaluation, and Reporting* (1992).

Accounting for Learning:

What assessment and evaluation strategies already work for you and your children?

Accounting for Learning: **BECOMING RESEARCHERS**

Involving children in the assessment and evaluation process enhances their learning and helps you build a comprehensive picture of each child's abilities and accomplishments. The steps outlined here introduce children to the processes of collecting evidence and using multiple sources of data:

1. Talk to the children about what things they would like to know more about.

2. Have students make curiosity webs or lists to record their topics or interests.

3. Let students discuss their choices with a partner, then select the one item they wish to pursue. (Supply different colored highlighters so they can mark their choices.)

4. Have the children record their choices on a chart. For example, "We want to find out about…"

5. Meet with the whole class. Talk about the choices everyone has made. Ask: "If you want to find out about some thing what do you usually do?" (Typical responses include "Look in a book" or "Ask someone who knows.")

6. Ask: "What if you can't find any information in a book or don't know anyone who could help? For example, maybe all the books in the library about budgies are being used and no one here knows about budgies. What could you do then?" (If you are patient, someone will eventually suggest, "You could watch a budgie or a video about budgies.")

Summarize these first six steps by doing the following: Draw and label a triangle on paper or on the chalkboard, while saying, "So you could talk, read, and watch. This is the same way teachers find out about children in their classes. I talk to you and ask you what you've done or how you do something. I watch you while you are working and playing. I look at the things you write and make. While you do your projects on the things you choose to learn about, my project is to learn about our class." Continue the process:

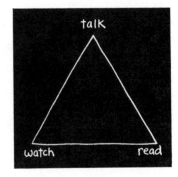

7. To model and help your students organize their investigations give each a sheet of paper. Have them fold the sheet in three and turn up the bottom edge to form a research folder.

Explain that for the first research project everyone will work together as a group to get used to and learn about researching. Use your projects as the model. For example, ask: "Who can I talk to to find out about you? Who can you talk to to find out about your topic?"

Name: Siobhan   **Topic:** Cats

I can talk to...	I can observe...	I can collect...
my parents the vet the cat club president 477-MEOW my friends who have cats	my cat the neighbors cat video on cats	pamphlets at vets cat books from library cat pictures

Reproducible master in appendix A

Talk sheet

Research folder

Name: Siobhan   **Date:** Nov 12, 1993

When I talked to...

the vet I learned:
cats need check ups
they get diseases like lukemia
fleas can make them sick
their whiskers tell them how
big a space they can go through

Reproducible master in appendix A

Name: Siobhan   **Date:** _____

When I watched _____ my cat
_____ I learned ___ *she
washes a lot
* likes to be in warm places

* likes my mom better
than my dad

Reproducible master in appendix A

8. Give the students "talk sheets." Tell them to keep these in their research folders.

After children have had time to talk to their informants (this could be done in class or at home) ask them to share their information.

Repeat this step for the other two ways children can gather information: observation and reading.

9. When the children have gathered their information for each section have them, with partners, look for information that appears in more than one section. This information is well documented and will appear in their final presentation under a title such as "Findings." Information that appears in only one area is put in another section titled, "Unanswered Questions" and needs to be further investigated. Last, "New Questions" is for those questions that arose during the investigation.

Observation sheet

10. Have students present their findings in some form—written reports, labeled posters, labeled models, or oral presentations.

As the children present their findings, take time for specific compliments. Conclude with a final question, "What did you find out about being a researcher?"

Explain that as the teacher you will be doing research all year long because your job is to learn about the people in your class. Tell the children: "You can help me with my job by letting me learn about you. For our next research project I'm going to ask you to do a research study about yourself. This will help you learn the different ways you can learn about and tell others about your learning. Let's create new folders and start the cycle again, "this time the subject is you!"

Name: _____

Date: _____

When learning how to be a researcher, I learned

_____
_____
_____
_____
_____
_____
_____
_____

☐ Next time I will do these things again because they worked.

☐ Next time I won't do these things because they weren't helpful.

Research evaluation

Reproducible master in appendix A

Accounting for Learning: ASKING STUDENTS

Sometimes teachers spend lots of time trying to figure out why children do what they do or trying to assess what children know. We have found that asking students why they do what they do or asking them to show us what they know increases our knowledge of them and answers some of our questions about their learning.

Through self-evaluation children

- ☞ find out what they know
- ☞ inform their teacher and parents about their learning
- ☞ develop pride in their efforts and accomplishments
- ☞ set new learning goals

The example, right, shows one way children can collect and organize information about their own learning.

Name __Evelyn__ Date __June 9, 99__

A book that is easy for me to read is

Ronix Day maG

If I don't know a word when I first see it I can

1. Look at the next word.

2. Sou ned it out.

3. ask a patner.

4. Look at the Pitcher.

5. ASK a fhien frst

6. look at the ~~frst~~ Letter.

Reading evaluation form

Reproducible master in appendix A

Accounting for Learning: OBSERVING OURSELVES AND OTHERS

Focusing on learning is an integral part of a teacher's day—observations that are recorded and dated create a record of the learning that has taken place. We used to think teachers had to do all the observing and recording. We've learned that it is everyone's responsibility. Share this task by having prepared frames for children to use and library pockets on the front of each assessment file book or on a chart on the wall. Have children complete, date, and file their observations of their own learning as well as the learning of other students in their class. Students and teachers can work together to decide what characteristics they are observing.

Observation frames

Name _____ Jessie _____

Date _____ Dec. 12 93 _____

helpful   hard working
considerate   thoughtful
respectful   caring
knowledgeable   encouraging to others

Situation

Africa performance

Comments

I noticed Jessie and Alicia worked really hard to get ready for their performance.

        Kaileen

Name _____ Heidi _____

Date _____

Today I finished my africa project. It was a lot of work! I really liked our presentation. I worked with Allison and Kathleen.

Name _____ Kaileen _____

Date _____ Dec. 15 _____

Focus | Division |

I want you to know
        that I know how to divide with decimals!

Name _____ Susan _____

Date _____ Oct. 12 _____

Eureka!
Now I can

Serve over the net in volleyball.

Name _____ J.C. _____

Date _____ Dec. 3 _____

Goal | not talking out |

Evidence
    I listened to Jamie tell about prehistoric times.
    I remembered to go to Evan's desk to talk to him. You said I did really well.

ACCOUNTING FOR LEARNING: FINDING TIME TO OBSERVE

One of the most frequent concerns of teachers wanting to observe their students is finding the time for observation. If you are always teaching, you don't have time to observe. But if you can establish a balance of whole-class instruction, small-group work, and individual activity you can use the group and individual time to interact with and observe students.

Norma Mickelson (University of Victoria) taught us that when we let students get on with their learning, we can get on with ours—the important task of kid-watching that Yetta and Ken Goodman write about. To establish what times in the day you can observe, we suggest an activity we learned in a session conducted by Brian Cambourne and Jan Turbill.

1. Fold a sheet of paper lengthwise into three sections.

2. In the first column list the events that take place in your school day.

3. In the second column note the times you could use for observation.

4. In the third column note what your focus for the observation could be.

5. Review the second column to see if you could, by shifting your use of time, increase the amount of time you have for observations.

Running-Record of Day	Possible Observation Time	Focus for Observations
Entry		
Exploration		record who works with whom
Group Meeting		
Math	make notes during independent practice	5 year olds' number recognition
Recess		
Math		
Readers' + Writers' Workshops	Conference time	meet with Sam, Mac, Chandra
Computer		
Lunch		
Storytime	Ask student teacher to read story	take notes on how Mike and Jordan focus
Project time/ Theme time		
Gym	Observe at indoor hockey area	Who is a leader? Who cooperates?

Observation sheet

Authentic data is collected while children are learning. When you tell children what information you are collecting and why, you are committed to actually collecting the information, and the students are more likely to inform you about their learning.

Five ways to keep track of what you are observing are

☛ Post-it notes and file folders in which to stick them
☛ notebook with a tabbed page for each child (setting the goal of observing and reflecting on two children each day makes us feel less overwhelmed)
☛ grid, with a square for each child, in which you jot notes
☛ slips of papers and library pockets with children's names on them
☛ having children record for you. (Start the day by saying: "Today we will be looking for…" Have children respond by making written observations of themselves and others.)

***Accounting for Learning:* READING COMPLIMENTS**

The more children think about learning processes, the more information they have to help themselves improve. Giving compliments helps children focus on the reading process, and children are consistently reinforcing the qualities of being a good reader. Students' first attempts to give a compliment to a peer often result in vague "he did a good job" responses. With a teacher prompting ("What made it good?") and modeling compliments ("I like the way he lowered his voice in the scary part" or "I notice when Jordan read house for horse he realized his error and went back—that's called self-correction" or "When Amy didn't know a word she looked at the pictures") children soon become expert at giving specific compliments.

Listen in: Four children have just finished doing a readers' theater for the class. When the teacher invites them to ask for compliments their classmates respond:

> Roslyn: *I like the way you all spoke loudly so we could hear you.*
> Rasool: *The hats you wore really matched your characters.*
> Kevin: *You all came in at the right places.*

The performers often respond with compliments to the audience such as: "You were very quiet while we read"; "You sat still and didn't fool around."

Good Readers
* think
* ask "does it make sense?"
* look at the pictures
* sound out words
* skip words they don't know then return to them when they know what the rest means
* ask friends for help
* read lots of books

"What Do Good Readers Do?"

Compliments become a way of life in the classroom. Guest speakers are not just thanked; they get compliments that let them know how they contributed: "The things you brought helped us know about how people in the north stay warm."

Another way to prepare children to think about their reading is to ask: "What do good readers do?" Brainstorm and record their responses on the chalkboard.

This process can also work especially well with the following activities, which generate criteria for behaviors such as

- cleaning up
- speaking to a group
- being an audience member
- participating in activities such as music or gym
- putting on plays

When each student knows what is expected of him or her by all class members and seeks to be recognized for positive learning behaviors, children of all ages can help one another progress in all areas by complimenting successes and shaping positive behaviors.

Accounting for Learning: **PROGRESS FOLIOS**

Portfolios are one effective way of displaying student work; however, the way they are organized often makes it difficult to see progress over time. Although portfolios may contain wonderful examples of student's work, they do not provide us, our students, or their parents

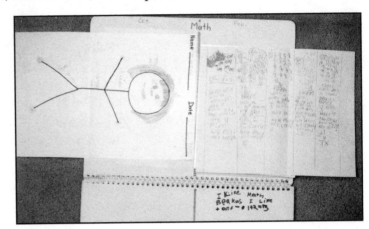

with the "aha" feeling that comes with graphically seeing the changes in key aspects of learning in reading, writing, spelling, mathematics, and the fine arts.

We know that how information is displayed facilitates communication. With that in mind, we developed an idea that we believe to be an alternative or practical extension of portfolios—the Progress Folio.[1]

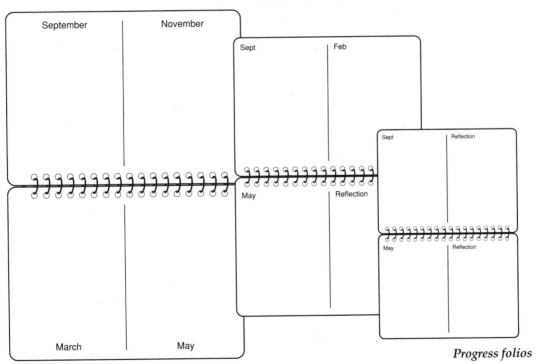

Progress folios

---

1. Our thanks to Darcy Carter for sharing her "Learning Frontiers" system of organizing portfolios.

Use a scrapbook or large booklet made from paper. Begin with a web or resumé introducing the student and a Table of Contents. The next several double-page spreads each feature an important area of student learning.

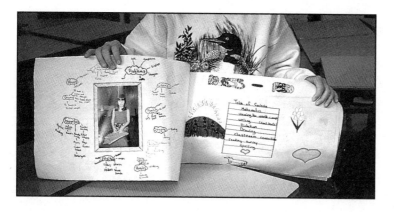

Select the categories for each of the double-page spreads. For example, the first double-page spread may be for mathematics, the second for reading, the third for writing, and so on, depending on the areas selected and known to be of interest to parents (see photo page 89). How each double spread is sectioned depends upon how many times a year you want the students to demonstrate their growth and development. Some teachers choose to collect samples four times a year, some three, while others choose to collect twice a year.

Set aside time during class to collect representative samples in each of the agreed upon categories. These samples are dated and glued into the Progress Folios. When the second set of samples are collected and placed in the Progress Folios you might ask students to reflect verbally or in writing about the significance or quality of their efforts.

Many teachers use Progress Folios for their ongoing assessment and also have students show them to parents during conference times throughout the year. Each double-page spread of the Progress Folio provides parents with a direct comparison between what their child could do and what the child is now able to do.

Remaining pages in the Progress Folio provide children with an area to save memorable or significant pieces of their own choice. Some teachers include an envelope or file folder for parent responses and storage space for audio cassettes and videotapes. The categories chosen and the additional items included depend entirely upon your needs and the needs of your students and their parents.

The bonus of using Progress Folios is that once items are collected in each of the categories, they can be set aside until the next collection date. Rather than being cumbersome and time-consuming, Progress Folios meet the goal of demonstrating student learning in a practical and manageable way.

Accounting for Learning: POWERFUL AND PAINLESS REPORTING

Types of reports vary in form and frequency between jurisdictions. Regardless of the format there are some things that can improve the quality of reports. Building on the ideas described in the British Columbia Primary Program documents, we write reports about our children that

- ☞ describe what children are able to do
- ☞ indicate learning and developmental needs
- ☞ suggest ways to support or challenge each learner

Reports are more effective when we

- ☞ have a collection of evidence (notes, portfolios) upon which to base our observations

- ☞ support what we say with samples of classroom activity (e.g., "Mackenzie's mathematical ability was clearly demonstrated when he kept the accounts for our class garage sale.")
- ☞ include quotations from students' work (e.g., "At five-and-a-half years old, Reva's growing power over language was obvious when she wrote, 'My favorite skool tim is storee.'")
- ☞ use quotations from children (e.g., "When Matthew was asked about his favorite activities he said, 'I really like building patterns and doing graphs.'")
- ☞ put the report card in perspective by also providing samples of children's work
- ☞ have the child listen to the report before it goes home and ask, "Is it fair? Have I missed anything? Is there anything you would like added?"

To make your reporting more learner-centered, use a process of summary reporting. Combine collecting evidence of learning, informal reporting, and student reflection to form a foundation for a conference with the child, parents, and teacher where all participants meet to discuss the students' abilities and achievements, learning needs, and future learning plans. To prepare for this conference, students, parents, and teachers are asked to make notes about the student's learning as part of an informal report (see below for older child sample; page 94, top left, for younger child sample). Rather than present parents with a written report to be discussed at the conference, the conference note s are a record of the significant points agreed upon by all parties and form the draft of the report (see page

Informal Report Sample (Intermediate)

Learning Focus September-November 1993	Eric's Perspective

Themes: Building our Community and Canada

Activities and Skill Builders

Building Our Community
• overnight camp at Camp Gilwell, focus on leadership, cooperative teams, appreciating variety of talents, created skits, created name posters & painted rocks, listening to, respecting and helping one another

Setting Expectations
• class meetings, keeping focused, completing assigned work on time, able to set and meet goals, learning log consistently used, homework done and in on time, neat, well-presented work, focuses on proofreading & handwriting for final copy, notes organized and up-to-date, daily thinking skills

Canada and the Election
• map work accurate, neat, increasing knowledge of places as well as Canadian government, reading and learning about Canadian authors, writing biographies, spelling key theme words, listens and comprehends novels read aloud, designing campaign posters, replicating Canadian artists' work

Reading Work
• in-class and home reading, learning different ways to respond to literature, keeping reading log, reading orally to class, listening to other people read, practice, poetry for assembly, listens to news, takes notes, presents information, advertises great books

Writing Work
• brainstorm/pre-writing, organizing work, using a ruler, using all the space, first person story, book reports, spelling and editing, acrostic poetry, grammar (me and I)

Mathematics Work
• pre- and post-test results, addition & subtraction, multiplication & division, mad minutes, graphing, problem solving, independent work, home practice & Wednesday after-school math club

Physical Education
• soccer, throwing, catching, scoopball, volleyball, fitness, focusing on participation, cooperation, practicing new skills,

Computers
• using for writing and math practice

Music
• working on a project, opportunity to be a member of choir

What's Next?
• more division & geometry, reading science fiction, reading nonfiction about space, astronomy theme, more writing, audiotape presentation, more spelling, mini-grammar lessons, notetaking and research skills, learning about mythology, readers' theater, more work habits, study habits, test-taking skills

Strengths:

- P.E. I'm good at over hand serving the volley ball
- Math 92 and 82 percent on my tests.
- Neat in my work
- Getting bucks & have 13
- Books organized
- Nice Writing
- I cooperate a lot
- I help as much as I can in computers
- I'm good at spelling

Improvement or Challenges Needed:

① My brain goes too fast
② I need to do tests faster
③ Not talking as much
④ Proofreading

Possible Goals for Next Term:

① Proofreading Better
② Not Talking as much

94, right). Each report is then checked by the teacher and given to the child and parents. This process is fully described in our book *Together Is Better: Collaborative Assessment, Evaluation, and Reporting* (1992).

When school time is not available for conferences, the reporting process can still be a record of the conference between teacher and child.

Ms. Mahabir & Ms. Davies' Perspective	Parent(s)' Perspective
Strengths: - Eric is a responsible learner; he can work well independently or in groups; shows leadership potential - is a cooperative class member; polite and fair, yet fun - work done meticulously — writing & map work are examples; notebooks are organized - excellent listening, study skills & note taking; Elections test 96%; Math + - (92%); multiplication improved from 59 - 82% - able to take brief but informative notes for news; excellent participation in discussions - works hard in P.E. with resulting good skills and sportsmanship - good spelling; answers are thorough; has solid grasp of capitals, punctuation & grammar; - writing is descriptive	**Strengths:** at home: - Eric is responsible about doing chores and homework - he does his homework carefully and neatly - studies and practices for tests - reads novels & nonfiction and watches the news with interest Eric always asks perceptive questions that show he thinks hard about things - likes to learn
Improvement or Challenges Needed: - proofread carefully for those lingering spelling errors - when coloring, color all the same way for neatness - can become distracted – likes to know all that is going on in the classroom *	**Improvement or Challenges Needed:** - Eric can slow down and think before he speaks or writes
Possible Goals for Next Term: ① Work on proofreading & editing & trying to expand creative writing for length and details ② Try to avoid being distracted by peers *	**Possible Goals for Next Term:** - concentrate on work at school perhaps sitting in a less chatty group - some way of being helpful to friend without disrupting ?

Name Marcie   **Nov. 8, 1993**

Strengths

REDING
WRITING
GAMs
MY MEMRE
KILRING
MATH
COMPYOUTR
LIBERE
FECING
PLAWING
SER

Needs

KIDS BEING NIS
DOT BE BOSE
LOSING MY MEMRE

Plans

I HAF TO BE NIS
I HAF TO ET
I HAF TO WRK MOR

Stewart

Strengths – reading – using lots of good
strategies
– is skipping over & check later...
use pictures.
– intense, wants to read & do well
Responsible for self & stuff
group meeting, listening, attending, following instructions
Writing –

Math – numbers to 1000
add / subtract
gym – basketball, hockey
needs –
reading – read a lot, time to read
learn new strategies
– write more at school and home
– using some standard spelling
– practice to solidify skills & understanding
plans – continue to read in morning
– draw & write in journal with a balance...
don't leave out either but try more
writing than drawing?
– use a pencil

Teacher's preconference notes

Conference Guide for Collaborative Report
(Teacher and Student)

Questions to be posed to child:	Answers:
1. What would you like to have written about your strengths?	
2. Let's look at your work collection. What does it show about you? [*Each child is asked to have a sample of something that shows his or her reading skill and a collection of work ready to bring to the conference.*]	
3. What about [*subject*]? [*For example, "What about mathematics?"*]	
4. What did you select to read? Why? [*Child reads a sample.*] What do you do well when you read? Is there anything you need to work on?	
5. When you think about your learning, are there things you want or need to do better or learn about?	
6. How can you help yourself? How can I help you?	

Reproducible master in appendix A

Edit a draft of the conference notes and then add a summary statement. Show the final draft to the student, then send a copy home to parents along with work samples and an invitation to parents to respond to their child's learning.

Conference guide for collaborative reports

The goals of the Primary Program are to provide a variety of experiences that foster the child's

- Aesthetic and Artistic Development
- Physical Development
- Emotional and Social Development
- Social Responsibility
- Intellectual Development
- Social Development

All goals are emphasized throughout the entire Primary Program

---

March 1993

When we talked about J's strengths we noted:

• the progress he has made in becoming an independent reader. This was highlighted one morning when he read the posted agenda to himself and told us that "lunch" was not written. An example of a book J can read is *Green Eggs and Ham.*

• he is developing skill as a writer. He is proud of his ability to write whatever he needs to say.

• he is eager to learn and makes great connections between what we are doing and what he remembers. One day he connected talk about New York to *Home Alone Two* taking place in New York.

• J is a hard worker. He is neat and can show his ideas through speaking, drawing, and writing. He can write anything with help and is becoming increasingly independent about writing by himself.

• gym is fun for him. He is a good sport and practices to improve his skills.

• in mathematics he is able to understand new concepts quickly. His abilities to use numbers are obvious when he offers suggestions during "Number of the Day."

When we talked about goals for J we agreed:

• he will work on being a better listener during group time. He said he would not talk and that he would ignore others if someone was speaking.

• he would work on being able to write more on his own.

We would like to add:

• we are pleased with J's progress. He is experiencing success at school and his insightful comments make our class a more interesting place to be.

• we are particularly pleased with the positive choices J is making about his behavior and group participation.

Sample of primary report

Above, and on the following pages, are examples of final reports that resulted from the process of summary reporting. Reports are completed after evidence of learning is collected, and conference notes produced.

The goals of the Intermediate Program are to provide a variety of experiences that foster the child's

- Aesthetic and Artistic Development
- Physical Development
- Emotional and Social Development
- Social Responsibility
- Intellectual Development
- Social Development

All goals are emphasized throughout the entire Intermediate Program

Summary of November (1993) Conference

Strengths

Some of the strengths H noted were "read the more challenging books," "enjoys writing," "I am creative. I like painting and using charcoal," and "I like to do challenging things." H's parents wrote, "We are really pleased with your ability and progress in all areas, especially Math and Art!!" and noted that a strength for H was "attention to detail."

We agree with all the above and note that:

- H's Bateman replica is absolutely fabulous!! You are a talented person, H.
- We're glad that you are pleased with yourself. You have accomplished a lot this term.
- H has been speaking out in class on behalf of her group and expressing her ideas. We are pleased that she is practicing.
- Mathematics test results have been good (addition and subtraction 88% and multiplication 98%) and we have been especially pleased with the independent practice that H has undertaken during class working sessions.
- H has increased her notetaking speed during CBC News and writes clear summaries—an improvement since September.
- H's printing is neat and the pages are neatly laid out with date, name, and title. We appreciate the thrifty use of space.
- Work is done on time. Her writing work shows knowledge of punctuation and capitals (see dictation).
- She's increasing her knowledge and improving her mental map of North America.
- Election spelling test 19.5/20.

We expect she will do better on future tests.

- The end-of-unit Election test mark was 74%. H was away for two weeks during this unit.
- She did a fabulous Ripple Rock trip map.
- We really enjoy working with H. She is calm, sensible, friendly, and hardworking.

Improvement or Challenges Needed

H suggested that she needed to speak out in class discussions, practice notetaking and decimals. H's parents suggested that H needs more challenging reading, help with time management, and more practice with letter-writing skills. We agreed that H needs to carefully consider her goals as it is important that she look for challenges as well as improvement.

In summary we want H to know how much we appreciate her strengths. We're not sure we spent enough time during our conference acknowledging all the wonderful strengths H brings to her learning. H meets or exceeds the widely held expectations for children her age and has the work habits to support her learning. She is obviously building upon a solid foundation of learning and is well able to meet the challenges of this year. We are enjoying having her be a part of our class—she is a positive and productive member!

Goal(s) and Action Plan

1. Proofread regularly
2. Focus on study skills
3. Find more challenging reading material

Parents – help with proofreading & studying
Teacher – recommend challenging "horse" & other material for reading
Student – accept help willingly; proofread without reminding; practice study skills

Hannah	Ca Davies	A Wadarsky	DB Singleton
Student's Signature	Teacher's Signature	Parent's Signature	Principal's Signature

Sample of intermediate report

The goals of the Intermediate Program are to provide a variety of experiences that foster the child's

- Aesthetic and Artistic Development
- Physical Development
- Emotional and Social Development
- Social Responsibility
- Intellectual Development
- Social Development

All goals are emphasized throughout the entire Intermediate Program

Summary of November (1993) Conference

Strengths

E's personal inventory of strengths include "I'm good at overhand serving the volleyball, math, neatness, getting bucks. I'm organized, cooperative and helpful." His parents noted that "E is responsible about doing homework carefully and neatly" and he "always asks perceptive questions that shows he thinks hard about things."

In addition to agreeing with the above comments, we would like to note:

• E is a responsible learner; he can work equally well independently or in groups; shows leadership potential—has shared many worthy ideas in Club T and class discussions
• is a cooperative class member; polite and fair, yet fun
• work done meticulously—writing and map work are examples; notebooks are organized; vast improvement in drawing map of North America
• excellent listening, study skills, and notetaking; Elections test 90%
• good general knowledge and ability to learn new information; able to take brief but informative notes for news; excellent participation in discussions
• works hard in P.E. with resulting good skills and sportsmanship
• good spelling; answers are thorough; has solid grasp of capitals, punctuation, and grammar; writing is descriptive
• Math 92%; multiplication improved from 59% to 82%.

Improvement or Challenges Needed

E's summary is that "my brain goes too fast!" He would like to work on doing tests faster, proofreading, and not talking as much in class. We agree with these, E. It was a good idea of yours to sit alone until a group activity arises for you to join in.

E's knowledge and skills meet or exceed the widely held expectations for students his age. He has a large capacity for knowledge and is quick to share and help others. We appreciate your enthusiasm, good manners, and excellent work.

Goal(s) and Action Plan

1. Proofread written material
2. Try to avoid being distracted by peers

Parent – Encourage Eric to proofread
Teacher – proofreading time set aside, reminders
   – encourage Eric to use options
Student – proofread without needing reminding
   – find suitable place to work quietly

Eric	a Davies	B St John	T.E. Singleton
Student's Signature	Teacher's Signature	Parent's Signature	Principal's Signature

Sample of intermediate report

As we involve our students and their parents more and more in the reporting process, we are developing assessment and evaluation roles that reflect their increasing contribution to the process. Two

Frame for collaborative report

Date _____ *March 1/93* _____   Teacher _____ *Mahabir/Schellinck* _____

Topics	Student's Notes
Work Habits – organization and neatness – learning log; homework, communication – use of time; class + lunch; involvement – social skills; cooperation, resolving conflict	I have been better organized. I write and print neat unless I am doing a draft! I show my Learning Log to my parents, and I have gotten my homework in on time. Lately I have been using my time wisely.
Language Arts – use of writing strategies – imagery, descriptive writing – spelling, proofreading – mechanics (punctuation, paragraphs, quotations, grammar, capital letters)	I'd like to use all of those a bit more to make my stories better. In my spelling I have done well. I think I proofread as I go along because I always know what to write next. I would like to use quotation a bit more.
Reading/Literature – books read / class average; goals met? – character interview – book talk; favorite novel – Novel Study – comprehension	I have read 29 books, this above the class average which is 27! I have met all my goals this year. I was Charlotte from Charlotte's Web.
Social Studies – Study skills, test taking – research skills; categorizing; notetaking; bibliography; written material; final product – understanding of other cultures	I study with the skills that we have learned, but at tests I get nervous. I can categorize and take thourough notes and I'm satisfied with my final product. I now understand what it is like in another culture!
Thinking Skills – questioning skills – knowledge vs. opinion – visual imagery; imagining – word games – participation in discussion; sharing thoughts	I know the difference, but it is hard for me to ask an opinion question. I hope to make more imagery in my stories. I like doing word games they are challenging.
Fine Arts/Physical Education – Art – drawing, pastels, mosaic, plasticine – Drama – Readers' Theater, Islam Role Play – P.E. – volleyball, dodgeball, skiing, basketball, fitness; skills, participation	I love doing art, I like to color and it is fun! I like Dodgeball because I just like it! I also liked the ski trip that was AWESOME!!
Mathematics – Basic facts – Multiplication of Decimals – Long Division – Problem solving – Geometry	I know all my basic facts off by heart. I am able to do both short and long division well. I have only one error in the entire test. I am on chapter 6 now from chapter 3!
Science – Research project; following criteria – Electricity – predicting – observing	I got 88%, but 26½ out of 30! I enjoy electricity and after predicting I am sometimes amazed at the end result!
Other – Computers; keyboarding, use as a tool in research and class work (Math, S.S.) – Français – Personal Safety · Decision making	I use the propper fingerings, but sometimes I have to look at the keys. I am able to get 50 wpm. I can use CPG creating stories and news letters. Tim Burke has taught me about taxes, construction, and what disasters can do

Signatures _____ *Ken Haddad* _____

teachers, Marina Mahabir and Charlie Schellinck, used the following frame to report with students and parents.

Student	Ken Haddad

Teachers' Notes	Parent's Comments
- notebooks are well-organized; very neat - L.L. used extremely well; good communication - time use better recently - went through a bit of a slump - likeable, enthusiastic about most activities, very involved in sports; avoids conflict	This is a very important area, Kenny, and we're glad you are trying so hard — especially using your time more wisely.
- has definite "Kenny" style - very light, up beat, humorous; flows well, pleasant to read; strong vocabulary - excellent imagery & use of strategies - punctuation excellent; paragraphs well used - spelling terrific	Yes, we enjoy these stories very much!!
- meeting reading goals; keeping up with log well - interview — well prepared, knowledge of character's feelings, good expression (acted like a spider!) - Book talk - explained book in expressive way, humorous.	Kenny, we're glad you are enjoying your reading - we'd like to see you with a book in your hands more often.
- Tests Judaism 43% Islam 64% - quite low for Ken's ability; strive for better results! - notes are accurate & neat, mapwork very good, understands study strategies - Rome project - excellent, well organized	Yes, you do have good notes, Kenny, and you worked hard on your project. We think you could be better prepared, too, for tests. How can we help?
- able to ask both types of questions; offers both knowledge & opinions during discussion; willing participant - good visualizer - able to solve many word games - had "ways" of finding answers	Isn't it great to challenge ourselves — we're glad you're interested in doing that, Kenny.
- some excellent drawings & art projects - enjoys drama activities, participates enthusiastically, with confidence - P.E. excellent skills	Great that you are enjoying your art and P.E.
- Excellent knowledge of basic facts - is able to do long division, multiplication of decimals, and draw, measure geometric angles & figures - good problem solver	It is a real pleasure to know you are making the most of your math skills.
- good report. Some minor items such as neatness and editing skills should be addressed - works well in small groups predicting/testing	We have enjoyed hearing about your electricity unit, Kenny.
- enjoys using the computer - good speed and fingering of the keyboard - could challenge himself to learn more difficult keys	We are all enjoying our new computer and we know you are really comfortable with the computer — how about that extra challenge?

Alona Haddad

Accounting for Learning: **PICTURE THIS!**

A wonderful way to communicate successful learning to parents and/or guardians is to use photographs of students working at school and two or three lines describing what they are doing.

Picture This

Picture This!

This is me. I am writing a letter. isn't it neat.

I'd like you to know that

* I love writing

* I send a letter to Nana

* I made a card for Mr. Gordon

Michelle

Accounting for Learning: READING AND MATH GO HOME

Having children take home selected learning activities involves parents in their child's learning and provides them with a sampling of ways they can encourage their children to practice and learn. Many parents are unable to come into the classroom; these home activities provide a "window" into the classroom and help build positive relationships between home and school. We need to take the pressure off busy families by assuring them that these activities are a choice, not an assignment.

Home activity sheets

Dear ___Mom and Dad___

I've been practicing my math facts at school. While you watch me I am going to

* throw the dice and answer four questions

* throw the dice and create three equations that have that number for the answer

Please record 2 things you observe about my work and one question you'd like to ask me.

Love,
Mackenzie

- -

Response

I notice that you are really quick adding and subtracting! What do you want to learn next?

Mom

_____

Dear _____

Writers monitor their writing and make needed corrections. At school we've been practicing effective proofreading strategies. When I am proofreading written work my favorite strategies are:

* mumble read

* check for capitals and periods

* have a partner check my work

Watch me do the Daily Edit and please give me a compliment and a wish:

from

___Jordan___

Daily Edit

during this year   are clas is wrkin one inproving are editting, it taks lots of concentation to read for speling as we a fore misused synonyns! punctuation, and capilals? as ~~when year~~ I'm doin my homwork you can ask me to proofread som of my work! when I'm doing a project I ned help proofreading thak you?

Compliment

Wish

Accounting for Learning: TAKING MUSIC HOME

Specialist teachers who work with our classes sometimes find it difficult to communicate students' learning to their parents. One of our colleagues, Mary Weiler, developed this informal report, which has proven successful. Please adapt it to suit your needs.

Informal music report

Name ___Laurie___

Informal Music Report

We are exploring rhythm, melody, and form through listening, singing, and playing the recorder. As students gain insight into the elements of a piece of music they see how the parts fit together in the total composition.

Students are encouraged to develop good posture (essential for good tone production) and are constantly expanding their playing range and reading ability.

Students have rated each piece: difficult, moderate, or easy, and underlined the piece they will play for you. Please listen and enjoy. Your response is welcome.

Musically yours,

Mrs. Weiler

Mrs. Weiler

		Rating
I will play:	White Coral Bells	*hard*
	Donkey Riding	*moderate*
	Four Strong Winds	*moderate*
	Simple Gifts	*moderate*
	Oats, Peas, Beans	*1st TIME - 8.5 2nd TIME - 9.0 easy*

and _____ (optional)

As I'm playing please note that:

1. ___my feet are flat___
2. ___recorder is infront of my teeth___
3. ___and I play slowly___

Parent Comment

After listening to you play I would like to compliment you on: ___The time you spent practicing your music, Greg. Also, you have a good sense of rhythm that makes listening to your music a pleasant experience.___

I'd also like to add: ___I'm looking forward to hearing a new piece of music from the list above.___

Please sign and return to

C. Santos	*Laurie Santos*	*Mrs. Weiler*	*DR Singleton*
Parent's signature	Student's signature	Teacher's signature	Principal's signature

---

Accounting for Learning: REFLECTING ON LEARNING

Reflection is the foundation for self-evaluation; investing in time for reflection pays off in all aspects of classroom life. Reflection needs to become a regular part of every day. This can be done by having students tell a partner one thing they liked about their activity or writing reflections on specific aspects of the learning process. You can help students reflect on their learning by taking a few minutes before an activity begins to discuss what successful learners do. Some stems for reflection are

- ☞ When I was reading I…
- ☞ I worked well with others because…
- ☞ At cleanup I…
- ☞ When I got stuck I…

SUMMARY

In our book, *Together Is Better: Collaborative Assessment, Evaluation, and Reporting,* we provide a comprehensive plan for assessing, evaluating, and reporting learning. In this chapter we have built upon that work by adding new strategies and ideas that are particularly suitable for educators who work with a wide range of learners. The questions we ask to clarify our thinking about assessment, evaluation, and reporting are:

- ☞ What time have I allocated to observe and record?
- ☞ What system do I use to manage the "stuff" I collect?
- ☞ How can I help my students understand and be included in the assessment and evaluation process?
- ☞ What ongoing activities do I have to keep parents informed?
- ☞ How have I structured the reporting process to include and inform students and their parents?

Anyone who works in a classroom soon comes to appreciate efforts, accomplishments, and abilities of each child. Our challenge is to help parents understand their child's strengths and learning needs. In the next chapter we offer ideas that let us work together to invite further learning.

What's one new idea you can incorporate into your practice? What can you give up to have the time and energy for something new?

8

INFORMING, INVITING, AND INCLUDING OTHERS

Multi-age classes exist within a larger context—a community of learners and colleagues, parents, and residents. By inviting, including, and informing others, we gain their understanding and support. This gives us the comfort and security we need to take risks for learning. When others in our community understand and appreciate multi-age classes and the experiences such classes provide for students, we can get on with the learning.

Change creates anxiety. Because multi-age classes may be different from familiar graded organizations, everybody needs to be reassured that students are learning the basics and that grouping students in a multi-age classroom is positive for students and their learning. Our goal in inviting, informing, and including others, then, is to help them understand that the intent of multi-age classes (MAC) is to *M*aximize *A*dvantages for *C*hildren.

As well as providing parents and colleagues with information about multi-age classes, we're learning that they can be valuable sources of information. When we ask parents and colleagues what they think and listen to their responses, we are often taken way beyond our original notions. In addition to contributing ideas, parents and colleagues are able to support our work when they know what we are trying to do.

What do you do to help your parent community feel comfortable about your classroom?

Informing, Inviting, and Including Others:

Informing, Inviting, and Including Others: SUBJECT SPECIALTY NIGHTS

To reassure parents and give the children an opportunity to demonstrate their skills, we developed evening meetings for parents and children at which parents can see what and how their children are learning specific information. All sessions follow the same format:

1. Children and parents doing together

2. Parents watching children doing

3. Teacher being available for questions and/or comments

4. Tea, coffee, cookies, and wishes for a good night

Mainly Math is an example of one session we conduct.

Because many parents think math is taught in a sequential way, it is hard for them to imagine how children at different ages can learn together. We have used the following agenda to show the kind of learning that is possible in multi-age classrooms:

Welcome to Mainly Math

6:30 p.m.: Together, children and parents try problem-solving tasks, use math manipulatives, and play.

7:00: Participants clean up and move to a central meeting area. Small chalkboards and chalk are available so the children can show how they make good use of transition time to get ready for the number of the day, a math activity that involves that day's date.

7:05: The children demonstrate their usual activities with the calendar and then contribute all the equations that equal the number of the day of the month (see page 30). These are recorded by the teacher or children on chart paper, chalkboard, or overhead transparency. The children conclude this activity by suggesting where this number might be found "in the real world." For example, if sixteen is the number of the day, they might respond: "Sixteen are the corners on four squares" or "There are sixteen days until Christmas" or "There are sixteen boys in our class."

7:20: Excuse some children to work on independent and small-group activities while you show the parents how it is possible to do a lesson to develop concepts with one group (for example, regrouping, using unit blocks on the overhead projector).

7:30: The children who have been working independently return to the whole group. Have someone volunteer to describe what he or she was doing during the work time.

7:45: Have children whose ages when added to their parents' ages equal even numbers say "Good night." Have children whose ages plus their parents' ages equal odd numbers say "Good night." Give parents a response sheet to take home.

Parent Response

At the math evening I noticed _____

_____

_____

I was pleased to see _____

_____

_____

I'd like to know more about _____

_____

_____

Response sheet

Having children work with their parents followed by a teacher-led demonstration works well in many curriculum areas and helps parents understand how their children are being taught. Depending on what parents are interested in, highlight science explorations, reading/writing activities, social studies projects, or use of fine arts materials. You might call your evening session "Simply Science," "Really Reading," "Spotlight on Social Studies," or "Focus on the Fine Arts."

We have learned that when the children are invited to attend the parent night, attendance skyrockets. An intermediate teacher, Lora Beth Le Garff, warned us that when older students have their special night, parents need to be asked to leave younger siblings at home as they have a tendency to steal the spotlight.

Informing, Inviting, and Including Others: KIDS' PERFORMANCE NIGHT

A parents' night often centers on a performance by children—typically rehearsed fine arts activities such as choirs, plays, and dances. We have successfully adapted the format used in these performances

to other curriculum areas, enabling parents and others to observe and appreciate the children's successes in subjects such as language arts. When parents know their children, not the teacher, will be performing, they are more willing to come to learn about what is happening at school. The following is a description of one such evening.

Munchies and Memories

Preparation

Each family was asked to bring a potluck *hors d'oeuvres* and whatever else they wanted for refreshments. We supplied name tags, cups, glasses, coffee, tea, napkins, and paper plates. When people arrived they set out their snacks.

6:30 p.m.–7:00 p.m.: Everyone enjoyed eating and conversing.

7:00–7:30: Children demonstrated Nine *P*s Reading (see chapter 5, page 59) to show how well they read. Having children work with partners or in small groups lets everyone give a successful performance in a short time. After each reading, we encouraged the children to give compliments. This gave us an opportunity to point out the strategies the children had learned to apply to reading and the ways they had learned to comment on the variety of materials read.

7:40–7:45: With music playing in the background, we showed slides of the children "in action."

7:45–8:00: Snacks.

8:00: Good night.

Informing, Inviting, and Including Others: PARENTS RESPONDING TO READING

Leon Politano sends home the letter below, asking parents to listen to their child give a specially prepared reading of the class's current favorite book. Other times he varies the request, asking parents to read the story to their child. This "home learning" gives students and their parents an opportunity to talk about school and learning together in a concrete way. It also gives students an audience for their reading, while parents get to hear how well their child reads aloud.

Dear Parents:

After sharing this book with _____*Alicia*_____ could you please give him/her two stars and a wish for their reading. (Ask your child to explain.)

★ *Alicia's reading has greatly improved since September. She has a sudden interest in chapter books, which seem to give her a real sense of accomplishment.*

★ *Alicia loves to be read to when it comes to a book that may be beyond her reading level (eg. Anne of Green Gables which we've been working on for months). It is tough reading. However she is very interested in the character of Anne. Therefore her enthusiasm for the story is ongoing.*

Wish *Our wish for Alicia is that her interest and enthusiasm for reading continues to grow, and that she becomes comfortable reading fiction and nonfiction alike.*

Please send this sheet back to school along with the book.

Barbara Hughes

"Two Stars and a Wish" note

Reading request note

Dear Parents:

We've read the book _The Very Last First Time by Jan Andrews_ and your child is ready to read it to you. Find a comfortable chair and enjoy!

When your child has finished reading, please take a few moments and share your response by writing a note. Please tell a couple of things that pleased you about your child's reading and anything else you'd like to add.

Best wishes,

Leon

Informing, Inviting, and Including Others: PARENT LETTER TO ACCOMPANY WORK SAMPLES

We often send collections of work home with students in a portfolio, a scrapbook, or large envelope. We include a letter so that parents understand the significance of what they are viewing and how they are to respond. A colleague glued this letter into the front of each child's scrapbook.

Informing, Inviting, and Including Others:
INVITING INFORMATION FROM PARENTS ABOUT CHILDREN

Inviting parents to tell you what they know about their child provides you with valuable information and lets them know you value their input. You can do this by letter. Some teachers also send along information about themselves: how long they have been teaching, their interests, information about their families, and their hopes for the upcoming year. The following samples created by our colleagues can be adapted for your use.

Letter to parents

RE: Student Portfolio

Dear Parents:

Throughout the year your child will be collecting samples of work and saving them in this scrapbook. The main purpose of this portfolio is to track development. It is not a "showpiece" for display; nor is it just a random collection of work. A student portfolio contains systematic, dated evidence of your child's work and growth. It helps your child become involved in self-evaluation and also gives you a chance to talk about the different kinds of work your child is doing. As the year goes on you can read about how your child evaluates or feels about his or her learning.

Most of the items in the portfolio have been chosen by your child. At times, I add items I feel are important. Each item in the folder has a cover sheet attached to it telling who decided to save it and why.

We invite you to respond to your child's growth and progress in the section marked "Comments."

Several times this year, your child's portfolio will be sent home. Please review this folder with your child and respond in the COMMENTS section.

As you look through the portfolio pages, please look for at least "one star and a wish."

A STAR IS A COMPLIMENT. You might compliment your child on the mastery of a skill—knowing how to read certain words, neatness, imaginative drawings, an improvement in a certain area, and so on. COMPLIMENTS help us recognize when we have done something well. We feel good about ourselves, we accept challenges more readily and enthusiastically, and learning becomes easier.

After listening to your compliments, your child will be ready to listen to your wish.

WISHES INDICATE AN AREA FOR IMPROVEMENT. Only one wish is required, as too many wishes may do more harm than good. Pick out one area in which you feel your child is capable of improving.

Please be sure to respond in the COMMENTS section and return the whole scrapbook to school. This information from you provides valuable feedback for me.

This portfolio technique will become a useful and powerful technique with your help.

Thank you for taking the time to do this.

Should you have any questions or concerns, please make comments in your child's portfolio or contact me at school.

I plan to do this each month. Please return scrapbooks promptly.

Sincerely,

Vicki Dreger

Dear Parents/Guardian:

I am just beginning to get to know your child and would appreciate your insights to assist in program planning. As parents you know about your child's learning and how your child puts those skills into action outside school. I would like you to consider your child's abilities and interests as well as your own expectations. You can use the frame provided below or flip the page over and write what you want. Please return as soon as possible. Thank you.

Best wishes,

M. Mahabir + A. Davies

P.S. Our first open house of the year will be tomorrow, Thursday September 30. It begins at 7:00 p.m. in the gym and will be over at 8:00 p.m. I am looking forward to meeting you and your family.

Dear ___*Marina + Anne*___:

Our child is a talented youngster. The thing that ___*Sam*___ loves to do more than anything else is ___*draw*___.

When ___*Sam*___ starts talking about ___*hockey*___ he/she just can't seem to stop.
The other thing ___*Sam*___ is enthusiastic about is ___*any other sport*___.

I/we remember reading a book called ___*Good Night Moon*___ when ___*Sam*___ was little. We read that book over and over again. These days he/she likes to read ___*sports magazines and Hank The Cowdog adventures*___. Right now we are reading ___*Tales of a 4th Grade Nothing*___ to him/her.

We think it is important for ___*Sam*___ to learn about ___*communication*___ this year. We think the following skills are vital: ___*writing, speaking, and spelling*___
We are really busy but we will find ___*20*___ minutes each week to help ___*Sam*___ with school work.
Our preference would be to do ___*editing*___ work with him/her.

One thing ___*Sam*___ never likes to miss is ___*gym*___ but he/she would be quite happy to avoid ___*cleaning up*___. One thing you might not find out about ___*Sam*___ is ___*he also likes poetry*___.

___*Anne + Marina*___, our wish for ___*Sam*___ in the coming year is ___*that he be happy and try lots of new things*___. We hope that it is an excellent year for ___*Sam*___.
Please call ___*us at home*___ if you need to talk to us about ___*Sam*___'s learning at school!

Best wishes,

Martha & Joseph Geremia

Letter to parents with information request

Written response to letter

Dear Marina & Anne,

Nicky is a quiet, attentive student. She usually tackles her work with enthusiasm, and enjoys it. One thing she doesn't like is math, even though she does well at it. She enjoys science projects, story writing, computers; is an excellent speller (though I noticed some errors on her work samples for Open House.) You will probably find that Nicky is reluctant to speak up in class — this is something all her teachers have worked on, especially Mr. James. (Brian Goodenough told me when she was in his class he learned to read lips really well!) She certainly has no trouble making herself heard at home, especially when it comes to her brother. We feel Nicky is a very good role model, and she loves school! Our hope for her this year is that she is well prepared for junior high — we're sure she will be. She is very happy to be in your class, and we're sure she'll do very well this year.

Thank you,
L. Nettleton

Informing, Inviting, and Including Others: **LEARNING LOGS**

Having students' reflect on their learning—setting and resetting goals—helps them focus their energies. When this is shared with their parents they are giving their parents specific information about their daily activities and inviting their parents to respond.

Some teachers have students record this information in notebooks. Others prefer students to keep a separate journal or log for recording their learning. Some find students are most comfortable using mind maps and word webs to record their information and thinking. Others, such as our colleagues Marina Mahabir and Charlie Schellinck, prefer using a more structured framework, especially with older students. They have used with success, and taught us to use, this version of a learning log.

Weekly learning log

Weekly Learning Log   Week of _____

Goals for the Week _____

_____

	Activity	Homework	Daily Reflection
MON	Daily Edit Learning Log check Division Test Recess Fitness Music U.S.S.R. Centers Centers L.L.	Wrapping paper money due Wed. Gather center stuff. Read 30 minutes Good copy of thank you letter.	Today our couch arrived. It is very nice! We also worked on centers. My (and Lucy's) poster is up. It's WICKED! I am glad we are going to continue our math test—mine sure isn't done !!! Oh well. It will be done soon.
TUE	Class Meeting Math "The Game" Centers Computers Choir USSR Africa L.L.	Finish African problems · math stuff for Centers. Start Africa title page. Draw a African animal. Begin Africa map	Today we decided to do a mini-Africa study. I plan to make very good use of my time. Tonight alone I am finishing 2 of the 10 projects and starting my title page. I think I am really going to enjoy studying Africa. It's DOUBLE WICKED!
WED	Sponge Daily Edit math Move Desks "The Game" Centers Reading Africa Project	Africa assignments	I am achieving my "done fully and on time" goal in the Africa project, right, Ms. M? See, Mom and Dad? I am responsible. The charts Lacey and I are making is taking forever! HELP !!!!
THUR	Sponge music P.E. Story Centers/Letter USSR Africa Assignment L.L.	Swimming note Africa projects	Honestly, Club T gave me a HEADACHE today. It seemed like every grade 1, 2, and 3 was there. But it was worth it. Today alone I got 6 bucks! We had an awesome day, though. I really enjoyed it. My woodblock is coming along.
FRI	Kira Sponge Graphing News stories from Africa Africa projects Club T meeting Mrs. Taylor L.L. P.E.	Africa project (get story & art research done) Swimming money (#1.80)	Today, learning about Africa from Mrs. Taylor was really interesting. I did not know they tie-dyed their material. It look double wicked. I also did not know that elephant tusks are hollow — good for my Africa report.

Weekly Reflection _____

_____

Parent or Teacher Comment _____

_____

Teacher Signature _____   Parent Signature _____

Reproducible master in appendix A

Informing, Inviting, and Including Others: MONTHLY HIGHLIGHTS

Our students use story frames to retell the highlights of stories they had just read. We have adapted these frames to record information about other activities our students have shared during the month. The frames are simple enough for older children to complete on their own. For younger children, record the information for them or group them in threes or fours and have each group complete a frame.

"Reflecting on Learning"
frames

Two things I want to remember about this month are _____

_____

and _____

Next month I want to _____

_____

Two things I will remember about my three-way conference are:

1. *shows potential leadership skills in group work*

2. *notebooks neatly organized*

One thing I hope to achieve next month is *finishing my homework on time and not leaving for the last minute.*

Our class has enjoyed having _____

aloud. We've been practicing our reading by _____

_____ , _____

_____ , and _____

_____ .

One thing we tried this month has been _____ .

We had fun when _____

_____

We all tried to improve _____

_____ .

During *November* our class has been learning about _____

Astronomy and Division .

Three things I have learned are:

1. *The Phases of the Moon*

2. *The revolution of seasons*

3. *About the Earth and its axis*

---

s month our class has been learning about _____

_____ .

have put our knowledge of mathematics to use by _____

_____ .

Informing, Inviting, and Including Others: WEB OF THE MONTH

At the end of each month, we web the highlights. These webs are visual records that show parents and administrators how much we fit into our busy days. If we record the web on a transparency then we can photocopy it and send it home the same day. We invite children to use the back of the sheet to illustrate their personal highlights or to write about what they have learned and what their learning goals are for the upcoming month. Each month's web can be placed in a binder or posted in an area where classroom visitors can note some of the class's learning experiences.

Informing, Inviting, and Including Others: **TRIED AND TRUE**

Over the years we have developed many ways to invite, include, and inform others. It is important, however, that we remember some of the tried and true ways that have been especially effective.

Open house during school time, and sending home the daily agenda and short newsletters written by the teacher or teacher and students, are all methods that require little preparation but yield positive results. Phoning parents with good news is simple and effective. When a child has a great idea, shows thoughtfulness to others, or makes a breakthrough, call the parents that day and share. Keep a class list to make sure that everyone gets one or more calls during the year.

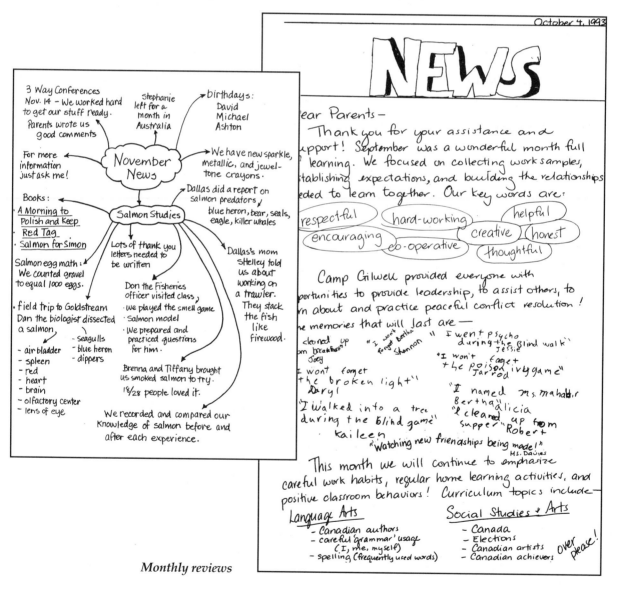

Monthly reviews

Informing, Inviting, and Including Others: NEWSLETTER POSSIBILITIES

Tammy Orthner, an inventive student teacher, created a newsletter that delighted parents and children. She established categories and collected information from the children during the week, printing the children's information as she went. The highly personal, friendly format gave a real sense of what was happening in the classroom and became a favorite source of reading material.

Sports and Friends

Philomena learned a new dance at dance cl...
Jordan went swimming with his dad and br...
D.J. went skating by his house.
William got to skate on his grass in the ba...
Catherine played with her friend Jenni...
David's friend Jenny was coming over to hi...

General News

Breanna sang, to our class, Santa Claus is ...
to Town.
Karl made a Christmas present for his mo...
Laura brought a doll-bracelet to class, whi...
got from her friends, Irene and Ivan.
Tiffany made a Rudolph the Red Nose Rei...
Christmas decoration.
Gemma made a connection between her four ca...
our new cat book.
Alison performed a play about a bank.
Megan received her first Christmas card of t...
Jenna discovered a book about cats, which ...
to the song The Twelve Days of Christmas.
Jessica went to a Brownie recital.

*Our toy sale made $18.09.

Class Page (Div. 12s)

week: Nov. 28 to Dec. 4, 1992

Birthdays

Ashton's birthday was November 30th.
She got a colour blaster and a barbie shop.
Amy's birthday was December 1st she received a beautiful flowered dress and shoes.
Bradley also had a birthday on December 4th his favourite present was a hockey stick.

Sick Kids

Matthew had the flu that seems to be going aroun... the same one Wishart.
Dallas was home sick with the flu and a cold.
Shane went home from school because he was not feelin... well.
*Please everyone, keep taking vitamins and get lots of rest!!

Reading Books

Patrick read 7 pages of a chapter book.
Andi made a connection about CoCo when Mrs. Leeson read The Fuzzy Rabbit's Christmas.
Shaun bought 4 books at the book fair.
Evelyn won a book from the book fair's draw.

Informing, Inviting, and Including Others: HOMEWORK BECOMES HOME LEARNING

Turn homework into home learning. This enables both the students and parents to make connections between school learning and the world outside school. You can do this by sending activities home that involve the children and their parents. Use topics that evolve from classroom work. Some activities you might suggest:

- ☞ Estimate the length, width, and depth of objects in your neighborhood or around your home.
- ☞ Interview your parents about their special place or something they did that seemed like a good idea at the time.
- ☞ Read *When I Was Young in the Mountains* by Cynthia Rylant then ask your parents for a story of when they were young.
- ☞ Create math problems to bring to class the next day.
- ☞ Find out when your parents use math. What kind do they do when they are shopping? Working? Banking? Playing?
- ☞ Create palindromes (a number that reads the same backwards or forwards such as 17071). Use your telephone number, street address, or birth date.

Informing, Inviting, and Including Others: BUILDING BRIDGES

Teachers of multi-age classes often make up only a small percentage of the school staff. To help us work through our questions and ideas while helping everyone understand our intentions, therefore, it is important that we share our work with others and give others opportunities to share with us. A web is one method that has worked for us.

Administrators need to be informed of what goes on in multi-age classes so that they can understand and be prepared to help others understand multi-age classes. Following are some of the ways we share the excitement of MAC:

- ☞ We send our administrator copies of all notes and newsletters that we send home.
- ☞ We invite them to classroom open houses and parents' evenings.
- ☞ We have children show them projects, written work, and "polished" reading.
- ☞ We share books and articles that help explain the MAC.

have an area for posting samples of parent letters/newsletter by copying machine

team-teaching and co-planning

cross-age buddying

holding staff meetings in different classrooms

have a "trade classes" for a morning/day

Consider...

Use a preparation period to visit another teacher's class and invite them to yours

go on a field trip with another class

Combine classes for gym period

Putting a sign-up sheet in the staffroom to share materials and ideas

sharing books and materials between classes

Share centers and have common activity times

Idea web

Substitute teachers are often nervous when called to a multi-age, learner-centered classroom—routines and procedures are quite different from what they are used to. One practical way of letting substitute teachers know what you would like done in your absence is to provide a written description of the class routines and an update of current plans. This method can be used over and over and it gives the substitute teacher an idea of how the class works.

You can prepare a folder in a few hours with the necessary information or, have the children produce a booklet, which will build their awareness of important information.

Substitute folder

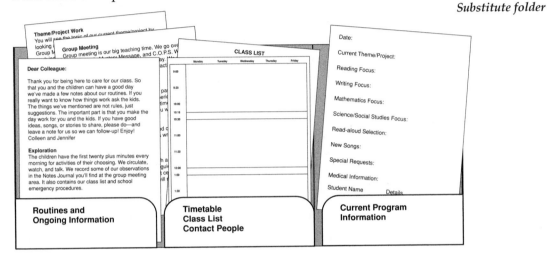

Routines and Ongoing Information

Timetable Class List Contact People

Current Program Information

Dear Colleague:

Thank you for being here to care for our class. So that you and the children can have a good day we've made a few notes about our routines. If you really want to know how things work ask the kids. The things we've mentioned are not rules, just suggestions. The important part is that you make the day work for you and the kids. If you have good ideas, songs, or stories to share, please do—and leave a note for us so we can follow-up! Enjoy! Colleen and Jennifer

Exploration
The children have the first twenty plus minutes every morning for activities of their choosing. We circulate, watch, and talk. We record some of our observations in the Notes Journal you'll find at the group meeting area. It also contains our class list and school emergency procedures.

Clean-up
We give a five minute warning before clean up. When a child has cleaned his or her own area he or she is asked to help others. We put on music for clean up. Children like to play "beat that song!"

Group Meeting
Group meeting is our big teaching time. We go over the agenda, do Mystery Message, and C.O.P.S. We try to work in a story and/or poem every day. We use this time to set expectations for whatever activity is to follow.

Music
As well as singing for the fun of it and as part of our themes, we have two scheduled music periods with Mr. Stewart. This is teacher preparation time—you are welcome to join in or use this time as you wish.

Readers' and Writers' Workshop
The routines for both of these are posted on charts at the Group Meeting Area. The children's writing files are kept in the Assessment Center.

Math Workshop
Our typical routine for math begins with a mini-lesson on our current topic, followed by brief guided practice and children working independently at centers or agreed-upon activities. The agenda will note our math topic.

Theme/Project Work
You will see the topic of our current theme/project by looking at the display and books collected in our Group Meeting Area. This is the time children use to work individually or in small groups on their theme-related projects.

Quick Attention Signal
A hand in the air indicates that everyone needs to stop and listen for directions, information, instructions. The children know that if someone doesn't pick up on the signal, it is their job to give them silent help.

Washrooms
Children use the washrooms when they need to. For safety purposes we ask younger students to let someone know and older students to sign out when they leave the class.

(Computer, gym, reflection time, and other daily activities are described in a similar way.)

Detail: Routines and Ongoing Information

SUMMARY

Together *is* better—when we work alongside our parents and colleagues on behalf of children we all benefit! In this chapter we have added to the possibilities for inclusion described in both *Together Is Better: Collaborative Assessment, Evaluation, and Reporting* and *Making Themes Work.* We know that when we promote shared understanding of our intentions and purposes, our ability to achieve our goals is enhanced. When we think about how we are inviting, informing, and including others we ask:

- ☞ What things have I done to help others understand the goals of our classroom?
- ☞ How have I let others know I value their suggestions and ideas?
- ☞ What invitations have I given to encourage others to see our class in action?
- ☞ What different forms of representation have I used to communicate information about our learning?

As we invite, inform, and include others we enter into a dialogue. This *can* be intimidating, but we have learned the value of the questions people ask. Every question provides us with an opportunity to explain our intentions, our hopes, and our dreams more fully.

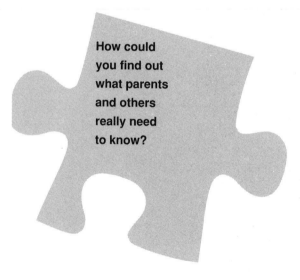

How could you find out what parents and others really need to know?

RESPONDING TO QUESTIONS

We've learned that questions are our friends. The questions teachers and parents ask inform us about their concerns. Because the same questions about multi-age classes arise again and again, in this chapter we give our answers to some of the most frequently asked. We hope these will help you when you respond to questions and engage in dialogue with parents, colleagues, and community members.

We take concerns seriously and seek to address them in a realistic fashion within the constraints of a school setting, as well as within the framework of a multi-age learning experience. Listening to understand and then working together to address concerns lead to better learning for students and a stronger community for us all.

Can't I do all this great stuff in a single-age classroom?

Of course you can. We believe that all classrooms contain a wide diversity of learners and learning needs. Diversity exists in every class, and every teacher needs to consider it. The challenge of multi-age classes pushes our thinking and acts as a signal to open up instruction. Our challenge is to constantly recognize and plan for diversity. Our experiences in multi-age classrooms have shown us that differences are strengths, and that teaching to those differences is not only valid but essential, no matter what the age range of your students.

What is the difference between family grouping or multi-age classes and split grades?

We use family grouping as a synonym for multi-age classes. Like family members, children in multi-age classrooms vary in age but share similar needs. The role of the family or class is to support one another's learning. In a multi-age class or family grouping we view the curriculum from a broader perspective. For example, instead of having the grade-four students do a unit on the Haida Nation and the students in grade five do a unit on the Inuit, we have all children learn about cultures whose survival is based on a strong relationship with the environment.

With split grades, students are taught the grade-three curriculum in grade three and the grade-four curriculum in grade four. Even teachers in areas with strict state or provincial requirements for each grade find they are able to combine their classes for most activities by reframing expectations and focusing on what is similar.

What are the advantages of multi-age classes?

As soon as you have a mixture of ages you put an emphasis on individuals and take the emphasis off comparisons. Single-grade classes encourage sameness. Children who do "too much" or "too little" are perceived to be different, and being different is perceived as negative. When children are in mixed-age classes everyone is different so everyone can get on with learning.

As principal Trevor Calkins said: "If you walk into a classroom thinking 'this is grade five,' you expect ten-year-olds and you bring all your beliefs about what ten-year-olds can and cannot do. Your plans are shaped by your notions of what grade five is and what ten-year-olds are. As soon as you know you've got eight-, nine-, and ten-year-olds, you seek ways to increase the scope of the activities. The children's range of ages acts as a constant signal to rethink your instructional plans."

How long do children stay with one teacher?

There are as many possibilities for placing children as there are classrooms; where a child is placed depends on the way the school is able to organize classes from year to year. Every child, however, needs to be placed in the best environment for his or her learning. We prefer to keep our children for at least two years so that the children who have been the younger or the middle have the opportunity to be the oldest. Other people have had success with keeping children for three or more years. We feel it might be advantageous for children to have access to another teacher and his or her talents after two years. Whatever the decision, it needs to be made with the children's best interests as the key factor.

Don't older children get bored or end up spending their time helping the younger children instead of learning?

Many people assume this, and that only the younger students will benefit from the multi-age class arrangement. When we focus on individual talents and abilities, however, children tend not to be categorized by age but rather by who can do what needs to be done right now. For example, we have watched five-year-olds helping eight-year-olds organize equipment and eight-year-olds helping ten-year-olds edit their writing drafts. Children in such learning situations come to appreciate the talents that exist within the group regardless of age. And while it is true that older children work with the younger children, this gives them opportunities for leadership and for practicing their skills with a real audience.

How do multi-age classes fit with state or provincial requirements?

As long as children are actively learning they are prepared to demonstrate what they know and can do. As teachers become more comfortable with sharing the state or provincial expectations with children, students are better prepared to be assessed and evaluated according to clear criteria. By letting children know what they are expected to learn, they can put their energies towards learning rather than towards guessing what needs to be learned. We have also learned to write proposals and, where necessary, prepare waivers to school districts and departments of education so we can get on with meeting children's learning needs in the best possible ways.

How do you handle the range from children who are barely reading to children who are able to read anything and everything?

Reading, whether learning about reading or reading for a variety of purposes, is a critical component of our learning with children. It's a chunk of our instructional practice that needs to work successfully or everything feels out of kilter. The examples we've provided in chapter 5 exemplify ways to foster more and better reading among a diverse group of learners. Strategies for teaching reading are selected because they meet the criteria that are essential for all classes: they encourage and provide for open-ended reading experiences and responses.

What about younger children who are more able than older children?

One of the many advantages of a multi-age class is younger children are not held back by the confines of grade expectations. Because individual strengths and talents are accepted and valued, a six-year-old who reads chapter books or relishes solving problems that require multiplication becomes an accepted part of classroom life. When sameness isn't expected, older children are not threatened by a younger child's exceptional abilities.

The multi-age classroom allows talented young children to behave like the "little kids" they are yet to learn according to their abilities.

What about when children move to classrooms that are organized as single grades?

Classroom configurations are not the final determinants of the quality of an educational experience. Any classroom can offer students positive experiences if each child's strengths and needs are both recognized and appreciated and if the curriculum is viewed as something to be constructed with a group of students rather than something to be covered in spite of the students.

How do you handle curriculum requirements for two or three grade levels in one classroom?

There are many different definitions of curriculum. Publishers' programs are often confused with curriculum documents or assumed to be the same as state or provincial curriculum documents. They are not. State and provincial curricula are external sets of expectations or guidelines that explain what is expected to be taught at a particular age level. Most jurisdictions have curriculum development teams comprised of teachers and researchers in any given area. Most curriculum documents give enough flexibility so that teachers can best meet student needs. One of the first tasks of a teacher of a multi-age class is to locate the actual curriculum documents mandated in his or her jurisdiction.

Curriculum documents address both the actual content (knowledge and information) and the different processes (researching, writing, computing, reading/thinking, editing) through which we construct knowledge and take action in our world. Both content and process are important.

Teachers of multi-age classes need to analyze the content of their curriculum documents to determine what is continuous from year to year and what needs to be added (see page 19). We find there is tremendous overlap from year to year—commercial publishers of educational materials might have you believe otherwise because that is how they justify so many books, skill packages, extension ideas, and kits.

Curriculum content is designed to be spiral in nature. The same area (for example, reading, problem solving, basic math facts—both content and process) is revisited year after year with extensions being made over time. Current curriculum design, in fact, supports multi-age classes because students are able to work with a two- or three-year chunk and move along at their own pace.

Difficulties may arise when poorly designed standardized-norm or criterion-referenced tests and district-wide tests are administered. These may not accurately reflect the classroom curriculum expectations, respect the multitude of different ways students represent what they know and can do, or take place at appropriate times. No one can effectively prepare for a poorly conceived and poorly designed test—students cannot afford to waste valuable learning time preparing for a test that does not measure a significant portion of what they have learned. Many jurisdictions are redesigning their state or provincial assessments to align them more closely to their stated expectations.

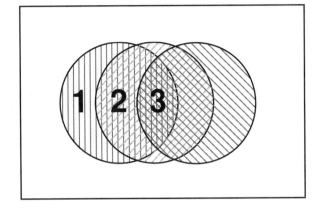

Have there been difficulties when students have transferred in from programs that are different?

We have found it important to assure children who come from graded schools that, even though the class is ungraded, they still have available all the learning opportunities for children of their age. We give them help so they can explain or describe their classroom learning environment to others.

We also make sure parents of new students know why we have chosen a multi-age class organization and how it benefits students and their learning. We invite parents to join us in class so they can see, firsthand, children of all ages learning the attitudes, skills and processes, and knowledge that are taught and learned throughout our daily activities.

What about students with special needs?

Multi-age classes are open to *all* children in the given age range. Students who have been identified as having special needs are accommodated, as are all children, by assessing their strengths and learning needs; then working with parents, school, and district personnel as well as the child to develop a learning plan, and to gain appropriate resources and support. For example, some children need a full-time assistant, others may need an intervener for sign language, while others benefit from technological aids.

What happens to children who haven't been successful with their learning?

We do not retain, fail, or keep back children. Studies show that students who fail or are retained have a 50 percent chance of eventually dropping out of school. Repeating more than one grade pushes their dropout probability rate to over 90 percent. We already knew the short-term effects of retention were not beneficial, so when we learned of these long-term effects of failing or being retained in a grade we could no longer support these practices. This led us to look at what action we could take to support student learning.

Our practice is to identify a child's strengths, be clear and specific about areas of concern, and develop a cooperative action plan with the child, his or her parents, and other school personnel. By combining ages, abilities, and interests within a multi-age class, children have the time and positive enabling environment in which to continue their learning.

Parents have expressed concern that having different age groups in the room means their child has fewer same-age playmates to choose among. Is this a problem? How do you deal with it?

Our students have buddies with other multi-age classes, trade around classes, and are grouped with other children of the same age to work on projects together for a week or two. In situations where a specialist is available (for example, music), children of a similar age range have some of their music time together. Each of these possibilities gives students a chance to interact with children of the same age and more choices for out-of-class playtime partners.

What questions do you have now?

Who could you connect with to discover the answers?

Do children who stay for more than one year in a multi-age class repeat material? How do they benefit?

Curricula are a complex mixture of knowledge, skills, processes, and attitudes that are constructed, refined, and extended over time and represented in different ways. Learning is a process of building a repertoire of ways to know, understand, respond to, and represent understandings and knowledge of our world. For example, children will read every year, and with the ever-increasing availability of reading materials, skill, and changing interests, the possibilities for what to read is endless. As children encounter and re-encounter concepts, they gain a richer and deeper understanding of the meaning of the materials they are reading and using. One child said, "Last year I could do this but this year I really know how it works."

CONCLUSION

In *Multi-Age and More* we share our dreams for all children: schooling that works for a lifetime and that takes advantage of the wonder and curiosity each child brings. We also want to maximize advantages for teachers. Our experience in multi-age classes has taught us that the more we observe, understand, and appreciate our children and shape our practice to support their needs, the more rewarding our teaching becomes.

Your teaching can be as enjoyable for you as it is beneficial for your students, as you learn to recognize the expert within. We encourage you to construct the knowledge you need about multi-age classes.

We hope you found more ideas in this book than you would ever use in a year. Be assured that we don't use them all with any one class. So take another look, then select, adapt, or modify those ideas that best fit your situation and your learning community!

We enjoy conducting workshops and institutes. If you would like further information regarding these, or if you would like to contact us about anything in this book, please write to us:

c/o Peguis Publishers
318 McDermot Avenue
Winnipeg, Manitoba
Canada R3A 0A2

APPENDIX—
REPRODUCIBLE MASTERS

Term _____

Theme _____

	Language Arts/Drama/Art/Computers	Maths/Computers	Social Studies/Science	Physical Ed.
Attitudes				
Skills/Processes				
Knowledge				

Page 23: Planning frame

Mathematics: Concept—

Mini-Lesson—

Guided Practice—

Independent Practice—

Beginning   **Developing**   **Extending**

Activity	Activity	Activity	Activity

Student's Concluding Reflection:
During this mathematics class we practiced _____

_____ **I completed** _____

Page 66: Math lesson plan

Three things I can tell you about _____ **are**

_____

_____

_____

Two things I like are

_____

_____

One thing I'll always remember is _____

_____

_____

At first _____

Then _____

Next _____

Finally _____

Once there was a _____

who _____

and _____

at last _____

_____

_____

Page 79: Sentence frames

Name: _____ **Topic:** _____

I can talk to...	I can observe...	I can collect...

FOLD

Page 84: Research folder

Name: _____ **Date:** _____

When I talked to…

_____

_____

_____

_____

_____

_____

_____

_____

_____

_____

Page 84: Talk sheet

Name: _____ **Date:** _____

When I watched _____

_____ **I learned** _____

_____

_____

_____

_____

_____

_____

_____

_____

_____

_____

Page 84: Observation sheet

Name: _____

Date: _____

When learning how to be a researcher, I learned

_____

_____

_____

_____

_____

_____

_____

_____

☐ Next time I will do these things again because they worked.

☐ Next time I won't do these things because they weren't helpful.

Page 85: Research evaluation

Name _____ **Date** _____

A book that is easy for me to read is

If I don't know a word when I first
see it I can

1.

2.

3.

Page 85: Reading evaluation form

Name _____

Date _____

Situation

Comments

Name _____

Date _____

Situation

Comments

Name _____

Date _____

Situation

Comments

Page 86: Observation frames

Name _____

Date _____

Today I

Name _____

Date _____

Eureka!
Now I can

Name _____

Date _____

Focus [   ]

I want you to know

Name _____

Date _____

Goal [   ]

Evidence

Page 86: Observation frames

Learning Focus _____	Perspective _____	Perspective _____	Parent(s)' Perspective
	Strengths:	**Strengths:**	**Strengths:**
	Improvement or Challenges Needed:	**Improvement or Challenges Needed:**	**Improvement or Challenges Needed:**
	Possible Goals for Next Term:	**Possible Goals for Next Term:**	**Possible Goals for Next Term:**

From: Building Connections: Multi-Age and More by Politano/Davies © 1994. May be reproduced for classroom use.   Note: This figure may be enlarged to 11" x 17" by setting your photocopier to 155%.

Page 92: Informal report form

Conference Guide for Collaborative Report
(Teacher and Student)

Questions to be posed to child:	Answers:
1. What would you like to have written about your strengths?	
2. Let's look at your work collection. What does it show about you? [*Each child is asked to have a sample of something that shows his or her reading skill and a collection of work ready to bring to the conference.*]	
3. What about [*subject*]? [*For example, "What about mathematics?"*]	
4. What did you select to read? Why? [*Child reads a sample.*] What do you do well when you read? Is there anything you need to work on?	
5. When you think about your learning, are there things you want or need to do better or learn about?	
6. How can you help yourself? How can I help you?	

Page 94: Conference guide for collaborative reports

Date _____ Teacher _____ Student _____

Topics	Student's Notes	Teachers' Notes	Parent's Comments
Work Habits			
Language Arts			
Reading/Literature			
Social Studies			
Thinking Skills			
Fine Arts/Physical Education			
Mathematics			
Science			
Other			

Signatures _____ _____

Page 98–99: Frame for collaborative report

Picture This!

This is me. ______________________________

____

____

____

I'd like you to know that

- ✷ ______________________________
- ✷ ______________________________
- ✷ ______________________________

Page 100: Picture This

Dear _____

I've been practicing my math facts at school.
While you watch me I am going to

Please record 2 things you observe about my work
and one question you'd like to ask me.

Love,

_____

- -

Response

Page 101: Home activity sheet

Dear Parents:

We've read the book _____
and your child is ready to read it to you. Find a comfortable chair
and enjoy!

When your child has finished reading, please take a few moments
and share your response by writing a note. Please tell a couple of
things that pleased you about your child's reading and anything else
you'd like to add.

Best wishes,

Dear Parents:

We've read the book _____
and your child is ready to read it to you. Find a comfortable chair
and enjoy!

When your child has finished reading, please take a few moments
and share your response by writing a note. Please tell a couple of
things that pleased you about your child's reading and anything else
you'd like to add.

Best wishes,

Page 109: Reading request note

Dear Parents:

After sharing this book with _____ could you please give him/her two stars and a wish for their reading. (Ask your child to explain.)

★

★

Wish

Please send this sheet back to school along with the book.

_____

Page 109: "Two Stars and a Wish" note

Weekly Learning Log

Week of _____

Goals for the Week _____

_____

	Activity	Homework	Daily Reflection
M O N			
T U E			
W E D			
T H U R			
F R I			

Weekly Reflection _____

_____

Parent or Teacher Comment _____

_____

Teacher Signature _____   Parent Signature _____

Page 112: Weekly learning log

Two things I want to remember about this month are _____

_____

and _____ .

Next month I want to _____

_____ .

Our class has enjoyed having _____ read

aloud. We've been practicing our reading by _____

_____ , _____

_____ , and _____ _____

_____ .

During _____ our class has been learning about _____

_____ .

Three things I have learned are:

1. _____

2. _____

3. _____

Page 113: "Reflecting on Learning" frames

Two things I will remember about my three-way conference are:

1. _____

2. _____

One thing I hope to achieve next month is _____

_____ .

One thing we tried this month has been _____ .

We had fun when _____

_____ .

We all tried to improve _____

_____ .

This month our class has been learning about _____

and _____ .

We have put our knowledge of mathematics to use by _____

_____

_____ .

Page 113: "Reflecting on Learning" frames

APPENDIX— BIBLIOGRAPHY

American Association of School Administrators. *The Non-Graded Primary: Making Schools Fit Children.* Stock No. 21 00192, Library of Congress Catalogue 0-87652-184-7, 1992.

Atwell, Nancie. *Side by Side: Essays on Teaching to Learn.* Portsmouth, NH: Heinemann, 1991.

Atwell, Nancie, ed. *Coming to Know: Writing to Learn in the Intermediate Grades.* Portsmouth, NH: Heinemann, 1990.

Barrell, John. *Teaching for Thoughtfulness: Classroom Strategies to Enhance Intellectual Development.* New York: Longman, 1991.

Bialostok, Steven. *Raising Readers: Helping Your Child to Literacy.* Winnipeg, MB: Peguis Publishers, 1992.

Bissex, G. *GNYS at WRK: A Child Learns to Write and Read.* Cambridge, MA: Harvard University Press, 1980.

Braun, Carl. *Looking, Listening, and Learning: Observing and Assessing Young Readers.* Winnipeg, MB: Peguis Publishers, 1993.

Bredekamp, S., and T. Rosegrant, eds. *Reaching Potentials: Appropriate Curriculum and Assessment for Young Children, Volume One.* Washington, DC: National Association for Education of Young Children (NAEYC), 1993.

Brown, Janet. *Valuing Diversity: The Primary Years.* Washington, DC: National Association for Education of Young Children (NAEYC), 1992.

Brownlie, F., S. Close, and L. Wingren. *Tomorrow's Classroom Today.* Markham, ON: Pembroke Publishing, 1990.

Bruner, J. London. *The Process of Education.* Cambridge, MA: Harvard University Press, 1960.

Burns, M. *About Teaching Mathematics: A K-8 Resource.* White Plains, NY: Math Solutions Publications Cuisenaire Company of America, 1992.

Caine, R., and G. Caine. *Making Connections: Teaching and the Human Brain.* Alexandria, VA: Association for Supervision and Curriculum Development, 1991.

Cambourne, Brian, and Jan Turbill. *Coping With Chaos.* Rozelle, Australia: Primary English Teaching Association, 1987.

Cambourne, B. *The Whole Story.* New York, Ashton Scholastic, 1988.

Clay, M. *Becoming Literate.* Auckland, NZ: Heinemann, 1991.

Davies, A., C. Politano, and C. Cameron. *Making Themes Work.* Building Connections series. Winnipeg, MB: Peguis Publishers, 1993.

Davies, A., C. Cameron, C. Politano, and K. Gregory. *Together Is Better: Collaborative Assessment, Evaluation, and Reporting.* Winnipeg, MB: Peguis Publishers, 1992.

Donaldson, M. *Children's Minds.* London: Collins, 1978.

Eisner, E. *Educational Imagination* (3rd edition). London: Collier Books, 1985.

Gardner, H. *Frames of Mind: The Theory of Multiple Intelligence.* New York: Basic Books, 1985.

Goodman, K. *What's Whole in Whole Language?* Toronto, ON: Scholastic, 1986.

Guba, E., and Y. Lincoln. *Effective Evaluation: Improving the Usefulness of Evaluation Results Through Responsive and Naturalistic Approaches.* London: Jossey-Bass Publishers, 1981.

Harste, J., K. Short, with C. Burke. *Creating Classrooms for Authors.* Portsmouth, NH: Heinemann, 1988.

Healy, Jane. *Endangered Minds: Why Children Don't Think and What We Can Do About It.* New York: Simon and Schuster, 1990.

Heard, Georgia. *For the Good of the Earth and the Sun.* Portsmouth, NH: Heinemann, 1989.

Hill, Susan. *Becoming Responsible Learners.* Portsmouth, NH: Heinemann, 1991.

Hill, Susan, and Joelie Hancock. *Reading and Writing Communities: Cooperative Literacy Learning in the Classroom.* Armadale, Australia: Eleanor Curtain Publishing, 1993.

Johnson, Terry, et al. *The Tiger's Kiss: Assessment and Evaluation in the Classroom.* (In press)

Johnson, Terry, and Daphne Louis. *Bringing It All Together.* Richmond Hill, ON: Scholastic, 1990.

———. *Literacy Through Literature.* Richmond Hill, ON: Scholastic, 1987.

Kagen, S. *Cooperative Learning.* San Juan, Capistrano, CA: Kagen Cooperative Learning, 1992.

Kasten, W., and B. Clarke. *The Multi-Age Classroom: A Family of Learners.* Katonah, NY: Richard Owen, 1993.

Katz, Lilian, D. Evangelou, and J. A. Hartman. *The Case for Mixed-Age Grouping in Early Education.* Washington, DC: National Association for Education of Young Children (NAEYC), 1990.

Katz, L. G., and S. Chard. Meeting at the Child Study Center, University of British Columbia, August 1991.

Kropp, Paul. *The Reading Solution: Making Your Child a Reader for Life.* New York: Random House, 1993.

Lemke, J. L. *Using Language in the Classroom.* Don Mills, ON: Oxford University Press, 1989.

Ministry of Education, Province of British Columbia. *Primary Program (Foundation Document)* (GC0279). Victoria, BC, 1991.

Ministry of Education, Province of British Columbia. *Supporting Learning: Understanding and Assessing the Progress of Children* (document #RB 0018). Victoria, BC, 1991.

N.C.T.M Professional Standards for Teaching Mathematics. Reston, VA: The National Council of Teachers of Mathematics, 1991.

Nebraska Department of Education. *Learning in the Heartland.* Lincoln, NE: Nebraska Department of Education, Iowa Department of Education, and Iowa Area Education Agencies, 1993.

Piaget, J. *To Understand Is to Invent.* New York: Penguin, 1977.

Pigdon, Keith, and Marilyn Woolley, eds. *The Big Picture: Integrating Children's Learning.* Armadale, Australia: Eleanor Curtain Publishing, 1992.

Short, Kathy, and Carolyn Burke. *Creating Curriculum: Teachers and Students as a Community of Learners.* Portsmouth, NH: Heinemann, 1991.

Smith, F. *The Role of Prediction in Reading.* Toronto, ON: Paper presented at the Reading '74 Conference, February 1974.

Smith, Frank. *Understanding Reading* (4th edition). New York: Teachers College Press, Columbia University, 1988.

Vygotsky, L. S. *Mind in Society.* Cambridge, MA: Harvard University Press, 1978.

Wells, G. *The Meaning Makers.* Portsmouth, NH: Heinemann, 1986.

my recipes

America's FAVORITE Food

myrecipes

America's FAVORITE Food

200 top-rated recipes from the country's best magazines

Oxmoor House®

ISBN-13: 978-0-8487-3716-0
ISBN-10: 0-8487-3716-4
Library of Congress Control Number: 2012941381

Printed in the United States of America
First Printing 2012

Oxmoor House

VP, Publishing Director: Jim Childs
Editorial Director: Leah McLaughlin
Creative Director: Felicity Keane
Brand Manager: Vanessa Tiongson
Senior Editor: Rebecca Brennan
Managing Editor: Rebecca Benton

MyRecipes *America's Favorite Food*

Editor: Nichole Aksamit
Project Editor: Emily Chappell
Assistant Designer: Allison Sperando Potter
Director, Test Kitchen: Elizabeth Tyler Austin
Assistant Directors, Test Kitchen: Julie Christopher, Julie Gunter
Recipe Developers and Testers: Wendy Ball, R.D.; Victoria E. Cox; Stefanie Maloney; Callie Nash; Leah Van Deren
Recipe Editor: Alyson Moreland Haynes
Food Stylists: Margaret Monroe Dickey, Catherine Crowell Steele
Photography Director: Jim Bathie
Senior Photo Stylist: Kay E. Clarke
Photo Stylist: Katherine Eckert Coyne
Assistant Photo Stylist: Mary Louise Menendez
Senior Production Manager: Greg A. Amason

Contributors

Content Editor: Pam Hoenig
Recipe Developers and Testers: Tamara Goldis, Tonya Johnson, Kyra Moncrief, Kathleen Royal Phillips
Copy Editors: Julie Bosche, Barry Wise Smith
Proofreader: Polly Linthicum
Indexer: Mary Ann Laurens
Interns: Erin Bishop; Mackenzie Cogle; Jessica Cox, R.D.; Laura Hoxworth
Photographer: Johnny Autry
Photo Stylist: Anna Pollock

MyRecipes.com

General Manager, Time Inc. Lifestyle Digital: Tina Imm
Content Director: Jason Burnett
Senior Editor: Anne Chappell Cain, M.S., R.D.
Production Manager: Jim Sheetz
Nutrition Editor: Holley Johnson Grainger, M.S., R.D.
Associate Editors/Producers: Emily Shepherd, Ashley Kappel

Time Home Entertainment Inc.

Publisher: Richard Fraiman
VP, Strategy & Business Development: Steven Sandonato
Executive Director, Marketing Services: Carol Pittard
Executive Director, Retail & Special Sales: Tom Mifsud
Director, Bookazine Development & Marketing: Laura Adam
Executive Publishing Director: Joy Butts
Finance Director: Glenn Buonocore
Associate General Counsel: Helen Wan

To order additional publications, call
1-800-765-6400 or **1-800-491-0551**.

For more books to enrich your life,
visit **oxmoorhouse.com**.

To search, savor, and share thousands of recipes,
visit **MyRecipes.com**.

Front cover: Grilled Cilantro Chicken with Pickled Tomato and Avocado Salsa, page 68
Back cover: Coconut Cupcakes with Lime Buttercream Frosting (left), page 240; Peach and Gorgonzola Chicken Pizza (right), page 195

contents

page 21

page 33

page 172

page 211

WHAT THE RECIPE LABELS MEAN

 5 Ingredients or Less
uses five or fewer ingredients, not including salt, pepper, water, ice, cooking spray, and optional garnishes

 30 Minutes or Less
done in half an hour, from start to finish

 Gluten-Free
contains no wheat, barley, oats, bran, grits, flour, beer, breads, crackers, cakes, pastas, broth, soy sauce, hoisin, or ingredients that commonly contain gluten*

 Grill It!
designed to be made on the grill

 Kid-Friendly
modestly spiced, no alcohol, and likely enjoyed by little ones

 Low-Calorie
at or below low-calorie benchmarks**

 Make-Ahead
includes complete instructions for making now and serving later

 **Slow Cooker**
designed or adapted to be made in the slow cooker

*Due to variability among brands and changes in formulation, some prepared products may contain gluten or be processed in facilities that process products with gluten. Always check labels to be sure.

**Per serving: 40 calories for beverages, snacks, appetizers, cookies, and sauces; 120 calories for breads, cereals, and sides; 200 calories for main-dish proteins and desserts; 400 calories for protein-plus-side main dishes; 500 calories for one-dish meals with protein and two sides

Now we're cooking!

That's how I feel whenever something new comes along that makes cooking a little bit easier. I felt it the first time I tried a microwave, used a stove with gas burners, and fired up my very own grill. I can't help but feel it now as I flip through *America's Favorite Food*. Truly, it is a cookbook like no other.

For starters, it's the first from MyRecipes.com—the online home of more than 65,000 recipes, from *Cooking Light*, *Southern Living*, *Sunset*, *All You*, *Real Simple*, *Coastal Living*, Oxmoor House, and *Health*. The cookbook features only the best of the best—200 recipes created by these trusted brands and top-rated by the more than 6 million home cooks who use MyRecipes.com each month. It's also packed with insights about how the recipes work for picky eaters, flavor seekers, calorie counters, and time-pressed cooks in real American homes.

In the pages that follow, you'll find delicious 4- and 5-star dishes for everything from parties and potlucks to breakfasts, lunches, dinners, and desserts. They're the most-tried and best-rated recipes, served up with advice from pros and suggestions from MyRecipes.com users to help you cook with what's in your pantry, save time, and find dishes sure to delight your family, friends, and coworkers. Labels make it easy to spot kid-friendly, gluten-free, and low-calorie recipes, as well as dishes that can be made in a slow cooker, on the grill, in 30 minutes, or with 5 ingredients or less.

What's more, *America's Favorite Food* is the first cookbook with Scan-It/Cook-It™ technology. Invisible watermarks in more than 130 images bring the recipes to life, delivering videos, bonus recipes, menus, and other features directly to your smartphone.

This is a small but incredibly helpful innovation. Should you get stuck mid-recipe—wondering how exactly to peel shrimp, perhaps, or the best way to skin a peach—step-by-step video is at your fingertips. It's also easy and fun to use. Just download the free app (see next page for details) and use it on SCAN THIS boxes and photos in each chapter. I bet you say "Ooh!" when your first scan loads. What I said went a little something like this: "*Now* we're cooking!"

Nichole Aksamit

Nichole Aksamit
Editor

P.S. As a special bonus, we've created a **customizable online version** of this amazing recipe collection that you can use to get shopping lists with grocery sale prices in your area, as well as to sort, rate, review, and share the recipes you've tried. Get scanning to get yours.

SCAN THIS BOOK for the online version.

How to use the Scan-It/Cook-It™ digital features in this book

1. Download and open the Digimarc Discover app on your smartphone. It's free and available at the iTunes store for Apple devices and at the Google Play market for Android devices.

2. Position the phone 4 to 7 inches above any photo or box with a SCAN THIS label (shown at right) as if you are about to take its picture. Use the phone's camera flash if necessary. If you have access to a Wi-Fi connection, downloads will be faster.

3. Hold the phone steady for a second or two. The app will click and buzz when it recognizes the image and then begin downloading the described feature directly to your phone.

HOW IT WORKS Invisible watermarks embedded in the page act as portals to bonus content. With the Digimarc Discover app, your phone recognizes the watermarks, opens the portals, and delivers the content.

WHAT TO LOOK FOR

Maroon labels like this one identify *photos* you can scan for bonus content:

SCAN THIS PHOTO for video on how to prepare this recipe.

Orange labels like this one identify *boxes* you can scan for bonus content:

SCAN THIS BOX for more cooking know-how from our experts.

WHAT YOU GET WHEN YOU SCAN

How-to videos that walk you through a recipe, step by step, so you know just what to do

Technique videos that show you a procedure, such as how to poach eggs or cut up a chicken

Collections of similar recipes, such as more chicken chili recipes or kid-friendly breakfasts

Weeknight Meal Planners with a menu and a combined shopping list for five weeknight recipes, including the one you just scanned

Expert answers to common cooking questions and an easy way to submit your own

A customizable online version of the entire recipe collection

starters

MyRecipes.com users know how to get a party started: with a no-fail appetizer and a great cocktail. Here, we've gathered their favorite recipes for beverages (alcoholic and otherwise), dips, and finger foods—including our best-rated recipe in any category: Grilled Stuffed Jalapeños.

To use the exclusive **Scan-It/Cook-It**™ features in this chapter, look for the smartphone symbol (shown at left). For detailed instructions, please see page 7.

GRILLED STUFFED JALAPEÑOS
page 16

Make-Ahead

myrecipes users suggest:
• zipping it up by adding 1 teaspoon Tabasco sauce, 1 tablespoon Worcestershire sauce, 2 tablespoons lemon juice, and 1 tablespoon prepared horseradish

from Cooking Light

Spinach-and-Artichoke Dip

2 cups (8 ounces) shredded part-skim mozzarella cheese, divided
½ cup fat-free sour cream
¼ cup (1 ounce) grated fresh Parmesan cheese, divided
¼ teaspoon black pepper
3 garlic cloves, crushed
1 (14-ounce) can artichoke hearts, drained and chopped

1 (8-ounce) block ⅓-less-fat cream cheese, softened
1 (8-ounce) block fat-free cream cheese, softened
½ (10-ounce) package frozen chopped spinach, thawed, drained, and squeezed dry
1 (13.5-ounce) package baked tortilla chips (about 16 cups)

1. Preheat oven to 350°.
2. Combine 1½ cups mozzarella, sour cream, 2 tablespoons Parmesan, and next 6 ingredients in a large bowl; stir until well blended. Spoon mixture into a 1½-quart baking dish. Sprinkle with remaining ½ cup mozzarella and remaining 2 tablespoons Parmesan.
3. Bake at 350° for 30 minutes or until bubbly and golden brown. Serve with tortilla chips.

Note: To make ahead, assemble as directed up to 2 days ahead of serving; cover and refrigerate. Bake as directed in step 3.

Makes 5½ cups ▪ Prep time: 10 minutes ▪ Total time: 40 minutes

For complete nutritional information on this and other *Cooking Light* recipes, please turn to the appendix on pages 280–283.

> " I made this as an appetizer for Thanksgiving. Everyone kept coming into the kitchen to tell me how much they loved it!"
>
> —liafinney
> ★★★★★

from COASTAL LIVING

Hot Caramelized Onion Dip with Bacon and Gruyère

2 teaspoons butter
1 teaspoon vegetable oil
2 Spanish onions (about 1 pound), halved and thinly sliced
¼ teaspoon sugar
¼ teaspoon sea salt
1 tablespoon sherry vinegar

½ teaspoon minced fresh thyme
3 applewood-smoked bacon strips
¾ cup (3 ounces) shredded Gruyère cheese
½ cup sour cream
½ cup mayonnaise
¼ teaspoon freshly ground black pepper

1. Preheat oven to 400°. Melt butter with oil in a large skillet over medium-high heat. Add onions, sugar, and salt; cook, stirring occasionally, 8 minutes or until onions soften and just begin to turn golden. Reduce heat to medium, and cook, stirring often, 20 minutes or until onions turn deep golden brown. Stir in vinegar, scraping bottom of skillet to deglaze pan. Cook, stirring often, until vinegar is reduced by half. Stir in thyme.
2. Cook bacon in a large skillet over medium-high heat 8 to 10 minutes or until crisp. Drain on paper towels; finely crumble.
3. Combine cheese and next 3 ingredients in a medium bowl. Stir in onion mixture and bacon. Transfer to a 2-cup baking dish.
4. Bake at 400° for 20 minutes or until mixture bubbles and top is lightly golden.

Makes 2 cups ■ Total time: 1 hour, 10 minutes

30 Minutes
or Less

 I used two cloves of garlic, left out the jalapeño, and used a couple of shots of Sriracha sauce for kick. Awesome!"

—gary1950

★★★★★

myrecipes users suggest:
- using three-bean mixture (kidney, black, and pinto beans) instead of plain black beans
- thinning the mixture by using sesame oil and a little water instead of tahini
- making it less spicy by putting the jalapeño in whole instead of chopped and/or omitting the crushed red pepper

SCAN THIS PHOTO
for 7 more recipes
that use black beans.

from CookingLight

Spicy Black Bean Hummus

1 garlic clove, peeled
2 tablespoons fresh lemon juice
1 tablespoon tahini (roasted sesame seed paste)
1 teaspoon ground cumin
¼ teaspoon salt
1 (15-ounce) can black beans, rinsed and drained

1 small jalapeño pepper, chopped (about 2 tablespoons)
Dash of crushed red pepper
2 teaspoons extra-virgin olive oil
Dash of ground red pepper
1 (6-ounce) bag pita chips

1. Place garlic in a food processor; process until finely chopped. Add lemon juice, tahini, cumin, salt, black beans, jalapeño, and crushed red pepper; process until smooth.

2. Spoon bean mixture into a medium bowl, and drizzle with oil. Sprinkle with ground red pepper. Serve with pita chips.

Makes 8 servings ■ Prep time: 10 minutes ■ Total time: 15 minutes

For complete nutritional information on this and other *Cooking Light* recipes, please turn to the appendix on pages 280–283.

from CookingLight

Hot Crab Dip

1 cup fat-free cottage cheese
½ teaspoon grated lemon rind
2 tablespoons lemon juice
1 tablespoon Dijon mustard
1½ teaspoons Worcestershire sauce
1 teaspoon hot sauce
½ teaspoon salt
⅛ teaspoon freshly ground black pepper
1 garlic clove, minced

1 (8-ounce) block ⅓-less-fat cream cheese, softened
2 tablespoons chopped green onion
1 pound lump crabmeat, shell pieces removed
Cooking spray
2 tablespoons grated fresh Parmesan cheese
¼ cup dry breadcrumbs

1. Preheat oven to 375°.
2. Combine first 9 ingredients in a food processor; process until smooth.
3. Combine cottage cheese mixture, cream cheese, and onion in a large bowl; gently fold in crab. Place crab mixture in an 11 x 7–inch baking dish coated with cooking spray. Bake at 375° for 30 minutes. Sprinkle with Parmesan and breadcrumbs. Bake for another 15 minutes or until lightly golden.

Makes 20 servings ■ Prep time: 15 minutes ■ Total time: 1 hour

For complete nutritional information on this and other *Cooking Light* recipes, please turn to the appendix on pages 280–283.

please turn to the appendix on pages 280–283.

myrecipes users suggest:
- making it with canned crabmeat
- topping it with grated white Cheddar
- tossing in some cooked salad shrimp and a dash of curry

" This didn't taste light at all, and it was perfect with melba toasts and whole grain pita chips. It would be great for a holiday party appetizer."

—MeMyselfAndPie
★★★★

SCAN THIS PHOTO for 7 more recipes that use Cheddar.

5 Ingredients or Less   **Make-Ahead**

from *Sunset*

Salt-and-Pepper Cheese Puffs

1½ cups water
½ cup butter, cut into chunks
1½ cups all-purpose flour
6 large eggs, beaten to blend

1¼ cups shredded sharp Cheddar cheese
1½ teaspoons freshly ground black pepper
Parchment paper
Coarse sea salt

1. Preheat oven to 400°. In a 3- to 4-quart pan over high heat, bring water and butter to a full, rolling boil. Remove from heat, add flour all at once, and stir until mixture is a smooth, thick paste with no lumps. Add one-quarter of beaten eggs at a time, stirring vigorously after each addition until dough is no longer slippery. Stir in cheese and pepper.
2. Spoon dough into a large pastry bag fitted with a plain ½-inch round tip. Pipe in 48 equal mounds on two parchment paper-lined or buttered 12 x 15–inch baking sheets. (Alternatively, drop dough on sheets in slightly rounded tablespoon-size portions.) Sprinkle each mound with a few grains of coarse sea salt.
3. Bake at 400° until dry and well browned, about 30 minutes. Serve warm.

Note: To make ahead, bake the puffs, cool, then freeze in an airtight container up to 1 month. Reheat thawed puffs, uncovered, in a 375° oven until crisp and hot, about 5 minutes.

Makes 48 puffs ■ Prep time: 30 minutes ■ Total time: 1 hour

For complete nutritional information on this and other *Sunset* recipes, please turn to the appendix on pages 280–283.

> ❝ Delicious! It is quite a workout, but everyone loved these. Mine puffed beautifully. I used a smoked sea salt, and it really took it to the next level.”
>
> —KelliAnne
> ★★★★★

⊙ QUICK TIP

Use assertive cheeses such as aged white Irish, English, or Canadian Cheddar for best flavor.

---

myrecipes users suggest:
- adding crisp-cooked, well-blotted, crumbled thick-cut bacon when you add the cheese
- placing the dough in a zip-top plastic bag and snipping off a corner to pipe the puffs if you don't have a pastry bag
- stuffing the baked puffs with crab salad

Grill It! **Make-Ahead**

from CookingLight.

Grilled Stuffed Jalapeños

2 slices center-cut bacon
½ cup (4 ounces) cream cheese, softened
½ cup (4 ounces) fat-free cream cheese, softened
¼ cup (1 ounce) shredded extra-sharp Cheddar cheese
¼ cup minced green onions
1 teaspoon fresh lime juice

¼ teaspoon kosher salt
1 small garlic clove, minced
14 jalapeño peppers, halved lengthwise and seeded
Cooking spray
2 tablespoons chopped fresh cilantro
2 tablespoons chopped seeded tomato

1. Preheat grill to medium-high heat.
2. Cook the bacon in a skillet over medium heat until crisp. Remove bacon from pan, and drain on paper towels. Crumble bacon. Combine crumbled bacon, cheeses, and next 4 ingredients in a bowl, stirring to combine. Divide cheese mixture evenly and fill the pepper halves. Place peppers, cheese side up, on grill rack or grill grate coated with cooking spray. Cover and grill peppers 8 minutes or until bottoms of peppers are charred and cheese mixture is lightly browned. Place the peppers on a serving platter. Sprinkle with cilantro and tomato.

Note: To make ahead, stuff the peppers, cover, and chill. Grill just before your guests arrive.

Makes 14 servings ■ Prep time: 30 minutes ■ Total time: 40 minutes

For complete nutritional information on this and other *Cooking Light* recipes, please turn to the appendix on pages 280–283.

---

myrecipes users suggest:
- using a melon baller to remove seeds from halved jalapeños
- leaving in some of the membranes of the jalapeño for a little more heat
- using 1 (8-ounce) package of ⅓-less-fat cream cheese instead of the full-fat and fat-free mixture
- leaving off the cilantro and tomato topping

❝ If you like jalapeño poppers, you'll love this dish. It is truly a kicked-up version. I added a little more bacon than the recipe called for, but you can never have too much bacon."

—Jimprince123
★★★★★

SCAN THIS PHOTO for video on how to seed jalapeños.

 QUICK TIP

Firm peaches work best; if they're too soft, they'll make the tortillas soggy. Placing the fillings on one side of the tortilla and folding the other half over (like a taco) makes the quesadillas easier to handle.

myrecipes users suggest:
- adding sliced grilled pork to make it into a main dish
- substituting apple slices for the peaches
- grilling the quesadillas instead of cooking them on the stovetop

from CookingLight

Peach and Brie Quesadillas with Lime-Honey Dipping Sauce

Sauce:
2 tablespoons honey
2 teaspoons fresh lime juice
½ teaspoon grated lime rind
Quesadillas:
1 cup thinly sliced peeled firm ripe peaches (about 2 large)

1 tablespoon chopped fresh chives
1 teaspoon brown sugar
3 ounces Brie cheese, thinly sliced
4 (8-inch) fat-free flour tortillas
Cooking spray
Chive strips (optional)

1. To prepare sauce, combine first 3 ingredients, stirring with a whisk; set aside.
2. To prepare quesadillas, combine peaches, chives, and sugar, tossing gently to coat. Heat a large nonstick skillet over medium-high heat. Arrange one-fourth of cheese and one-fourth of peach mixture over half of each tortilla; fold tortillas in half. Coat pan with cooking spray. Place 2 quesadillas in pan; cook 2 minutes on each side or until tortillas are lightly browned and crisp and cheese is melted. Remove from pan; keep warm. Repeat procedure with remaining quesadillas. Cut each quesadilla into 3 wedges; serve with sauce. Garnish with chive strips, if desired.

Makes 6 servings ▪ Prep time: 20 minutes ▪ Total time: 30 minutes

For complete nutritional information on this and other *Cooking Light* recipes, please turn to the appendix on pages 280–283.

> **"** Very good! The 20 minutes in the freezer is essential; otherwise the coating falls off in the oil."
>
> —Agiola78
>
> ★★★★

from COASTAL LIVING

Coconut Shrimp with Maui Mustard Sauce

18 large fresh shrimp (16/20 count)
1 cup coconut milk
2 tablespoons chopped fresh cilantro
2 tablespoons fresh lime juice
1 cup all-purpose flour
¾ cup beer

1 (7-ounce) package sweetened flaked coconut
½ cup fine, dry breadcrumbs
Peanut oil
Salt
Maui Mustard Sauce

1. Peel shrimp, leaving tails on. Butterfly shrimp by making a deep slit down the back of each from the large end to the tail, cutting to, but not through, inside curve of shrimp.
2. Stir together coconut milk, cilantro, and lime juice in a large bowl. Add shrimp, tossing gently to coat. Cover and chill 30 minutes. Drain shrimp from mixture (do not pat dry).
3. Whisk together flour and beer in a small bowl. Combine coconut and breadcrumbs in a shallow dish. Dip shrimp into beer batter; dredge in coconut mixture, pressing onto shrimp. Place shrimp on a baking sheet; freeze 20 minutes.
4. Pour oil to depth of 2 inches in a Dutch oven, and heat to 350°. Cook shrimp, in batches, 2 to 3 minutes or until golden. Drain on paper towels, and sprinkle lightly with salt. Serve immediately with Maui Mustard Sauce.

Makes 10 to 12 servings ■ Prep time: 30 minutes ■ Total time: 1 hour, 30 minutes

Maui Mustard Sauce

⅓ cup pineapple preserves
⅓ cup apricot preserves

¼ cup stone-ground mustard

Stir together all ingredients in a small bowl. Cover and chill.

Makes about 1 cup ■ Prep time: 5 minutes ■ Total time: 15 minutes

SCAN THIS PHOTO
for video on peeling
and butterflying shrimp.

5
5 Ingredients or Less

30 Minutes or Less

Kid-Friendly

from CookingLight

Blackberry Limeade

6 cups water, divided
3 cups fresh blackberries
1 cup sugar

⅔ cup fresh lime juice (about 4 limes)
8 thin lime slices
Fresh blackberries (optional)

1. Place 1 cup water and blackberries in a blender; process until smooth. Press blackberry puree through a sieve into a large pitcher; discard solids. Add remaining 5 cups water, sugar, and lime juice to pitcher; stir until sugar dissolves.
2. Place ice, 1 lime slice, and a few blackberries, if desired, into each of 8 glasses; pour about 1 cup limeade into each glass.

Makes 8 servings ■ Prep time: 15 minutes ■ Total time: 15 minutes

For complete nutritional information on this and other *Cooking Light* recipes, please turn to the appendix on pages 280–283.

> The best way to describe this is 'summer in a glass.' It is unbelievably refreshing and delicious!"

—LauraLeigh8

★★★★★

myrecipes users suggest:
• cutting the sugar to ⅔ cup if you like it on the tart side
• using superfine sugar instead granulated sugar for faster dissolving

ask the expert

Should I refrigerate lemons, limes, and oranges?

While you can store citrus fruit out on the counter, it won't last nearly as long there as it will in the refrigerator. You can also store citrus fruit in a cool, dark place, which is better than on the counter—but again, refrigeration will extend its life significantly.

SCAN THIS BOX for more cooking know-how from our experts.

5
5 Ingredients
or Less

 30 Minutes
or Less

 Kid-
Friendly

❝ This is a perfect drink on a hot summer day—not too sweet and amazingly flavorful! Don't skip the mint or the citrus slices. They make the drink!"

—EVC7599

 ★★★★★

from **Southern Living**

Lemonade Iced Tea

3 cups water
2 family-size tea bags
1 (1-ounce) package fresh mint leaves
   (about 1 cup loosely packed)
½ cup sugar

4 cups cold water
1 (6-ounce) can frozen lemonade
   concentrate, thawed
Garnish: fresh citrus slices

1. Bring 3 cups water to a boil in a 2-quart saucepan. Remove from heat, add tea bags, and stir in mint. Cover and steep 10 minutes.
2. Remove and discard tea bags and mint. Stir in sugar until dissolved.
3. Pour tea into a 3-quart container, and stir in 4 cups cold water and lemonade concentrate. Serve over ice. Garnish, if desired.

Makes 8 cups ▪ Prep time: 10 minutes ▪ Total time: 25 minutes

SCAN THIS PHOTO for 11 more refreshing iced tea recipes.

> **my**recipes users suggest:
> - substituting pink lemonade or limeade concentrate for the raspberry lemonade concentrate
> - using a beer with lime flavor
> - adding a can of lemon-lime soda (such as Sprite) to the mixture

> " I made this for an evening pool-side party, and it was a huge hit! I served it in Mason jars with wedges of lemon and lime, and a frozen raspberry in each. It was very pretty and very refreshing, and I will certainly make it again."
>
> —emilyclare
>
> ★★★★★

from Southern Living

Raspberry-Beer Cocktail

1 (12-ounce) container frozen raspberry
   lemonade concentrate, thawed
½ cup vodka

¾ cup frozen or fresh raspberries
3½ (12-ounce) bottles beer, chilled
Garnish: lemon and lime slices

Stir together first 4 ingredients. Serve over ice. Garnish, if desired.

Note: To make ahead, stir together the raspberry lemonade concentrate and vodka in a large container. Chill up to 3 days. Stir in raspberries and beer just before serving. Garnish, if desired.

Makes 6 servings ■ Prep time: 5 minutes ■ Total time: 5 minutes

5 Ingredients or Less

Kid-Friendly

Make-Ahead

👁 **QUICK TIP**

For a grown-up version, substitute 1 (750-milliliter) bottle extra-dry Champagne and ¼ cup orange liqueur for the club soda.

myrecipes users suggest:
- freezing some of the punch in ice cube trays, then floating the cubes in the punch along with fresh mint sprigs

from Southern Living

Sparkling Punch

1 (12-ounce) can frozen pink lemonade concentrate, thawed
4 cups white cranberry juice cocktail

1 quart club soda, chilled
Garnish: fresh mint sprigs

1. Stir together lemonade concentrate and cranberry juice cocktail in a large pitcher. Cover and chill at least 1 hour or up to 24 hours.
2. Stir in club soda just before serving. Garnish, if desired.

Makes about 9 cups ■ Prep time: 5 minutes ■ Total time: 1 hour, 5 minutes

" I served this at my granddaughter's birthday party. To dress it up, I made an ice ring the night before with water, in which I put whole strawberries with the green tops and fresh mint leaves."

—bluedogwriter77
★★★★★

SCAN THIS PHOTO
for a video on how to
juice citrus fruit.

👁 **QUICK TIP**

Hibiscus blossoms,
or flor de Jamaica (pro-
nounced ha-MY-ca), can
be found at Latin grocery
stores, some health food
stores, and online.

from CookingLight

Jamaica Margaritas

1 cup (about 2 ounces) dried hibiscus
   blossoms
3 cups water
¾ cup sugar

1¼ cups tequila
½ cup fresh lime juice
⅓ cup Triple Sec (orange-flavored liqueur)
8 lime slices

1. Place blossoms in a strainer; rinse under cold water. Combine blossoms, water,
and sugar in a medium saucepan; bring to a boil. Reduce heat, and simmer 10
minutes. Strain; discard blossoms. Cover and chill hibiscus mixture.
2. Combine hibiscus mixture, tequila, lime juice, and Triple Sec. Serve over ice.
Garnish with lime slices.

Makes 8 servings ■ Prep time: 15 minutes ■ Total time: 45 minutes

For complete nutritional information on this and other *Cooking Light* recipes, please turn to the appendix on pages
280–283.

⏱ 30 Minutes or Less   ⑤ 5 Ingredients or Less

from CookingLight

Watermelon Margaritas

2 teaspoons plus 2 tablespoons sugar
1 lime wedge
3½ cups cubed seeded watermelon
½ cup tequila
3 tablespoons fresh lime juice

1 tablespoon Triple Sec (orange-flavored liqueur)
3 cups crushed ice
Lime wedges or watermelon balls (optional)

1. Place 2 teaspoons sugar in a saucer. Rub the rims of 6 glasses with 1 lime wedge; spin rim of each glass in sugar to coat. Set prepared glasses aside.
2. Combine watermelon, tequila, lime juice, Triple Sec, and remaining 2 tablespoons sugar in a blender; process until smooth. Fill each prepared glass with ½ cup crushed ice. Add ½ cup margarita to each glass. Garnish with lime wedges or melon balls, if desired.

Makes 6 servings ■ Prep time: 10 minutes ■ Total time: 10 minutes

For complete nutritional information on this and other *Cooking Light* recipes, please turn to the appendix on pages 280–283.

myrecipes users suggest:
- freezing the watermelon slightly before putting it in the blender
- blending the margarita mixture with ice for a slushy drink

❝ I love these. I am allergic to tequila, so I used golden rum instead. I made several batches the night before my 4th of July party, froze them, and thawed them for about an hour before serving. No need to add ice!"

—BethPB
★★★★★

soups & sandwiches

In the mood for a bowl of comfort? These top-rated soups satisfy. The range includes purees that can be ready in minutes, stews that simmer all day in the slow cooker, and chili, a perennial favorite at MyRecipes.com. We've also included top-rated sandwiches to pair with your soup du jour.

 To use the exclusive **Scan-It/Cook-It**™ features in this chapter, look for the smartphone symbol (shown at left). For detailed instructions, please see page 7.

**BUTTERNUT SQUASH
AND APPLE SOUP**
page 30

Kid-Friendly

Low-Calorie

myrecipes users suggest:
- using vegetable broth instead of chicken broth to make it vegetarian

from **Health**

Butternut Squash and Apple Soup (pictured on page 29)

1½ teaspoons unsalted butter
1¼ cups chopped Vidalia or other sweet onion (about ½ large onion)
1 large garlic clove, smashed and peeled
1⅓ cups cubed peeled Braeburn apple
1¼ pounds peeled cubed butternut squash
¼ teaspoon dried rubbed sage
½ teaspoon kosher salt, plus pinch

¼ teaspoon freshly ground black pepper
⅛ teaspoon ground nutmeg
2 cups fat-free, less-sodium chicken broth
½ cup fat-free evaporated milk, divided
8 mini pumpkins, tops and seeds removed (optional)
¼ cup crème fraîche
Fresh sage leaves

1. Melt butter in large saucepan over medium heat. Add onion; sauté 3 minutes. Add garlic and apple; cook, stirring constantly, 1 minute. Add squash and next 4 ingredients; stir 30 seconds or until well combined. Add broth, and bring to a simmer. Reduce heat to medium-low; simmer 20 minutes or until squash and vegetables are tender.
2. Place half of squash mixture in a blender with ¼ cup evaporated milk. Remove center of blender lid (to let steam escape); secure lid. Place clean towel over opening to avoid splatters; blend until smooth. Pour into bowl. Repeat with remaining squash and evaporated milk.
3. Spoon ½ cup soup into small bowl or mini pumpkin. Swirl in ¾ teaspoon crème fraîche and garnish with fresh sage leaves, if desired. Serve immediately.

Makes 8 servings ▪ Prep time: 15 minutes ▪ Total time: 35 minutes

For complete nutritional information on this and other *Health* recipes, please turn to the appendix on pages 280–283.

> " I've made other butternut squash soups before and always found them boring. I made this in my pressure cooker, and it was wonderful! It was easy, simple, healthy, and flavorful!"
>
> —burbgirl
> ★★★★★

Kid-
Friendly

Low-
Calorie

from *Cooking Light*

Broccoli and Cheese Soup

Cooking spray
1 cup chopped onion
2 garlic cloves, minced
3 cups fat-free, less-sodium chicken broth
1 (16-ounce) package broccoli florets

2½ cups 2% reduced-fat milk
⅓ cup all-purpose flour
¼ teaspoon black pepper
8 ounces light processed cheese, cubed
  (such as Velveeta Light)

1. Heat a large nonstick saucepan coated with cooking spray over medium-high heat. Add onion and garlic; sauté 3 minutes or until tender. Add broth and broccoli. Bring broccoli mixture to a boil over medium-high heat. Reduce heat to medium; cook 10 minutes.
2. Combine milk and flour, stirring with a whisk until well blended. Add milk mixture to broccoli mixture. Cook 5 minutes or until slightly thick, stirring constantly. Stir in pepper. Remove from heat; add cheese, stirring until cheese melts.
3. Place one-third of soup in a blender or food processor, and process until smooth. Return pureed soup mixture to pan.

Makes 6 servings ■ Prep time: 20 minutes ■ Total time: 35 minutes

For complete nutritional information on this and other *Cooking Light* recipes, please turn to the appendix on pages 280–283.

☺ Kid-Friendly GF Gluten-Free LC Low-Calorie

from **Cooking Light**

Summer Squash and Corn Chowder

myrecipes users suggest:
- making it with fresh corn (cut from 3 ears) instead of frozen
- adding cubed cooked chicken
- substituting yellow onion for green onions

 I absolutely loved this low-fat, low-cal chowder. I am making it again this weekend with all the yellow squash from my garden."

—coloradojenn

★★★★★

2 slices applewood-smoked bacon
¾ cup sliced green onions, divided
¼ cup chopped celery
1 pound yellow summer squash, chopped
1 pound frozen white and yellow baby corn kernels, thawed and divided

2¼ cups 1% low-fat milk, divided
1 teaspoon chopped fresh thyme
½ teaspoon plus ⅛ teaspoon salt
¼ teaspoon freshly ground black pepper
¼ cup (1 ounce) shredded extra-sharp Cheddar cheese

1. Cook bacon in a large Dutch oven over medium-high heat until crisp. Remove bacon from pan, reserving 2 teaspoons drippings in pan. Crumble bacon, and set aside. Add ½ cup onions, celery, and squash to drippings in pan; sauté 8 minutes or until vegetables are tender.
2. Reserve 1 cup corn; set aside. Place remaining corn and 1 cup milk in a blender; process until smooth. Add remaining 1¼ cups milk, thyme, ½ teaspoon salt, and pepper to blender; process just until combined. Add pureed mixture and reserved 1 cup corn to pan. Reduce heat to medium; cook 5 minutes or until thoroughly heated, stirring constantly. Stir in remaining ⅛ teaspoon salt.
3. Ladle about 1½ cups soup into each of 4 bowls; top each serving with about 1 tablespoon bacon, 1 tablespoon remaining onions, and 1 tablespoon cheese.

Makes 4 servings ■ Prep time: 40 minutes ■ Total time: 40 minutes

For complete nutritional information on this and other *Cooking Light* recipes, please turn to the appendix on pages 280–283.

 **SCAN THIS PHOTO** for video on how to prepare this recipe.

30 Minutes or Less · **LC Low-Calorie** · **Kid-Friendly**

> " This was so easy to make and very satisfying for a light meal, served with a salad and crusty bread. I used canned tomatoes seasoned with basil, garlic, and oregano, and it was great—and even better the next day."
>
> —judybsmith
>
> ★★★★

from

Tomato Soup with White Beans and Pasta

2 tablespoons olive oil
2 garlic cloves, finely chopped
¼ teaspoon dried oregano
2 (15-ounce) cans diced tomatoes
28 ounces low-sodium chicken broth
½ cup tubetini, elbow macaroni, or other small pasta

1 (15-ounce) can cannellini beans, drained and rinsed
Salt and black pepper
2 tablespoons finely chopped fresh parsley

1. Warm oil in a large saucepan over medium-high heat. Add garlic and cook, stirring frequently, until fragrant, about 1 minute. Add oregano, stir once, then add tomatoes with juice and broth. Bring to a boil.
2. Add pasta, stir, and cook until just tender, about 8 minutes. Stir in beans, reduce heat, and simmer until warmed through, about 5 minutes. Season with salt and pepper, stir in parsley, and divide among 4 bowls, drizzling each portion with additional olive oil if desired.

Makes 4 servings ■ Prep time: 10 minutes ■ Total time: 25 minutes

For complete nutritional information on this and other *All You* recipes, please turn to the appendix on pages 280–283.

from **CookingLight**

Two-Bean Soup with Kale

30 Minutes or Less   Low-Calorie

3 tablespoons olive oil
1 cup chopped onion
½ cup chopped carrot
½ cup chopped celery
½ teaspoon salt, divided
2 garlic cloves, minced
4 cups organic vegetable broth, divided
7 cups stemmed, chopped kale (about 1 bunch)

2 (15-ounce) cans no-salt-added cannellini beans, rinsed, drained, and divided
1 (15-ounce) can no-salt-added black beans, rinsed and drained
½ teaspoon freshly ground black pepper
1 tablespoon red wine vinegar
1 teaspoon chopped fresh rosemary

1. Heat a large Dutch oven over medium-high heat. Add oil to pan; swirl to coat. Add onion, carrot, and celery, and sauté 6 minutes or until tender. Stir in ¼ teaspoon salt and garlic; cook 1 minute. Stir in 3 cups broth and kale. Bring to a boil; cover, reduce heat, and simmer 3 minutes or until kale is crisp-tender.
2. Place half of cannellini beans and remaining 1 cup broth in a blender or food processor; process until smooth. Add pureed bean mixture, remaining cannellini beans, black beans, and pepper to soup. Bring to a boil; reduce heat, and simmer 5 minutes. Stir in remaining ¼ teaspoon salt, vinegar, and rosemary.

Makes 6 servings ■ Prep time: 25 minutes ■ Total time: 30 minutes

For complete nutritional information on this and other *Cooking Light* recipes, please turn to the appendix on pages 280–283.

 QUICK TIP

For a heftier dish, add rotisserie chicken or Italian sausage.

myrecipes users suggest:
- making it with beef broth instead of vegetable broth
- adding hot sauce or crushed red pepper
- adding a blend of fresh mushrooms

" Amazing! Such a good recipe. I added sausage, and it turned out great. When making, I usually double the recipe and freeze whatever we don't eat for dinner the first night. It freezes and defrosts very well!"

—ChicagoChef82
★★★★★

Kid-Friendly

Slow Cooker

from **Southern Living**

Hearty Potato Soup

6 potatoes, peeled and cut into ½-inch
    cubes (2½ pounds)
2 medium onions, diced
2 carrots, thinly sliced
2 celery stalks, thinly sliced
2 (14.5-ounce) cans low-sodium fat-free
    chicken broth

1 teaspoon dried basil
1 teaspoon salt
½ teaspoon black pepper
¼ cup all-purpose flour
1½ cups fat-free half-and-half
Garnish: fresh celery leaves

1. Combine first 8 ingredients in a 4½-quart slow cooker.
2. Cook, covered, at HIGH 3 hours or until vegetables are tender.
3. Stir together flour and half-and-half; stir into soup. Cover and cook 30 minutes or until thoroughly heated. Garnish, if desired.

Makes 8½ cups ∎ Prep time: 10 minutes ∎ Total time: 3 hours, 40 minutes

> **"** I served this to my family last night and got rave reviews. My mother called me this morning and said that it deserved 6 stars!"
>
> —JasonBurn
> ★★★★★

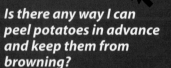

ask the expert

Is there any way I can peel potatoes in advance and keep them from browning?

Peel your potatoes up to two hours ahead and keep them submerged in cold water to retain their creamy white color. The potato flesh turns brown when exposed to air—but they are still just as safe and tasty.

SCAN THIS BOX for more cooking know-how from our experts.

myrecipes users suggest:

- adding broccoli, spicy Italian sausage, and a whole bay leaf
- frying some bacon, sautéeing mushrooms in the bacon fat, and adding both to the soup along with the half-and-half
- adding ground sausage and a bag of fresh spinach

SCAN THIS PHOTO
for video on how to
make a roux.

from Southern Living

Chicken-and-Sausage Gumbo

1 pound andouille sausage, cut into
 ¼-inch-thick slices
4 skinless, bone-in chicken breasts
Vegetable oil
¾ cup all-purpose flour
1 medium onion, chopped
½ green bell pepper, chopped
2 celery stalks, sliced
2 quarts hot water
3 garlic cloves, minced

2 bay leaves
1 tablespoon Worcestershire sauce
2 teaspoons Creole seasoning
½ teaspoon dried thyme
½ to 1 teaspoon hot sauce
4 green onions, sliced
Filé powder (optional)
Hot cooked rice
Garnish: chopped green onions

1. Cook sausage in a Dutch oven over medium heat, stirring constantly, 5 minutes or until browned. Drain on paper towels, reserving drippings in Dutch oven. Set sausage aside.

2. Cook chicken in reserved drippings in Dutch oven over medium heat 5 minutes or until browned. Remove to paper towels, reserving drippings in Dutch oven. Set chicken aside.

3. Add enough oil to drippings in Dutch oven to measure ½ cup. Add flour, and cook over medium heat, stirring constantly, 20 to 25 minutes, or until roux is chocolate-colored.

4. Stir in onion, bell pepper, and celery; cook, stirring often, 8 minutes or until tender. Gradually add hot water, and bring mixture to a boil; add chicken, garlic, and next 5 ingredients. Reduce heat to low, and simmer, stirring occasionally, 1 hour. Remove chicken; let cool.

5. Add sausage to gumbo; cook 30 minutes. Stir in green onions; cook for 30 more minutes.

6. Bone chicken, and cut meat into strips; return chicken to gumbo, and simmer 5 minutes. Remove and discard bay leaves.

7. Remove gumbo from heat. Sprinkle with filé powder, if desired. Serve over hot cooked rice. Garnish, if desired.

Makes 4 to 6 servings ▪ Prep time: 55 minutes ▪ Total time: 3 hours, 55 minutes

myrecipes users suggest:
• substituting poblano pepper for bell pepper
• adding okra

“ My sister gave me this recipe, and I have made it many times. It does take a lot of time, but it is well worth it. I always double it so I can freeze some. I follow the recipe to a T, and it always comes out delish!”

—Kelmcd

30 Minutes
or Less

  Excellent! Tastes
  like you spent all
day preparing it. I used
a chunky salsa verde,
added a squeeze of
lime, and sprinkled
with cheese and diced
avocado in addition to
the other condiments.
I'll make this again!"

—Mars418

★★★★★

from **REAL**SIMPLE

Southwestern Chicken Soup

1 (12-ounce) jar salsa verde
3 cups cooked chicken pieces (1 small
  deli-counter rotisserie chicken or leftovers)
1 (15-ounce) can cannellini beans, drained
3 cups chicken broth

1 teaspoon ground cumin (optional)
2 green onions, chopped
½ cup sour cream
Tortilla chips (optional)

1. Place salsa in a large saucepan. Cook 2 minutes over medium-high heat, then add chicken, beans, broth, and cumin (if desired). Bring to a boil, lower heat to a simmer, and cook for 10 minutes, stirring occasionally.
2. Divide among 4 bowls and top each with a sprinkling of onions, a dollop of sour cream, and some tortilla chips (if desired).

Makes 4 servings ▪ Prep time: 5 minutes ▪ Total time: 20 minutes

For complete nutritional information on this and other *Real Simple* recipes, please turn to the appendix on pages 280–283.

5
5 Ingredients
or Less

LC
Low-
Calorie

Slow
Cooker

ask the expert

How long can I leave food in the slow cooker after it is done without it spoiling?

As with food cooked any other way, cooked slow-cooker foods should be refrigerated within 2 hours of cooking or being removed from an appliance that keeps them warm (or within 1 hour if the room temperature is over 90°).

SCAN THIS BOX
for more cooking know-how from our experts.

myrecipes users suggest:
- adding 2 cloves garlic
- using chicken broth instead of vegetable broth
- substituting a leftover roasted turkey leg or 2 boneless, skinless chicken breasts (1 pound) for the smoked turkey leg

from **Oxmoor House®**

Smoked Turkey-Lentil Soup

6 cups organic vegetable broth
1 (8-ounce) smoked turkey leg
½ pound dried lentils, rinsed and drained
1 (8-ounce) container refrigerated pre-chopped celery, onion, and bell pepper mix

2 teaspoons chopped fresh or ½ teaspoon dried oregano
½ teaspoon freshly ground black pepper
Nonfat Greek yogurt (optional)
Fresh oregano sprigs (optional)

1. Place first 6 ingredients in a 3- to 4-quart slow cooker. Cover and cook on LOW 8 to 10 hours or until lentils are tender and turkey falls off the bone.
2. Remove turkey leg from cooker. Remove and discard skin. Shred meat; return to cooker, discarding bone. Ladle soup into bowls; garnish with yogurt and oregano sprigs, if desired.

Makes 8 servings ■ Prep time: 5 minutes ■ Total time: 8 hours, 5 minutes

For complete nutritional information on this and other Oxmoor House recipes, please turn to the appendix on pages 280–283.

from CookingLight

Kid-Friendly   Low-Calorie

Beef-Barley Soup

Cooking spray
¾ pound boneless chuck roast, trimmed
    and cut into ½-inch pieces
1½ cups thinly sliced carrot
1½ cups thinly sliced celery
⅔ cup chopped onion

1 (8-ounce) package presliced mushrooms
4 cups fat-free, less-sodium beef broth
1 bay leaf
⅔ cup uncooked pearl barley
½ teaspoon salt
½ teaspoon black pepper

1. Heat a Dutch oven over medium-high heat. Coat pan with cooking spray. Add beef to pan; cook 4 minutes or until browned, stirring frequently. Remove beef from pan. Add carrot, celery, onion, and mushrooms to pan; cook 6 minutes or until liquid almost evaporates. Add beef, broth, and bay leaf. Bring to a simmer over medium-high heat. Cover, reduce heat, and simmer 1½ hours or until beef is tender, stirring occasionally.
2. Stir in pearl barley; cover and simmer 30 minutes or until pearl barley is tender. Stir in salt and pepper. Discard bay leaf.

Makes 4 servings ■ Prep time: 20 minutes ■ Total time: 2 hours, 20 minutes

For complete nutritional information on this and other *Cooking Light* recipes, please turn to the appendix on pages 280–283.

> " My husband and my 2-year-old loved it and requested it several times. The meat is so flavorful, and the barley makes it so filling."

—JessicaLuu
★★★★★

SCAN THIS PHOTO for 14 more recipes using barley.

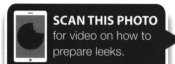

SCAN THIS PHOTO for video on how to prepare leeks.

myrecipes users suggest:
- using 2 cups skim milk instead of the water and evaporated milk, and increasing chicken broth to 1½ cups

from **Oxmoor House**®

Sweet Potato, Leek, and Ham Soup

Olive oil-flavored cooking spray
1 cup diced cooked ham
1½ cups sliced leek (about 1 large)
2 tablespoons water (optional)
3 cups refrigerated cubed peeled
    sweet potato

1 cup fat-free, less-sodium chicken broth
2 cups water
1 (5-ounce) can evaporated fat-free milk
¼ teaspoon freshly ground black pepper
Thinly sliced leek (optional)
Thinly sliced green onions (optional)

1. Heat a large Dutch oven over medium heat. Coat pan with cooking spray. Add ham; cook 3 to 4 minutes or until browned, stirring frequently. Remove ham from pan; set aside.
2. Add leek to pan; coat with cooking spray. Cook leek, covered, 5 minutes or until very tender, stirring occasionally. Add water to pan, if needed, to prevent burning.
3. Add sweet potato and next 4 ingredients, scraping pan to loosen browned bits; bring mixture to a boil. Cover, reduce heat, and simmer 15 minutes or until sweet potato is very tender.
4. Place half of potato mixture in a blender or food processor. Remove center piece of blender lid (to allow steam to escape); secure blender lid on blender. Place a clean towel over opening in blender lid (to avoid splatters). Process until smooth. Pour puree into a large bowl. Repeat procedure with remaining mixture. Return pureed mixture to pan. Stir in ¾ cup reserved ham. Ladle soup into bowls; top servings evenly with remaining ¼ cup ham. Garnish with sliced leek and onions, if desired.

Makes 4 servings ■ Prep time: 20 minutes ■ Total time: 40 minutes

For complete nutritional information on this and other Oxmoor House recipes, please turn to the appendix on pages 280–283.

from CookingLight

Bacon-Corn Chowder with Shrimp

30 Minutes or Less

LC Low-Calorie

6 slices center-cut bacon, chopped
1 cup prechopped onion
½ cup prechopped celery
1 teaspoon chopped fresh thyme
1 garlic clove, minced
4 cups fresh or frozen corn kernels, thawed

2 cups fat-free, lower-sodium chicken broth
¾ pound peeled and deveined medium shrimp
⅓ cup half-and-half
¼ teaspoon black pepper
⅛ teaspoon salt

1. Heat a large Dutch oven over medium-high heat. Add bacon to pan; sauté 4 minutes or until bacon begins to brown. Remove and reserve a third of the bacon. Drain on paper towels. Add onion and next 3 ingredients to pan, and sauté for 2 minutes. Add corn, and cook 2 minutes, stirring occasionally. Add broth; bring to a boil, and cook for 4 minutes.

2. Place 2 cups of corn mixture in a blender. Remove center piece of blender lid (to allow steam to escape), and secure lid on blender. Place a clean towel over opening in blender lid (to avoid splatters). Blend until smooth. Return pureed corn mixture to pan. Stir in shrimp; cook 2 minutes or until shrimp are done. Stir in half-and-half, pepper, and salt. Crumble reserved bacon over soup.

Makes 4 servings ■ Prep time: 20 minutes ■ Total time: 20 minutes

For complete nutritional information on this and other *Cooking Light* recipes, please turn to the appendix on pages 280–283.

myrecipes users suggest:
- adding chopped red bell peppers and diced potatoes, plus crushed red pepper to taste
- throwing in some frozen green peas

> " I absolutely loved this recipe! It was easy to make (dare I say fun?) and incredibly delicious. I used frozen grilled shrimp, which I sautéed in a skillet prior to adding to the chowder. So good!"
>
> —meganhalv
> ★★★★★

SCAN THIS PHOTO for 7 more recipes using fresh corn.

SCAN THIS PHOTO for video on how to prepare this recipe.

30 Minutes or Less   **LC** Low-Calorie

from *Cooking Light*

Prosciutto, Fresh Fig, and Manchego Sandwiches

4 teaspoons Dijon mustard
8 (¾-ounce) slices Italian bread, toasted
1 cup baby arugula
2 ounces very thinly sliced prosciutto

2 ounces Manchego cheese, shaved
8 fresh figs, cut into thin slices
2 tablespoons fig jam

1. Spread 1 teaspoon mustard over 4 bread slices. Arrange ¼ cup arugula over each slice. Divide prosciutto evenly over bread slices; top evenly with cheese and fig slices.
2. Spread 1½ teaspoons jam over remaining 4 bread slices. Place 1 bread slice, jam side down, over fig slices.

Makes 4 servings ■ Prep time: 20 minutes ■ Total time: 20 minutes

For complete nutritional information on this and other *Cooking Light* recipes, please turn to the appendix on pages 280–283.

> " Now this is a great take on the classic ham and cheese! Having an abundance of figs from our yard, I am looking for different ways to use them. And for a quick, weeknight meal, this is perfect."

—Kimmimz
★★★★★

 QUICK TIP

Use a vegetable peeler to shave the Manchego. The Spanish cheese is similar to pecorino Romano, which you can substitute in a pinch.

30 Minutes or Less

30 Minutes or Less | **LC Low-Calorie**

myrecipes users suggest:
• using sourdough bread
• spreading the bread with Dijon mustard before sprinkling on the cheese

❝ **These were tasty and easy to make. I served the sandwiches with white bean chili.**❞

—Jessie123

★★★★★

from **Cooking Light**

Grown-Up Grilled Cheese Sandwiches

Cooking spray
1 cup vertically sliced red onion
1 large garlic clove, minced
1 cup (4 ounces) shredded reduced-fat
    sharp white Cheddar cheese
8 (1½-ounce) slices hearty white bread
    (such as Pepperidge Farm)
2 cups fresh spinach leaves
8 (¼-inch-thick) slices tomato
6 slices center-cut bacon, cooked

1. Heat a large nonstick skillet over medium-low heat. Coat pan with cooking spray. Add onion and garlic; cook for 10 minutes or until tender and golden brown, stirring occasionally.
2. Sprinkle 2 tablespoons cheese over each of 4 bread slices. Top each slice with ½ cup spinach, 2 tomato slices, 2 tablespoons onion mixture, and 1½ bacon slices. Sprinkle each with 2 tablespoons cheese; top with the remaining 4 bread slices.
3. Heat skillet over medium heat. Coat pan with cooking spray. Place sandwiches in pan, and cook for 3 minutes on each side or until golden brown and cheese melts.

Makes 4 servings ▪ Prep time: 15 minutes ▪ Total time: 20 minutes

For complete nutritional information on this and other *Cooking Light* recipes, please turn to the appendix on pages 280–283.

30 Minutes or Less

LC
Low-Calorie

SCAN THIS PHOTO for video on how to prepare this recipe.

> " This was great! My husband wants to know when we are having it again."

—kateford

★★★★★

---

myrecipes users suggest:
- doubling all the ingredients except the chicken, rolls, and pickles, and cooking it in a slow cooker on LOW for 4 to 5 hours
- adding ½ cup chicken broth and cooking it in a pressure cooker

---

from *CookingLight*

Black Pepper and Molasses Pulled Chicken Sandwiches

3 tablespoons ketchup
1 tablespoon cider vinegar
1 tablespoon prepared mustard
1 tablespoon molasses
¾ teaspoon chili powder
½ teaspoon ground cumin
¼ teaspoon freshly ground black pepper

⅛ teaspoon ground ginger
12 ounces skinless, boneless chicken thighs, cut into 2-inch pieces
4 (2-ounce) sandwich rolls, cut in half horizontally
12 dill pickle chips

1. Combine first 9 ingredients in a medium saucepan; bring to a boil. Reduce heat to medium-low; cover and cook, stirring occasionally, 23 minutes or until chicken is done and tender. Remove from heat; shred chicken with 2 forks to measure 2 cups meat.
2. Place ½ cup chicken on bottom half of each roll. Top each with 3 pickle chips and top half of roll.

Makes 4 servings ■ Prep time: 5 minutes ■ Total time: 30 minutes

For complete nutritional information on this and other *Cooking Light* recipes, please turn to the appendix on pages 280–283.

from

Spicy Chicken Sandwiches with Cilantro-Lime Mayo

Mayo:
¼ cup reduced-fat mayonnaise
2 tablespoons chopped fresh cilantro
1 teaspoon fresh lime juice
1 garlic clove, minced
Chicken:
¼ cup egg substitute
3 tablespoons hot sauce
1 teaspoon dried oregano

½ teaspoon salt
2 (6-ounce) skinless, boneless chicken
   breast halves
4½ ounces baked tortilla chips (about 6 cups)
2 tablespoons olive oil
Remaining ingredients:
4 (2-ounce) Kaiser rolls, split
12 (⅛-inch-thick) red onion slices
4 lettuce leaves

1. To prepare mayo, combine the first 4 ingredients.
2. To prepare chicken, combine egg substitute, hot sauce, oregano, and salt in a large zip-top plastic bag. Cut chicken breast halves in half horizontally to form 4 cutlets. Add chicken to bag; seal. Marinate in refrigerator 2 hours or up to 8 hours, turning bag occasionally.
3. Place tortilla chips in a food processor; process 1 minute or until ground. Place ground chips in a shallow dish.
4. Working with 1 cutlet at a time, remove chicken from marinade, allowing excess to drip off. Coat chicken completely in chips. Set aside. Repeat procedure with remaining chicken and chips.
5. Heat a large nonstick skillet over medium heat. Add oil to pan, swirling to coat. Add chicken to pan; cook 3 minutes on each side or until browned and done.
6. Spread mayo evenly over cut sides of rolls. Layer bottom half of each roll with 3 onion slices, 1 lettuce leaf, and 1 chicken cutlet; top with top halves of rolls.

Makes 4 servings ■ Prep time: 30 minutes ■ Total time: 2 hours, 30 minutes

For complete nutritional information on this and other *Cooking Light* recipes, please turn to the appendix on pages 280–283.

 Delicious! My husband is still raving about them. They would also be a good brown-bag lunch option."

—Monica3

myrecipes users suggest:
- using 2 egg whites instead of egg substitute
- substituting plain Greek-style yogurt for the mayonnaise
- adding 1 teaspoon finely shredded lime zest to the mayonnaise

30 Minutes or Less

LC Low-Calorie

" Delicious! A great, fast, and easy weeknight meal. My teenager asked me to make them again— and again and again."

—jupett

★★★★★

from Cooking Light

Turkey Reuben Sandwiches

2 tablespoons Dijon mustard
8 slices rye bread
4 (1-ounce) slices reduced-fat, reduced-sodium Swiss cheese

8 ounces smoked turkey, thinly sliced
⅔ cup sauerkraut, drained and rinsed
¼ cup fat-free Thousand Island dressing
1 tablespoon canola oil, divided

1. Spread about ¾ teaspoon mustard over each bread slice. Place 1 cheese slice on each of 4 bread slices. Divide turkey evenly over cheese. Top each serving with 2½ tablespoons sauerkraut and 1 tablespoon dressing. Top each serving with 1 bread slice, mustard side down.

2. Heat 1½ teaspoons oil in a large nonstick skillet over medium-high heat. Add 2 sandwiches to pan; top with another heavy skillet. Cook 3 minutes on each side or until golden; remove sandwiches from pan, and keep warm. Repeat procedure with remaining 1½ teaspoons oil and sandwiches.

Makes 4 servings ■ Prep time: 10 minutes ■ Total time: 20 minutes

For complete nutritional information on this and other *Cooking Light* recipes, please turn to the appendix on pages 280–283.

30 Minutes or Less   **Kid-Friendly**   **Low-Calorie**

from CookingLight

Chipotle Sloppy Joes

Cooking spray
2½ cups presliced Vidalia or other
    sweet onion
1 (7-ounce) can chipotle chiles in
    adobo sauce
1 pound ground sirloin
½ cup prechopped green bell pepper
2 tablespoons tomato paste
1 teaspoon kosher salt
½ teaspoon ground cumin
1 (8-ounce) can no-salt-added tomato sauce
5 (1½-ounce) hamburger buns, toasted

1. Heat a small nonstick skillet over medium-high heat. Coat pan with cooking spray. Add onion to pan; cover and cook 8 minutes or until golden brown, stirring frequently. Remove from heat; set aside.
2. Remove 1 teaspoon adobo sauce from can; set aside. Remove 1 chipotle chile from can; chop and set aside. Reserve remaining chiles and adobo sauce for another use.
3. Heat a large nonstick skillet over medium-high heat. Coat pan with cooking spray. Add beef to pan; cook 4 minutes or until browned, stirring to crumble. Add bell pepper to pan; sauté 2 minutes. Stir in chopped chipotle chile, adobo sauce, tomato paste, and next 3 ingredients; cook 3 minutes, stirring occasionally.
4. Spoon ½ cup beef mixture over bottom half of each bun, and top evenly with onions and top half of bun.

Makes 5 servings ■ Prep time: 10 minutes ■ Total time: 20 minutes

For complete nutritional information on this and other *Cooking Light* recipes, please turn to the appendix on pages 280–283.

myrecipes users suggest:
- making it with ground buffalo, adding a minced garlic clove along with the green pepper, and draining the buffalo after browning
- mixing a little of the chipotle adobo sauce with mayonnaise and spreading on the hamburger buns before adding the sloppy joe mixture

" I am a vegetarian, so I made this with soy 'beef.' The sweet onions on top just took them to another level."

—Veggiecook11

★★★★★

 SCAN THIS PHOTO for video on how to prepare this recipe.

poultry

Chicken rules the roost at MyRecipes.com. It's the top ingredient search term on the site. From grilled thighs and roasted whole birds to chicken chili and casseroles, the recipes here represent the best of the flock. We've also included our most popular roast turkey recipes and a downright delicious duck cassoulet.

 To use the exclusive **Scan-It/Cook-It™** features in this chapter, look for the smartphone symbol (shown at left). For detailed instructions, please see page 7.

EASY CHICKEN AND DUMPLINGS
page 78

5 5 Ingredients or Less
🕐 30 Minutes or Less
☺ Kid-Friendly

❝ The sweetness of the apricot spread goes very well with the curry powder, and the lemon juice added a great subtle tang to the dish. I would definitely make this again.❞

—Bradsbabe

 ★★★★★

from Oxmoor House®

Apricot-Lemon Chicken

1 teaspoon curry powder
½ teaspoon salt
¼ teaspoon freshly ground black pepper
4 (6-ounce) skinless, boneless chicken breast halves
Cooking spray

⅓ cup apricot spread (such as Polaner All Fruit)
2 tablespoons fresh lemon juice
2 tablespoons water
2 teaspoons grated lemon rind

1. Combine first 3 ingredients in a small bowl; rub mixture over chicken.
2. Place a large nonstick skillet over medium-high heat. Coat pan with cooking spray. Cook chicken 6 minutes on each side or until done. Remove chicken from pan, and keep warm.
3. Add apricot spread, lemon juice, and water to pan, stirring until smooth. Cook over medium heat 1 minute. Spoon sauce over chicken; sprinkle with lemon rind.

Makes 4 servings ■ Prep time: 5 minutes ■ Total time: 20 minutes

For complete nutritional information on this and other Oxmoor House recipes, please turn to the appendix on pages 280–283.

LC
Low-Calorie

> " I think the fennel seeds made a huge difference. My husband loved it as well, and I will be trying the seasonings from the chicken on a pork tenderloin next!"
>
> —heckysue
>
> ★★★★★

from **CookingLight**

Roast Chicken with Balsamic Bell Peppers

¾ teaspoon salt, divided
¾ teaspoon fennel seeds, crushed
½ teaspoon black pepper, divided
¼ teaspoon garlic powder
¼ teaspoon dried oregano
4 (6-ounce) skinless, boneless chicken breasts
2 tablespoons olive oil, divided

Cooking spray
2 cups thinly sliced red bell pepper
1 cup thinly sliced yellow bell pepper
½ cup thinly sliced shallot (about 1 large)
1½ teaspoons chopped fresh rosemary
1 cup fat-free, less-sodium chicken broth
1 tablespoon balsamic vinegar

1. Preheat oven to 450°.
2. Heat a large skillet over medium-high heat. Combine ½ teaspoon salt, fennel seeds, ¼ teaspoon black pepper, garlic powder, and oregano. Brush chicken with 1½ teaspoons oil; sprinkle spice rub over chicken. Add 1½ teaspoons oil to pan. Add chicken; cook 3 minutes or until browned. Turn chicken over; cook 1 minute. Arrange chicken in an 11 x 7–inch baking dish coated with cooking spray. Bake at 450° for 10 minutes or until done.
3. Heat remaining olive oil over medium-high heat. Add bell peppers, shallot, and rosemary; sauté 3 minutes. Stir in broth, scraping pan to loosen browned bits. Reduce heat; simmer 5 minutes. Increase heat to medium-high. Stir in vinegar, ¼ teaspoon salt, and ¼ teaspoon pepper; cook 3 minutes, stirring frequently. Serve bell pepper mixture over chicken.

Makes 4 servings ■ Prep time: 15 minutes ■ Total time: 40 minutes

For complete nutritional information on this and other *Cooking Light* recipes, please turn to the appendix on pages 280–283.

5 Ingredients or Less   30 Minutes or Less   **GF** Gluten-Free

myrecipes users suggest:
- using Madeira or dry sherry instead of Marsala
- swapping baby portabellas for the shiitake mushrooms

" This has become a weeknight go-to recipe for us. It is absolutely delicious—vibrant, flavorful, and rich but never heavy."

—CherCooks411

from **Oxmoor House®**

Chicken and Shiitake Marsala

4 (6-ounce) skinless, boneless
  chicken breast halves
Cooking spray
¼ teaspoon salt
¼ teaspoon black pepper
2 (3.5-ounce) packages shiitake
  mushrooms, sliced

½ cup Marsala wine
2 green onions, finely chopped
  (about ⅓ cup), divided
2 tablespoons butter

1. Place each chicken breast half between 2 sheets of heavy-duty plastic wrap; pound to ½-inch thickness using a meat mallet or small heavy skillet.
2. Heat a large nonstick skillet over medium-high heat. Coat pan with cooking spray. Sprinkle chicken evenly with salt and pepper. Add chicken to pan. Cook 5 to 6 minutes on each side or until done. Remove chicken and drippings from pan; set aside, and keep warm.
3. Heat pan over medium-high heat; coat pan with cooking spray. Add mushrooms. Coat mushrooms with cooking spray; cook 2 minutes or until tender, stirring frequently. Add wine and 3 tablespoons onions. Cook 30 seconds over high heat. Reduce heat; add butter, stirring until butter melts.
4. Add chicken and drippings to pan, stirring gently. Place chicken on platter. Spoon mushroom sauce over chicken; sprinkle with remaining onions.

Makes 4 servings ▪ Prep time: 10 minutes ▪ Total time: 25 minutes

For complete nutritional information on this and other Oxmoor House recipes, please turn to the appendix on pages 280–283.

from

Mexican Slow-Cooker Chicken

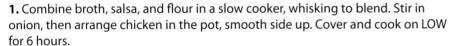

¾ cup chicken broth
½ cup green or red salsa, plus more for
   serving
⅓ cup flour
1 large onion, chopped
2½ pounds skinless, boneless chicken
   breast halves

⅔ cup reduced-fat sour cream
4 ounces sharp Cheddar or Monterey Jack
   cheese, shredded
1 can (15-ounce) red beans, heated
2 cups shredded iceberg lettuce
Soft, fresh corn tortillas, warmed for serving

1. Combine broth, salsa, and flour in a slow cooker, whisking to blend. Stir in onion, then arrange chicken in the pot, smooth side up. Cover and cook on LOW for 6 hours.

2. Remove chicken breast halves to a plate. Ladle sauce from pot into a blender and puree. Stir in sour cream. Return sauce and chicken to the pot. Keep warm until ready to serve.

3. Arrange chicken on plates and top with shredded cheese. Serve with beans, lettuce, additional salsa, and tortillas.

Makes 6 servings ■ Prep time: 10 minutes ■ Total time: 6 hours, 10 minutes

For complete nutritional information on this and other *All You* recipes, please turn to the appendix on pages 280–283.

LC **Low-Calorie**   **Slow Cooker**

myrecipes users suggest:
- adding a can of green chiles for more heat
- using pepper Jack cheese instead of Cheddar

" I make this all the time, and my husband and I both love it! I add cilantro, cumin, and some crushed red pepper just to give it a little more spice, and it always comes out great."

—Chilburn1212

★★★★★

SCAN THIS PHOTO
for 21 more chicken
slow-cooker recipes.

from **Southern Living**

Creamy Slow-Cooker Chicken

6 skinless, boneless chicken breasts
   (about 2½ pounds)
2 teaspoons seasoned salt
2 tablespoons canola oil
1 (10.75-ounce) can reduced-fat
   cream of mushroom soup

1 (8-ounce) package ⅓-less-fat cream cheese
½ cup dry white wine
1 (0.7-ounce) envelope Italian dressing mix
1 (8-ounce) package sliced fresh mushrooms

1. Sprinkle chicken with seasoned salt. Cook chicken, in batches, in hot oil in a large skillet over medium-high heat 2 to 3 minutes on each side or just until browned. Transfer chicken to a 5-quart slow cooker, reserving drippings in skillet.
2. Add soup, cream cheese, wine, and Italian dressing mix to hot drippings in skillet. Cook over medium heat, stirring constantly, 2 to 3 minutes or until cheese is melted and mixture is smooth.
3. Arrange mushrooms over chicken in slow cooker. Spoon soup mixture over mushrooms. Cover and cook on LOW 4 hours. Stir well before serving.

Note: To make it ahead, prepare recipe as directed. Transfer to a 13 x 9-inch baking dish, and let cool completely. Freeze up to 1 month. Thaw in refrigerator 8 to 24 hours. To reheat, cover tightly with aluminum foil, and bake at 325° for 45 minutes. Uncover and bake about 15 minutes, until thoroughly heated.

Makes 6 servings ▪ Prep time: 10 minutes ▪ Total time: 4 hours, 25 minutes

> " I used cream of chicken soup instead of cream of mushroom, and it was a hit with my husband and kids. This would make a great potluck dish or entrée to serve company. Very elegant and rich-tasting."

—CherylO
★★★★★

30 Minutes or Less **Kid-Friendly**

" Excellent one-dish meal. It was hard to stop eating this. My husband had three helpings!"

—Lovestoeatsoup

★★★★★

from **all you**

Chicken Fried Rice with Vegetables

½ (12-ounce) chicken breast, chopped
2 tablespoons soy sauce
2 teaspoons sesame oil
¼ cup vegetable oil
¾ cup chopped onion
½ (10-ounce) package frozen mixed
    vegetables, thawed

4 cups cooked white rice
3 eggs
Kosher salt
Black pepper

1. In a medium bowl, toss chicken with soy sauce and sesame oil. Cover and marinate at room temperature for 10 minutes.
2. Heat a large nonstick skillet over medium-high heat. Add chicken and marinade, and stir-fry until chicken is cooked through, 3 to 4 minutes. Transfer chicken to a plate. Add vegetable oil to skillet and heat over medium heat. Add onion and cook for 3 minutes. Stir in vegetables and cook for 1 minute. Increase heat to medium-high; stir in rice until incorporated and cooked through, 3 minutes.
3. Using a wooden spoon, form a well in mixture. Add eggs and scramble within well just until soft. Then break apart and mix into rice; season with salt and pepper. Let cook undisturbed until a golden crust forms, about 1 minute. Turn rice with a spatula and cook other side. Repeat 2 or 3 times until rice is uniformly golden. Add chicken and stir to combine. Serve warm.

Makes 4 servings ▪ Prep time: 10 minutes ▪ Total time: 25 minutes

For complete nutritional information on this and other *All You* recipes, please turn to the appendix on pages 280–283.

5 5 Ingredients or Less   **30 Minutes** or Less   **GF** Gluten-Free

SCAN THIS PHOTO for video on how to pound chicken.

myrecipes users suggest:
- using red onion instead of shallots
- substituting chicken broth or Chardonnay for sherry
- using oregano instead of marjoram

from Oxmoor House.

Mushroom-Herb Chicken

4 (6-ounce) skinless, boneless
   chicken breast halves
¼ teaspoon salt
¼ teaspoon black pepper
Cooking spray

3 large shallots, peeled (about 1 cup)
1 (8-ounce) package presliced mushrooms
⅓ cup dry sherry
1 teaspoon dried marjoram, crushed
Freshly ground black pepper (optional)

1. Place each chicken breast half between 2 sheets of heavy-duty plastic wrap; pound to ⅓-inch thickness using a meat mallet or small heavy skillet. Sprinkle chicken evenly with salt and pepper; coat with cooking spray. Heat a large non-stick skillet over medium-high heat. Add chicken to pan; cook 5 to 6 minutes on each side or until browned.
2. While chicken cooks, cut shallots vertically into thin slices. Remove chicken from pan. Coat pan with cooking spray. Add mushrooms and shallots to pan; coat vegetables with cooking spray. Cook 1 minute, stirring constantly. Stir in sherry and marjoram. Return chicken to pan; cover and cook 3 to 4 minutes or until mushrooms are tender and chicken is done. Transfer chicken to a platter. Pour mushroom mixture over chicken; sprinkle with freshly ground pepper, if desired. Serve immediately.

Makes 4 servings ▪ Prep time: 5 minutes ▪ Total time: 20 minutes

For complete nutritional information on this and other Oxmoor House recipes, please turn to the appendix on pages 280–283.

Kid-
Friendly

 I never thought
I could make
moist, tender chicken
fingers without frying.
Marinating them in
the buttermilk mixture
makes for such a
delicious chicken
tender. Yum!"

—ItalianCook79
★★★★★

from

Buttermilk Chicken Tenders

½ cup buttermilk
¾ teaspoon Tabasco sauce
1⅓ pounds chicken tenders
¾ cup all-purpose flour
2 teaspoons kosher salt

⅛ teaspoon cayenne pepper
2 eggs
2 tablespoons water
2 cups bread crumbs
¾ cup vegetable oil

1. Mix buttermilk and Tabasco in a resealable plastic bag. Add chicken tenders and marinate for at least 1 hour or up to 1 day.
2. Preheat oven to 225°. In a shallow dish, mix flour, salt, and cayenne pepper. In a shallow bowl, beat together eggs with water. Place bread crumbs in a separate shallow dish. Line a baking sheet with wax paper.
3. Remove chicken tenders from buttermilk, draining any excess, and dredge individually in flour mixture, shaking off excess; then dip into egg, draining any excess. Next, dip chicken in bread crumbs, pressing gently into crumbs to coat. Place on baking sheet.
4. In a large skillet, heat ¼ cup vegetable oil over medium-high heat. When hot, add one-third of chicken tenders and cook, turning, until golden, about 4 minutes. Transfer to a baking sheet and keep warm. Wipe out pan and repeat cooking procedure in 2 more batches with remaining oil and tenders.

Makes 6 servings ▪ Prep time: 20 minutes ▪ Total time: 1 hour, 35 minutes

For complete nutritional information on this and other *All You* recipes, please turn to the appendix on pages 280–283.

> **"** My husband and I both loved this excellent soup—easy to make and delicious. I used fresh corn shaved off the ear and put it in at the end—what a taste difference!"
>
> —Angelina823
>
> ★★★★★

myrecipes users suggest:
- using taco seasoning instead of chili powder
- adding a can of black beans for more heft
- garnishing with chopped fresh cilantro and avocado and a dollop of sour cream

from **all you**

Spicy Chicken Stew

2 baking potatoes (about 1½ pounds), peeled and cut into chunks (3⅓ cups)
1 (10-ounce) package frozen sweet corn
2 celery stalks, chopped
2 carrots, peeled and cut into chunks (1 cup)
1 onion, thickly sliced
2 garlic cloves, minced
1 (12.5-ounce) jar salsa
2 teaspoons kosher salt

1½ teaspoons ground cumin
1 teaspoon chili powder
½ teaspoon black pepper
1 skinless, boneless chicken breast, halved (about 1 pound)
4 skinless, boneless chicken thighs (about 10½ ounces)
2½ cups chicken broth
4 (6-inch) fresh corn tortillas, cut into strips

1. Place potatoes, corn, celery, carrots, onion, and garlic in slow cooker. Stir in salsa, salt, cumin, chili powder, and pepper. Distribute chicken evenly on top of vegetables and pour broth over chicken. Cover slow cooker and cook stew on HIGH for 4 hours.

2. Transfer chicken to a plate and shred with two forks into bite-size chunks; return to slow cooker. Mix tortilla strips into stew. Serve warm.

Makes 6 servings ■ Prep time: 15 minutes ■ Total time: 4 hours, 15 minutes

For complete nutritional information on this and other *All You* recipes, please turn to the appendix on pages 280–283.

Kid-Friendly   Low-Calorie   Slow Cooker

White Bean and Chicken Chili

2 (15-ounce) cans white beans, rinsed and drained
4 cups low-sodium chicken broth
1 tablespoon vegetable oil
2 whole bone-in chicken breasts (3 pounds)
Salt and black pepper

2 onions, chopped
4 garlic cloves, chopped
2 (4-ounce) cans roasted green chiles, drained
1 cup water
1 tablespoon ground cumin

1. Place beans and broth in a slow cooker. Cover and cook on HIGH until beans are tender, 2 hours.
2. Warm oil in skillet over medium-high heat. Sprinkle chicken with salt and pepper. Place chicken skin side down in skillet; cook until brown, about 4 minutes. Turn and cook for 2 minutes more. Transfer to a plate; remove and discard skin. Drain all but 2 tablespoons fat from skillet. Add onions and garlic; cook until softened, 5 minutes. Add onion mixture, chiles, water, and cumin to slow cooker. Stir; add chicken.
3. Cook on LOW for 6 hours, stirring twice. Remove 1 cup beans plus ½ cup liquid from slow cooker. Puree in a blender; return to slow cooker. Remove chicken, shred it, and return to slow cooker. Spoon into individual bowls and serve.

Makes 6 servings ■ Prep time: 30 minutes ■ Total time: 8 hours, 30 minutes

For complete nutritional information on this and other *All You* recipes, please turn to the appendix on pages 280–283.

myrecipes users suggest:
- adding sliced carrots and chopped celery
- stirring in sliced mushrooms and fresh spinach at the end and cooking, covered, until heated through
- adding chili powder, ground coriander, green chile powder, and/or chopped fresh jalapeño

SCAN THIS PHOTO for 9 more chicken chili recipes.

GF Gluten-Free · Grill It!

from *Sunset*

Grilled Cilantro Chicken with Pickled Tomato and Avocado Salsa

Salsa:
1 pound medium beefsteak-type tomatoes, quartered, seeds squeezed out
2 serrano chiles, thinly sliced
½ cup thinly sliced green onions
½ cup distilled white vinegar
2½ tablespoons packed light or dark brown sugar
1½ teaspoons kosher salt
4 teaspoons minced fresh ginger
1 tablespoon minced garlic
2 teaspoons mustard seeds
2 teaspoons freshly cracked black pepper
2 teaspoons ground cumin
1 teaspoon cayenne pepper
½ teaspoon turmeric
½ cup extra-virgin olive oil
2 firm-ripe avocados, peeled and cut into ¾-inch chunks

Chicken:
¼ cup extra-virgin olive oil
¼ cup fresh lime juice
½ cup chopped fresh cilantro
1 tablespoon ground cumin
½ teaspoon kosher salt
½ teaspoon freshly ground black pepper
4 bone-in, skin-on chicken breast halves (2½ pounds total)

1. Make salsa: In a bowl, combine tomatoes, chiles, and green onions. In a medium saucepan over high heat, bring vinegar to a boil. Add sugar and salt and cook, stirring, until dissolved, about 1 minute. Remove from heat. Put ginger, garlic, and next 5 ingredients in a bowl. In another medium saucepan, heat olive oil over medium-high heat until rippling. Add ginger mixture and cook, stirring, until fragrant, 1 minute. Remove from heat, stir in seasoned vinegar, and pour over tomato mixture.
2. Let salsa cool, then cover and chill at least 1 hour and up to 4 hours. About 1 hour before serving, stir avocados into salsa and bring to room temperature.
3. Make chicken: In a large bowl, combine olive oil, lime juice, cilantro, cumin, salt, and pepper. Turn chicken in mixture to coat. Let stand at room temperature, turning occasionally, for 30 to 45 minutes.
4. Heat grill to high heat (450° to 550°; you can hold your hand 5 inches above cooking grate only 2 to 4 seconds). Lift chicken from marinade (discard marinade) and grill chicken with cover closed, turning often to prevent scorching, until no longer pink in center, 15 to 20 minutes.
5. Transfer chicken to a platter and spoon salsa on top, saving half of liquid for another use (such as salad dressing).

Makes 4 servings ▪ Prep time: 30 minutes ▪ Total time: 2 hours, 15 minutes

For complete nutritional information on this and other *Sunset* recipes, please turn to the appendix on pages 280–283.

myrecipes users suggest:
• serving the salsa over grilled or oven-roasted halibut instead of chicken
• omitting the cayenne and/or seeding the serrano chile if you like less heat
• using cherry tomatoes instead of beefsteak

" The chicken comes out a little crispy on the outside and delicious in its own right. With the salsa, it's killer."

—candisanne
★★★★★

SCAN THIS PHOTO for video on how to prepare an avocado.

30 Minutes or Less   GF Gluten-Free

 What an easy, tasty chicken dish. I suggest lining the broiler pan with aluminum foil so cleanup is easy. The sauce is very sticky—but good!"

—madjack96

★★★★

from Cooking Light

Spicy Honey-Brushed Chicken Thighs

2 teaspoons garlic powder
2 teaspoons chili powder
1 teaspoon salt
1 teaspoon ground cumin
1 teaspoon paprika

½ teaspoon ground red pepper
8 skinless, boneless chicken thighs
Cooking spray
6 tablespoons honey
2 teaspoons cider vinegar

1. Preheat broiler.
2. Combine first 6 ingredients in a large bowl. Add chicken to bowl; toss to coat. Place chicken on a broiler pan coated with cooking spray. Broil chicken 5 minutes on each side.
3. Combine honey and vinegar in a small bowl, stirring well. Remove chicken from oven; brush ¼ cup honey mixture on chicken. Broil 1 minute. Remove chicken from oven and turn over. Brush chicken with remaining honey mixture. Broil 1 additional minute or until chicken is done.

Makes 4 servings ▪ Prep time: 10 minutes ▪ Total time: 20 minutes

For complete nutritional information on this and other *Cooking Light* recipes, please turn to the appendix on pages 280–283.

from **Sunset**

White Wine Coq au Vin

4½ tablespoons flour
¾ teaspoon kosher salt, divided
½ teaspoon freshly ground black pepper, divided
1 teaspoon herbes de Provence
4 slices bacon (¼ pound), chopped
1½ pounds skinless, boneless chicken thighs
2 tablespoons olive oil

1½ cups peeled baby carrots
3 celery stalks
1 medium onion
1⅓ cups Chardonnay
2 cups reduced-sodium chicken broth
½ cup lightly packed fresh flat-leaf parsley sprigs
¼ cup lightly packed fresh tarragon sprigs

1. In a plastic bag, shake flour with ½ teaspoon salt, ¼ teaspoon pepper, and the herbes de Provence; set aside.
2. In a 5- to 6-quart pan over medium-high heat, brown the bacon, stirring occasionally, 6 to 7 minutes. Meanwhile, cut chicken into 1-inch chunks, then shake half at a time in flour to coat.
3. With a slotted spoon, transfer bacon from pan to paper towels. Brown half the chicken in bacon fat, stirring occasionally, 3 to 5 minutes. Transfer to a plate. Repeat with remaining chicken, adding oil to pan. Meanwhile, cut carrots in half lengthwise and cut celery into diagonal slices. Chop onion.
4. Add vegetables to pan with remaining salt and pepper and sauté until onion is golden, about 5 minutes. Meanwhile, in a microwave-safe bowl, microwave wine and broth until steaming, about 3 minutes.
5. Add broth mixture, chicken, and bacon to pan, stirring to loosen browned bits. Cover and bring to a boil over high heat. Reduce heat and simmer until vegetables are tender, about 15 minutes. Meanwhile, coarsely chop parsley and tarragon. Stir them into stew.

Makes 4 servings ▪ Prep time: 20 minutes ▪ Total time: 1 hour, 5 minutes

For complete nutritional information on this and other *Sunset* recipes, please turn to the appendix on pages 280–283.

SCAN THIS PHOTO for video on how to cut up chicken.

from **REAL**SIMPLE

Chicken Cacciatore

¼ cup all-purpose flour
1¼ teaspoons kosher salt, divided
¾ teaspoon black pepper, divided
1 (3½- to 4-pound) chicken, cut into pieces
¼ cup olive oil
1 medium yellow onion, roughly chopped
1 carrot, diced

1 celery stalk, diced
4 garlic cloves, finely chopped
3 sprigs fresh thyme
1 bay leaf
1 (28-ounce) can plum tomatoes
⅓ cup dry red wine
¼ cup fresh flat-leaf parsley, roughly chopped

1. In a shallow bowl, combine the flour, 1 teaspoon of the salt, and ½ teaspoon of the pepper. Pat chicken dry with paper towels. Working in batches, lightly coat the chicken with the flour mixture, shaking off any excess.
2. Heat the oil in a Dutch oven or large saucepan over medium heat. Add some of the chicken to the pan and cook until browned, 4 to 5 minutes per side. Transfer to a plate; set aside. Repeat with the remaining chicken.
3. Add the onion to the pan and cook for 2 minutes. Add the carrot, celery, garlic, thyme, and bay leaf. Cook, stirring occasionally, for 10 minutes.
4. Crush the tomatoes in the can with a large spoon and stir them into the vegetables along with the wine and the remaining salt and pepper. Bring to a simmer. Add the chicken, reduce heat, and cover. Simmer for 45 minutes, turning the pieces occasionally. Remove and discard the bay leaf. Stir in the parsley.

Makes 4 servings ■ Prep time: 30 minutes ■ Total time: 1 hour, 30 minutes

For complete nutritional information on this and other *Real Simple* recipes, please turn to the appendix on pages 280–283.

> **"** This was an amazing dish. I'm Italian, and it tastes as authentic as it gets!"
> —101angelica
> ★★★★★

GF
Gluten-Free

Grill It!

Make-Ahead

> Don't leave the cumin out! Trust me, that's what makes this recipe so different and so yummy."

—wannabecook

★★★★★

from **Sunset**

Grilled Buttermilk Chicken

1 quart buttermilk	1 tablespoon ground cumin
½ cup minced shallots	1 teaspoon black pepper
2 tablespoons chopped garlic	6 chicken thighs (about 2½ pounds)
2 tablespoons kosher salt	6 chicken drumsticks (about 1¾ pounds)
2 tablespoons sugar	

1. In a large bowl, mix buttermilk, shallots, garlic, salt, sugar, cumin, and pepper.
2. Rinse chicken thighs and drumsticks and pat dry. Trim off excess fat. Submerge chicken pieces in buttermilk brine. Cover and chill at least 4 hours, or up to 1 day.
3. Lift chicken from brine; discard brine. Wipe excess brine from chicken with paper towels.
4. Lay chicken pieces on a grill over medium coals or medium heat on a gas grill (you can hold your hand at grill level only 4 to 5 seconds); close lid on gas grill. Cook, turning frequently, until browned on both sides and no longer pink at the bone (cut to test), 20 to 30 minutes. Serve hot or cold.

Note: To make ahead, brine the chicken up to 1 day before grilling; grill up to 1 day before serving. Refrigerate in an airtight container.

Makes 6 servings ■ Prep time: 45 minutes ■ Total time: 4 hours, 45 minutes

For complete nutritional information on this and other *Sunset* recipes, please turn to the appendix on pages 280–283.

SCAN THIS PHOTO for video on how to mince shallots.

SCAN THIS PHOTO for video on how to prepare this recipe.

" This may be my favorite new Mexican recipe. Easy to make, no special ingredients to buy, and tasty."

—twinsucf

★★★★★

from Cooking Light

Chicken Tamale Casserole

1 cup (4 ounces) preshredded 4-cheese Mexican blend cheese, divided
⅓ cup fat-free milk
¼ cup egg substitute
1 teaspoon ground cumin
⅛ teaspoon ground red pepper
1 (14.75-ounce) can cream-style corn
1 (8.5-ounce) box corn muffin mix (such as Martha White)

1 (4-ounce) can chopped green chiles, drained
Cooking spray
1 (10-ounce) can red enchilada sauce (such as Old El Paso)
2 cups shredded cooked chicken breast
½ cup fat-free sour cream

1. Preheat oven to 400°.
2. Combine ¼ cup cheese and next 7 ingredients in a large bowl, stirring just until moist. Pour mixture into a 13 x 9–inch baking dish coated with cooking spray.
3. Bake for 15 minutes or until set. Pierce entire surface liberally with a fork; pour enchilada sauce over top. Top with chicken; sprinkle with remaining ¾ cup cheese. Bake for 15 minutes or until cheese melts. Remove from oven; let stand 5 minutes. Cut into 8 pieces; top each serving with 1 tablespoon sour cream.

Makes 8 servings ■ Prep time: 10 minutes ■ Total time: 45 minutes

For complete nutritional information on this and other *Cooking Light* recipes, please turn to the appendix on pages 280–283.

myrecipes users suggest:
- kicking up the heat by using a 7-ounce can of chiles, hot red enchilada sauce, and/or doubling the cayenne
- trading the chicken for sautéed vegetables for a vegetarian twist

from Southern Living

King Ranch Chicken Casserole

1 (4½- to 5-pound) whole chicken
2 celery stalks, cut into 3 pieces each
2 carrots, cut into 3 pieces each
2½ to 3 teaspoons salt
2 tablespoons butter
1 medium onion, chopped
1 medium-size green bell pepper, chopped
1 garlic clove, pressed
1 (10.75-ounce) can cream of mushroom soup
1 (10.75-ounce) can cream of chicken soup

2 (10-ounce) cans diced tomatoes and green chiles, drained
1 teaspoon dried oregano
1 teaspoon ground cumin
1 teaspoon Mexican-style chili powder (can be substituted with 1 teaspoon regular chili powder and ⅛ teaspoon ground red pepper)
3 cups grated sharp Cheddar cheese
12 (6-inch) fajita-size corn tortillas, cut into ½-inch strips

1. Remove any giblets from chicken, and reserve for another use.
2. Place chicken, celery, carrots, and salt in a large Dutch oven with water to cover. Bring to a boil over medium-high heat; reduce heat to low. Cover and simmer 50 minutes to 1 hour or until chicken is done. Remove from heat. Remove chicken from broth; cool 30 minutes. Remove and reserve ¾ cup cooking liquid. Strain any remaining cooking liquid, and reserve for another use.
3. Preheat oven to 350°. Melt butter in a large skillet over medium-high heat. Add onion, and sauté 6 to 7 minutes or until tender. Add bell pepper and garlic, and sauté 3 to 4 minutes. Stir in reserved ¾ cup cooking liquid, cream of mushroom soup, and next 5 ingredients. Cook, stirring occasionally, 8 minutes.
4. Skin and bone chicken; shred meat into bite-size pieces. Layer half of chicken in a lightly greased 13 x 9–inch baking dish. Top with half of soup mixture and 1 cup Cheddar cheese. Cover with half of corn tortilla strips. Repeat layers once. Top with remaining 1 cup cheese.
5. Bake at 350° for 55 minutes to 1 hour or until bubbly. Let stand 10 minutes before serving.

Makes 8 to 10 servings ■ Prep time: 30 minutes ■ Total time: 3 hours, 30 minutes

My family adored this! My husband and high school son had three helpings and made me commit to keeping it in the repertoire."

—DebinAZ
★★★★★

Kid-Friendly

QUICK TIP

To make it faster, substitute 1 (2-pound) skinned, boned, and shredded deli-roasted chicken for whole chicken, 3 cups coarsely crumbled lime-flavored white corn tortilla chips for corn tortillas, and ¾ cup chicken broth for cooking liquid. Omit celery, carrots, and salt. Prepare recipe as directed, beginning with Step 3.

Kid-Friendly

SCAN THIS PHOTO for video on how to slice and dice carrots.

" This recipe is so delicious. My only complaint is that there wasn't enough. Next time I will double the recipe."

—Kcfields

★★★★★

 QUICK TIP

One roasted chicken yields about 3 cups of meat.

from Southern Living

Easy Chicken and Dumplings

1 (32-ounce) container low-sodium
   chicken broth
3 cups shredded cooked chicken
   (about 1½ pounds)
1 (10.75-ounce) can reduced-fat
   cream of chicken soup

¼ teaspoon poultry seasoning
1 (10.2-ounce) can refrigerated jumbo
   buttermilk biscuits
2 carrots, diced
3 celery stalks, diced

1. Bring first 4 ingredients to a boil in a Dutch oven over medium-high heat. Cover, reduce heat to low, and simmer, stirring occasionally, 5 minutes. Increase heat to medium-high; return to a low boil.
2. Place biscuits on a lightly floured surface. Roll or pat each biscuit to ⅛-inch thickness; cut into ½-inch-wide strips.
3. Drop strips, 1 at a time, into boiling broth mixture. Add carrots and celery. Cover, reduce heat to low, and simmer 15 to 20 minutes, stirring occasionally to prevent dumplings from sticking.

Makes 4 to 6 servings ■ Prep time: 30 minutes ■ Total time: 40 minutes

from Southern Living

Sugar-and-Spice Cured Turkey

1 (12-pound) whole turkey
¼ cup firmly packed light brown sugar
2 tablespoons kosher or coarse-grain sea salt
1 teaspoon onion powder
½ teaspoon garlic powder
½ teaspoon ground allspice
½ teaspoon ground cloves

½ teaspoon ground mace
1 large onion, quartered
2 (14-ounce) cans low-sodium chicken broth
Additional chicken broth
2 tablespoons all-purpose flour
Garnishes: fresh rosemary sprigs,
   apple slices, nuts

1. Remove and discard giblets and neck; rinse turkey with cold water. Pat dry. Tie legs together with string; tuck wing tips under. Combine brown sugar and next 6 ingredients. Rub over turkey. Cover with plastic wrap; chill 8 hours.
2. Preheat oven to 325°. Place turkey on a rack in a roasting pan, breast side up. Arrange onion quarters around turkey. Pour 2 cans broth into bottom of pan.
3. Bake, loosely covered with foil, at 325° for 1½ hours. Uncover and bake 1½ more hours or until meat thermometer registers 180°. (Cover with foil to prevent excessive browning, if necessary.) Remove onion; discard, reserving pan drippings. Let turkey stand 15 minutes before carving.
4. Combine pan drippings and enough broth to equal 2 cups in a saucepan over medium heat. Whisk in flour and cook, whisking constantly, 5 minutes or until thickened. Serve with turkey. Garnish, if desired.

Makes 8 to 10 servings ■ Prep time: 10 minutes ■ Total time: 11 hours, 30 minutes

ask the expert

How do I know if the turkey's done?

An accurate thermometer used correctly is the most reliable way to ensure the meat is cooked safely but is not overcooked and dry.

Here's how to do it: Insert the thermometer into the inner thigh. Make sure the tip of the probe is at the thickest part of the thigh without touching the bone, which can give a falsely hot reading. Also insert the thermometer into the thickest part of the breast.

Although some recipes still advise cooking dark meat to 180° for tenderness, the bird is safe to consume when the temperature hits 165°. If the bird is stuffed, you must also make sure that a thermometer stuck into the center of the stuffing registers 165°. (For optimal safety, the USDA recommends cooking stuffing separately.)

SCAN THIS BOX for more cooking know-how from our experts.

ask the expert

What's the best way to thaw my turkey?

There are two good ways to thaw your turkey: (1) in the refrigerator, which takes several days, depending on the size of the turkey, and (2) submerged in cold water. In both cases, leave the turkey in its original wrapper. When thawing in the refrigerator, place the turkey on a large tray or pan to catch the leaking juices. Once thawed, the turkey can safely last in the refrigerator another two days before cooking.

Thawing in cold water is quicker, but requires more of your attention. Make sure the wrapping is secure. If you think it is not watertight, wrap over the existing wrapper with additional plastic until it is. Submerge your wrapped turkey in a big bowl (or sink) of very cold tap water. (Avoid the temptation to use warmer water: The inside will still be frozen and the outside will become a breeding ground for bacteria.) Change the water every 30 minutes, again using very cold tap water and submerging the turkey.

SCAN THIS BOX for more cooking know-how from our experts.

from *Sunset*

Dry-Cured Rosemary Turkey

3 tablespoons sea salt or kosher salt
3 tablespoons dried marjoram
3 tablespoons dried thyme
3 tablespoons dried juniper berries
1 tablespoon black peppercorns
2 teaspoons anise seeds
1 (14- to 15-pound) turkey

12 fresh rosemary sprigs (3 inches each)
12 garlic cloves, peeled
½ cup unsalted butter, at room temperature, divided
Cooking spray
Pan Gravy (next page)

1. Three days before serving, in a blender or spice grinder, finely grind salt, marjoram, thyme, juniper berries, peppercorns, and anise seeds.
2. Remove and discard leg truss from turkey. Pull off and discard any lumps of fat. Remove giblets and neck. Discard giblets; save neck for gravy. Rinse turkey inside and out; pat dry. Cut off wing tips to the first joint and reserve for gravy. Rub half the herb mixture all over turkey; sprinkle remaining in body cavity. Cover and chill for 3 days.
3. Preheat oven to 325° (convection not recommended). Put rosemary sprigs and garlic inside turkey body cavity. Gently push your hand between skin and turkey breast to separate skin from breast. Spread about half the butter over breast under skin. Melt remaining butter and brush lightly over top of turkey. Coat a V-shaped rack with cooking spray and set in a 12 x 17–inch roasting pan. Place turkey, breast down, on the rack. Roast turkey for 1 hour, 45 minutes.
4. Meanwhile, cook turkey wing tips and neck for pan gravy as directed. Remove turkey from oven and turn breast side up. Return to oven. Roast until a meat thermometer inserted straight down through thickest part of breast to the bone registers 165°, 45 to 60 minutes longer.
5. Tip turkey to drain juices from cavity into pan, and transfer to a platter. Let stand in a warm place, uncovered, for 15 to 30 minutes. Finish gravy, then carve turkey.

Note: To grind the salt and herbs together, use a mortar and pestle or a clean coffee grinder. For best results, use a turkey that hasn't been infused with broth, saline solution, or butter.

Makes 14 servings ■ Prep time: 45 minutes ■ Total time: 3 days, 3 hours, 30 minutes

Pan Gravy

2 tablespoons vegetable oil
Turkey wing tips and neck
4½ cups reduced-sodium chicken broth
Pan juices from roast turkey
Melted butter as needed

1 garlic clove, minced
½ cup flour
1 cup whipping cream
Salt

1. Pour oil into 5- to 6-quart pan over medium-high heat. Add turkey wing tips and neck and brown well, 4 to 7 minutes. Add broth and bring to a boil; cover, reduce heat, and simmer about 1 hour.

2. Remove wings and neck. While turkey rests, pour juices from roasting pan into a 1- to 2-quart glass measuring cup. Skim off and reserve fat. Add simmered broth to pan juices to make 4 cups; if you don't have enough, add water.

3. Return ⅓ cup fat (if not enough, add enough melted butter to make up the difference) and garlic to unwashed roasting pan; set over two burners at medium-high heat. Add flour and cook, stirring, until bubbly and smooth. Stir in broth and cream; scrape pan sides and bottom to loosen browned bits. Cook gravy, whisking, until smooth and boiling, 4 to 7 minutes. Add salt to taste.

Makes 5½ cups ■ Prep time: 25 minutes ■ Total time: 1 hour, 25 minutes

> I've been making this turkey recipe for more than two years now. When I'm not making a turkey, I make a scaled-down version with a roasting chicken."
>
> —Chell962
> ★★★★★

SCAN THIS PHOTO for video on how to carve a turkey.

Kid-Friendly

from **REAL**SIMPLE

Turkey and Roasted Red Pepper Meat Loaf

1½ pounds ground turkey
1 small yellow onion, chopped
½ cup bread crumbs
1 egg, beaten
1 cup grated Parmesan
2 tablespoons plus 2 teaspoons
   Dijon mustard

1 cup fresh flat-leaf parsley, chopped
1 (7-ounce) jar roasted red peppers,
   cut into ½-inch pieces
Kosher salt and black pepper
1 tablespoon white wine vinegar
3 tablespoons extra-virgin olive oil
6 cups mixed greens

1. Preheat oven to 400°. Combine the turkey, onion, bread crumbs, egg, Parmesan, 2 tablespoons mustard, the parsley, red peppers, ¾ teaspoon salt, and ½ teaspoon pepper in a large bowl. Shape the meat into an 8-inch loaf and place in a baking dish.

2. Bake at 400° until no trace of pink remains (internal temperature should be 165°), about 45 minutes. Transfer to a cutting board and let rest 15 minutes before slicing.

3. Whisk together the remaining mustard, the vinegar, oil, ¼ teaspoon salt, and ¼ teaspoon pepper in a small bowl.

4. Divide the greens among individual plates, and drizzle the vinaigrette over the top. Serve with the sliced meat loaf.

Makes 4 servings ■ Prep time: 15 minutes ■ Total time: 1 hour, 15 minutes

For complete nutritional information on this and other *Real Simple* recipes, please turn to the appendix on pages 280–283.

SCAN THIS PHOTO for a Weeknight Meal Planner.

SCAN THIS PHOTO for video on how to prepare this recipe.

myrecipes users suggest:
- adding hot sauce, chopped jalapeño, or chipotle chile powder
- adding a can of black beans or swapping the kidney beans for chickpeas or pinto beans
- serving over rice instead of spaghetti or using it to make chili dogs

from Cooking Light

Cincinnati Turkey Chili

4 ounces uncooked spaghetti
Cooking spray
8 ounces lean ground turkey
1½ cups prechopped onion, divided
1 cup chopped green bell pepper
1 tablespoon bottled minced garlic
1 tablespoon chili powder
2 tablespoons tomato paste
1 teaspoon ground cumin
1 teaspoon dried oregano
¼ teaspoon ground cinnamon

⅛ teaspoon ground allspice
½ cup fat-free, less-sodium chicken broth
1 (15-ounce) can kidney beans, rinsed and drained
1 (14.5-ounce) can diced tomatoes, undrained
2½ tablespoons chopped semisweet chocolate
¼ teaspoon salt
¾ cup (3 ounces) shredded sharp Cheddar cheese

1. Cook pasta according to package directions, omitting salt and fat. Drain; set aside.
2. Heat a Dutch oven over medium-high heat. Coat pan with cooking spray. Add turkey; cook 3 minutes, stirring to crumble. Add 1 cup onion, bell pepper, and garlic; sauté 3 minutes. Stir in chili powder and next 5 ingredients; cook 1 minute. Add broth, beans, and tomatoes; bring to a boil. Cover, reduce heat, and simmer 20 minutes, stirring occasionally. Remove from heat; stir in chocolate and salt. Serve chili over spaghetti; top with remaining ½ cup onion and cheese.

Makes 4 servings ■ Prep time: 20 minutes ■ Total time: 40 minutes

For complete nutritional information on this and other *Cooking Light* recipes, please turn to the appendix on pages 280–283.

Kid-Friendly Low-Calorie

 Definitely dry the excess water off the veggies. I've made this several times and love it, as does my boyfriend."

—dena9472

from **REAL SIMPLE**

Turkey Burgers with Grated Zucchini and Carrot

¾ pound ground turkey
1 medium zucchini, grated
1 medium carrot, grated
2 garlic cloves, finely chopped
¾ teaspoon dried thyme
¾ teaspoon kosher salt
¼ teaspoon black pepper

1 large egg
3 tablespoons olive oil, divided
4 slices crusty bread
4 small leaves Boston lettuce
¼ cup mayonnaise (optional)
2 teaspoons fresh lemon juice (optional)

1. Heat broiler. In a large bowl, combine turkey, zucchini, carrot, garlic, thyme, salt, pepper, and egg. Form mixture into 4 patties.
2. Heat 1 tablespoon oil in a large skillet over medium heat. Cook patties, turning once, until no trace of pink remains, 4 to 5 minutes per side.
3. Meanwhile, place bread on a baking sheet and brush with remaining oil. Broil until golden brown and crisp, about 1½ minutes. Transfer bread to individual plates. Top with lettuce leaves and burgers. If using, combine mayonnaise and lemon juice in a small bowl, and serve with burgers.

Makes 4 servings ■ Prep time: 15 minutes ■ Total time: 25 minutes

For complete nutritional information on this and other *Real Simple* recipes, please turn to the appendix on pages 280–283.

from *CookingLight*

LC
Low-
Calorie

Duck and Black-Eyed Pea Cassoulet

6 slices applewood-smoked bacon, chopped
6 (10-ounce) duck leg quarters, skinned
1 teaspoon salt, divided
1 teaspoon freshly ground black pepper, divided
1 cup finely chopped yellow onion
¼ cup chopped garlic (about 7 cloves)
1½ cups chopped cremini mushrooms
1 cup finely chopped celery
½ cup finely chopped carrot
6 cups fat-free, less-sodium chicken broth
6 cups frozen black-eyed peas, thawed
2 tablespoons chopped fresh thyme, divided
2 tablespoons chopped fresh flat-leaf parsley, divided

1. Cook bacon in a large Dutch oven over medium heat until crisp. Remove bacon, reserving 3 tablespoons drippings in pan; set bacon aside. Increase heat to medium-high.

2. Sprinkle duck with ½ teaspoon salt and ½ teaspoon pepper. Add 3 duck legs to drippings in pan; cook 3 minutes on each side or until browned. Remove from pan. Repeat procedure with remaining duck. Add onion and garlic to pan; sauté 3 minutes. Add remaining ½ teaspoon salt, remaining ½ teaspoon pepper, mushrooms, celery, and carrot. Cover, reduce heat to low, and cook 20 minutes or until very tender, stirring occasionally.

3. Stir in broth, peas, 1 tablespoon thyme, and 1 tablespoon parsley. Return duck to pan; bring to a boil. Reduce heat, and simmer 1 hour and 20 minutes or until duck is tender, slightly mashing beans occasionally with a fork or potato masher. Remove duck from pan; cool slightly. Remove meat from bones; shred. Discard bones. Return meat to pan. Simmer 20 minutes or until mixture is thick, stirring occasionally. Stir in remaining 1 tablespoon thyme and remaining 1 tablespoon parsley. Sprinkle with bacon.

Makes 8 servings ■ Prep time: 40 minutes ■ Total time: 2 hours, 40 minutes

For complete nutritional information on this and other *Cooking Light* recipes, please turn to the appendix on pages 280–283.

myrecipes users suggest:
- substituting turkey drumsticks for the duck leg quarters

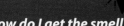
ask the expert

How do I get the smell of garlic off my hands?

After you wash your hands with soap and water, rub them on a stainless steel surface. It can be your kitchen sink, faucet, stovetop, or anything you have in your house that is stainless steel.

Even better: buy a stainless steel "soap" that is made just for this. It is a piece of stainless formed to look like a piece of soap, and it can easily be stored near or under your sink. It is useful for both garlic and onion smell, and it really does work.

SCAN THIS BOX for more cooking know-how from our experts.

meats 🔍

Ground beef is popular, but for the home cooks who use MyRecipes.com, the versatile pork chop is still No. 1 among meats. Here, we've corralled our most popular pork chop dishes, as well as top-rated recipes for burgers, steaks, roasts, and stews of beef, pork, and lamb.

 To use the exclusive **Scan-It/Cook-It™** features in this chapter, look for the smartphone symbol (shown at left). For detailed instructions, please see page 7.

PORK CHOPS WITH APRICOT SAUCE
page 105

30 Minutes
or Less

❝ Yum. My husband said that he would pay money for this in a restaurant."

—Debbie17

★★★★★

from Cooking Light

Chipotle Barbecue Burgers with Slaw

½ cup dry breadcrumbs
2 tablespoons barbecue sauce
1 tablespoon chopped chipotle chiles, canned in adobo sauce
1 teaspoon bottled minced garlic
1 pound lean ground beef
1 large egg
Cooking spray

2 cups cabbage-and-carrot coleslaw
1 tablespoon reduced-fat mayonnaise
1 tablespoon reduced-fat sour cream
1 teaspoon sugar
1 teaspoon cider vinegar
⅛ teaspoon salt
⅛ teaspoon black pepper
4 (1½-ounce) hamburger buns

1. Combine first 6 ingredients. Divide mixture into 4 equal portions, shaping each into a ½-inch-thick patty.
2. Heat a large nonstick skillet over medium-high heat. Coat pan with cooking spray. Add patties to pan; cook for 4 minutes on each side or until a meat thermometer registers 160°.
3. Combine coleslaw and next 6 ingredients in a large bowl; toss well. Place 1 patty on bottom half of each bun; top each serving with ½ cup coleslaw mixture and top half of bun.

Makes 4 servings ■ Prep time: 10 minutes ■ Total time: 20 minutes

For complete nutritional information on this and other *Cooking Light* recipes, please turn to the appendix on pages 280–283.

30 Minutes or Less

Grill It!

> *This* is the burger that will blow you away. The red onion jam is phenomenal. "
>
> —LIMarc
>
> ★★★★

from Cooking Light

Cheddar Burgers with Red Onion Jam

Jam:
1 teaspoon olive oil
4 cups vertically sliced red onion
4 teaspoons sugar
4 teaspoons red wine vinegar
¾ teaspoon chopped fresh thyme

Burgers:
¾ teaspoon chopped fresh oregano
½ teaspoon salt
¼ teaspoon garlic powder
1 pound extra-lean ground round
Cooking spray
4 (½-ounce) slices white Cheddar cheese
4 (1½-ounce) hamburger buns, toasted
4 teaspoons canola mayonnaise

1. Preheat grill to medium-high heat.
2. To prepare jam, heat a large nonstick skillet over medium-high heat. Add oil to pan; swirl to coat. Add onion; sauté 5 minutes. Reduce heat to medium-low; stir in sugar, vinegar, and thyme. Cover and cook 10 minutes or until onion is very tender. Remove from heat.
3. To prepare burgers, combine oregano, salt, garlic powder, and beef. Divide mixture into 4 equal portions, shaping each into a ½-inch-thick patty. Place on grill rack coated with cooking spray; cook 2 minutes. Turn patties over. Place 1 cheese slice on each patty; cook 2 minutes or until done.
4. Spread cut sides of each bun with ½ teaspoon mayonnaise. Place 1 patty on bottom half of each bun; top each with ¼ cup onion jam and bun top.

Makes 4 servings ■ Prep time: 20 minutes ■ Total time: 30 minutes

For complete nutritional information on this and other *Cooking Light* recipes, please turn to the appendix on pages 280–283.

5 Ingredients or Less

LC Low-Calorie

" Great flavor! I can't wait to make it again! I accidentally used balsamic vinaigrette instead of vinegar, and it was still awesome!"

—KathyTX

★★★★★

from CookingLight

Grilled Balsamic Skirt Steak

¼ cup balsamic vinegar
1 tablespoon Worcestershire sauce
2 teaspoons dark brown sugar
1 garlic clove, minced
1 pound skirt steak, trimmed and cut into 4 pieces

Cooking spray
½ teaspoon kosher salt, divided
¼ teaspoon freshly ground black pepper

1. Combine first 4 ingredients in a large zip-top plastic bag. Add steak, turning to coat; seal and marinate at room temperature 25 minutes, turning once. Remove steak from bag; discard marinade.
2. Heat a large grill pan over medium-high heat. Coat pan with cooking spray. Sprinkle both sides of steak with ¼ teaspoon salt and pepper. Add steak to pan; cook 3 minutes on each side or until desired degree of doneness. Remove steak from pan; sprinkle with remaining ¼ teaspoon salt. Tent with foil; let stand 5 minutes. Cut steak diagonally across the grain into thin slices.

Makes 4 servings ■ Prep time: 10 minutes ■ Total time: 40 minutes

For complete nutritional information on this and other *Cooking Light* recipes, please turn to the appendix on pages 280–283.

from CookingLight

Mongolian Beef

2 tablespoons lower-sodium soy sauce
1 teaspoon sugar
1 teaspoon cornstarch
2 teaspoons dry sherry
2 teaspoons hoisin sauce
1 teaspoon rice vinegar
1 teaspoon chile paste with garlic (such as sambal oelek)

¼ teaspoon salt
2 teaspoons peanut oil
1 tablespoon minced peeled fresh ginger
1 tablespoon minced garlic
1 pound sirloin steak, thinly sliced across the grain
16 medium green onions, cut into 2-inch pieces

1. Combine first 8 ingredients, stirring until smooth.
2. Heat peanut oil in a large nonstick skillet over medium-high heat. Add ginger, garlic, and beef; sauté for 2 minutes or until beef is browned. Add green onion pieces; sauté 30 seconds. Add soy sauce mixture; cook 1 minute or until thickened, stirring constantly.

Makes 4 servings ■ Prep time: 15 minutes ■ Total time: 20 minutes

For complete nutritional information on this and other *Cooking Light* recipes, please turn to the appendix on pages 280–283.

myrecipes users suggest:
- substituting hot sauce, prepared chile sauce, or chile oil for the chile paste with garlic
- adding sliced red bell peppers, broccoli, and/or mushrooms
- serving it over Asian noodles, rice, or whole-wheat spaghetti

SCAN THIS PHOTO for video on how to prepare this recipe.

30 Minutes or Less   Kid-Friendly   Low-Calorie

myrecipes users suggest:
- using lamb instead of beef
- using shiitake mushrooms instead of baby bellas
- adding extra shallots and garlic

from Cooking Light

Steak Tips with Peppered Mushroom Gravy

2 cups uncooked egg noodles
Cooking spray
1 pound top sirloin steak, cut into ¾-inch pieces
1 tablespoon butter
2 tablespoons finely chopped shallots
1 (8-ounce) package presliced baby bella mushrooms

1 teaspoon minced garlic
1 tablespoon lower-sodium soy sauce
3 tablespoons all-purpose flour
1½ cups fat-free, lower-sodium beef broth
½ teaspoon black pepper
¼ teaspoon salt
3 fresh thyme sprigs
1 teaspoon fresh thyme leaves (optional)

1. Cook noodles according to package directions, omitting salt and fat; drain.
2. While noodles cook, heat a large nonstick skillet over medium-high heat. Coat pan with cooking spray. Add steak; sauté 5 minutes, browning on all sides. Remove from pan; cover.
3. Melt butter in pan over medium-high heat. Add shallots and mushrooms; sauté 4 minutes. Add garlic; sauté 30 seconds. Stir in soy sauce. Sprinkle flour over mushroom mixture; cook 1 minute, stirring constantly. Gradually add broth, stirring constantly. Add pepper, salt, and thyme sprigs. Bring to a boil; cook 2 minutes or until thickened. Return beef to pan; cook 1 minute or until thoroughly heated. Discard thyme sprigs.
4. Serve over noodles. Garnish with thyme leaves, if desired.

Makes 4 servings ■ Prep time: 20 minutes ■ Total time: 20 minutes

For complete nutritional information on this and other *Cooking Light* recipes, please turn to the appendix on pages 280–283.

 SCAN THIS PHOTO for a Weeknight Meal Planner.

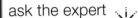

30 Minutes or Less Kid-Friendly **LC** Low-Calorie

myrecipes users suggest:
- making it with thinly sliced flank or sirloin steak and adding sliced onions

ask the expert

How do I choose the freshest broccoli?

October through April are the peak months for fresh broccoli. You always want to look for firm stalks with tightly bunched heads. Don't choose broccoli with a head that shows signs of buds turning yellow; those little green trees are over the hill.

You can store fresh broccoli in the fridge (in a plastic bag) up to four days.

SCAN THIS BOX for more cooking know-how from our experts.

from

Beef and Broccoli Stir-Fry

1 pound pre-cut beef for stir-fry
2 garlic cloves, smashed
1 tablespoon minced fresh ginger
2 tablespoons soy sauce
1 bunch broccoli (about 1 pound)
1 carrot

2 tablespoons vegetable oil, divided
½ cup water
1½ cups beef broth
2 tablespoons cornstarch
1 cup fresh mung bean sprouts

1. Combine beef, garlic, ginger, and soy sauce in a bowl and let stand.
2. Wash broccoli thoroughly and cut into florets. Trim and peel stems and cut into ¼-inch-thick slices. Wash and peel carrot. Halve lengthwise, and cut into ¼-inch-thick diagonal slices.
3. Heat 1 tablespoon oil in a large nonstick skillet or wok over high heat, add broccoli florets and stems; stir-fry for 2 minutes. Add water and stir until water evaporates. Transfer broccoli and carrots to a plate.
4. Add remaining oil to pan, add beef mixture, and stir-fry for 3 minutes. Stir together broth and cornstarch, add to meat, and stir-fry until sauce is thickened, about 3 minutes longer. Add broccoli, carrots, and bean sprouts, then cook, stirring, until heated through, about 2 minutes.

Makes 4 servings ▪ Prep: 15 minutes ▪ Total time: 25 minutes

For complete nutritional information on this and other *All You* recipes, please turn to the appendix on pages 280–283.

Slow
Cooker

❝ We've tried several different recipes over the years, and this is the one to keep. I added a little balsamic with the wine. The taste was rich and hearty."

—GoTigers

★★★★

from **REAL**SIMPLE

Classic Beef Stew

4 pounds bottom round, well trimmed and cut into 2-inch pieces
1 cup all-purpose flour
⅓ cup olive oil (plus more if needed)
2 large onions, diced (2 cups)
1 (6-ounce) can tomato paste
1 cup dry red wine
1 pound potatoes, cut into 2-inch pieces (about 4 cups)

½ pound baby carrots (about 2 cups)
2 cups beef broth
1 tablespoon kosher salt
1 teaspoon dried thyme leaves
1 bay leaf
1 cup frozen peas, thawed

1. Coat the beef in flour. Heat a few tablespoons of the oil in a large skillet over medium-high heat. Brown meat, a few pieces at a time, adding more oil as necessary. Transfer to a 4- to 6-quart slow cooker.
2. Add onions to skillet and cook over medium heat until tender, about 10 minutes. Stir in tomato paste and coat onions; transfer to cooker.
3. Pour wine into skillet and scrape up any browned bits; add to cooker. Stir in potatoes, carrots, broth, salt, thyme, and bay leaf. Cover and cook on LOW for 7½ hours or on HIGH for 4 hours.
4. Add peas and heat through.

Makes 8 to 10 servings ■ Prep time: 35 minutes ■ Total time: 8 hours, 15 minutes

For complete nutritional information on this and other *Real Simple* recipes, please turn to the appendix on pages 280–283.

5 Ingredients or Less **Slow Cooker**

 QUICK TIP

An oval slow cooker
works best for this recipe
because of the shape of
the meat. If you don't own
an oval slow cooker, cut
the meat in half to fit the
one you have.

myrecipes users suggest:
- adding baby carrots or
  lima beans
- substituting red wine for
  the beer
- making soft tacos with
  any leftovers

from **Oxmoor House®**

Beer-Braised Beef

1 cup refrigerated prechopped onion
Cooking spray
1 pound boneless top round steak, trimmed
1 (14.5-ounce) can diced tomatoes with basil,
    garlic, and oregano, undrained

½ cup light beer
2 tablespoons molasses
¼ teaspoon salt

1. Place onion in a 3- to 3½-quart slow cooker coated with cooking spray.
2. Heat a large nonstick skillet over medium-high heat; coat pan with cooking
spray. Add steak; cook 3 minutes on each side or until browned. Place steak over
onion in cooker; pour tomatoes and beer over steak. Cover and cook on LOW for
8 hours or until steak is very tender.
3. Shred steak with 2 forks in slow cooker; stir in molasses and salt. Let steak
stand 10 minutes before serving.

Makes 4 servings ■ Prep time: 10 minutes ■ Total time: 8 hours, 20 minutes

For complete nutritional information on this and other Oxmoor House recipes, please turn to the appendix on pages
280–283.

GF
Gluten-Free

Slow Cooker

from **all you**

Coconut-Curry Beef

2 tablespoons vegetable oil
2 pounds beef chuck roast, cut into
   2-inch pieces
Salt
2 large onions, each cut into 8 wedges
4 garlic cloves, finely chopped

2 tablespoons finely chopped fresh ginger
1 (12-ounce) can light coconut milk
2 tablespoons packed light brown sugar
1 tablespoon curry powder
1 teaspoon cayenne pepper
1 pint cherry tomatoes

1. In a large skillet, warm oil over medium-high heat. Sprinkle beef with salt, and brown on all sides, in batches if necessary, about 8 minutes total. Transfer to slow cooker along with onions, garlic, and ginger.
2. Whisk together coconut milk, brown sugar, curry powder, and cayenne, and pour over meat. Cover and cook on LOW until meat is fork-tender, 4 to 5 hours. Stir in cherry tomatoes and let them warm and soften in stew for 15 minutes. Adjust seasonings and serve.

Makes 6 servings ▪ Prep time: 15 minutes ▪ Cook: 5 hours, 25 minutes

For complete nutritional information on this and other *All You* recipes, please turn to the appendix on pages 280–283.

> " I have made this twice now, and my family devours it. There are no leftovers with this one. I make brown rice and serve the beef over it. I leave out the tomatoes and cut the cayenne in half. Yummo!"
>
> —7475hill
> ★★★★★

SCAN THIS PHOTO
for video on how to prepare fresh ginger.

from Cooking Light

30 Minutes or Less

LC
Low-Calorie

Beef Tagine with Butternut Squash

2 teaspoons paprika
1 teaspoon ground cinnamon
¾ teaspoon salt
½ teaspoon ground ginger
½ teaspoon crushed red pepper
¼ teaspoon freshly ground black pepper
1 (1-pound) beef shoulder roast or petite tender roast, trimmed and cut into 1-inch cubes

1 tablespoon olive oil
4 shallots, quartered
4 garlic cloves, chopped
½ cup fat-free, lower-sodium chicken broth
1 (14.5-ounce) can no-salt-added diced tomatoes, undrained
3 cups (1-inch) cubed peeled butternut squash (about 1 pound)
¼ cup chopped fresh cilantro

1. Combine first 6 ingredients in a medium bowl. Add beef; toss well to coat.
2. Heat oil in a Dutch oven over medium-high heat. Add beef and shallots; cook 4 minutes or until browned, stirring occasionally. Add garlic; cook 1 minute, stirring frequently. Stir in broth and tomatoes; bring to a boil. Cook 5 minutes. Add squash; cover, reduce heat, and simmer 15 minutes or until squash is tender. Sprinkle with cilantro.

Makes 4 servings ■ Prep time: 10 minutes ■ Total time: 30 minutes

For complete nutritional information on this and other *Cooking Light* recipes, please turn to the appendix on pages 280–283.

myrecipes users suggest:
- adding 2 tablespoons ground cumin and omitting the salt
- increasing the cinnamon, paprika, and red pepper by half, using minced fresh ginger instead of ground ginger, and adding ¼ cup dried cranberries along with the squash
- using beef sirloin or venison roast instead of beef shoulder roast

 It smelled amazing as it was cooking, and my family loved it! The kids even asked for seconds."

—MeganGomez
★★★★★

Slow Cooker

from **all you**

Beef Stroganoff

¾ teaspoon salt
Black pepper
2 teaspoons paprika, divided
1½ pounds beef stew meat, cut into cubes
1 tablespoon vegetable oil
2 cups sliced shiitake mushrooms (6 ounces) or white mushrooms

3 shallots, thinly sliced
1½ cups low-sodium beef broth
½ cup sour cream
Chopped fresh dill or parsley (optional)
¾ teaspoon salt

1. Sprinkle ¾ teaspoon salt, pepper, and 1 teaspoon paprika all over beef. Warm oil in a large skillet over medium-high heat. Cook beef, stirring occasionally, until browned on all sides, about 8 minutes. Transfer meat to a slow cooker.
2. Add mushrooms, shallots, and remaining 1 teaspoon paprika to skillet; season with salt and cook for 3 minutes, stirring often. Combine broth and sour cream, pour into pan with mushrooms and shallots, and cook for 2 minutes, scraping up any browned bits from bottom of pan. Pour mixture over beef in slow cooker, cover, and cook on LOW until beef is tender, 6 hours. If desired, sprinkle with dill or parsley before serving.

Makes 4 servings ■ Prep time: 15 minutes ■ Total time: 6 hours, 15 minutes

For complete nutritional information on this and other *All You* recipes, please turn to the appendix on pages 280–283.

> **"** The meat was so tender it fell apart. I did add a little bit of flour to thicken it up, but overall it was fantastic! I have a picky son when it comes to food, and he loved it!"
>
> —5638552056
>
> ★★★★★

from *Sunset*

Brandied Cranberry Short-Rib Stew

6 pounds bone-in beef short ribs, cut into
    2-inch pieces
About 2 teaspoons kosher salt, divided
About 1 teaspoon black pepper
3 tablespoons vegetable oil, divided
3 pounds kabocha squash (1 small), seeded,
    cut into 2-inch wedges, and peeled
2 medium onions, finely chopped
⅓ cup flour
4 garlic cloves, minced

3 tablespoons Dutch-processed bittersweet
    cocoa powder or 1 square (1 ounce)
    bittersweet chocolate, chopped
5 cups reduced-sodium beef broth
½ cup brandy
½ cup dried cranberries
2 tablespoons minced candied ginger
1 tablespoon finely shredded orange zest
1½ cups fresh cranberries

1. Preheat oven to 500°. Dry ribs on paper towels and sprinkle with 1 teaspoon
each salt and pepper. In a large, heavy ovenproof pot, heat 1 tablespoon oil over
medium-high heat. In 4 batches, brown ribs all over. Transfer to a bowl.
2. Cut squash wedges crosswise, put on a baking sheet, and toss with remaining
oil. Roast until caramelized, 10 minutes. Remove from oven and lower heat to 300°.
3. Add onions and remaining 1 teaspoon salt to pot and cook over medium-high
heat, stirring often, until softened, about 3 minutes. Add flour and cook, stirring,
until deep golden brown, about 5 minutes. Stir in garlic and cocoa; cook 1 minute.
Stir in broth and brandy. Add dried cranberries, ginger, and orange zest, and
bring mixture to a boil. Return short ribs to pot, cover, and bake 2½ hours.
4. Remove pot from oven and spoon off fat. (Or chill overnight before skimming;
return to a simmer before continuing.) Stir in fresh cranberries and kabocha.
Cover and bake until kabocha is tender and meat pulls away from the bone,
about 30 minutes.

Makes 8 servings ▪ Prep time: 50 minutes ▪ Total time: 4 hours

For complete nutritional information on this and other *Sunset* recipes, please turn to the appendix on pages 280–283.

---

ask the expert

Do I have to remove the green stem in the middle of the garlic clove?

You don't have to, but you may want to. Though, it is not poisonous or toxic, that green sprout can impart a bitter flavor. It certainly indicates your garlic has been around awhile, and the clove itself may have a milder flavor.

 SCAN THIS BOX for more cooking know-how from our experts.

myrecipes users suggest:
- making the stew the night before and refrigerating, then scraping the fat off the top, reheating, and serving
- substituting a Sugar Pie pumpkin for the kabocha squash
- using ground ginger instead of candied ginger

Kid-
Friendly

Slow
Cooker

from

Tangy Asian Meatballs

1 pound ground pork
⅓ cup panko breadcrumbs
3 scallions, white and light-green parts,
   chopped
1 large egg
1 tablespoon soy sauce
1 tablespoon finely chopped fresh ginger

2 garlic cloves, finely chopped
Cooking spray
½ cup barbecue sauce
¼ cup jarred Chinese plum sauce
   or duck sauce
2 tablespoons hoisin sauce

1. Combine pork, panko, scallions, egg, soy sauce, ginger, and garlic in a large bowl; mix gently but thoroughly with your fingers. Roll into 1-inch balls.
2. Mist slow cooker with cooking spray. Add meatballs. In a small bowl, whisk together barbecue sauce, plum sauce, and hoisin sauce; pour over meatballs. Gently stir to coat.
3. Cover and cook on LOW until meatballs are cooked through, 3 to 5 hours.

Makes 4 servings ■ Prep time: 15 minutes ■ Total time: 3 hours, 15 minutes

For complete nutritional information on this and other *All You* recipes, please turn to the appendix on pages 280–283.

 This was delicious, and the ginger flavor came out even more in the leftovers the next day."

—sugarkewb
★★★★

myrecipes users suggest:
• browning the meatballs on the stovetop, then adding the sauce to the pan and simmering until the meatballs are cooked through, instead of using a slow cooker
• using ground beef instead of pork

Kid-
Friendly

 After inhaling the meat, my 4-year-old said, 'Try dipping the broccoli in the gravy!' That's a ringing endorsement if I ever heard one. We will definitely make this again."

—cesamsel

★★★★★

from CookingLight

Pork Chops with Country Gravy

¼ cup all-purpose flour (about 1 ounce)
¾ teaspoon salt
¼ teaspoon dried marjoram
¼ teaspoon dried thyme
¼ teaspoon dried rubbed sage

4 (4-ounce) boneless center-cut loin pork chops (about ¾ inch thick)
1 tablespoon butter
Cooking spray
1½ cups 1% low-fat milk

1. Lightly spoon flour into a dry measuring cup; level with a knife. Place flour, salt, marjoram, thyme, and sage in a shallow dish. Dredge pork in flour mixture, turning to coat; shake off excess. Reserve remaining flour mixture.
2. Melt butter in a large nonstick skillet coated with cooking spray over medium-high heat. Add pork to pan; cook 2 minutes on each side or until browned. Reduce heat, and cook for 10 minutes or until done, turning pork once. Remove pork from pan; keep warm.
3. Combine reserved flour mixture and milk in a small bowl, stirring with a whisk until blended. Add milk mixture to pan; place over medium-high heat. Bring to a boil, scraping pan to loosen browned bits. Reduce heat, and simmer 2 minutes or until slightly thickened, stirring constantly. Serve with chops.

Makes 4 servings ■ Prep time: 15 minutes ■ Total time: 40 minutes

For complete nutritional information on this and other *Cooking Light* recipes, please turn to the appendix on pages 280–283.

SCAN THIS PHOTO for video on how to prepare this recipe.

30 Minutes
or Less

" Ordinarily, we are not fond of sweet sauces with meat, but this was the exception. Sweet potato fries along with steamed broccoli rounded out an easy weekday dinner."

—hikerbuck
★★★★

from

Pork Chops with Apricot Sauce

Cooking spray
4 (10-ounce) center-cut, bone-in pork chops
Salt and black pepper
2 tablespoons vegetable oil

½ cup low-sodium chicken broth
½ cup strained apricot jam
2 tablespoons Dijon mustard

1. Preheat oven to 350°. Mist a baking dish with cooking spray. Season pork chops with salt and pepper. Warm oil in a large skillet over medium-high heat until hot but not smoking. Add chops and cook until nicely browned, about 3 minutes per side. Transfer chops to prepared baking dish, and bake 7 to 10 minutes or until cooked through.

2. Pour off fat from skillet and add broth. Bring to a boil over high heat, stirring with a wooden spoon or heatproof spatula to pick up any browned bits on bottom of skillet. Boil rapidly until liquid is reduced by half, 3 to 5 minutes. Add apricot jam and bring mixture back to a boil. Cook sauce, stirring, until thick and syrupy, about 2 minutes. Stir in mustard.

3. Lower heat on stove to medium and return cooked pork chops to skillet along with any accumulated juices in baking dish. Turn pork chops several times in sauce to coat. Spoon remaining sauce over chops, and serve hot.

Makes 4 servings ▪ Prep time: 10 minutes ▪ Total time: 25 minutes

For complete nutritional information on this and other *All You* recipes, please turn to the appendix on pages 280–283.

myrecipes users suggest:
- broiling the pork instead of grilling, or baking in a 350° oven for about an hour
- preparing the rub and sauce ahead of time and reheating the sauce while the pork grills
- rubbing the spice mixture over the pork the night before and refrigerating until ready to grill

" I served the pork and sauce as sliders on sweet Hawaiian rolls. I definitely will make again."

—chilipebs
★★★★★

from Cooking Light

Spice-Rubbed Pork Tenderloin with Mustard Barbecue Sauce

Sauce:
2 bacon slices, finely chopped
1 cup chopped onion
½ cup prepared yellow mustard
5 tablespoons honey
3 tablespoons ketchup
2 tablespoons cider vinegar
¼ teaspoon chili powder
¼ teaspoon ground cumin

Pork:
1 tablespoon light brown sugar
1 tablespoon smoked paprika
2 teaspoons chili powder
1 teaspoon garlic powder
1 teaspoon ground cumin
¾ teaspoon salt
½ teaspoon freshly ground black pepper
⅛ teaspoon ground red pepper
2 (1-pound) pork tenderloins, trimmed
Cooking spray

1. Prepare grill.

2. To prepare sauce, cook bacon in a medium saucepan over medium-high heat 4 minutes or until almost crisp, stirring occasionally. Add onion to pan; cook 4 minutes, stirring frequently. Add mustard and next 5 ingredients to pan, and bring to a boil. Reduce heat, and simmer for 4 minutes or until slightly thick, stirring occasionally.

3. To prepare pork, combine brown sugar and next 7 ingredients in a small bowl, stirring well; rub mixture evenly over pork. Place pork on grill rack coated with cooking spray. Grill 20 minutes or until a thermometer registers 155° (slightly pink), turning once. Let pork stand 10 minutes. Cut pork crosswise into ½-inch-thick slices. Serve with sauce.

Makes 8 servings ■ Prep time: 15 minutes ■ Total time: 50 minutes

For complete nutritional information on this and other *Cooking Light* recipes, please turn to the appendix on pages 280–283.

Gluten-Free   Slow Cooker

from Southern Living

Spicy-Sweet Ribs and Beans

2 (16-ounce) cans pinto beans, drained
4 pounds country-style pork ribs, trimmed
1 teaspoon garlic powder
½ teaspoon salt
½ teaspoon black pepper

1 medium onion, chopped
1 (10.5-ounce) jar red jalapeño jelly
1 (18-ounce) bottle hickory-flavored
  barbecue sauce
1 teaspoon green hot sauce

1. Place beans in a 5-quart slow cooker; set aside.
2. Cut ribs apart; sprinkle with garlic powder, salt, and pepper. Place ribs on a broiling pan.
3. Broil 5½ inches from heat 18 to 20 minutes or until browned, turning once. Add ribs to slow cooker, and sprinkle with onion.
4. Combine jelly, barbecue sauce, and hot sauce in a saucepan; cook over low heat until jelly melts. Pour over ribs; stir gently.
5. Cover and cook on HIGH 5 to 6 hours or on LOW 9 to 10 hours. Remove ribs. Drain bean mixture, reserving sauce. Skim fat from sauce. Arrange ribs over bean mixture; serve with sauce.

Makes 8 servings ■ Prep time: 30 minutes ■ Total time: 5 hours, 50 minutes

> " Broiling the ribs prior to putting them in the slow cooker adds so much flavor and a really nice crust on the outside of the meat. The beans were much better than canned baked beans."
>
> —Lindsayglacy
> ★★★★★

SCAN THIS PHOTO
for video on how to chop an onion.

Grill It!

❝ The red wine sauce is a definite must. We drizzled it over bread when we ran out of pork!"

—Mom2Kate

from Southern Living

Molasses Pork Tenderloin with Red Wine Sauce

1 cup reduced-sodium soy sauce
1¼ cups molasses
¼ cup fresh lemon juice
¼ cup olive oil

3 tablespoons minced fresh ginger
2 large garlic cloves, minced
3 (¾-pound) pork tenderloins
Red Wine Sauce (optional)

1. Combine first 6 ingredients in a shallow dish or heavy-duty zip-top plastic bag; add tenderloins. Cover or seal, and chill 8 hours.
2. Preheat grill to medium-high heat (350° to 400°). Remove tenderloins from marinade, discarding marinade.
3. Grill tenderloins, covered with grill lid 20 minutes or until a meat thermometer inserted into thickest portion registers 160°, turning occasionally. Meanwhile, make the Red Wine Sauce, if desired. Let meat stand 10 minutes before slicing. Serve with sauce, if desired.

Makes 6 to 8 servings ▪ Prep time: 10 minutes ▪ Total time: 8 hours, 40 minutes

Red Wine Sauce

½ small sweet onion, minced
2 tablespoons butter
½ cup dry red wine

1 (14.5-ounce) can beef broth
¼ cup water
2 tablespoons cornstarch

1. Sauté onion in butter in a large saucepan over medium-high heat 3 minutes or until browned. Add wine, and cook 3 minutes. Add broth; bring to a boil, and cook 5 minutes.
2. Stir together water and cornstarch; add to broth mixture, stirring constantly, 1 minute or until mixture thickens. Remove from heat, and serve over tenderloin.

Makes 1¼ cups ▪ Prep time: 15 minutes ▪ Total time: 15 minutes

Kid-Friendly

Slow Cooker

myrecipes users suggest:
- using pork tenderloin, beef chuck roast, or boneless chicken breasts and thighs instead of Boston butt
- making Chinese dumplings out of any leftover pork or serving it in flour tortillas

 My family didn't eat this—they inhaled it. My extremely picky daughter devoured it. The meat was flavorful and tender and even had a bit of an Indian flavor."

—cataloger

★★★★★

from CookingLight

Slow-Cooker Char Siu Pork Roast

¼ cup low-sodium soy sauce
¼ cup hoisin sauce
3 tablespoons ketchup
3 tablespoons honey
2 teaspoons bottled minced garlic
2 teaspoons grated peeled fresh ginger

1 teaspoon dark sesame oil
½ teaspoon five-spice powder
2 pounds boneless Boston butt pork roast, trimmed
½ cup fat-free, less-sodium chicken broth

1. Combine first 8 ingredients in a small bowl, stirring well with a whisk. Place in a large zip-top plastic bag. Add pork to bag; seal. Marinate in refrigerator at least 2 hours, turning occasionally.
2. Place pork and marinade in a slow cooker. Cover and cook on LOW for 8 hours.
3. Remove pork from slow cooker using a slotted spoon; place on a cutting board or work surface. Cover with aluminum foil; keep warm.
4. Add broth to sauce in slow cooker. Cover and cook on LOW for 30 minutes or until sauce thickens. Shred pork with 2 forks; serve with sauce.

Makes 8 servings ■ Prep time: 10 minutes ■ Total time: 10 hours, 40 minutes

For complete nutritional information on this and other *Cooking Light* recipes, please turn to the appendix on pages 280–283.

SCAN THIS PHOTO for a Weeknight Meal Planner.

> " What a good dinner this made! We served it over sticky rice. Tonight we will make nachos with the leftovers."
>
> —schapstick
> ★★★★

from *Sunset*

Salsa Verde Braised Pork

1 (3½-pound) bone-in pork shoulder (pork butt)
1 (15-ounce) bottle salsa verde
1 medium onion, finely chopped
3 cups reduced-sodium chicken broth
2 teaspoons cumin seeds

2 teaspoons coriander seeds
1 teaspoon dried oregano
½ cup chopped fresh cilantro, plus some leaves
Salt
Tortillas and additional salsa verde

1. Trim excess pork fat. Put meat in a large casserole or Dutch oven with salsa, onion, broth, cumin seeds, coriander seeds, and oregano. Bring to a boil over high heat; reduce heat, cover, and simmer until meat is very tender when pierced, about 3 hours.

2. Preheat oven to 375°. With 2 wide spatulas, transfer meat to a rimmed baking pan. Bake until richly browned, 30 minutes.

3. Meanwhile, skim and discard fat from pan juices. Boil juices, stirring, until reduced to 2¾ cups, 8 to 10 minutes.

4. With 2 forks, tear meat into large shreds. Add to pan and stir in chopped cilantro. Season with salt. Spoon into a serving bowl and sprinkle with cilantro leaves. Serve with tortillas and more salsa verde.

Note: To make this in the slow cooker, put trimmed pork in a 5- to 6-quart slow cooker and turn heat to HIGH. In a pan, bring salsa, onion, broth, cumin seeds, coriander seeds, and oregano to a boil. Pour over pork, cover, and cook until meat is very tender when pierced and registers at least 165° on an instant-read thermometer, at least 7 or up to 9 hours. Continue recipe with Step 2, using a large pot for Step 3.

Makes 6 servings ▪ Prep time: 20 minutes ▪ Total time: 4 hours

For complete nutritional information on this and other *Sunset* recipes, please turn to the appendix on pages 280–283.

30 Minutes or Less   **Gluten-Free** **LC Low-Calorie**

 My hubs and I fought over the last meatball. The sauce was a tad spicy—but still really good!"

—Saecca

★★★★★

from *Cooking Light*

Quick Lamb Kofta with Harissa Yogurt Sauce

Rice:
1 (3.5-ounce) bag boil-in-bag jasmine rice
1 teaspoon saffron threads
2 tablespoons thinly sliced green onions

Kofta:
2 tablespoons minced fresh cilantro
2 tablespoons grated fresh onion
2 tablespoons 2% Greek-style plain yogurt
1 teaspoon ground cumin
1 teaspoon ground coriander
1 teaspoon turmeric
2 teaspoons bottled minced garlic
½ teaspoon salt
¼ teaspoon black pepper
1 pound lean ground lamb
Cooking spray

Sauce:
½ cup 2% Greek-style plain yogurt
¼ cup chopped bottled roasted red bell pepper
1 teaspoon ground cumin
1 teaspoon ground coriander
2 teaspoons bottled minced garlic
½ teaspoon crushed red pepper
¼ teaspoon salt

1. To prepare rice, cook boil-in-bag jasmine rice and saffron in boiling water according to package directions. Drain; fluff rice with a fork. Sprinkle with green onions.

2. While rice cooks, prepare kofta. Combine cilantro and next 9 ingredients; shape into 12 oblong patties.

3. Heat a large nonstick skillet over medium-high heat. Coat pan with cooking spray. Add patties to pan; cook 10 minutes or until done, turning occasionally to brown on all sides.

4. While kofta cooks, prepare sauce. Combine ½ cup yogurt and remaining ingredients. Serve sauce with kofta and rice.

Makes 4 servings ■ Prep time: 10 minutes ■ Total time: 20 minutes

For complete nutritional information on this and other *Cooking Light* recipes, please turn to the appendix on pages 280–283.

from Cooking Light

Guinness Lamb Stew

8 teaspoons olive oil, divided
2 cups chopped onion
1 tablespoon chopped fresh thyme
1½ teaspoons chopped fresh rosemary
3 tablespoons all-purpose flour
2½ pounds boneless leg of lamb, trimmed and cut into 1-inch cubes
1 teaspoon salt, divided
¾ teaspoon freshly ground black pepper, divided

2 cups Guinness stout
1 tablespoon tomato paste
3 cups fat-free, lower-sodium beef broth
1 bay leaf
2 cups cubed peeled Yukon gold potato
2 cups 1-inch-thick diagonally sliced carrot
8 ounces baby turnips, peeled and quartered
1 tablespoon whole-grain Dijon mustard
⅓ cup chopped fresh parsley

1. Heat a large Dutch oven over medium-high heat. Add 2 teaspoons oil to pan; swirl to coat. Add onion, thyme, and rosemary; sauté for 5 minutes, stirring occasionally. Place onion mixture in a large bowl. Place flour in a shallow dish. Sprinkle lamb evenly with ½ teaspoon salt and ½ teaspoon pepper. Dredge lamb in flour, and shake off excess. Return pan to medium-high heat. Add 1 tablespoon oil to pan; swirl to coat. Add half of lamb mixture to pan; sauté for 6 minutes, turning to brown on all sides. Add browned lamb to onion mixture. Repeat the procedure with remaining lamb and remaining 1 tablespoon oil.
2. Add stout to pan; bring to a boil, scraping pan to loosen browned bits. Cook until reduced to 1 cup (about 5 minutes). Return onion mixture and lamb to pan. Stir in the tomato paste; cook 30 seconds. Add broth and bay leaf; bring to a boil. Cover, reduce heat, and simmer for 1 hour and 15 minutes, stirring occasionally. Uncover and stir in potato, carrot, and turnips. Simmer, uncovered, for 1½ hours or until meat and vegetables are tender. Stir in remaining ½ teaspoon salt, remaining ¼ teaspoon pepper, and mustard. Ladle about 1 cup stew into each of 7 bowls; sprinkle evenly with parsley.

Makes 7 servings ■ Prep time: 35 minutes ■ Total time: 3 hours, 20 minutes

For complete nutritional information on this and other *Cooking Light* recipes, please turn to the appendix on pages 280–283.

LC
Low-Calorie

SCAN THIS PHOTO
for 7 more recipes using beer.

QUICK TIP

Try another dark beer if you can't find or don't care for Guiness.

" I strayed from the original by using boneless chuck roast in place of the boneless leg of lamb."

—Laurie18
★★★★★

seafood

America adores salmon and shrimp. Favorites on MyRecipes.com include salmon that's been glazed, planked, or broiled, and shrimp that's been grilled, sautéed, or turned into burgers. We've reeled in the best of the rest as well—our users' top picks for halibut, cod, tilapia, scallops, and crab.

To use the exclusive **Scan-It/Cook-It**™ features in this chapter, look for the smartphone symbol (shown at left). For detailed instructions, please see page 7.

BROILED SALMON WITH MARMALADE-DIJON GLAZE
page 128

🕐 **30 Minutes or Less** ☺ **Kid-Friendly**

myrecipes users suggest:

- using flounder, orange roughy, halibut, black cod, or tilapia
- adding grated Parmesan to the breadcrumbs
- lining the pan with aluminum foil for easy cleanup

❝ Delicious! I didn't feel like bothering with fresh breadcrumbs, so I used panko crumbs that I had on hand. The topping was nice and crunchy.❞

—Tamcooks
★★★★

from Cooking Light

Easy Baked Fish Fillets

1½ pounds grouper or other white fish fillets
Cooking spray
1 tablespoon fresh lime juice
1 tablespoon light mayonnaise
⅛ teaspoon onion powder

⅛ teaspoon black pepper
½ cup fresh breadcrumbs
1½ tablespoons butter or stick margarine, melted
2 tablespoons chopped fresh parsley

1. Preheat oven to 425°.
2. Place fish in an 11 x 7–inch baking dish coated with cooking spray. Combine lime juice, mayonnaise, onion powder, and pepper in a small bowl, and spread over fish. Sprinkle with breadcrumbs; drizzle with butter. Bake at 425° for 20 minutes or until fish flakes easily when tested with a fork. Sprinkle with parsley.

Makes 4 servings ▪ Prep time: 5 minutes ▪ Total time: 25 minutes

For complete nutritional information on this and other *Cooking Light* recipes, please turn to the appendix on pages 280–283.

30 Minutes
or Less

myrecipes users suggest:
- using cod, tilapia, mahi mahi, halibut, or catfish instead of the red snapper fillets
- adding chopped jalapeño to the crema

" These were so good! My son, who hates fish, even chowed down on these!"

—lasvegasmomma

★★★★★

from Cooking Light

Fish Tacos with Lime-Cilantro Crema

Crema:
¼ cup thinly sliced green onions
¼ cup chopped fresh cilantro
3 tablespoons fat-free mayonnaise
3 tablespoons reduced-fat sour cream
1 teaspoon grated lime rind
1½ teaspoons fresh lime juice
¼ teaspoon salt
1 garlic clove, minced

Tacos:
1 teaspoon ground cumin
1 teaspoon ground coriander
½ teaspoon smoked paprika
¼ teaspoon ground red pepper
⅛ teaspoon salt
⅛ teaspoon garlic powder
1½ pounds red snapper fillets
Cooking spray
8 (6-inch) corn tortillas
2 cups shredded cabbage

1. Preheat oven to 425°.
2. To prepare crema, combine first 8 ingredients in a small bowl; set aside.
3. To prepare tacos, combine cumin and next 5 ingredients in a small bowl; sprinkle spice mixture evenly over both sides of fish. Place fish on a baking sheet coated with cooking spray. Bake for 9 minutes or until fish flakes easily with a fork or until desired degree of doneness. Place fish in a bowl; break into pieces with a fork. Heat tortillas according to package directions. Divide fish evenly among tortillas; top each with ¼ cup cabbage and 1 tablespoon crema.

Makes 4 servings ■ Prep time: 15 minutes ■ Total time: 25 minutes

For complete nutritional information on this and other *Cooking Light* recipes, please turn to the appendix on pages 280–283.

30 Minutes
or Less

 users suggest:
- substituting cod or mahi mahi for the halibut
- trading the pecans for pistachios
- using light cream instead of heavy cream

❝ This was easy to make and tasted absolutely delicious—would be a great dish to make for guests. I skipped the sauce and just served Dijon mustard on the side.❞

—London1

★★★★★

from COASTAL LIVING

Pecan-Crusted Halibut with Dijon Cream Sauce

1 cup all-purpose flour
½ teaspoon sea salt
¾ teaspoon freshly ground black pepper
2 teaspoons coarse-grained Dijon mustard
2 large eggs
1¼ cups pecans, finely chopped
1¼ cups fresh or dried breadcrumbs
8 (6-ounce) skinless halibut fillets
¼ cup butter
Dijon Cream Sauce

1. Combine flour, salt, and pepper in a shallow bowl. Whisk mustard and eggs in another shallow bowl. Combine pecans and breadcrumbs in a third shallow bowl.
2. Preheat oven to 350°. Dredge each halibut fillet in flour mixture, shaking off excess. Dip halibut in egg mixture to coat; drain excess. Place halibut in pecan mixture, pressing slightly to coat both sides of the fillet.
3. Melt 2 tablespoons butter over medium heat. Add fillets, in batches, and cook 2 minutes on each side or until lightly browned, adding additional butter as needed.
4. Arrange fillets on a foil-lined baking sheet. Bake at 350° for 10 minutes or until done. Serve with Dijon Cream Sauce.

Makes 8 servings ▪ Prep time: 5 minutes ▪ Total time: 30 minutes

Dijon Cream Sauce

1 cup heavy whipping cream
½ cup coarse-grained Dijon mustard
Sea salt
Freshly ground black pepper

Combine cream and mustard in a medium saucepan. Whisk constantly over low heat 3 minutes or until heated. Season to taste with salt and pepper.

Makes 1½ cups ▪ Prep time: 5 minutes ▪ Total time: 5 minutes

SCAN THIS PHOTO for video on how to prepare this recipe.

30 Minutes
or Less

from  CookingLight

Halibut with Coconut-Red Curry Sauce

2 teaspoons canola oil, divided
4 (6-ounce) halibut fillets
1 cup chopped onion
½ cup chopped green onions
1 tablespoon grated peeled fresh ginger
1 cup light coconut milk

1 tablespoon sugar
1 tablespoon fish sauce
¾ teaspoon red curry paste
½ teaspoon ground coriander
1 tablespoon chopped fresh basil
2 teaspoons fresh lime juice

1. Heat 1 teaspoon oil in a large nonstick skillet over medium-high heat. Add fish to pan; cook 5 minutes on each side or until fish flakes easily when tested with a fork or until desired degree of doneness. Remove fish from pan; keep warm.
2. Add remaining 1 teaspoon oil to pan. Add onion, green onions, and ginger; sauté 2 minutes. Stir in coconut milk and next 4 ingredients. Bring to a boil; cook 1 minute. Remove from heat. Stir in basil and lime juice.

Makes 4 servings ■ Prep time: 15 minutes ■ Total time: 30 minutes

For complete nutritional information on this and other *Cooking Light* recipes, please turn to the appendix on pages 280–283.

> " All three of my kids under the age of 5 usually balk at fish. They ate every bit! My husband said I could make this once a week it was so yummy. Positively outstanding!"

—GJohnson

myrecipes users suggest:
• substituting mahi mahi or tilapia for halibut
• using chicken instead of fish
• doubling the ginger and substituting 1 tablespoon curry powder for the red curry paste

ask the expert

How can I cook fish without smelling up my whole house?

There are three things you can do to help avoid the dreaded "fish stink."

First, make sure you are cooking really fresh fish. This is especially important with oilier fish, which tend to be more odorific.

Second, open the window or turn on the fan before you start cooking.

Finally, if all else fails and your house smells, simmer white vinegar on the stove until the smell goes away.

SCAN THIS BOX for more cooking know-how from our experts.

" Our family, from 4 years old to 55 years old, loves this. I triple the sauce for 9 fillets and serve over roasted garlic couscous."

—pamsy10

★★★★★

 myrecipes users suggest:
• substituting capers for the green peppercorns

SCAN THIS PHOTO for 6 more popular recipes using tilapia.

from *Cooking Light*

Sautéed Tilapia with Lemon-Peppercorn Pan Sauce

¾ cup fat-free, less-sodium chicken broth
¼ cup fresh lemon juice
1½ teaspoons drained brine-packed green peppercorns, lightly crushed
3 teaspoons butter, divided
1 teaspoon vegetable oil

2 (6-ounce) tilapia or sole fillets
¼ teaspoon salt
¼ teaspoon freshly ground black pepper
¼ cup all-purpose flour
Lemon wedges (optional)

1. Combine first 3 ingredients.
2. Melt 1 teaspoon butter with oil in a large nonstick skillet over low heat.
3. While butter melts, sprinkle fish fillets with salt and pepper. Place flour in a shallow dish. Dredge fillets in flour; shake off excess flour.
4. Increase heat to medium-high; heat 2 minutes or until butter turns golden brown. Add fillets to pan; sauté 3 minutes on each side or until fish flakes easily when tested with a fork. Remove fillets from pan. Add broth mixture to pan, scraping to loosen browned bits. Bring to a boil; cook until reduced to ½ cup (about 3 minutes). Remove from heat. Stir in remaining 2 teaspoons butter with a whisk. Serve sauce over fillets. Garnish with lemon wedges, if desired.

Makes 2 servings ▪ Prep time: 25 minutes ▪ Total time: 30 minutes

For complete nutritional information on this and other *Cooking Light* recipes, please turn to the appendix on pages 280–283.

30 Minutes or Less Gluten-Free Grill It! Low-Calorie

from Cooking Light

Snapper with Grilled Mango Salsa

6 (½-inch-thick) mango wedges (1 mango)
3 (¼-inch-thick) slices red onion
2 teaspoons olive oil, divided
Cooking spray
¼ cup diced peeled avocado
1 tablespoon chopped fresh mint
2 teaspoons fresh lemon juice

½ teaspoon salt, divided
¼ teaspoon freshly ground black pepper, divided
4 (6-ounce) yellowtail snapper or other firm white fish fillets
Fresh mint sprigs (optional)

1. Preheat grill to medium-high heat.
2. Brush mango and onion with 1 teaspoon oil. Place mango and onion on grill rack coated with cooking spray; cover and grill 3 minutes on each side or until tender. Chop mango and onion. Combine mango, onion, avocado, chopped mint, lemon juice, ¼ teaspoon salt, and ⅛ teaspoon pepper in a medium bowl.
3. Brush fish with remaining 1 teaspoon oil; sprinkle with remaining ¼ teaspoon salt and ⅛ teaspoon pepper. Place fish on grill rack; grill 4 minutes on each side or until fish flakes easily when tested with a fork or until desired degree of doneness. Serve with mango salsa. Garnish with mint sprigs, if desired.

Makes 4 servings ▪ Prep time: 15 minutes ▪ Total time: 30 minutes

For complete nutritional information on this and other *Cooking Light* recipes, please turn to the appendix on pages 280–283.

myrecipes users suggest:
- adding a chopped jalapeño or chopped pineapple to the salsa
- grilling the avocado before dicing it

 Instead of grilling it, I made this recipe completely on the stove with a skillet. It turned out wonderful."

—Jessica87
★★★★★

5
5 Ingredients
or Less

30 Minutes
or Less

Kid-
Friendly

> **Really fantastic!
> My edits: Use
> grouper, and add a
> little unsalted butter
> and brown sugar to
> your pan."**
>
> —goodsgirl

★★★★

QUICK TIP

Try this pecan breading on other fish, such as cod, halibut, or catfish.

from CookingLight

Pecan-Crusted Trout

¼ cup pecan halves
¼ cup panko (Japanese breadcrumbs)
1 tablespoon olive oil, divided

4 (6-ounce) rainbow trout fillets, halved
¼ teaspoon salt
¼ teaspoon freshly ground black pepper

1. Place pecans in a mini chopper or food processor; pulse until pecans are finely ground. Combine pecans and panko in a shallow dish.
2. Heat 1½ teaspoons oil in a large nonstick skillet over medium-high heat. Sprinkle fish evenly with salt and pepper. Dredge tops of fish in nut mixture, pressing gently to adhere. Place half of fish, breading side down, in pan; cook 4 minutes or until browned. Turn fish over; cook 4 minutes or until fish flakes easily with a fork or until desired degree of doneness. Remove fish from pan; cover and keep warm. Repeat procedure with remaining 1½ teaspoons oil and remaining fish.

Makes 4 servings ▪ Prep time: 10 minutes ▪ Total time: 30 minutes

For complete nutritional information on this and other *Cooking Light* recipes, please turn to the appendix on pages 280–283.

30 Minutes or Less **Gluten-Free** **Low-Calorie**

from **REALSIMPLE**

Chili-Roasted Cod

Cooking spray
1½ pounds fresh cod fillets
1 teaspoon chili powder
½ teaspoon dried oregano

½ teaspoon salt
2 tablespoons butter
¼ teaspoon ground cumin
Juice of 1 lime

1. Preheat oven to 450°. Lightly coat a roasting pan with cooking spray. Arrange cod fillets skin side down. Sprinkle with chili powder, oregano, and salt. Roast 5 to 7 minutes or until cod is just opaque and flakes easily when tested with a fork.
2. Meanwhile, melt butter in a small skillet over medium-low heat. Cook, swirling constantly, just until it begins to brown. Add cumin and lime juice and continue to cook, swirling, 1 minute longer.
3. Remove cod from oven. Drizzle cumin-lime butter over cod. Serve.

Makes 4 servings ■ Prep time: 10 minutes ■ Total time: 15 minutes

For complete nutritional information on this and other *Real Simple* recipes, please turn to the appendix on pages 280–283.

For complete nutritional information on this and other *Real Simple* recipes, please turn to the appendix on pages 280–283.

ask the expert

How can I tell when fish is cooked enough but not overcooked?

Check for doneness when the fish looks like it is no longer translucent, when it feels somewhat more firm when you press the top center with your fingertip, and/or when it has cooked the equivalent of about 8 minutes per inch, if you can't tell at all from the first two. (That happens, for example, when you bake fish smothered in tomatoes, onions, and olives: You can't really see the fish well.)

The ultimate check for doneness is to peek into the center of the thickest part of the fish. To do this and not serve fish with a big gash mark in the center, slide a butter knife straight down through one of the existing seams in the flesh (those little parallel lines that run through the fish). Gently pry the flesh back and determine if the fish has just lost its translucency. You should see lots of moisture, but the fish will be nearly opaque. If you see just the tiniest bit of translucency in the center, take it off the heat—by the time you serve it, the fish will be cooked through.

 SCAN THIS BOX for more cooking know-how from our experts.

Gluten-Free

Grill It!

QUICK TIP

If you aren't able to grill it, here's an oven method. Prepare the salmon as directed, then roast on the cedar plank in a 325° oven for about 25 minutes.

from **REALSIMPLE**

Cedar-Plank Salmon

1 (2-pound) salmon fillet, skin on
1 cedar plank, soaked in water 20 minutes
½ cup brown sugar

2 tablespoons canola oil
1 tablespoon dried thyme leaves
1 teaspoon cayenne pepper

1. Preheat a gas grill to high; adjust to medium-low after 15 minutes. (If cooking over charcoal, allow coals to burn until they are covered with white ash.) Place salmon, skin side down, on cedar plank.
2. Combine brown sugar, oil, thyme, and cayenne in a bowl. Spread over salmon. Place planked salmon on grilling grate and cook, with grill covered, about 40 minutes or just until surface fat begins to turn white.

Makes 4 servings ■ Prep time: 10 minutes ■ Total time: 1 hour, 5 minutes

For complete nutritional information on this and other *Real Simple* recipes, please turn to the appendix on pages 280–283.

" This was our first grilled-fish-on-a-plank experience, and we'll definitely repeat it. I had a 1.3-lb fillet of wild salmon, so I halved the amount of brown sugar. This will be a go-to salmon rub recipe for us going forward!"

—kvluv2cook
★★★★★

SCAN THIS PHOTO for video on how to cook fish on a plank.

Kid-
Friendly

5 Ingredients
or Less

30 Minutes
or Less

Gluten-
Free

" I didn't have any orange marmalade, so I used a mango spread instead. It turned out great!"

—4Joanie4

★★★★★

from Cooking Light

Broiled Salmon with Marmalade-Dijon Glaze

½ cup orange marmalade
1 tablespoon Dijon mustard
½ teaspoon garlic powder
½ teaspoon salt

¼ teaspoon black pepper
⅛ teaspoon ground ginger
4 (6-ounce) salmon fillets
Cooking spray

1. Preheat broiler.
2. Combine first 6 ingredients in a small bowl, stirring well. Place fish on a jelly-roll pan coated with cooking spray. Brush half of marmalade mixture over fish; broil 6 minutes. Brush fish with remaining marmalade mixture; broil for 2 minutes or until fish flakes easily when tested with a fork or until desired degree of doneness.

Makes 4 servings ■ Prep time: 5 minutes ■ Total time: 15 minutes

For complete nutritional information on this and other *Cooking Light* recipes, please turn to the appendix on pages 280–283.

from CookingLight

Grilled Orange-and-Bourbon Salmon

¼ cup bourbon
¼ cup fresh orange juice
¼ cup low-sodium soy sauce
¼ cup packed brown sugar
¼ cup chopped green onions

3 tablespoons chopped fresh chives
2 tablespoons fresh lemon juice
2 garlic cloves, chopped
4 (6-ounce) salmon fillets (about 1 inch thick)
Cooking spray

1. Combine first 8 ingredients in a large zip-top plastic bag, and add salmon to bag. Seal and marinate in refrigerator 1½ hours, turning bag occasionally.
2. Prepare grill or broiler.
3. Remove salmon from bag. Transfer marinade to a heat-proof bowl, and microwave on HIGH 3 minutes or until heated through. Place salmon on a grill rack or broiler pan coated with cooking spray. Cook 6 minutes on each side or until fish flakes easily when tested with a fork, basting frequently with reserved and heated marinade.

Makes 4 servings ■ Prep time: 15 minutes ■ Total time: 1 hour, 45 minutes

For complete nutritional information on this and other *Cooking Light* recipes, please turn to the appendix on pages 280–283.

myrecipes users suggest:
• using halibut or Hawaiian opah instead of salmon

" This is beyond outstanding. It is such an elegant entrée. I have used this recipe no less than 5 times this year alone—a list topper when I want to serve fish."

—Camillka
★★★★★

SCAN THIS PHOTO for a seafood grilling guide and recipes.

5 Ingredients or Less

30 Minutes or Less

from **Oxmoor House®**

Maple-Glazed Salmon

1 tablespoon maple syrup
1 tablespoon hoisin sauce
1 teaspoon Dijon mustard

¼ teaspoon coarsely ground black pepper
2 (6-ounce) salmon fillets (about 1 inch thick)
Cooking spray

1. Preheat broiler.
2. Combine first 4 ingredients in a small bowl; stir with a whisk.
3. Place salmon, skin side down, on a broiler pan coated with cooking spray. Brush with maple mixture. Broil 10 to 12 minutes or until fish flakes easily when tested with a fork, brushing with maple mixture after 5 minutes and again after 10 minutes.

Makes 2 servings ■ Prep time: 5 minutes ■ Total time: 20 minutes

For complete nutritional information on this and other Oxmoor House recipes, please turn to the appendix on pages 280–283.

SCAN THIS PHOTO for a Weeknight Meal Planner.

30 Minutes
or Less

SCAN THIS PHOTO
for video on how to
prepare this recipe.

" This was my first attempt at fresh salmon burgers, and they turned out perfect! They were a big hit with the family and a very healthy dish."

—JoJoA0808

from Cooking Light

Fresh Salmon-Cilantro Burgers

Mayonnaise:
¼ cup reduced-fat mayonnaise
1 tablespoon chopped fresh cilantro
1 tablespoon fresh lime juice
⅛ teaspoon salt
⅛ teaspoon freshly ground black pepper

Burgers:
1 (1-pound) salmon fillet, skinned and cut into 1-inch pieces
¼ cup dry breadcrumbs
2 tablespoons fresh cilantro leaves

2 tablespoons chopped green onions
1 tablespoon chopped seeded jalapeño pepper
2 tablespoons fresh lime juice
½ teaspoon salt
¼ teaspoon freshly ground black pepper
Cooking spray
4 (1½-ounce) hamburger buns with sesame seeds, toasted
12 (¼-inch-thick) slices English cucumber
4 leaf lettuce leaves

1. Combine first 5 ingredients in a small bowl; cover and chill.
2. Place salmon in a food processor; pulse until coarsely chopped. Add breadcrumbs and next 6 ingredients; pulse 4 times or until well blended. Divide salmon mixture into 4 equal portions, shaping each into a ¾-inch-thick patty.
3. Heat a grill pan over medium-high heat. Coat pan with cooking spray. Add patties to pan; cook 2 minutes. Carefully turn patties over; cook 2 minutes or until done.
4. Spread about 1 tablespoon mayonnaise mixture over bottom half of each hamburger bun. Top each serving with 1 salmon patty, 3 cucumber slices, 1 lettuce leaf, and top half of bun.

Makes 4 servings ▪ Prep time: 10 minutes ▪ Total time: 20 minutes

For complete nutritional information on this and other *Cooking Light* recipes, please turn to the appendix on pages 280–283.

from CookingLight

Crab Cakes with Spicy Rémoulade

Make the rémoulade
1 day ahead to allow the flavors to marry.

QUICK TIP

myrecipes users suggest:
- substituting green onions for the chives
- making appetizer-size crab cakes using a 2-tablespoon coffee measure
- adding more mustard and red pepper to the rémoulade

Crab cakes:
2 tablespoons finely chopped fresh chives
1 tablespoon chopped fresh flat-leaf parsley
1½ tablespoons canola-based mayonnaise
½ teaspoon grated lemon rind
1 tablespoon fresh lemon juice
¼ teaspoon freshly ground black pepper
⅛ teaspoon ground red pepper
1 large egg
⅓ cup panko (Japanese breadcrumbs)
1 pound lump crabmeat, drained and shell pieces removed
1 tablespoon olive oil, divided

Rémoulade:
¼ cup canola-based mayonnaise
1 tablespoon chopped shallots
1½ tablespoons capers, drained and chopped
2 teaspoons Creole mustard
1 teaspoon fresh lemon juice
¼ teaspoon ground red pepper
⅛ teaspoon kosher salt

1. To prepare crab cakes, combine first 8 ingredients. Add panko and crab, tossing gently to combine. Cover and refrigerate 30 minutes.
2. Fill a ⅓-cup dry measuring cup with crab mixture. Invert onto work surface; gently pat into a ¾-inch-thick patty. Repeat procedure with remaining crab mixture, forming 8 cakes.
3. Heat 1½ teaspoons oil in a large skillet over medium-high heat. Add 4 crab cakes to pan; cook 4 minutes or until bottoms are golden. Carefully turn cakes; cook 4 minutes or until bottoms are golden and crab cakes are thoroughly heated. Remove cakes from pan; keep warm. Wipe pan dry with paper towels. Heat remaining 1½ teaspoons oil. Repeat procedure with remaining 4 crab cakes.
4. To prepare rémoulade, combine ¼ cup mayonnaise and remaining ingredients in a small bowl; stir with a whisk. Serve with crab cakes.

Makes 4 servings ■ Prep time: 15 minutes ■ Total time: 1 hour

For complete nutritional information on this and other *Cooking Light* recipes, please turn to the appendix on pages 280–283.

30 Minutes or Less **LC Low-Calorie**

 Excellent and simple recipe! If you have to use previously frozen scallops, pat them dry. This will keep the scallops from steaming in the pan and will give you a good sear."

—combatTVgirl

★★★★★

from CookingLight

Seared Scallops with Warm Tuscan Beans

2 tablespoons olive oil, divided
1½ pounds sea scallops
¼ teaspoon salt
1 cup prechopped onion
⅛ teaspoon crushed red pepper
2 garlic cloves, minced

¼ cup dry white wine
1 cup fat-free, less-sodium chicken broth
1 (19-ounce) can cannellini beans or other white beans, rinsed and drained
1 (6-ounce) package fresh baby spinach
2 tablespoons chopped fresh basil

1. Heat 1 tablespoon oil in a large nonstick skillet over medium-high heat. Sprinkle scallops evenly with salt. Add scallops to pan; cook 2 minutes on each side or until done. Remove scallops from pan; keep warm.
2. Add remaining 1 tablespoon oil and onion to pan; sauté 2 minutes. Add red pepper and garlic; cook 20 seconds, stirring constantly. Stir in wine; cook 1 minute or until most of liquid evaporates. Stir in broth and beans; cook 2 minutes. Add spinach; cook 1 minute or until spinach wilts. Remove from heat; stir in basil.

Makes 4 servings ▪ Prep time: 15 minutes ▪ Total time: 20 minutes

For complete nutritional information on this and other *Cooking Light* recipes, please turn to the appendix on pages 280–283.

SCAN THIS PHOTO for video on how to prepare this recipe.

from *Southern Living*

Cajun Shrimp Casserole

2 pounds large fresh shrimp
¼ cup butter
1 small red onion, chopped
½ cup chopped red bell pepper
½ cup chopped yellow bell pepper
½ cup chopped green bell pepper
4 garlic cloves, minced
2 cups fresh or frozen sliced okra
1 tablespoon lemon juice

1½ teaspoons salt
1 (10.75-ounce) can cream of shrimp soup
½ cup dry white wine
1 tablespoon soy sauce
½ teaspoon cayenne pepper
3 cups cooked long-grain rice
¼ cup grated Parmesan cheese
Garnishes: quartered lemon slices, fresh
   flat-leaf parsley sprigs

1. Peel shrimp; devein, if desired. Preheat oven to 350°.
2. Melt butter in large skillet over medium-high heat. Add onion and next 3 ingredients; sauté 7 minutes or until tender. Add garlic, and sauté 1 minute. Stir in okra, lemon juice, and salt; sauté 5 minutes. Add shrimp, and cook 3 minutes or until shrimp turn pink. Stir in soup and next 4 ingredients until blended. Pour into a lightly greased 11 x 7–inch baking dish. Sprinkle evenly with Parmesan cheese.
3. Bake at 350° for 15 to 20 minutes or until casserole is bubbly and cheese is lightly browned. Garnish, if desired.

Note: To make ahead, prepare casserole as directed, omitting Parmesan cheese; do not bake. Cover tightly, and freeze. Let stand at room temperature 30 minutes before baking. Bake, covered, at 350° for 50 minutes. Uncover; sprinkle evenly with Parmesan, and bake 10 more minutes or until cheese is lightly browned.

Makes 6 servings ■ Prep time: 20 minutes ■ Total time: 35 minutes

ask the expert

Is it necessary to devein shrimp?

There is no good health reason to remove the vein from fresh shrimp. Contrary to what you may have heard, the vein's color comes from the sediment on which the shrimp feeds: It is not a concentrated source of contaminants, according to Tim Fitzgerald, Senior Policy Analyst at the Environmental Defense Fund.

However, many people find it unsightly, and removing it is an aesthetic decision. In very large shrimp, the veins tend to be more visually prominent and may also contain bits of gritty sand: In that case they should certainly be removed.

SCAN THIS BOX
for more cooking
know-how from
our experts.

SCAN THIS PHOTO
for a video on how to
zest citrus.

30 Minutes or Less Gluten-Free Grill It! Low-Calorie

Mojito Shrimp

1 to 1½ pounds peeled, deveined shrimp
   (21 to 30 per pound, tails on)
Mojito Marinade

2 tablespoons fresh lime juice
Fresh mint sprigs

1. Prepare a gas or charcoal grill for high heat. (Grill is ready when you can hold your hand 1 to 2 inches above cooking grate only 1 to 2 seconds.) Meanwhile, put shrimp in a 1-gallon resealable plastic bag and pour in marinade. Seal and marinate at room temperature 15 to 20 minutes.
2. Remove shrimp, reserving marinade. Thread shrimp onto 6 or 7 (10- to 14-inch) metal or bamboo skewers.
3. Arrange shrimp on grill and baste with marinade (dab some mint and shallot from marinade onto shrimp); close lid. Cook until shrimp are just beginning to brown, 1 to 2 minutes. Turn shrimp over, baste again, and close lid. Cook 1 to 2 minutes until browned but still moist in center (cut to check). Transfer shrimp to a platter, drizzle with lime juice, and garnish with mint sprigs.

Makes 4 to 6 servings ▪ Prep time: 15 minutes ▪ Total time: 25 minutes

Mojito Marinade

20 fresh mint leaves, chopped
⅓ cup sugar
1 shallot, thinly sliced
⅓ cup light rum

3 tablespoons fresh lime juice
1 tablespoon vegetable oil
1 teaspoon grated lime zest
1 teaspoon coarse kosher salt

1. In a medium bowl, combine mint, sugar, and shallot. Pound with a wooden spoon to crush coarsely.
2. Whisk in rum, lime juice, oil, lime zest, and salt. Whisk until salt dissolves.

Makes 1½ cups ▪ Prep time: 5 minutes ▪ Total time: 5 minutes

For complete nutritional information on this and other *Sunset* recipes, please turn to the appendix on pages 280–283.

 QUICK TIP

Don't over-marinate
or the rum and lime juice will "cook" the shrimp and ruin their texture.

> " I cooked these on a grill pan, and the sugar and shallots caramelized, which I think made them even better."

—Cansas
★★★★★

myrecipes users suggest:

- using chicken andouille, turkey sausage, or chorizo instead of regular andouille
- substituting frozen crawfish tails for the shrimp
- adding cayenne and chopped fresh cilantro to taste

    Very delicious!
Not too spicy—
my whole family
(including four kids)
'yummed' it right up!"

—Lorraine34

★★★★★

from CookingLight

Jambalaya with Shrimp and Andouille Sausage

1 tablespoon olive oil
1 cup chopped onion
1 cup chopped red bell pepper
1 tablespoon minced garlic
6 ounces andouille sausage, sliced
1 cup uncooked long-grain white rice
1 teaspoon paprika
1 teaspoon freshly ground black pepper
1 teaspoon dried oregano
½ teaspoon onion powder
½ teaspoon dried thyme

¼ teaspoon garlic salt
1 bay leaf
2 cups fat-free, less-sodium chicken broth
¾ cup water
1 tablespoon tomato paste
½ teaspoon hot pepper sauce
1 (14.5-ounce) can no salt-added diced tomatoes, undrained
½ pound peeled, deveined medium shrimp
2 tablespoons chopped fresh parsley

1. Heat oil in a large Dutch oven over medium-high heat. Add onion, bell pepper, garlic, and sausage; sauté 5 minutes or until vegetables are tender.
2. Add rice and next 7 ingredients; cook 2 minutes. Add broth, water, tomato paste, hot pepper sauce, and tomatoes; bring to a boil. Cover, reduce heat, and simmer 20 minutes. Add shrimp; cook 5 minutes. Let stand 5 minutes. Discard bay leaf. Stir in parsley.

Makes 4 servings ■ Prep time: 10 minutes ■ Total time: 45 minutes

For complete nutritional information on this and other *Cooking Light* recipes, please turn to the appendix on pages 280–283.

30 Minutes or Less **Kid-Friendly**

from COASTAL LIVING

Cheesy Shrimp and Grits

3 cups chicken broth
1 cup uncooked quick-cooking grits
½ teaspoon salt
¼ teaspoon freshly ground pepper
2 tablespoons butter
2 cups (8 ounces) shredded Cheddar cheese
6 slices bacon, chopped

2 pounds medium shrimp, peeled and deveined
1 tablespoon fresh lemon juice
2 teaspoons Worcestershire sauce
2 tablespoons chopped fresh parsley
6 green onions, chopped
2 garlic cloves, minced

1. Bring broth to a boil over medium-high heat; stir in grits. Cook, stirring occasionally, 5 to 7 minutes or until thickened. Remove from heat; stir in salt and next 3 ingredients. Set aside, and keep warm.
2. Cook bacon in a large nonstick skillet over medium-high heat 3 minutes or until crisp; remove bacon from pan.
3. Cook shrimp in same pan over medium-high heat 3 minutes or until almost pink, stirring occasionally. Add lemon juice and next 4 ingredients, and cook 3 minutes. Stir in bacon.
4. Spoon grits onto individual plates or into shallow bowls; top with shrimp mixture. Serve immediately.

Makes 4 servings ■ Prep time: 10 minutes ■ Total time: 25 minutes

myrecipes users suggest:
• cutting the cheese back to ¾ cup
• using smoked Gouda instead of Cheddar

" This is one of the best dishes my husband and I have ever made. I never thought I cared much for grits, but this recipe changed my mind."

—GinnieHand01
★★★★★

Grill It!

from Southern Living

Shrimp Burgers with Sweet 'n' Spicy Tartar Sauce

1¼ pounds medium-size raw shrimp
   (31/40 count)
Cooking spray
1 large egg, lightly beaten
1 tablespoon mayonnaise
2 teaspoons lemon juice
½ teaspoon salt
⅛ teaspoon ground red pepper
3 tablespoons finely chopped celery

2 tablespoons chopped green onion
1 tablespoon chopped fresh parsley
1¼ cups crushed cornbread crackers
   (about 1 sleeve or 24 crackers)
4 Kaiser rolls with poppy seeds, split
Sweet 'n' Spicy Tartar Sauce
4 Bibb lettuce leaves
Garnish: grilled lemon halves

1. Peel shrimp; devein, if desired. Cut each shrimp into thirds.
2. Line a 15 x 10–inch jelly-roll pan with aluminum foil. Coat with cooking spray.
3. Stir together egg and next 4 ingredients until blended; stir in celery, green onion, and parsley. Fold in shrimp and cracker crumbs (mixture will be very thick). Shape into 4 (4-inch-wide, 1-inch-thick) patties. Place patties on prepared pan. Cover and chill 1 to 24 hours. Transfer to freezer, and freeze 30 minutes.
4. Coat cold cooking grate of grill with cooking spray, and place on grill. Preheat grill to 350° to 400° (medium-high) heat. Grill burgers, covered with grill lid, 4 to 5 minutes or until burgers lift easily from cooking grate using a large spatula. Turn burgers, and grill 4 to 5 minutes or until shrimp turn pink and burgers are cooked through and lightly crisp.
5. Grill buns, cut sides down, 1 to 2 minutes or until lightly toasted. Serve burgers on buns with Sweet 'n' Spicy Tartar Sauce and lettuce. Garnish, if desired.

Note: We tested with Keebler Town House Bistro Corn Bread Crackers.

Makes 4 servings ▪ Prep time: 25 minutes ▪ Total time: 2 hours, 5 minutes

Sweet 'n' Spicy Tartar Sauce

1 cup mayonnaise
2 tablespoons chopped fresh parsley
2 tablespoons horseradish

1½ teaspoons Cajun seasoning
1½ teaspoons lemon juice
¼ teaspoon paprika

Stir together all ingredients in a bowl. Cover and chill 30 minutes to 24 hours.

Makes about 1⅓ cup ▪ Prep time: 5 minutes ▪ Total time: 35 minutes

---

myrecipes users suggest:
- substituting round, buttery crackers for cornbread crackers
- baking in a 350° oven instead of grilling
- serving on French bread instead of buns

I made these into sliders instead of full-sized burgers. My family loved them, and I would definitely make them again. The Sweet 'n' Spicy Tartar Sauce also makes a good dip for fries."

—KyGirl1981
★★★★★

SCAN THIS PHOTO
for 7 more recipes
using shrimp.

meatless mains

Here's where to turn when you're in a veggie state of mind: our top-ranked meat-free dinner recipes. Whether you want to please a vegetarian guest or add a "meatless Monday" option to your repertoire, we've got you covered. Find even more meatless options in the soup and pasta chapters.

 To use the exclusive **Scan-It/Cook-It**™ features in this chapter, look for the smartphone symbol (shown at left). For detailed instructions, please see page 7.

**SUMMER LEMON-
VEGETABLE RISOTTO**
page 159

LC
Low-Calorie

→
Make-Ahead

from CookingLight.

Black Bean Burrito Bake

1 (7-ounce) can chipotle chiles in adobo sauce
½ cup reduced-fat sour cream
1 (15-ounce) can black beans, rinsed and drained, divided
1 cup frozen whole-kernel corn, thawed

4 (8-inch) flour tortillas
Cooking spray
1 cup bottled salsa
½ cup (2 ounces) shredded Monterey Jack cheese

1. Preheat oven to 350°.
2. Remove one chile from can. Chop chile. Reserve remaining adobo sauce and chiles for another use. Combine sour cream and chile in a medium bowl; let stand 10 minutes.
3. Place half of beans in a food processor; process until finely chopped. Add chopped beans, remaining beans, and corn to sour cream mixture.
4. Spoon ½ cup bean mixture down the center of each tortilla. Roll up tortillas; place, seam side down, in an 11 x 7–inch baking dish coated with cooking spray. Spread salsa over tortillas; sprinkle with cheese. Cover and bake at 350° for 20 minutes or until thoroughly heated.

Note: To make ahead, assemble as directed (up to baking) up to 8 hours in advance and refrigerate; bring it back to room temperature before baking.

Makes 4 servings ■ Prep time: 20 minutes ■ Total time: 40 minutes

For complete nutritional information on this and other *Cooking Light* recipes, please turn to the appendix on pages 280–283.

SCAN THIS PHOTO for video on how to prepare this recipe.

Low-Calorie   Slow Cooker

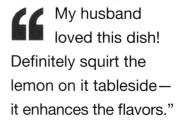 My husband loved this dish! Definitely squirt the lemon on it tableside—it enhances the flavors."

—drm0426

★★★★★

from Cooking Light

Vegetable and Chickpea Curry

1 tablespoon olive oil
1½ cups chopped onion
1 cup (¼-inch-thick) slices carrot
1 tablespoon curry powder
1 teaspoon brown sugar
1 teaspoon grated peeled fresh ginger
2 garlic cloves, minced
1 serrano chile, seeded and minced
3 cups cooked chickpeas (garbanzo beans)
1½ cups cubed peeled baking potato

1 cup diced green bell pepper
1 cup (1-inch) cut green beans
½ teaspoon salt
¼ teaspoon black pepper
⅛ teaspoon ground red pepper
1 (14.5-ounce) can diced tomatoes, undrained
1 (14-ounce) can vegetable broth
3 cups fresh baby spinach
1 cup light coconut milk
6 lemon wedges

1. Heat oil in a large nonstick skillet over medium heat. Add onion and carrot; cover and cook 5 minutes or until tender. Add curry powder, sugar, ginger, garlic, and chile; cook 1 minute, stirring constantly.
2. Place onion mixture in a 5-quart slow cooker. Stir in chickpeas and next 8 ingredients. Cover and cook on HIGH 6 hours or until vegetables are tender. Add spinach and coconut milk; stir until spinach wilts. Serve with lemon wedges.

Makes 6 servings ■ Prep time: 15 minutes ■ Total time: 6 hours, 15 minutes

For complete nutritional information on this and other *Cooking Light* recipes, please turn to the appendix on pages 280–283.

Low-Calorie

Make-Ahead

SCAN THIS PHOTO
for video on how to
cut a pineapple.

 QUICK TIP

Purchase precut,
fresh pineapple in the produce section to save time.

" This dish has wonderful flavors. I've made it twice, and my meat-eating boyfriend and his vegetarian sister both love it as much as I do."

—GBlondieP

from CookingLight

Cuban Black Bean Patties with Pineapple Rice

Rice:
1 (3.5-ounce) bag boil-in-bag long-grain rice
2 teaspoons butter
1 cup diced fresh pineapple
2 tablespoons chopped fresh cilantro
¼ teaspoon salt
Patties:
2 cups rinsed, drained canned black beans
    (1 [15-ounce] can), divided
½ teaspoon bottled minced garlic

¼ teaspoon ground cumin
⅛ teaspoon salt
1 large egg white
½ cup (2 ounces) shredded Monterey Jack
    cheese with jalapeño peppers
¼ cup chopped red onion
¼ cup cornmeal
Cooking spray
¼ cup reduced-fat sour cream

1. To prepare rice, cook rice according to package directions, omitting salt and fat. Drain; place rice in a large bowl. Melt butter in a nonstick skillet over medium-high heat. Add pineapple; sauté 4 minutes or just until pineapple begins to brown. Add pineapple mixture, cilantro, and ¼ teaspoon salt to rice in bowl; cover and keep warm. Wipe pan clean with paper towels.
2. To prepare patties, place 1½ cups beans, garlic, cumin, and ⅛ teaspoon salt in a bowl; partially mash with a fork. Place remaining ½ cup beans and egg white in a food processor; process 30 seconds or until well combined. Add bean puree to mashed beans in bowl, and stir until combined. Add cheese and onion to bean mixture; stir until combined. Divide bean mixture into 4 equal portions, shaping each into a ½-inch-thick patty. Place cornmeal in a shallow dish. Dredge both sides of each patty in cornmeal.
3. Heat pan over medium-high heat. Coat pan with cooking spray. Add patties; cook 3 minutes on each side or until browned. Spoon about ½ cup rice onto each of 4 plates; top each serving with 1 patty and 1 tablespoon sour cream.

Note: To make ahead, assemble and dredge the patties as directed; cover and refrigerate up to 8 hours. Continue with step 3 when ready to serve.

Makes 4 servings ■ Prep time: 40 minutes ■ Total time: 40 minutes

For complete nutritional information on this and other *Cooking Light* recipes, please turn to the appendix on pages 280–283.

LC
Low-Calorie

Make-Ahead

Slow Cooker

from *Sunset*

Moroccan Vegetable Stew

2 tablespoons olive oil
3 garlic cloves, peeled and crushed
   with the side of a knife
1 teaspoon ground coriander
1 teaspoon ground cumin
½ teaspoon cayenne pepper
¼ teaspoon ground cinnamon
5 cups vegetable broth
4 carrots (12 ounces total), peeled
   and cut into ½-inch lengths

2½ cups diced peeled eggplant
2½ cups (½-inch-thick) sliced zucchini
2 cups cauliflower florets
1 cup diced onion (about 5 ounces)
2 (14.5-ounce) cans stewed tomatoes
1 (15-ounce) can garbanzos, drained
   and rinsed
¾ cup dried currants
1 cup chopped toasted almonds
½ tablespoon kosher salt

1. Pour oil into a small frying pan over medium-low heat. Add garlic and spices and cook, stirring often, until fragrant, 1 to 2 minutes, being careful not to scorch garlic. Scrape mixture into a slow cooker (at least 5 quarts). Add broth, carrots, eggplant, zucchini, cauliflower, onion, stewed tomatoes (with juices), garbanzos, currants, almonds, and salt, and stir to combine. Cover slow cooker and cook on HIGH until vegetables are tender to bite and flavors are blended, 8 to 9 hours.
2. Ladle about 3 cups of vegetable mixture into a blender. Holding lid down with a towel and taking care to avoid steam, whirl until smooth. Return purée to slow cooker and stir to blend. Ladle stew into a tureen or individual bowls.

Note: To make ahead, cook the spices and chop the vegetables the night before. Refrigerate in the crock overnight, then start it in the morning. Serve with couscous and plain yogurt.

Makes 6 to 8 servings ■ Prep time: 15 minutes ■ Total time: 8 hours, 15 minutes

For complete nutritional information on this and other *Sunset* recipes, please turn to the appendix on pages 280–283.

> " This stew was awesome and surprisingly easy to make! I purchased my vegetables pre-chopped and put them straight into the slow cooker with the canned goods and broth. It was a hit at my work lunch."
>
> —kathigh
> ★★★★★

5 5 Ingredients or Less   **30 Minutes or Less**   **GF** Gluten-Free   **LC** Low-Calorie

---

QUICK TIP

Poblano chiles grown in a hot, dry climate can be more intense than others, so the spiciness of this dish hinges on the heat of your peppers.

---

myrecipes users suggest:

- substituting corn kernels for the rice
- adding chopped olives to the filling mixture
- mixing the cheese in with the filling mixture instead of sprinkling it on top

---

from **Oxmoor House**

Refried Bean Poblanos with Cheese

4 medium poblano chiles, halved and seeded
1 (16-ounce) can fat-free refried beans
1 (8.8-ounce) pouch microwaveable cooked long-grain rice (such as Uncle Ben's Original Ready Rice)
½ cup picante sauce
1 cup (4 ounces) preshredded reduced-fat 4-cheese Mexican blend cheese
Chopped fresh cilantro (optional)

1. Place chile halves, cut sides up, on a round microwave-safe plate. Cover with wax paper; microwave at HIGH 3 minutes.
2. While chiles cook, combine beans, rice, and picante sauce in a medium bowl, stirring well. Spoon bean mixture evenly into chile halves. Cover with wax paper; microwave at HIGH 2 minutes. Uncover chiles, sprinkle each half with 2 table-spoons cheese, and microwave at HIGH 1 to 2 minutes or until cheese melts. Sprinkle evenly with cilantro, if desired.

Makes 4 servings ■ Prep time: 10 minutes ■ Total time: 10 minutes

For complete nutritional information on this and other Oxmoor House recipes, please turn to the appendix on pages 280–283.

> **"** After stuffing the peppers and topping them with cheese, I put them on the grill on low for about 8 minutes. I will definitely be putting this at the top of my meatless menus list!"
>
> —heidimotsch
> ★★★★★

" Superb! The home-made enchilada sauce makes all the difference."

—Ebiniku

from CookingLight

Black Bean, Corn, and Zucchini Enchiladas

1 teaspoon canola oil
2 cups diced zucchini
1 (10-ounce) package frozen whole-kernel corn
1 (15-ounce) can black beans, rinsed and drained

3 cups Enchilada Sauce, divided
Cooking spray
8 (8-inch) whole-wheat tortillas
2 cups (8 ounces) shredded reduced-fat Cheddar cheese, divided

1. Preheat oven to 350°.
2. Heat oil in a large nonstick skillet over medium-high heat. Add zucchini and corn; sauté for 5 minutes or until vegetables are tender. Remove from heat, and stir in beans.
3. Spread 1 cup Enchilada Sauce in bottom of a 13 x 9–inch baking dish coated with cooking spray. Spoon about ½ cup zucchini mixture down center of 1 tortilla; sprinkle with 2 tablespoons cheese, and roll up. Place, seam side down, in baking dish. Repeat procedure with remaining tortillas and zucchini mixture, and 14 tablespoons cheese. Spread remaining 2 cups sauce evenly over enchiladas.
4. Cover with foil; bake at 350° for 30 minutes. Uncover; top with remaining 1 cup cheese. Bake, uncovered, for 10 minutes or until cheese melts.

Makes 8 servings ■ Prep time: 20 minutes ■ Total time: 1 hour

Enchilada Sauce

1 teaspoon canola oil
½ cup diced red onion
1 teaspoon minced garlic
½ cup organic vegetable broth (such as Swanson Certified Organic)
1 tablespoon chili powder

1 tablespoon honey
1 teaspoon ground cumin
½ teaspoon salt
1 (28-ounce) can crushed tomatoes, undrained

Heat oil in a large saucepan over medium heat. Add onion and garlic; sauté 5 minutes or until onion is tender. Stir in broth and remaining ingredients. Reduce heat, and simmer 30 minutes.

Note: You can prepare the Enchilada Sauce a few days ahead of time, and refrigerate.

Makes 3 cups ■ Prep time: 5 minutes ■ Total time: 35 minutes

For complete nutritional information on this and other *Cooking Light* recipes, please turn to the appendix on pages 280–283.

SCAN THIS PHOTO for 14 more meatless main bean dishes.

30 Minutes or Less Low-Calorie

from

Black Bean Burgers

2 tablespoons vegetable oil
1 celery stalk, chopped
1 onion, finely chopped
1 garlic clove, minced
1 (15-ounce) can black beans, rinsed
  and drained

1 large egg, lightly beaten
1 tablespoon ground cumin
½ cup plain breadcrumbs
Salt and black pepper
4 whole-grain buns
Lettuce, tomato, sliced red onion

1. Preheat oven to 375°. Line a large, rimmed baking sheet with foil; grease lightly.
2. Warm oil in a large skillet over medium-high heat. Add celery and onion and cook, stirring often, until softened, 3 to 5 minutes. Add garlic and sauté 1 minute longer.
3. Pour beans into a large bowl and use a fork or potato masher to mash into a thick paste. Scrape vegetables from skillet into bowl. Stir in egg, cumin, and breadcrumbs. Season with salt and pepper. Use your fingers to form into 4 patties (do not overmix). Place patties on baking sheet and bake at 375° until firm and set, about 10 minutes on each side. Serve on whole-grain buns with lettuce, tomato, and sliced red onion, if desired.

Makes 4 servings ▪ Prep time: 10 minutes ▪ Total time: 30 minutes

For complete nutritional information on this and other *All You* recipes, please turn to the appendix on pages 280–283.

30 Minutes or Less | **Kid-Friendly** | **Low-Calorie**

" This makes a lot, so I froze about four portions. This will be my go-to chili recipe from now on. My husband eats meat, so he just added ground beef to his. Voilà! Works for both of us!"

—cookinfabulous

★★★★★

SCAN THIS PHOTO for a Weeknight Meal Planner.

from **CookingLight**

Jane's Vegetarian Chili

1 tablespoon olive oil
2 cups chopped onion
3 garlic cloves, minced
4 cups water, divided
2 tablespoons sugar
2 tablespoons chili powder
2 tablespoons Worcestershire sauce
2 (14.5-ounce) cans diced tomatoes, undrained
1 (15.5-ounce) can chickpeas (garbanzo beans), rinsed and drained

1 (15-ounce) can black beans, rinsed and drained
1 (15-ounce) can kidney beans, rinsed and drained
1 (16-ounce) can cannellini or other white beans, rinsed and drained
1 (6-ounce) can tomato paste
½ cup (2 ounces) reduced-fat shredded Cheddar cheese (optional)

1. Heat oil in a large Dutch oven over medium-high heat. Add onion and garlic; sauté 3 minutes or until tender. Add 3 cups water and next 8 ingredients, stirring to combine.
2. Combine remaining 1 cup water and tomato paste in a bowl, stirring with a whisk until blended. Stir tomato paste mixture into bean mixture. Bring to a boil; reduce heat, and simmer 5 minutes or until thoroughly heated. Ladle into bowls. Top with cheese, if desired.

Makes 8 servings ■ Prep time: 25 minutes ■ Total time: 25 minutes

For complete nutritional information on this and other *Cooking Light* recipes, please turn to the appendix on pages 280–283.

Gluten-Free Low-Calorie

> **This is great with a cucumber-yogurt-based salad for no-meat night.**
>
> —buckeye11
>
> ★★★★★

from Cooking Light

Moroccan Chickpea Chili

2 teaspoons olive oil
1 cup prechopped onion
¾ cup chopped celery
½ cup chopped carrot
1 teaspoon bottled minced garlic
2 teaspoons ground cumin
2 teaspoons paprika
1 teaspoon ground ginger
½ teaspoon ground turmeric
¼ teaspoon freshly ground black pepper
¼ teaspoon salt

⅛ teaspoon ground cinnamon
⅛ teaspoon ground red pepper
1½ cups water
2 tablespoons no-salt-added tomato paste
2 (15.5-ounce) cans chickpeas (garbanzo beans), rinsed and drained
1 (14.5-ounce) can no-salt-added diced tomatoes, undrained
2 tablespoons chopped fresh cilantro
1 tablespoon fresh lemon juice

Heat oil in a large saucepan over medium-high heat. Add onion, celery, carrot, and garlic to pan; sauté 5 minutes. Stir in cumin and next 7 ingredients; cook 1 minute, stirring constantly. Add water, tomato paste, chickpeas, and tomatoes; bring to a boil. Cover, reduce heat, and simmer 20 minutes. Stir in cilantro and lemon juice.

Makes 4 servings ■ Prep time: 15 minutes ■ Total time: 35 minutes

For complete nutritional information on this and other *Cooking Light* recipes, please turn to the appendix on pages 280–283.

LC
Low-Calorie

Kid-Friendly

from Cooking Light

Red Lentil-Rice Cakes with Simple Tomato Salsa

Salsa:
3 cups finely chopped plum tomato
  (about 6 tomatoes)
¼ cup chopped fresh basil
1 tablespoon balsamic vinegar
2 teaspoons capers
¼ teaspoon salt
Cakes:
5 cups water, divided
1 cup dried small red lentils
½ cup uncooked basmati rice
2 tablespoons olive oil, divided

½ cup finely chopped red bell pepper
½ cup finely chopped red onion
½ teaspoon fennel seeds, crushed
2 garlic cloves, minced
¾ cup (3 ounces) shredded part-skim
  mozzarella cheese
¼ cup dry breadcrumbs
1 tablespoon chopped fresh basil
1 teaspoon salt
¼ teaspoon freshly ground black pepper
2 large egg whites, lightly beaten

1. To prepare salsa, combine first 5 ingredients; set aside at room temperature.
2. To prepare cakes, bring 4 cups water and lentils to a boil in a medium saucepan. Reduce heat, and simmer for 20 minutes or until tender. Drain and rinse with cold water; drain. Place lentils in a large bowl.
3. Combine remaining 1 cup water and rice in pan; bring to a boil. Cover, reduce heat, and simmer 18 minutes or until liquid is absorbed. Cool 10 minutes. Add rice to lentils.
4. Heat 1 teaspoon oil in a large nonstick skillet over medium-high heat. Add bell pepper, onion, fennel seeds, and garlic to pan; sauté 2 minutes or until tender. Cool 10 minutes. Add to rice mixture. Add mozzarella and remaining ingredients, stirring until well combined. Let stand for 10 minutes.
5. Wipe skillet clean with paper towels. Heat 2 teaspoons oil in skillet over medium heat. Spoon half of rice mixture by ⅓-cupfuls into pan, spreading to form 6 (3-inch) circles; cook 5 minutes or until lightly browned. Carefully turn cakes over; cook 5 minutes on other side. Remove cakes from pan. Repeat procedure with remaining 1 tablespoon oil and remaining rice mixture. Serve with salsa.

Makes 6 servings ■ Prep time: 55 minutes ■ Total time: 1 hour, 45 minutes

For complete nutritional information on this and other *Cooking Light* recipes, please turn to the appendix on pages 280–283.

QUICK TIP

If using cooked rice, you'll need about 1½ cups.

myrecipes users suggest:
- substituting cilantro for the basil in the salsa and cakes
- using fontina, feta, or emmenthaler cheese instead of mozzarella in the cakes
- using brown rice instead of basmati rice

" The flavors blended really well together. Even my 2-year-old cleaned his plate. I'll definitely make this again."

—melissaotero
★★★★★

5
5 Ingredients
or Less

30 Minutes
or Less

LC
Low-
Calorie

 This dish is a huge hit. I use it as a special-occasion dish for my vegetarian parents and as a way to get my husband who hates squash to eat some squash."

—LifesGood19

★★★★★

from **Oxmoor House®**

Creamy Butternut Squash Risotto

1¼ cups uncooked Arborio rice or other
   medium-grain rice
2 teaspoons olive oil
2½ cups fat-free, less-sodium vegetable broth
1 cup water
1 (12-ounce) package frozen pureed
   butternut squash (such as McKenzie's)

¼ teaspoon salt
¼ teaspoon freshly ground black
   pepper
6 tablespoons grated fresh Parmesan
   cheese
Grated Parmesan cheese (optional)
Fresh thyme sprigs (optional)

1. Combine rice and oil in a 1½-quart microwave-safe dish, stirring to coat. Microwave, uncovered, at HIGH 3 minutes.
2. Add broth and water to rice mixture; microwave, uncovered, at HIGH 9 minutes. Stir well; microwave, uncovered, at HIGH 6 minutes. Remove from microwave; let stand 5 minutes or until all liquid is absorbed.
3. While risotto stands, heat squash in microwave at HIGH 2 minutes or until warm. Add squash, salt, pepper, and Parmesan cheese to risotto. Stir well to combine. Garnish with additional cheese and thyme sprigs, if desired.

Makes 4 servings ■ Prep time: 8 minutes ■ Total time: 28 minutes

For complete nutritional information on this and other Oxmoor House recipes, please turn to the appendix on pages 280–283.

from CookingLight.

Summer Lemon-Vegetable Risotto (pictured on page 143)

8 ounces asparagus, trimmed and cut into 1-inch pieces
8 ounces sugar snap peas, trimmed and cut in half
5 teaspoons extra-virgin olive oil, divided
1 (8-ounce) zucchini, halved lengthwise and cut into ½-inch-thick slices
1 (8-ounce) yellow squash, halved lengthwise and cut into ½-inch-thick slices
4¾ cups organic vegetable broth

½ cup finely chopped shallots
1 cup uncooked Arborio rice
¼ cup dry white wine
½ cup (2 ounces) grated pecorino Romano cheese
¼ cup chopped fresh chives
1 teaspoon grated lemon rind
2 tablespoons fresh lemon juice
1 tablespoon unsalted butter
¼ teaspoon salt

1. Bring a large saucepan of water to a boil. Add asparagus and peas; cook for 3 minutes or until crisp-tender. Drain and rinse under cold water.
2. Heat a large nonstick skillet over medium-high heat. Add 2 teaspoons oil to pan; swirl to coat. Add zucchini and squash to pan; cook for 7 minutes or until lightly browned, stirring occasionally. Set aside.
3. Bring broth to a simmer in a medium saucepan (do not boil). Keep warm.
4. Heat remaining 1 tablespoon oil in a Dutch oven over medium heat. Add shallots, and cook for 3 minutes or until tender. Stir in rice, and cook for 1 minute, stirring constantly. Stir in wine; cook until liquid is absorbed (about 30 seconds), stirring constantly. Stir in 1 cup broth; cook 5 minutes or until liquid is nearly absorbed, stirring constantly. Reserve ¼ cup broth. Add remaining broth, ½ cup at a time, stirring constantly until each portion of broth is absorbed before adding the next (about 22 minutes total). Stir in vegetables; cook 1 minute or until thoroughly heated. Remove from heat; stir in reserved ¼ cup broth and remaining ingredients.

Makes 4 servings ■ Prep time: 1 hour ■ Total time: 1 hour

For complete nutritional information on this and other *Cooking Light* recipes, please turn to the appendix on pages 280–283.

> **myrecipes** users suggest:
> - substituting mushrooms for the squash
> - grilling the vegetables instead of boiling and sautéing to add more flavor
> - using regular onions instead of shallots
> - adding grilled shrimp marinated in lemon juice, olive oil, salt, pepper, and garlic powder

 The first time, I followed the recipe exactly. It was wonderful. The next two times, I used whatever vegetables were ripe in my garden at the moment. It's just a lovely dish. The lemon juice and lemon zest pull it all together."

—MalindaC
★★★★★

30 Minutes
or Less

LC
Low-Calorie

 My husband, who hates mushrooms and loves meat, gave this a bravo. (He also doesn't usually say bravo.)"

—vaughnac

★★★★★

from **Health**

Vegetarian Stuffed Mushrooms

4 large portobello mushroom caps
2 teaspoons olive oil
1½ tablespoons balsamic vinegar
¼ teaspoon coarse salt
½ teaspoon freshly ground black pepper, divided

1½ cups chopped tomato
⅓ cup chopped kalamata olives
1 cup fresh whole-grain breadcrumbs
½ cup (2 ounces) shredded fontina cheese
¼ cup chopped fresh chives

1. Preheat oven to 400°.
2. Place mushroom caps, gill sides up, on a rimmed baking sheet; drizzle with oil and vinegar, and season with salt and ¼ teaspoon pepper. Bake until caps are just tender, about 10 minutes.
3. Meanwhile, combine tomato, olives, breadcrumbs, cheese, and chives in a medium bowl. Season with remaining ¼ teaspoon pepper.
4. Divide tomato mixture evenly (about ½ cup per mushroom) among portobello caps. Bake at 400° for 10 to 12 minutes or until lightly browned and mushrooms are tender. Serve hot.

Makes 2 servings ■ Prep time: 10 minutes ■ Total time: 30 minutes

For complete nutritional information on this and other *Health* recipes, please turn to the appendix on pages 280–283.

from **Cooking Light**

Quinoa-Stuffed Poblano Chiles

4 (5-inch) poblano chiles
1½ cups water
¾ cup uncooked quinoa
Cooking spray
½ cup chopped green bell pepper
½ cup chopped red bell pepper
½ cup chopped onion
2 teaspoons minced seeded jalapeño pepper
2 garlic cloves, minced

2 tablespoons unsalted pumpkin seed kernels
½ cup minced green onions
1 tablespoon minced fresh or 1 teaspoon
  dried cilantro
1 tablespoon low-sodium soy sauce
1 tablespoon lime juice
2 cups tomato juice
1 cup (4 ounces) shredded reduced-fat sharp
  Cheddar cheese

1. Preheat oven to 350°.
2. Cut poblano chiles in half lengthwise; remove stems and seeds. Set aside.
Combine water and quinoa in a medium saucepan; bring to a boil. Cover, reduce
heat, and simmer 13 minutes or until liquid is absorbed. Set aside.
3. Spray a large nonstick skillet with cooking spray; place over medium-high heat
until hot. Add bell peppers, onion, jalapeño, and garlic; sauté 2 minutes. Add pumpkin seed kernels; sauté 2 minutes. Remove from heat; stir in quinoa, green onions,
cilantro, soy sauce, and lime juice. Spoon ⅓ cup quinoa mixture into each chile half.
4. Pour tomato juice into a 13 x 9–inch baking dish; place stuffed chiles in
dish. Cover and bake at 350° for 20 minutes. Sprinkle cheese over chiles; bake,
uncovered, an additional 10 minutes or until cheese melts and chiles are
thoroughly heated. Spoon tomato juice over chiles.

Makes 4 servings ■ Prep time: 15 minutes ■ Total time: 1 hour

For complete nutritional information on this and other *Cooking Light* recipes, please turn to the appendix on pages
280–283.

> This turned out
> great. Neither
my guests nor I had
tried quinoa before,
and everyone loved it."

—LauraWill
★★★★★

Low-Calorie Make-Ahead

" This dish was phenomenal. It was so flavorful and filling. It's hard to believe that it's low in calories. This casserole will become a regular in our rotation."

—NatalieC
★★★★★

from CookingLight

Artichoke and Goat Cheese Strata

1 teaspoon olive oil
½ cup finely chopped shallot (about 1 large)
1 (10-ounce) package frozen artichoke hearts, thawed
2 garlic cloves, minced
½ teaspoon dried herbes de Provence
1¾ cups 1% low-fat milk
½ teaspoon freshly ground black pepper
¼ teaspoon salt
4 large eggs
⅓ cup (about 1½ ounces) grated Parmigiano-Reggiano cheese
½ (1-pound) loaf country-style white bread, cut into 1-inch cubes (about 5 cups)
Cooking spray
¾ cup (3 ounces) crumbled goat cheese, divided
Parsley leaves

1. Heat a large nonstick skillet over medium heat. Add oil to pan; swirl to coat. Add shallot, and cook for 2 minutes, stirring frequently. Stir in artichoke hearts and garlic; cook for 8 minutes or until artichoke hearts begin to brown, stirring occasionally. Remove from heat, and stir in herbes de Provence. Cool 10 minutes.
2. Combine milk, pepper, salt, and eggs in a large bowl, stirring with a whisk. Add Parmigiano-Reggiano cheese and bread; toss gently to combine. Stir in artichoke mixture, and let stand for 20 minutes.
3. Preheat oven to 375°.
4. Spoon half of bread mixture into an 8-inch square glass or ceramic baking dish coated with cooking spray. Sprinkle with half of goat cheese, and top with remaining bread mixture. Sprinkle remaining goat cheese over top. Bake at 375° for 50 minutes or until browned and bubbly. Garnish with parsley.

Note: To make ahead, prepare through step 2, cover, and refrigerate. Let bread mixture stand at room temperature 10 minutes while the oven preheats. Then assemble and bake. The cook time will increase by about 10 minutes.

Makes 6 servings ■ Prep time: 30 minutes ■ Total time: 1 hour, 50 minutes

For complete nutritional information on this and other *Cooking Light* recipes, please turn to the appendix on pages 280–283.

SCAN THIS PHOTO
for 11 more recipes
using eggplant.

LC
Low-
Calorie

from CookingLight

Eggplant Parmesan

½ cup dry white wine
1 tablespoon dried basil
1 tablespoon dried oregano
4 (8-ounce) cans no-salt-added tomato sauce
1 (28-ounce) can no-salt-added whole
   tomatoes, undrained and chopped
1 (6-ounce) can tomato paste
2 garlic cloves, minced
2 (1-pound) eggplants, cut crosswise into
   ¼-inch-thick slices

¼ cup water
3 egg whites, lightly beaten
1¼ cups Italian-seasoned breadcrumbs
¼ cup grated Parmesan cheese
Cooking spray
3 cups (12 ounces) shredded part-skim
   mozzarella cheese
Fresh oregano sprigs (optional)

1. Combine first 7 ingredients in a large saucepan; bring to a boil. Reduce heat and simmer, uncovered, 20 minutes.
2. Place eggplant in a large bowl; add water to cover, and let stand 30 minutes. Drain well; blot dry with paper towels. Combine ¼ cup water and egg whites in a shallow bowl. Combine breadcrumbs and Parmesan cheese; stir well. Dip eggplant in egg white mixture, and dredge in breadcrumb mixture.
3. Preheat broiler. Place half of eggplant on a baking sheet coated with cooking spray, and broil 5 minutes on each side or until browned. Repeat procedure with remaining eggplant. Set eggplant aside.
4. Preheat oven to 350°. Spread half of tomato mixture in bottom of a 13 x 9–inch baking dish coated with cooking spray. Arrange half of eggplant over sauce; top with half of mozzarella cheese. Repeat layers with remaining sauce, eggplant, and cheese.
5. Bake at 350° for 30 minutes or until bubbly. Let stand 5 minutes before serving. Garnish with oregano sprigs, if desired.

Makes 8 servings ■ Prep time: 15 minutes ■ Total time: 2 hours

For complete nutritional information on this and other *Cooking Light* recipes, please turn to the appendix on pages 280–283.

> ❝ My husband's not an eggplant kind of guy, but he'll eat this. Since it's just the two of us, I cut the recipe in half and only use one eggplant. I still make the whole batch of sauce and freeze half for future use.❞
>
> —jameyadams
> ★★★★★

30 Minutes or Less

LC Low-Calorie

QUICK TIP

Don't have any sake?
You can use 1 tablespoon rice wine vinegar instead.

 I have been wanting to put more tofu in my diet, and this is a delicious way to do it. It's easy to tinker with the combination of soy/hoisin/sake to get it where you want it."

—ajknightfan

★★★★

from **CookingLight**

Tofu Fried Rice

2 cups uncooked instant rice
2 tablespoons vegetable oil, divided
1 (14-ounce) package reduced-fat firm tofu, drained and cut into (½-inch) cubes
2 large eggs, lightly beaten
1 cup (½-inch-thick) sliced green onions
1 cup frozen peas and carrots, thawed

2 teaspoons bottled minced garlic
1 teaspoon bottled minced fresh ginger
2 tablespoons sake (rice wine)
3 tablespoons low-sodium soy sauce
1 tablespoon hoisin sauce
½ teaspoon dark sesame oil
Thinly sliced green onions (optional)

1. Cook rice according to package directions, omitting salt and fat.
2. While rice cooks, heat 1 tablespoon oil in a large nonstick skillet over medium-high heat. Add tofu; cook 4 minutes or until lightly browned, stirring occasionally. Remove from pan. Add eggs to pan; cook 1 minute or until done, breaking egg into small pieces. Remove from pan. Add remaining 1 tablespoon oil to pan. Add 1 cup onions, peas and carrots, garlic, and ginger; sauté 2 minutes.
3. While vegetable mixture cooks, combine sake, soy sauce, hoisin sauce, and sesame oil. Add cooked rice to pan; cook 2 minutes, stirring constantly. Add tofu, egg, and soy sauce mixture; cook 30 seconds, stirring constantly. Garnish with sliced green onions, if desired.

Makes 4 servings ■ Prep time: 20 minutes ■ Total time: 30 minutes

For complete nutritional information on this and other *Cooking Light* recipes, please turn to the appendix on pages 280–283.

SCAN THIS PHOTO for video on how to prepare this recipe.

LC
Low-Calorie

SCAN THIS PHOTO for video on how to drain and press tofu.

from CookingLight

Tofu Steaks with Red Pepper–Walnut Sauce

1 (14-ounce) package water-packed reduced-fat extra-firm tofu
¼ cup finely chopped fresh basil
¼ cup water
2 tablespoons chopped fresh parsley
1 tablespoon chopped fresh thyme
2 tablespoons white wine vinegar
1 tablespoon Dijon mustard
½ teaspoon salt

½ teaspoon crushed red pepper
8 garlic cloves, minced
½ cup all-purpose flour
½ cup egg substitute
2 cups panko (Japanese breadcrumbs)
2 tablespoons olive oil
3 tablespoons chopped walnuts, toasted
1 (12-ounce) bottle roasted red peppers, drained

1. Cut tofu crosswise into 4 slices. Place tofu slices on several layers of heavy-duty paper towels; cover with additional paper towels. Let stand 30 minutes, pressing down occasionally.
2. Combine basil and next 8 ingredients in a large zip-top plastic bag. Add tofu to bag; seal. Marinate in refrigerator 1 hour, turning bag occasionally.
3. Place flour in a shallow dish. Place egg substitute in another shallow dish. Place panko in another shallow dish.
4. Remove tofu from marinade, reserving remaining marinade. Working with one tofu piece at a time, dredge tofu in flour, shaking off excess. Dip tofu in egg substitute, allowing excess to drip off. Coat tofu completely with panko, pressing lightly to adhere. Set aside. Repeat procedure with remaining tofu, flour, egg substitute, and panko.
5. Heat a large nonstick skillet over medium-high heat. Add oil to pan, swirling to coat. Add tofu to pan; reduce heat to medium, and cook for 4 minutes on each side or until browned. Remove tofu from pan, and keep warm.
6. Combine reserved marinade, walnuts, and roasted peppers in a blender; process until smooth (about 2 minutes). Pour roasted pepper mixture into pan; cook over medium-high heat 2 minutes or until thoroughly heated. Serve with tofu.

Makes 4 servings ■ Prep time: 30 minutes ■ Total time: 2 hours

For complete nutritional information on this and other *Cooking Light* recipes, please turn to the appendix on pages 280–283.

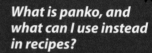
ask the expert

What is panko, and what can I use instead in recipes?

In Japanese, "pan" means bread and "ko" means small pieces: Panko is the Japanese name for sliver-shaped, coarse, crisp breadcrumbs that come from a specially prepared crustless bread. They add a distinctive crunchy texture to food, but the flavor is similar to that of most regular unseasoned breadcrumbs.

For similar flavor, regular breadcrumbs may be substituted, but for similar texture, coarsely ground corn flakes are a better choice.

SCAN THIS BOX for more cooking know-how from our experts.

30 Minutes or Less

LC Low-Calorie

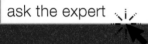

ask the expert

What can I substitute for black bean sauce?

The black bean sauce called for in many Asian recipes is often sold in the Asian foods section of the grocery store.

If you can't find it, use hoisin sauce instead. Hoisin is sweeter, so decrease the amount of any sugar or honey in the recipe.

SCAN THIS BOX for more cooking know-how from our experts.

 This recipe received a fabulous reception from my vegetarian daughter and vegan son-in-law. He said: 'This is one of the best tofu recipes I have ever had.'"

—ErikAnestad

★★★★★

from *Cooking Light*

Szechuan-Style Tofu with Peanuts

2 (3.5-ounce) bags boil-in-bag jasmine rice
1 (14-ounce) package water-packed firm tofu, drained and cut into 1-inch pieces
Cooking spray
½ cup less-sodium vegetable broth
1 tablespoon sambal oelek (ground fresh chile paste)
1 tablespoon less-sodium soy sauce
1 teaspoon cornstarch

2 teaspoons black bean garlic sauce
1 tablespoon canola oil
¼ teaspoon salt
1 (8-ounce) package presliced mushrooms
½ cup matchstick-cut carrots
1 tablespoon bottled ground fresh ginger
½ cup chopped green onions
¼ cup unsalted dry-roasted peanuts, chopped

1. Preheat broiler.
2. Cook rice according to package directions, omitting salt and fat.
3. Arrange tofu in a single layer on a foil-lined jelly-roll pan coated with cooking spray; broil 14 minutes or until golden.
4. While tofu cooks, combine broth and next 4 ingredients, stirring with a whisk; set aside.
5. Heat oil in a large nonstick skillet over medium-high heat. Add salt and mushrooms; sauté 4 minutes or until mushrooms begin to release liquid, stirring occasionally. Stir in carrots and ginger; cook 1 minute. Add broth mixture; cook 30 seconds or until sauce begins to thicken. Remove from heat; stir in tofu and onions. Serve over rice; sprinkle with peanuts.

Makes 4 servings ▪ Prep time: 15 minutes ▪ Total time: 30 minutes

For complete nutritional information on this and other *Cooking Light* recipes, please turn to the appendix on pages 280–283.

from **CookingLight**

Broccoli-Tofu Stir-Fry

1 (3.5-ounce) bag boil-in-bag brown rice
2 tablespoons low-sodium soy sauce
2 tablespoons oyster sauce
2½ teaspoons cornstarch
2 teaspoons rice vinegar
2 teaspoons dark sesame oil
2 teaspoons vegetable oil

1 pound firm tofu, drained and cut into
    ½-inch cubes
¼ teaspoon salt
2 cups broccoli florets
¾ cup water
1½ tablespoons bottled minced garlic

1. Cook the rice according to package directions.
2. While rice cooks, combine soy sauce and next 4 ingredients in a small bowl, stirring with a whisk; set aside.
3. Heat vegetable oil in a large nonstick skillet over medium-high heat. Add tofu, and sprinkle with salt. Cook 8 minutes or until golden brown, tossing frequently. Remove tofu from pan, and keep warm. Add broccoli, water, and garlic to pan. Cover and cook 4 minutes or until crisp-tender, stirring occasionally. Uncover; add soy sauce mixture and tofu, stirring gently to coat. Cook 2 minutes or until sauce thickens, stirring occasionally. Serve broccoli mixture over rice.

Makes 4 servings ▪ Prep time: 5 minutes ▪ Total time: 20 minutes

For complete nutritional information on this and other *Cooking Light* recipes, please turn to the appendix on pages 280–283.

30 Minutes
or Less

QUICK TIP

To cut preparation time, use precut broccoli florets. They're usually near the salad greens in supermarkets.

myrecipes users suggest:
• substituting fish sauce for the oyster sauce and sherry vinegar for the rice vinegar
• brushing the tofu with olive oil and broiling until golden, instead of browning it on the stove
• adding 1 tablespoon chopped peeled fresh ginger along with the garlic

❝ Really drying the tofu makes a big difference in the texture once it is cooked."

—paesanC
★★★★

pasta & pizza

When whipping up dinner with what's in your pantry, pasta is a great place to start. No wonder it's so popular on MyRecipes.com. Here, we've gathered our top-rated noodle dishes (including Asian-style and meat-free options) plus our users' favorite pizza and calzone recipes.

 To use the exclusive **Scan-It/Cook-It**™ features in this chapter, look for the smartphone symbol (shown at left). For detailed instructions, please see page 7.

**ORANGE-SESAME NOODLES
WITH GRILLED SHRIMP**
page 190

30 Minutes or Less   **LC Low-Calorie**

myrecipes users suggest:
- adding cooked chicken
- omitting the mint
- using grated Parmesan instead of Romano

from **Cooking Light**

Pasta with Zucchini and Toasted Almonds

2 cups cherry tomatoes, halved
2 tablespoons minced shallots
1 teaspoon minced fresh thyme
2 teaspoons fresh lemon juice
¾ teaspoon kosher salt
½ teaspoon freshly ground black pepper
¼ teaspoon sugar
5 teaspoons extra-virgin olive oil, divided

1 (9-ounce) package refrigerated linguine
1½ teaspoons bottled minced garlic
3 cups chopped zucchini (about 1 pound)
¾ cup fat-free, less-sodium chicken broth
3 tablespoons chopped fresh mint, divided
⅓ cup (1½ ounces) grated fresh pecorino Romano cheese
3 tablespoons sliced almonds, toasted

1. Combine first 7 ingredients in a medium bowl. Add 2 teaspoons of the oil, and toss to coat.
2. Cook pasta according to package directions, omitting salt and fat. Drain well.
3. Heat a large nonstick skillet over medium-high heat. Add the remaining oil to pan, swirling to coat. Add garlic to pan; sauté 30 seconds. Add zucchini; sauté 3 minutes or until crisp-tender. Add broth; bring to a simmer. Stir in pasta and 1½ tablespoons mint; toss well. Remove from heat; stir in tomato mixture.
4. Place 1½ cups pasta mixture in each of 4 bowls; top evenly with remaining 1½ tablespoons mint. Sprinkle each serving with 4 teaspoons cheese and 2 rounded teaspoons almonds.

Makes 4 servings ■ Prep time: 20 minutes ■ Total time: 20 minutes

For complete nutritional information on this and other *Cooking Light* recipes, please turn to the appendix on pages 280–283.

" My fiancé and I really loved this recipe—and he usually complains about vegetarian meals. This is definitely a keeper."

—Empac7

★★★★★

myrecipes users suggest:
- using more spinach and onion
- adding baby portobello mushrooms and artichoke hearts
- leaving the onion, spinach, and tomatoes raw, and serving as a cold pasta salad

from Cooking Light

Farfalle with Tomatoes, Onions, and Spinach

1 tablespoon plus ¼ teaspoon salt, divided
8 ounces uncooked farfalle pasta
2 tablespoons extra-virgin olive oil, divided
1 cup vertically sliced yellow onion
1 teaspoon dried oregano
5 garlic cloves, sliced
2 cups grape tomatoes, halved

1 tablespoon white wine vinegar
3 cups baby spinach
3 tablespoons shaved fresh Parmigiano-Reggiano cheese
¼ teaspoon freshly ground black pepper
¾ cup (3 ounces) crumbled feta cheese

1. Bring a large pot of water to a boil with 1 tablespoon salt. Add pasta, and cook according to package directions; drain.

2. Heat 1 tablespoon oil in a large nonstick skillet over medium-high heat. Add onion and oregano; sauté 12 minutes or until lightly browned. Add garlic; sauté 2 minutes. Add tomatoes and vinegar; sauté 3 minutes or until tomatoes begin to soften. Add pasta and spinach; cook 1 minute. Remove from heat, and stir in Parmigiano-Reggiano, remaining 1 tablespoon oil, remaining ¼ teaspoon salt, and pepper. Sprinkle with feta.

Makes 4 servings ■ Prep time: 20 minutes ■ Total time: 40 minutes

For complete nutritional information on this and other *Cooking Light* recipes, please turn to the appendix on pages 280–283.

SCAN THIS PHOTO for video on how to cook pasta.

> This is my new favorite home-made mac and cheese recipe. The kids thought the wine flavor was a bit too strong, so next time I will try ½ cup wine and ¾ cup chicken broth. Otherwise, I wouldn't change a thing!"
>
> —JeninND

★★★★★

  myrecipes users suggest:
- using Gewürztraminer wine and adding a little more spice
- substituting half-and-half for the heavy cream, and adding a package of cubed Canadian bacon

from *Sunset*

Ultimate Mac 'n' Cheese

8 ounces cavatappi, macaroni, or other tube-shaped pasta
½ teaspoon coarse salt, plus more for cooking pasta
3½ tablespoons butter, divided
½ cup finely chopped shallots
2 tablespoons all-purpose flour
1¼ cups dry white wine
⅔ cup heavy whipping cream

7 ounces Gruyère, grated
3 ounces aged gouda, grated
2 tablespoons plus 1 teaspoon minced fresh chives
1 tablespoon Dijon mustard
⅛ teaspoon cayenne pepper
⅛ teaspoon freshly grated nutmeg
4 ounces crusty sourdough bread (about ¼ loaf), torn into large pieces

1. Preheat oven to 400°. Cook pasta according to package directions in a large pot of boiling, well-salted water until tender to the bite, 7 to 12 minutes. Drain, but do not rinse.
2. In a large frying pan over medium-high heat, melt 2 tablespoons butter. Add shallots and cook until light golden, about 3 minutes. Sprinkle shallot-butter mixture with flour; cook, stirring often, 1 minute. Add wine and stir, picking up any browned bits from bottom of pan. Add cream and stir well. Sprinkle in cheeses, one large handful at a time, stirring until each handful is mostly melted before adding the next. Stir in 2 tablespoons chives, mustard, ¼ teaspoon salt, cayenne, and nutmeg. Stir cooked pasta into cheese mixture, then pour all into a 2-quart baking dish.
3. In a food processor, pulse bread with remaining 1½ tablespoons butter, 1 teaspoon chives, and ¼ teaspoon salt until coarse crumbs form. Sprinkle breadcrumbs over pasta and cheese and bake until top is browned and cheese is bubbling, 15 to 20 minutes.

Makes 6 servings ▪ Prep time: 25 minutes ▪ Total time: 50 minutes

For complete nutritional information on this and other *Sunset* recipes, please turn to the appendix on pages 280–283.

Baked Rigatoni with Ricotta and Collard Greens

1 (16-ounce) package rigatoni or penne pasta
¼ cup butter
1 medium onion, chopped (about 1 cup)
3 garlic cloves, minced
1 pound collard greens, washed, drained, and chopped
¼ cup all-purpose flour
1½ cups milk

1 cup shredded mozzarella
1 cup ricotta cheese
2 teaspoons sugar
2 teaspoons salt
½ teaspoon freshly ground black pepper
1 teaspoon red pepper flakes
½ cup grated Parmesan cheese

1. Prepare pasta according to directions. Drain and set aside. Preheat oven to 350°. Lightly grease a 13 x 9–inch baking dish.
2. Heat butter in a Dutch oven over medium-high heat; sauté onion 5 minutes or until just browned. Add garlic, and cook about 1 minute. Reduce heat to medium-low, and add greens; cover and cook 15 to 20 minutes or until greens are tender, stirring occasionally.
3. Sprinkle greens with flour. Cook uncovered, stirring constantly, 1 minute. Gradually add milk, stirring well. Cook 5 minutes, stirring often, until thickened and smooth. Remove from heat; stir in cooked pasta, mozzarella, and next 5 ingredients. Place in prepared dish, and sprinkle evenly with Parmesan.
4. Bake at 350° for 15 to 20 minutes.

Makes 8 to 10 servings ■ Prep time: 25 minutes ■ Total time: 55 minutes

ask the expert

How can I keep pasta from clumping in the pot?

Despite what you may have heard, adding oil to the water does nothing. A pinch of salt lends a little flavor—but again, does nothing to prevent clumping. The only way to prevent pasta from sticking as it cooks is to be sure you have plenty of vigorously boiling water.

When you think about the fact that pasta expands to about three times its size when it cooks, you can see why if you try to boil 1 cup of pasta in 2 cups of water, it's going to stick together. Now picture that same 1 cup of dry penne jumping around in 8 cups of boiling water—and you can just as easily see why it won't clump.

SCAN THIS BOX for more cooking know-how from our experts.

myrecipes users suggest:
• simmering the greens in chicken broth, instead of sautéing, for more flavor
• adding cut-up chicken breasts

Low-Calorie

> **I made this recipe with turkey bacon, and the saltiness works amazingly with the richness of the filling. Guests and the husband were impressed!"**
>
> —NikkeeB
> ★★★★

from

Butternut Squash Ravioli with Sage

1 (1-pound) butternut squash
Salt and black pepper
9 tablespoons unsalted butter, divided
⅓ cup finely chopped shallots
1 teaspoon finely chopped sage plus 2 tablespoons thinly sliced leaves and 8 whole leaves

¼ cup ricotta cheese
¼ cup plus 4 tablespoons Parmesan
Pinch of ground nutmeg
48 wonton skins
4 slices pancetta, chopped

1. Preheat oven to 450°. Halve squash and remove seeds. Season with salt and pepper and place, flesh side down, on a baking sheet. Bake until tender and a knife comes out easily, about 40 minutes. Use a spoon to scoop out flesh; puree in a food processor or blender until smooth.

2. Melt 1 tablespoon butter in a skillet. Add shallots and cook until tender, about 3 minutes. Add chopped sage, squash puree, ricotta, and ¼ cup Parmesan. Season with salt, pepper, and nutmeg, and cook for 1 minute. Remove from heat and allow to cool completely.

3. Place 1 wonton wrapper on work surface, keeping rest covered with a damp cloth. Brush wrapper with water and place 1 teaspoon squash mixture in center. Place another wrapper on top and seal together with fingers, taking care to push out air bubbles. Use a 3-inch round cookie cutter to cut filled ravioli into circles. Keep finished ravioli covered while you work.

4. In a skillet over medium heat, fry pancetta until crispy, about 5½ minutes. Remove from pan and drain on paper towels. Wipe skillet out.

5. Bring a large pot of salted water to a boil. Melt remaining 8 tablespoons butter in skillet over very low heat, then add sliced sage. Cook butter and sage until butter turns light golden brown, about 5 minutes; remove from heat. While butter is browning, add ravioli to boiling water, stirring gently so they don't stick together. Cook 4 minutes, then carefully drain.

6. Place 3 ravioli on each plate, top each with 1 tablespoon browned butter, and garnish with ½ tablespoon Parmesan, some crumbled pancetta, and 1 sage leaf. Serve hot.

Makes 8 servings ■ Prep time: 30 minutes ■ Total time: 1 hour, 10 minutes

For complete nutritional information on this and other *All You* recipes, please turn to the appendix on pages 280–283.

Kid-Friendly

Low-Calorie

Make-Ahead

QUICK TIP

To speed preparation, use precut onions, matchstick-cut carrots, and broccoli, in addition to precooked noodles.

" This is best after it sits for a day. I would recommend assembling it on a Saturday or Sunday when you have the time and then cooking it during the week for dinner. Excellent!"

—mcraven

★★★★★

from **Cooking Light**

Garden-Style Lasagna

Cooking spray
2 cups chopped onion
4 garlic cloves, minced
2 teaspoons olive oil, divided
2 cups (about 8 ounces) chopped zucchini
2 cups (about 8 ounces) chopped yellow squash
2 cups (about 8 ounces) thinly sliced carrot
2 cups (about 6 ounces) chopped broccoli
1 teaspoon salt, divided
½ cup all-purpose flour (about 2.25 ounces)
3½ cups 1% milk
1 cup (4 ounces) grated fresh Parmesan cheese, divided
¼ teaspoon freshly ground black pepper
Dash of ground nutmeg
1 (10-ounce) package frozen chopped spinach, thawed and drained
1½ cups 1% cottage cheese
2 cups (8 ounces) shredded part-skim mozzarella cheese, divided
12 precooked lasagna noodles, divided

1. Preheat oven to 375°.
2. Heat a large Dutch oven over medium-high heat. Coat pan with cooking spray. Add onion to pan; sauté 4 minutes or until lightly browned. Add garlic; sauté 1 minute. Spoon onion mixture into a large bowl.
3. Heat 1 teaspoon oil in pan over medium-high heat. Add zucchini and yellow squash; sauté 4 minutes or until tender and just beginning to brown. Add to onion mixture.
4. Heat remaining 1 teaspoon oil in pan over medium-high heat. Add carrot; sauté 4 minutes or until tender. Add broccoli; sauté 4 minutes or until crisp-tender. Add to onion mixture. Sprinkle with ½ teaspoon salt; toss well to combine.
5. Place flour in a medium saucepan. Gradually add milk, stirring with a whisk until blended. Bring to a boil over medium heat; cook 2 minutes or until thick, stirring constantly. Remove from heat. Add ½ cup Parmesan, remaining ½ teaspoon salt, pepper, and nutmeg; stir until smooth. Stir in spinach.
6. Combine cottage cheese and 1½ cups mozzarella; stir well. Spread ½ cup spinach mixture in bottom of a 13 x 9–inch baking dish coated with cooking spray. Arrange 4 noodles over spinach mixture in dish; top with half of cottage cheese mixture (about 1½ cups), half of vegetable mixture (about 2½ cups) and about 1 cup spinach mixture. Repeat layers, ending with noodles. Spread remaining spinach mixture over noodles; sprinkle with remaining ½ cup Parmesan and remaining ½ cup mozzarella.
7. Cover and bake at 375° for 20 minutes. Uncover and bake an additional 20 minutes or until cheese is bubbly and beginning to brown. Let stand 10 minutes before serving.

Note: To make ahead, prepare and bake as directed; let it cool completely, then cover and chill. The next day, heat single servings in the microwave. Freeze leftovers for dinner.

Makes 12 servings ■ Prep time: 50 minutes ■ Total time: 1 hour, 40 minutes

For complete nutritional information on this and other *Cooking Light* recipes, please turn to the appendix on pages 280–283.

SCAN THIS PHOTO
for 5 more low-cal
lasagna recipes.

30 Minutes or Less

Kid-Friendly

Low-Calorie

" My 5-year-old son told me that I could make this dinner any time I wanted to. Yay! It's become a weekly dinner because it's so light and easy to make."

—donnah35

from Cooking Light

Fettuccine Alfredo with Bacon

1 (9-ounce) package refrigerated fresh fettuccine
2 slices applewood-smoked bacon, chopped
1 teaspoon minced garlic
1 tablespoon all-purpose flour
1 cup 1% low-fat milk

⅔ cup (about 2½ ounces) grated Parmigiano-Reggiano cheese
½ teaspoon salt
2 tablespoons chopped fresh parsley
½ teaspoon freshly ground black pepper

1. Cook pasta according to package directions, omitting salt and fat. Drain in a colander over a bowl, reserving ¼ cup cooking liquid.
2. While pasta cooks, cook bacon in a large nonstick skillet over medium-high heat 4 minutes or until crisp, stirring occasionally. Remove bacon from pan, reserving drippings. Add garlic to drippings in pan; sauté 1 minute, stirring constantly. Sprinkle flour over garlic; cook 30 seconds, stirring constantly. Gradually add milk, stirring constantly; cook 2 minutes or until bubbly and slightly thick, stirring constantly. Reduce heat to low. Gradually add cheese, stirring until cheese melts. Stir in salt and reserved ¼ cup cooking liquid. Add hot pasta to pan; toss well to combine. Sprinkle with bacon, parsley, and pepper.

Makes 4 servings ■ Prep time: 20 minutes ■ Total time: 20 minutes

For complete nutritional information on this and other *Cooking Light* recipes, please turn to the appendix on pages 280–283.

LC
Low-Calorie

from **Cooking Light**

Pasta with Asparagus, Pancetta, and Pine Nuts

8 ounces uncooked cavatappi pasta
1 pound asparagus, trimmed and cut
   diagonally into 1½-inch pieces
1 teaspoon minced garlic
3 tablespoons pine nuts
2 ounces diced pancetta

2 tablespoons fresh lemon juice
2 teaspoons extra-virgin olive oil
½ teaspoon kosher salt
¼ teaspoon freshly ground black pepper
¼ cup (1 ounce) crumbled Parmigiano-
   Reggiano cheese

1. Preheat oven to 400°.
2. Cook pasta according to package directions, omitting salt and fat; add asparagus to pan during last 3 minutes of cooking. Drain. Sprinkle pasta mixture with garlic; return to pan, and toss well.
3. Arrange pine nuts in a single layer on a jelly-roll pan. Bake at 400° for 3 minutes or until golden and fragrant, stirring occasionally. Place in a small bowl.
4. Increase oven temperature to 475°.
5. Arrange pancetta on jelly-roll pan. Bake at 475° for 6 minutes or until crisp.
6. Combine lemon juice, oil, salt, and pepper, stirring with a whisk. Drizzle over pasta mixture; toss well to coat. Sprinkle with pine nuts, pancetta, and cheese.

Makes 4 servings ■ Prep time: 30 minutes ■ Total time: 40 minutes

For complete nutritional information on this and other *Cooking Light* recipes, please turn to the appendix on pages 280–283.

myrecipes users suggest:
- substituting prosciutto for the pancetta
- using elbow macaroni instead of cavatappi

❝ Fabulous!
Easy + tasty = something we'll make again and again! Make a double batch—you'll want extra."

—Bullwinkle
★★★★★

SCAN THIS PHOTO for video on how to prepare this recipe.

Kid-Friendly

 LC Low-Calorie

QUICK TIP

Ripe summer tomatoes are juicy and delicious and don't require seeding or peeling in this dish.

" My father had to get seconds. He said, 'This is so good,' every 5 seconds. Yummy and healthy!"

—sarahtutt

★★★★★

from CookingLight.

Fresh Tomato, Sausage, and Pecorino Pasta

8 ounces uncooked penne
8 ounces sweet Italian sausage
2 teaspoons olive oil
1 cup vertically sliced onion
2 teaspoons minced garlic
1¼ pounds tomatoes, chopped

6 tablespoons grated fresh pecorino
    Romano cheese, divided
¼ teaspoon salt
⅛ teaspoon black pepper
¼ cup torn fresh basil leaves

1. Cook pasta according to package directions, omitting salt and fat; drain.
2. Heat a large nonstick skillet over medium-high heat. Remove casings from sausage. Add oil to pan; swirl to coat. Add sausage and onion to pan; cook 4 minutes, stirring to crumble sausage. Add garlic; cook 2 minutes. Stir in tomatoes; cook 2 minutes. Remove from heat; stir in pasta, 2 tablespoons cheese, salt, and pepper. Sprinkle with remaining ¼ cup cheese and basil.

Makes 4 servings ▪ Prep time: 20 minutes ▪ Total time: 35 minutes

For complete nutritional information on this and other *Cooking Light* recipes, please turn to the appendix on pages 280–283.

 SCAN THIS PHOTO for video on how to prepare this recipe.

" I substituted ground turkey for the ground beef in this recipe, and my family absolutely loved it."

—momof1fromVA

★★★★★

from CookingLight

Beef, Cheese, and Noodle Bake

1 (8-ounce) package small elbow macaroni
Cooking spray
1 cup chopped onion
1 cup shredded carrot
2 teaspoons bottled minced garlic
1 pound lean ground sirloin
1 cup tomato sauce

1 teaspoon kosher salt, divided
½ teaspoon freshly ground black pepper
1 cup fat-free milk
2 tablespoons all-purpose flour
⅛ teaspoon ground nutmeg
1½ cups (6 ounces) 2% reduced-fat
    shredded sharp Cheddar cheese, divided

1. Preheat oven to 350°.
2. Cook pasta according to package directions, omitting salt and fat; drain.
Lightly coat pasta with cooking spray.
3. Heat a Dutch oven over medium-high heat. Coat pan with cooking spray. Add
onion and carrot, and sauté 4 minutes. Add garlic; sauté 1 minute. Add ground beef;
cook 5 minutes or until browned, stirring to crumble. Add tomato sauce, ½ teaspoon
salt, and pepper. Cook for 2 minutes or until most of the liquid evaporates.
4. Add pasta to beef mixture in pan, stirring to combine. Spoon pasta mixture
into an 11 x 7–inch baking dish coated with cooking spray.

5. Place milk, flour, nutmeg, and remaining ½ teaspoon salt in a medium saucepan; stir with a whisk until blended. Cook over medium heat 2 minutes or until
thickened, stirring constantly with a whisk. Add 1 cup cheese, stirring until
smooth. Pour cheese mixture over pasta mixture; stir. Top evenly with remaining
½ cup cheese. Bake at 350° for 20 minutes or until lightly browned. Let stand 5
minutes before serving.

Makes 8 servings ■ Prep time: 35 minutes ■ Total time: 1 hour

For complete nutritional information on this and other *Cooking Light* recipes, please turn to the appendix on pages
280–283.

myrecipes users suggest:
- preparing it with chicken instead of beef
- substituting udon noodles for the spaghetti
- garnishing with chopped peanuts

❝ My husband loved this! I didn't have a full 3 cups of broccoli, so I used vegetables on hand to make up a total of 3 cups: snow peas, celery, orange (bell) pepper, and carrots."

—Goodthots
★★★★★

from Cooking Light

Broccoli-Beef Lo Mein

4 cups hot cooked spaghetti (about 8 ounces uncooked pasta)
1 teaspoon dark sesame oil
1 tablespoon peanut oil
1 tablespoon minced peeled fresh ginger
4 garlic cloves, minced
3 cups chopped broccoli

1½ cups vertically sliced onion
1 (1-pound) flank steak, trimmed and cut across the grain into long, thin strips
3 tablespoons low-sodium soy sauce
2 tablespoons brown sugar
1 tablespoon oyster sauce
1 tablespoon chile paste with garlic

1. Combine pasta and sesame oil, tossing well to coat.
2. Heat peanut oil in a large nonstick skillet over medium-high heat. Add ginger and garlic; sauté 30 seconds. Add broccoli and onion; sauté 3 minutes. Add steak, and sauté 5 minutes or until done. Add pasta mixture, soy sauce, brown sugar, oyster sauce, and chile paste; cook 1 minute or until lo mein is thoroughly heated, stirring constantly.

Makes 6 servings ▪ Prep time: 20 minutes ▪ Total time: 35 minutes

For complete nutritional information on this and other *Cooking Light* recipes, please turn to the appendix on pages 280–283.

SCAN THIS PHOTO for 5 more Asian noodle recipes.

 QUICK TIP

You can bake the pasta in individual 8-ounce ramekins; bake at 425° for 15 minutes.

from *Cooking Light*

Three-Cheese Chicken Penne Florentine

1 teaspoon olive oil
Cooking spray
3 cups thinly sliced mushrooms
1 cup chopped onion
1 cup chopped red bell pepper
3 cups chopped fresh spinach
1 tablespoon chopped fresh oregano
¼ teaspoon freshly ground black pepper
1 (16-ounce) carton 2% cottage cheese
4 cups hot cooked penne (about 8 ounces uncooked tube-shaped pasta)

2 cups shredded roasted skinless, boneless chicken breast
1 cup (4 ounces) shredded reduced-fat sharp Cheddar cheese, divided
½ cup (2 ounces) grated fresh Parmesan cheese, divided
½ cup 2% milk
1 (10.75-ounce) can condensed reduced-fat, reduced-sodium cream of chicken soup, undiluted

1. Preheat oven to 425°.
2. Heat oil in a large nonstick skillet coated with cooking spray over medium-high heat. Add mushrooms, onion, and bell pepper; sauté 4 minutes or until tender. Add spinach, oregano, and black pepper; sauté 3 minutes or just until spinach wilts.
3. Place cottage cheese in a food processor; process until very smooth. Combine spinach mixture, cottage cheese, pasta, chicken, ¾ cup Cheddar cheese, ¼ cup Parmesan cheese, milk, and soup in a large bowl. Spoon mixture into a 2-quart baking dish coated with cooking spray. Sprinkle with remaining ¼ cup Cheddar cheese and remaining ¼ cup Parmesan cheese. Bake at 425° for 25 minutes or until lightly browned and bubbly.

Makes 8 servings ■ Prep time: 20 minutes ■ Total time: about 45 minutes

For complete nutritional information on this and other *Cooking Light* recipes, please turn to the appendix on pages 280–283.

> This is cheesy and creamy—the perfect comfort food. It even got my veggie-hating husband to eat spinach! This one's a keeper."
>
> —ScrapKat67
> ★★★★★

 from CookingLight

Chicken Tetrazzini

1 tablespoon butter
Cooking spray
1 cup finely chopped onion
⅔ cup finely chopped celery
1 teaspoon freshly ground black pepper
¾ teaspoon salt
3 (8-ounce) packages presliced mushrooms
½ cup dry sherry
⅔ cup all-purpose flour
3 (14.5-ounce) cans fat-free, less-sodium
   chicken broth

2¼ cups (9 ounces) grated fresh Parmesan
   cheese, divided
½ cup (4 ounces) ⅓-less-fat cream cheese
7 cups hot cooked vermicelli (about 1 pound
   uncooked pasta)
4 cups chopped cooked chicken breast
   (about 1½ pounds)
1 (1-ounce) slice white bread

1. Preheat oven to 350°.
2. Melt butter in large stockpot coated with cooking spray over medium-high heat. Add onion, celery, pepper, salt, and mushrooms; sauté 4 minutes or until mushrooms are tender. Add sherry; cook 1 minute.
3. Lightly spoon flour into a measuring cup; level with a knife. Gradually add flour to pan; cook 3 minutes, stirring constantly (mixture will be thick) with a whisk. Gradually add broth, stirring constantly. Bring to a boil. Reduce heat; simmer 5 minutes, stirring frequently. Remove from heat.
4. Add 1¾ cups Parmesan cheese and cream cheese, stirring with a whisk until cream cheese melts. Add pasta and chicken, and stir until blended. Divide pasta mixture between 2 (8-inch-square) baking dishes coated with cooking spray.
5. Place bread in food processor; pulse 10 times or until coarse crumbs form. Combine breadcrumbs and remaining ½ cup Parmesan cheese; sprinkle evenly over pasta mixture.
6. Bake at 350° for 30 minutes or until lightly browned. Remove casserole from oven; let stand 15 minutes.

Note: To make ahead, prepare through Step 5. Cool completely in refrigerator. Cover with plastic wrap, pressing to remove as much air as possible. Wrap with heavy-duty foil. Store in freezer for up to 2 months. To bake, thaw casserole completely in refrigerator (about 24 hours). Set foil aside; discard plastic wrap. Re-cover casserole with foil; bake at 350° for 30 minutes. Uncover and bake an additional 1 hour or until golden and bubbly. Let stand 15 minutes.

Makes 12 servings ■ Prep time: 30 minutes ■ Total time: 1 hour, 15 minutes

For complete nutritional information on this and other *Cooking Light* recipes, please turn to the appendix on pages 280–283.

 QUICK TIP

Breaking the vermicelli in half before cooking it makes it easier to toss the pasta and sauce.

 I made this with leftover turkey from Thanksgiving. My husband and I both loved it. This will become a tradition!"

—Suntuosabird
★★★★★

Kid-
Friendly

Make-
Ahead

from Southern Living

Chicken Cannelloni with Roasted Red Pepper Sauce

1 (8-ounce) package cannelloni or manicotti shells
4 cups finely chopped cooked chicken
2 (8-ounce) containers chive-and-onion cream cheese
1 (10-ounce) package frozen chopped spinach, thawed and well drained
1 cup (8 ounces) shredded mozzarella cheese
½ cup Italian-seasoned breadcrumbs
¾ teaspoon garlic salt
1 teaspoon seasoned pepper
Roasted Red Pepper Sauce
Garnish: chopped fresh basil or parsley

1. Cook pasta according to package directions; drain.
2. Preheat oven to 350°. Stir together chicken and next 6 ingredients.
3. Cut pasta shells lengthwise through one side. Spoon about ½ cup chicken mixture into each shell, gently pressing cut sides together. Place, cut sides down, in 2 lightly greased 11 x 7–inch baking dishes. Pour Roasted Red Pepper Sauce evenly over shells.
4. Bake, covered, at 350° for 25 to 30 minutes or until thoroughly heated. Garnish, if desired.

Note: To make ahead, prepare and stuff cannelloni shells as directed. Wrap tightly with wax paper; freeze until ready to serve. Let thaw in refrigerator. Unwrap and place in a baking dish; top with Roasted Red Pepper Sauce, or your favorite supermarket pasta sauce, and bake as directed.

Makes 6 to 8 servings ■ Prep time: 30 minutes ■ Total time: 1 hour

Roasted Red Pepper Sauce

2 (7-ounce) jars roasted red bell peppers, drained
1 (16-ounce) jar creamy Alfredo sauce
1 (3-ounce) package shredded Parmesan cheese

Process all ingredients in a blender until smooth, stopping to scrape down sides.

Makes 3½ cups ■ Prep time: 5 minutes ■ Total time: 5 minutes

" This is my favorite company recipe. I always get rave reviews. It freezes so well that I make it ahead of time, which makes for a less stressful meal. I would give it 6 stars if I could."

—LindaThiel
★★★★★

Kid-Friendly Low-Calorie Make-Ahead

SCAN THIS PHOTO
for more chicken
casserole recipes.

myrecipes users suggest:
- leaving out the chicken
  for a vegetarian entrée
- adding broccoli

" I used a rotisserie chicken to save time. The flavor was amazing, and everyone wanted seconds! It's a crowd-pleaser that you'll make again."

—lovetocook1

★★★★★

from **Oxmoor House**

Cheesy Chicken Spaghetti

9 ounces uncooked spaghetti
Cooking spray
1 cup frozen chopped onion
1 tablespoon bottled minced garlic
2 (14.5-ounce) cans stewed tomatoes, undrained and chopped
1 tablespoon low-sodium Worcestershire sauce

2 teaspoons dried Italian seasoning
¼ teaspoon salt
2 cups (8 ounces) shredded reduced-fat Cheddar cheese, divided
3 cups frozen chopped cooked chicken, thawed

1. Preheat oven to 350°.
2. Cook pasta according to package directions, omitting salt and fat. Drain.
3. Coat a nonstick skillet with cooking spray; place over medium-high heat until hot. Add onion and garlic; sauté 5 minutes. Add tomatoes, Worcestershire sauce, seasoning, and salt; bring to a boil. Reduce heat, and simmer, uncovered, 10 minutes. Stir in 1 cup cheese, cooked spaghetti, and chicken. Spoon into a 3-quart casserole coated with cooking spray.
4. Sprinkle with remaining 1 cup cheese. Bake at 350° for 15 minutes.

Note: To make ahead, prepare through step 3, cover, and refrigerate overnight. Uncover, sprinkle with remaining cheese, and bake at 350° for 25 minutes.

Makes 6 servings ■ Prep time: 25 minutes ■ Total time: 50 minutes

For complete nutritional information on this and other Oxmoor House recipes, please turn to the appendix on pages 280–283.

30 Minutes or Less

LC
Low-Calorie

from Cooking Light

Shrimp Pad Thai

8 ounces uncooked flat rice noodles (pad Thai noodles)
2 tablespoons dark brown sugar
2 tablespoons lower-sodium soy sauce
1½ tablespoons fish sauce
1½ tablespoons fresh lime juice
1 tablespoon Sriracha or chili garlic sauce

3 tablespoons canola oil
1 cup (2-inch) green onion pieces
8 ounces peeled and deveined large shrimp
5 garlic cloves, minced
1 cup fresh bean sprouts
¼ cup chopped unsalted dry-roasted peanuts
3 tablespoons thinly sliced fresh basil

1. Cook noodles according to package directions; drain.
2. Meanwhile, combine sugar and next 4 ingredients in a small bowl.
3. Heat a large skillet or wok over medium-high heat. Add oil to pan; swirl to coat. Add onion, shrimp, and garlic; stir-fry 2 minutes or until shrimp is almost done. Add cooked noodles; toss to combine. Stir in sauce; cook 1 minute, stirring constantly to combine. Arrange about 1 cup noodle mixture on each of 4 plates; top each serving with ¼ cup bean sprouts, 1 tablespoon peanuts, and 2 rounded teaspoons basil.

Makes 4 servings ■ Prep time: 25 minutes ■ Total time: 25 minutes

For complete nutritional information on this and other *Cooking Light* recipes, please turn to the appendix on pages 280–283.

myrecipes users suggest:
- making it with chicken instead of shrimp
- adding snow peas and shredded carrots
- substituting thin rice noodles for the pad Thai noodles

 This recipe is delicious! The presentation was beautiful! A keeper!"
—flowerpot916
★★★★★

30 Minutes
or Less

Grill It!

 QUICK TIP

Leave off the shrimp if you want to make this vegetarian. Or top with grilled chicken, pork, or steak instead of shrimp.

" Followed the recipe exactly except I used lower-carb angel hair pasta. I served it for friends, and they all wanted the recipe!"

—Peaster57

★★★★★

SCAN THIS PHOTO for a video on peeling and deveining shrimp.

from COASTAL LIVING

Orange-Sesame Noodles with Grilled Shrimp

Noodles:
¼ cup fresh orange juice
3 tablespoons tamari or soy sauce
3 tablespoons peanut butter
2 tablespoons toasted sesame oil
2 teaspoons freshly grated ginger
2 teaspoons grated orange zest
¼ teaspoon ground cayenne pepper

10 ounces soba noodles or spaghetti
1 cup snow peas
1 carrot, cut into matchsticks
Shrimp:
1½ pounds large shrimp, peeled and deveined
1 tablespoon toasted sesame oil

1. Combine first 7 ingredients in a large bowl. Preheat grill to medium heat.
2. Boil noodles according to package directions. Before draining, add snow peas and carrot. Let cook 30 seconds.
3. Drain pasta, peas, and carrot, and toss immediately with orange juice mixture. Set aside.
4. Brush shrimp with sesame oil, and grill 3 to 5 minutes.
5. Arrange pasta on serving plates, and top with shrimp.

Makes 4 servings ■ Prep time: 20 minutes ■ Total time: 20 minutes

Kid-Friendly

Low-Calorie

" This is the best tuna casserole recipe we have tried. Very creamy, and we loved the touch of Dijon."

—mauilover
★★★★

from Cooking Light

Tuna Noodle Casserole

8 ounces wide egg noodles
2 tablespoons olive oil
½ cup chopped yellow onion
⅓ cup chopped carrot
2 tablespoons all-purpose flour
2¾ cups fat-free milk
½ cup (4 ounces) ⅓-less-fat cream cheese, softened
2 tablespoons Dijon mustard
½ teaspoon salt
½ teaspoon freshly ground black pepper
1 cup frozen peas, thawed
½ cup (2 ounces) grated Parmigiano-Reggiano cheese, divided
2 (5-ounce) cans albacore tuna in water, drained and flaked
Cooking spray

1. Preheat broiler.
2. Cook noodles according to package directions, omitting salt and fat. Drain. Heat a large skillet over medium heat. Add oil to pan; swirl to coat. Add onion and carrot; cook 6 minutes or until carrot is almost tender, stirring occasionally. Sprinkle with flour; cook 1 minute, stirring constantly. Gradually stir in milk; cook 5 minutes, stirring constantly with a whisk until slightly thick. Stir in cream cheese, mustard, salt, and pepper; cook 2 minutes, stirring constantly.
3. Remove pan from heat. Stir in noodles, peas, ¼ cup Parmigiano-Reggiano cheese, and tuna. Spoon mixture into a shallow broiler-safe 2-quart baking dish coated with cooking spray; top with remaining ¼ cup Parmigiano-Reggiano cheese. Broil 3 minutes or until golden and bubbly. Let stand 5 minutes before serving.

Makes 6 servings ▪ Prep time: 30 minutes ▪ Total time: 40 minutes

For complete nutritional information on this and other *Cooking Light* recipes, please turn to the appendix on pages 280–283.

30 Minutes or Less **LC Low-Calorie**

 I made this for my girlfriend because she doesn't really like red sauce, and she loved it! I would suggest a bit less pepper and a bit more Parmigiano-Reggiano cheese, but other than that it was really good."

—tman5k

★★★★

from CookingLight

White Pizza

1 cup part-skim ricotta cheese
1 cup (4 ounces) shredded part-skim mozzarella cheese
¼ cup (1 ounce) grated Parmigiano-Reggiano cheese
1 (1-pound) Italian cheese-flavored pizza crust (such as Boboli)
1 cup thinly sliced fresh basil

½ cup thinly sliced shallots
½ cup finely chopped spinach
½ to 1 teaspoon crushed red pepper
½ teaspoon black pepper
½ teaspoon dried oregano
¼ teaspoon garlic powder
1 cup thinly sliced plum tomatoes

1. Preheat oven to 425°.
2. Combine first 3 ingredients in a medium bowl. Spread cheese mixture over pizza crust, leaving a ½-inch border around edge. Sprinkle with basil and next 6 ingredients. Arrange tomato slices in a single layer on top. Place pizza on baking sheet. Bake at 425° for 10 minutes. Remove pizza to cutting board; cut into 6 slices.

Makes 6 servings ■ Prep time: 10 minutes ■ Total time: 20 minutes

For complete nutritional information on this and other *Cooking Light* recipes, please turn to the appendix on pages 280–283.

SCAN THIS PHOTO for video on how to prepare this recipe.

30 Minutes or Less

LC Low-Calorie

SCAN THIS PHOTO
for video on how to toast nuts.

" Simply amazing! I bought the dough from a local pizza place, and I also added prosciutto after I layered the apples. So quick, easy, and delicious!"

—skinvail34

★★★★★

from Cooking Light

Apple, Goat Cheese, and Pecan Pizza

1 (1-pound) 6-grain pizza crust
Cooking spray
3 cups thinly sliced Fuji apple (about 8 ounces)
1 cup (4 ounces) crumbled goat cheese
2 teaspoons chopped fresh thyme
1 tablespoon extra-virgin olive oil

2 teaspoons Dijon mustard
1 teaspoon fresh lemon juice
1½ teaspoons honey
2 cups baby arugula
3 tablespoons chopped pecans, toasted

1. Preheat oven to 450°.
2. Place pizza crust on a baking sheet coated with cooking spray. Arrange apple slices evenly over pizza crust; top with cheese. Sprinkle thyme evenly over cheese. Bake at 450° for 8 minutes or until cheese melts and begins to brown.
3. Combine oil and next 3 ingredients in a medium bowl, stirring with a whisk. Add arugula; toss gently to coat. Sprinkle pecans evenly over pizza; top with arugula mixture. Cut pizza into 6 wedges.

Makes 6 servings ■ Prep time: 10 minutes ■ Total time: 20 minutes

For complete nutritional information on this and other *Cooking Light* recipes, please turn to the appendix on pages 280–283.

30 Minutes or Less   Low-Calorie

from CookingLight

Peach and Gorgonzola Chicken Pizza

1 (10-ounce) prebaked thin pizza crust (such as Boboli)
Cooking spray
1 teaspoon extra-virgin olive oil
½ cup (2 ounces) shredded part-skim mozzarella cheese, divided
1 cup shredded cooked chicken breast
⅓ cup (about 1½ ounces) crumbled Gorgonzola cheese
1 medium unpeeled peach, thinly sliced
⅓ cup balsamic vinegar
Arugula leaves and red onion slices (optional)

1. Preheat oven to 400°.
2. Place pizza crust on a baking sheet coated with cooking spray. Brush oil evenly over crust. Top evenly with ¼ cup mozzarella cheese, chicken, Gorgonzola cheese, and peach slices. Top with remaining ¼ cup mozzarella. Bake at 400° for 11 minutes or until crust browns.
3. Place vinegar in a small saucepan over medium-high heat; cook until reduced to 2 tablespoons (about 5 minutes). Drizzle balsamic reduction evenly over pizza. Cut pizza into 8 wedges. Garnish with arugula and red onion, if desired.

Makes 4 servings ■ Prep time: 20 minutes ■ Total time: 30 minutes

For complete nutritional information on this and other *Cooking Light* recipes, please turn to the appendix on pages 280–283.

> **"** My husband and I loved this pizza. I used home-made pizza dough and cooked it on the BBQ. So fabulous!"
>
> —Zendergirl
> ★★★★★

SCAN THIS PHOTO
for video on how to prepare this recipe.

Kid-Friendly

Low-Calorie

from Cooking Light

Chicago Deep-Dish Pizza

2 teaspoons sugar
1 package dry yeast (about 2¼ teaspoons)
1 cup warm water (100° to 110°)
1 tablespoon extra-virgin olive oil
2¾ cups all-purpose flour, divided
¼ cup yellow cornmeal
½ teaspoon salt
Cooking spray
2 cups (8 ounces) shredded part-skim mozzarella cheese, divided
2 precooked mild Italian chicken sausages (about 6 ounces), casings removed, chopped
1 (28-ounce) can whole tomatoes, drained
1½ teaspoons chopped fresh oregano
1½ teaspoons chopped fresh basil
2 cups (about 6 ounces) thinly sliced mushrooms
¾ cup chopped green bell pepper
¾ cup chopped red bell pepper

1. Dissolve sugar and yeast in warm water in a large bowl; let stand for 5 minutes. Stir in oil.

2. Lightly spoon flour into dry measuring cups; level with a knife. Combine about 2½ cups flour, cornmeal, and salt in a bowl. Stir flour mixture into yeast mixture until dough forms a ball. Turn dough out onto a lightly floured surface. Knead until smooth and elastic (about 5 minutes); add enough of remaining flour, 1 tablespoon at a time, to prevent dough from sticking to hands (dough will feel sticky).

3. Place dough in a large bowl coated with cooking spray, turning to coat top. Cover and let rise in a warm place (85°), free from drafts, 45 minutes or until doubled in size. (Gently press two fingers into dough. If indentation remains, dough has risen enough.) Punch dough down; cover and let rest 5 minutes. Roll dough into an 11 x 15–inch rectangle on a lightly floured surface. Place dough in a 13 x 9–inch baking dish coated with cooking spray; press dough up sides of dish. Spread 1½ cups cheese evenly over dough. Arrange chopped sausage evenly over cheese.

4. Preheat oven to 400°.

5. Chop tomatoes; place in a sieve. Stir in oregano and basil; drain tomato mixture 10 minutes.

6. Heat a large nonstick skillet over medium heat. Coat pan with cooking spray. Add mushrooms to pan; cook 5 minutes, stirring occasionally. Stir in bell peppers; cook for 8 minutes or until tender, stirring occasionally. Arrange vegetables over sausage; spoon tomato mixture evenly over vegetables and sausage. Sprinkle evenly with remaining ½ cup cheese. Bake at 400° for 25 minutes or until crust browns and cheese bubbles. Cool 5 minutes before cutting.

Makes 8 servings ■ Prep time: 55 minutes ■ Total time: 2 hours, 30 minutes

For complete nutritional information on this and other *Cooking Light* recipes, please turn to the appendix on pages 280–283.

myrecipes users suggest:
- substituting a store-bought whole-wheat crust for the homemade
- using hot pork Italian sausage or vegan Italian sausage, cooked and crumbled, instead of chicken sausage
- substituting frozen chopped spinach, thawed and squeezed out, for the mushrooms

" Wowzers!"

—CarieCPink
★★★★★

This is a favorite in our house, and my friends frequently ask for it. Great dish!"

—gingerdunnrd

★★★★★

from Cooking Light

Tex-Mex Calzones

8 ounces ground turkey breast
½ cup chopped onion
½ cup chopped green bell pepper
½ cup chopped red bell pepper
¾ teaspoon ground cumin
½ teaspoon chili powder
2 garlic cloves, minced

½ cup fat-free fire-roasted salsa verde
1 (11-ounce) can refrigerated thin-crust pizza dough
¾ cup (3 ounces) preshredded Mexican blend cheese
Cooking spray
¼ cup fat-free sour cream

1. Preheat oven to 425°.
2. Heat a large nonstick skillet over medium-high heat. Add ground turkey to pan; cook 3 minutes, stirring to crumble. Add onion and next 5 ingredients to pan; cook 4 minutes or until vegetables are crisp-tender, stirring mixture occasionally. Remove turkey mixture from heat; stir in salsa.
3. Unroll dough; divide into 4 equal portions. Roll each portion into a 6 x 4–inch rectangle. Working with one rectangle at a time, spoon about ½ cup turkey mixture on one side of dough. Top with 3 tablespoons cheese; fold dough over turkey mixture, and press edges together with a fork to seal. Place on a baking sheet coated with cooking spray. Repeat procedure with remaining dough and turkey mixture. Bake at 425° for 12 minutes or until browned. Serve with sour cream.

Makes 4 servings ■ Prep time: 25 minutes ■ Total time: 40 minutes

For complete nutritional information on this and other *Cooking Light* recipes, please turn to the appendix on pages 280–283.

SCAN THIS PHOTO for video on how to prepare this recipe.

30 Minutes or Less   Low-Calorie

🔍 **QUICK TIP**

A pizza cutter works well for dividing the refrigerated dough into 4 equal portions.

❝ Getting all that spinach in was a little tricky, but the end result was beautiful and tasty. I made some for the kids with a little marinara, mozzarella, and sausage. They loved their version, too!"

—Oblivity

★★★★★

from *Cooking Light*

Spinach Calzones with Blue Cheese

1 (10-ounce) can refrigerated pizza crust
Cooking spray
4 garlic cloves, minced
4 cups spinach leaves

8 (⅛-inch-thick) slices Vidalia or other sweet onion
1⅓ cups sliced cremini or button mushrooms
¾ cup (3 ounces) crumbled blue cheese

1. Preheat oven to 425°.
2. Unroll dough onto a baking sheet coated with cooking spray; cut into 4 quarters. Pat each quarter into a 6 x 5–inch rectangle. Sprinkle garlic evenly over rectangles. Top each rectangle with 1 cup spinach, 2 onion slices, ⅓ cup mushrooms, and 3 tablespoons cheese. Bring 2 opposite corners to center, pinching points to seal. Bring remaining 2 corners to center, pinching all points together to seal. Bake at 425° for 12 minutes or until golden.

Makes 4 servings ■ Prep time: 15 minutes ■ Total time: 30 minutes

For complete nutritional information on this and other *Cooking Light* recipes, please turn to the appendix on pages 280–283.

sides & salads

During the holidays, the humble sweet potato gets bragging rights as the most sought-after ingredient on MyRecipes.com. You'll find a beloved sweet potato casserole recipe here, as well as top-rated recipes for salads and other side dishes.

 To use the exclusive **Scan-It/Cook-It**™ features in this chapter, look for the smartphone symbol (shown at left). For detailed instructions, please see page 7.

SPAGHETTI SQUASH WITH
JALAPEÑO CREAM
page 209

Kid-
Friendly

Delicious! Even the people who don't like broccoli enjoyed this. Definitely no leftovers."

—hkw0003

★★★★

SCAN THIS PHOTO for 22 more casserole side-dish recipes.

from

Broccoli Casserole

Cooking spray
1 pound broccoli, cut into pieces
1 (10.75-ounce) can cream of mushroom soup
2 large eggs, lightly beaten
1 cup mayonnaise

1½ cups shredded Cheddar cheese
½ cup salted butter, cut into pieces
Black pepper
1 sleeve round, buttery crackers, crushed (⅓ of a 12-ounce box)

1. Preheat oven to 350°. Mist a 13 x 9–inch baking dish with cooking spray.
2. Steam broccoli until crisp-tender, 7 minutes. Transfer to a bowl of ice water.
3. Mix soup, eggs, mayonnaise, cheese, butter, and pepper in a saucepan and cook over medium-low heat, stirring constantly, until melted and combined.
4. Drain broccoli; spread evenly in baking dish. Pour cheese mixture on top. Sprinkle with crackers. Bake at 350° for 30 minutes.

Makes 10 servings ■ Prep time: 15 minutes ■ Total time: 45 minutes

For complete nutritional information on this and other *All You* recipes, please turn to the appendix on pages 280–283.

> **"** Neither my husband nor I had ever eaten Brussels sprouts, and we both loved this recipe. I'd totally serve this for company."
>
> —Goldberg
> ★★★★★

from **REAL SIMPLE**

Roasted Brussels Sprouts with Pecans

2 pounds Brussels sprouts, trimmed and halved
1 cup pecans, roughly chopped
2 tablespoons olive oil

2 garlic cloves, finely chopped
½ teaspoon kosher salt
¼ teaspoon black pepper

1. Preheat oven to 400°.
2. On a large rimmed baking sheet, toss Brussels sprouts, pecans, oil, garlic, salt, and pepper. Turn the Brussels sprouts cut side down. Roast at 400° until golden and tender, 20 to 25 minutes.

Makes 8 servings ■ Prep time: 10 minutes ■ Total time: 35 minutes

For complete nutritional information on this and other *Real Simple* recipes, please turn to the appendix on pages 280–283.

Make-Ahead

> **❝** I used a mixture of broccoli crowns and cauliflower, and it was excellent. The nuttiness of the Gruyère goes perfectly with the veggies, and it's even better left over."
>
> —kcnkate
>
>

from CookingLight

Gratin of Cauliflower with Gruyère

1 medium head cauliflower, trimmed and cut into florets (about 2 pounds)
Cooking spray
½ teaspoon kosher salt, divided
2 teaspoons butter
⅓ cup panko (Japanese breadcrumbs)
½ cup (2 ounces) shredded Gruyère cheese, divided

2 tablespoons finely chopped fresh chives
½ cup finely chopped onion
1 garlic clove, minced
3 tablespoons all-purpose flour
2 cups 2% reduced-fat milk
3 tablespoons chopped fresh flat-leaf parsley
¼ teaspoon freshly ground black pepper

1. Preheat oven to 400°.
2. Place cauliflower in a 2-quart broiler-safe baking dish lightly coated with cooking spray; coat cauliflower with cooking spray. Sprinkle with ¼ teaspoon salt; toss. Bake at 400° for 30 minutes or until almost tender. Cool 5 minutes.
3. Preheat broiler.
4. Melt butter in a saucepan over medium heat. Remove from heat. Stir in panko. Stir in ¼ cup cheese and chives.
5. Heat a medium saucepan over medium-high heat. Coat pan with cooking spray. Add onion to pan; sauté 4 minutes or until almost tender, stirring frequently. Add garlic; sauté 1 minute, stirring constantly. Add flour; cook 1 minute, stirring constantly. Gradually add milk, stirring with a whisk; bring to a boil. Cook 3 minutes or until thick, stirring constantly. Remove from heat; stir in remaining ¼ cup cheese, remaining ¼ teaspoon salt, parsley, and pepper. Pour milk mixture over cauliflower mixture; toss. Top evenly with panko mixture. Broil 3 minutes or until golden brown and thoroughly heated.

Note: To make ahead, prepare all the elements for the dish a day ahead. Refrigerate the sauce, the cauliflower, and the panko mixture separately, and assemble before baking as directed.

Makes 6 servings ▪ Prep time: 30 minutes ▪ Total time: 1 hour, 5 minutes

For complete nutritional information on this and other *Cooking Light* recipes, please turn to the appendix on pages 280–283.

" We ate this as tapas, and we'll be making it again. The chickpeas were crunchy and fabulous, and the caramelized cauliflower is a great way to work in veggies for the day."

—Namaste

★★★★★

⊙ QUICK TIP

Enjoy this as a side with sautéed fish or roast chicken, or serve it as the Spanish would, among a variety of other vibrantly flavored small plates.

SCAN THIS PHOTO for video on how to peel and mince garlic.

from CookingLight

Roasted Cauliflower, Chickpeas, and Olives

5½ cups cauliflower florets (about 1 pound)
24 green Spanish olives, pitted and halved
8 garlic cloves, coarsely chopped
1 (15-ounce) can chickpeas (garbanzo beans), rinsed and drained

3 tablespoons olive oil
½ teaspoon crushed red pepper
¼ teaspoon salt
3 tablespoons fresh flat-leaf parsley leaves

1. Preheat oven to 450°.
2. Combine first 4 ingredients in a small roasting pan. Drizzle with oil; sprinkle with red pepper and salt. Toss well to coat. Bake at 450° for 22 minutes or until cauliflower is browned and crisp-tender, stirring after 10 minutes. Sprinkle with parsley.

Makes 6 servings ■ Prep time: 10 minutes ■ Total time: 35 minutes

For complete nutritional information on this and other *Cooking Light* recipes, please turn to the appendix on pages 280–283.

from **Southern Living**

Au Gratin Potato Casserole

1 (32-ounce) package frozen Southern-style
   hash browns
1 (16-ounce) container sour cream
2 cups (8 ounces) shredded Cheddar cheese
1 (10.75-ounce) can cream of mushroom soup

1 small onion, finely chopped
¼ teaspoon black pepper
2 cups crushed cornflakes cereal
¼ cup butter, melted

1. Preheat oven to 325°. Stir together first 6 ingredients in a large bowl.
2. Spoon potato mixture into a lightly greased 13 x 9–inch baking dish. Sprinkle evenly with crushed cornflakes, and drizzle evenly with butter.
3. Bake at 325° for 1 hour and 20 minutes or until bubbly.

Makes 10 to 12 servings ■ Prep time: 10 minutes ■ Total time: 1 hour, 30 minutes

Kid-Friendly

myrecipes users suggest:
- using cream of chicken soup instead of cream of mushroom
- topping with crushed Ritz crackers or Chex cereal instead of the crushed cornflakes
- substituting cream of celery for the cream of mushroom soup

" I have been making this casserole for at least 25 years, and it never fails to get rave reviews—an exceptional side for any holiday or special event."

—MPhall
★★★★★

30 Minutes or Less   Gluten-Free   Low-Calorie

from Cooking Light

Corn and Summer Vegetable Sauté

1 tablespoon canola oil
½ cup chopped green onions (about 4)
1 garlic clove, minced
1 cup (about 4 ounces) sliced fresh okra
1 cup chopped red bell pepper (about 1)
1 jalapeño pepper, seeded and finely chopped

1 cup fresh corn kernels (about 2 ears)
1 (15-ounce) can black beans, rinsed and drained
⅓ cup minced fresh cilantro
⅛ teaspoon salt
⅛ teaspoon freshly ground black pepper

1. Heat oil in a large nonstick skillet over medium-high heat. Add onions and garlic; sauté 1 minute. Add okra; sauté 3 minutes. Reduce heat to medium. Add bell pepper and jalapeño; cook 5 minutes. Add corn; cook 5 minutes. Stir in beans; cook 2 minutes.
2. Remove from heat. Stir in cilantro; sprinkle with salt and black pepper.

Makes 6 servings ■ Prep time: 15 minutes ■ Total time: 30 minutes

For complete nutritional information on this and other *Cooking Light* recipes, please turn to the appendix on pages 280–283.

SCAN THIS PHOTO
for video on preparing spaghetti squash.

from *Sunset*

Spaghetti Squash with Jalapeño Cream

1 spaghetti squash (about 3 pounds)
2 cups milk
2 to 3 jalapeños, stemmed, seeded, and chopped

2 tablespoons butter, plus more for pans
3 tablespoons flour
1 teaspoon salt
1 cup shredded Jack cheese

1. Preheat oven to 375°. Cut squash in half lengthwise and use a spoon or melon baller to remove seeds and surrounding fiber. Put squash, cut side down, on a lightly buttered baking sheet and bake until tender when flesh is pierced with a fork, 30 to 40 minutes. Or poke several holes in skin of squash with a fork and microwave it on HIGH 10 minutes. Squash should be tender when pierced with a fork; if it isn't, microwave on HIGH in 1-minute intervals until tender. Let sit until cool.
2. Meanwhile, in a medium saucepan over medium heat, warm milk and jalapeños until bubbles form along edge of pan. Remove mixture from heat and let sit 15 minutes. Strain and discard jalapeños.
3. When squash is cool enough to handle, use a large spoon to scrape strands out of skin and into a large bowl.
4. In a medium saucepan over medium-high heat, melt 2 tablespoons butter. Whisk in flour and salt and cook, whisking, until flour smells cooked (like piecrust), about 3 minutes. Slowly pour in jalapeño-infused milk while whisking. Reduce heat to medium and continue whisking until mixture thickens slightly, about 3 minutes. Pour mixture over squash, and stir to combine. Transfer mixture to a buttered 2-quart baking dish. Sprinkle with Jack cheese and bake at 375° until bubbling and brown on top, about 30 minutes.

Makes 8 servings ■ Prep time: 30 minutes ■ Total time: 1 hour, 45 minutes

For complete nutritional information on this and other *Sunset* recipes, please turn to the appendix on pages 280–283.

> **"** I made this for my husband, who is extremely suspicious of all new vegetables. He ate half the pan! We had it as the main dish with a side salad. I think this would also be a great side dish."
>
> —Mediocrates
>
> ★★★★★

SCAN THIS PHOTO for video on slicing and dicing zucchini.

Zucchini Oven Chips

 Kid-Friendly   Low-Calorie

¼ cup dry breadcrumbs
¼ cup (1 ounce) grated fresh Parmesan
  cheese
¼ teaspoon seasoned salt
¼ teaspoon garlic powder

⅛ teaspoon freshly ground black pepper
2 tablespoons fat-free milk
2½ cups (¼-inch-thick) slices zucchini
  (about 2 small)
Cooking spray

1. Preheat oven to 425°.
2. Combine first 5 ingredients in a medium bowl, stirring with a whisk. Place milk in a shallow bowl. Dip zucchini slices in milk, and dredge in breadcrumb mixture. Place coated slices on an ovenproof wire rack coated with cooking spray; place rack on a baking sheet. Bake at 425° for 30 minutes or until browned and crisp. Serve immediately.

Makes 4 servings ■ Prep time: 10 minutes ■ Total time: 40 minutes

For complete nutritional information on this and other *Cooking Light* recipes, please turn to the appendix on pages 280–283.

> I loved these and am making them again tonight! My 2-year-old also liked them, which is awesome because he is super picky right now, and getting him to eat veggies is nearly impossible."

—hwinte87
★★★★★

myrecipes users suggest:
- cutting the zucchini thinner or thicker for crispier or chewier chips
- using panko instead of regular breadcrumbs and substituting 2 beaten egg whites for the milk
- substituting dill pickle chips for the zucchini

Kid-Friendly Slow Cooker

from Oxmoor House®

Sweet Potato Casserole with Pecan Topping

Casserole:
2 (29-ounce) cans sweet potatoes in syrup, drained and mashed (about 4 cups mashed)
⅓ cup butter, melted
½ cup granulated sugar
3 tablespoons light brown sugar
2 large eggs, lightly beaten
1 teaspoon vanilla extract
½ teaspoon ground cinnamon
¼ teaspoon ground nutmeg
⅓ cup heavy whipping cream
Topping:
¾ cup chopped pecans
¾ cup firmly packed light brown sugar
¼ cup all-purpose flour
2 tablespoons butter, melted

1. Combine first 8 ingredients in a large bowl; beat at medium speed with an electric mixer until smooth. Add whipping cream; stir well. Pour into a lightly greased 3-quart slow cooker.
2. Combine pecans and remaining 3 ingredients in a small bowl. Sprinkle over sweet potatoes.
3. Cover and cook on HIGH 3 to 4 hours.

Makes 8 servings ■ Prep time: 15 minutes ■ Total time: 3 hours, 15 minutes

ask the expert

How do I keep brown sugar from getting hard?

Here are two good ways:

Place a strip of orange peel in the sugar bag, roll the bag closed, and seal it with masking tape; place that bag inside a zip-top plastic bag and store at room temperature.

Soak a piece of terra-cotta in water and tuck it in any opened bag of brown sugar. (Many houseware stores sell terra-cotta discs for this purpose.)

If your brown sugar has hardened, microwave it on medium-low 1 to 2 minutes, or until it's soft. (Or, if you don't need to use the sugar right away, you can put an apple wedge in the bag and seal it overnight.)

SCAN THIS BOX for more cooking know-how from our experts.

SCAN THIS PHOTO for more sweet potato casserole recipes.

from CookingLight.

Swiss Chard Spanakopita Casserole

Cooking spray
2¼ cups minced white onion
¾ cup minced green onions
3 garlic cloves, minced
9 cups trimmed Swiss chard, chopped
(about 1½ pounds)
6 tablespoons chopped fresh parsley
3 tablespoons minced fresh mint

1 cup (4 ounces) crumbled feta cheese
½ cup (2 ounces) freshly grated Parmesan
cheese
½ teaspoon salt
¼ teaspoon black pepper
3 large egg whites
10 (18 x 14–inch) sheets frozen phyllo
dough, thawed

1. Preheat oven to 350°.
2. Heat a large nonstick skillet coated with cooking spray over medium-high heat. Add white onion; sauté 7 minutes or until golden. Add green onions and garlic, and sauté 1 minute. Stir in chard; cook 2 minutes or until chard wilts. Stir in parsley and mint, and cook 1 minute. Place in a large bowl; cool slightly. Stir in cheeses, salt, pepper, and egg whites.
3. Place 1 phyllo sheet on a large cutting board (cover remaining phyllo to prevent drying), and coat with cooking spray. Top with 1 phyllo sheet, and coat with cooking spray. Repeat procedure with 3 additional sheets.
4. Cut phyllo stack into a 14-inch square. Place square in center of a 13 x 9–inch baking dish coated with cooking spray, allowing phyllo to extend up long sides of dish. Cut 14 x 4–inch piece into 2 (7 x 4–inch) rectangles. Fold each rectangle in half lengthwise. Place a rectangle against each short side of dish. Spread chard mixture evenly over phyllo.
5. Place 1 phyllo sheet on a large cutting board (cover remaining phyllo to prevent drying), and coat with cooking spray. Top with 1 phyllo sheet, and coat with cooking spray. Repeat procedure with remaining phyllo sheets. Place 18 x 14–inch phyllo stack over chard mixture. Fold phyllo edges into center. Coat with cooking spray. Score phyllo by making 2 lengthwise cuts and 3 crosswise cuts to form 12 rectangles. Bake at 350° for 40 minutes or until golden.

Makes 12 servings ■ Prep time: 40 minutes ■ Total time: 1 hour, 20 minutes

For complete nutritional information on this and other *Cooking Light* recipes, please turn to the appendix on pages 280–283.

 I've made this three times, once with my over-abundant rainbow chard and twice with spinach. It's so easy and so good."

—parrotkabob
★★★★★

myrecipes users suggest:
• adding 2 sliced tomatoes and toasted pine nuts
• omitting the mint

Make-
Ahead

❝ We loved, loved,
loved this recipe
and intend to use it
as a dinner casserole
and not just a holiday
stuffing recipe.”

—jean64

from *Sunset*

Italian Chard Dressing

¾ loaf (¾ pound) French bread
1½ cups nonfat milk
2 pounds Italian sausages
1 cup chopped fresh flat-leaf parsley
1 garlic clove, minced or pressed
1 medium onion, chopped
½ cup finely chopped celery
1½ pounds green Swiss chard, stem ends
  trimmed, coarsely chopped

½ cup water
1½ cups freshly grated Parmesan cheese
1½ teaspoons dried basil
¼ teaspoon dried rubbed sage
¼ teaspoon dried rosemary
Salt

1. Cut bread into ½-inch slices. Place slices in a large bowl and add milk. Mix gently with a spoon to saturate with milk, and let stand about 30 minutes. Stir occasionally.

2. Meanwhile, place a 6- to 8-quart pot over high heat. Squeeze sausages from casings into pot. Discard casings. Cook meat, stirring often to crumble, until lightly browned, 10 to 15 minutes; discard fat. Add parsley, garlic, onion, and celery. Cook, stirring often, until vegetables are lightly browned, 5 to 8 minutes. Add chard and water and cook, stirring often, until wilted, about 5 minutes.

3. With your hands, squeeze bread slices to break them into tiny pieces. Add cooked meat mixture, Parmesan, basil, sage, and rosemary. Season with salt to taste.

4. Preheat oven to 350°. Spoon dressing into a shallow 3-quart (13 x 9–inch) casserole. For moist stuffing, cover with foil; for crusty dressing, do not cover. Bake at 350° until hot (at least 150° in center) or lightly browned, at least 30 minutes.

Note: To make ahead, assemble as directed through step 3 the day before; place in casserole, cover, and refrigerate. Allow about 1 hour to bake as directed.

Makes 16 servings ■ Prep time: 30 minutes ■ Total time: 1 hour, 30 minutes

For complete nutritional information on this and other *Sunset* recipes, please turn to the appendix on pages 280–283.

SCAN THIS PHOTO for video on how to mince parsley.

QUICK TIP

Out of light coconut milk?
You can substitute equal parts regular coconut milk and water.

" Best rice dish ever! This dish has so much flavor, and I would definitely make it again."

—satori56
★★★★★

from COASTAL LIVING

Coconut Curry Jasmine Rice

1¼ tablespoons butter
1 small onion, chopped
2 teaspoons curry powder
1 cup jasmine or long-grain rice
⅓ cup golden raisins

1 cup light coconut milk
½ cup vegetable broth
½ cup water
½ teaspoon salt
1 bay leaf

1. Melt butter in a medium saucepan. Add onion, and sauté until tender. Add curry powder and rice; cook 2 minutes. Stir in remaining ingredients.
2. Bring to a boil; cover, reduce heat, and simmer 20 minutes or until liquid is absorbed. Remove bay leaf.

Makes 3½ cups ■ Prep time: 15 minutes ■ Total time: 35 minutes

30 Minutes
or Less

Kid-
Friendly

SCAN THIS PHOTO
for 7 more recipes
using bacon.

" This is my
favorite
recipe right now.
Very impressive."

—rujoebanks
★★★★★

from CookingLight

Macaroni Salad with Bacon, Peas, and Creamy Dijon Dressing

Dressing:
½ cup (4 ounces) ⅓-less-fat cream cheese
¼ cup chopped shallots
¼ cup reduced-fat mayonnaise
2 tablespoons fat-free sour cream
2 tablespoons Dijon mustard
2 tablespoons lemon juice
1 tablespoon white wine vinegar
¾ teaspoon black pepper
½ teaspoon kosher salt

Salad:
8 ounces uncooked large elbow macaroni
⅔ cup fresh green peas
⅔ cup finely diced red bell pepper
⅔ cup finely diced red onion
½ cup thinly sliced green onions
¼ cup chopped fresh flat-leaf parsley
½ teaspoon grated lemon rind
3 lower-sodium bacon slices, cooked and
    crumbled

1. To prepare dressing, combine first 9 ingredients in a food processor, and process until smooth. Cover and chill.
2. To prepare salad, cook pasta according to package directions, omitting salt and fat; add peas during the last 3 minutes of cooking time. Drain; rinse with cold water. Drain. Combine pasta mixture, bell pepper, and next 4 ingredients in a large bowl. Toss pasta mixture with half of dressing. Cover and chill until ready to serve. Toss salad with remaining dressing, and sprinkle with crumbled bacon; serve immediately.

Makes 8 servings ▪ Prep time: 10 minutes ▪ Total time: 25 minutes

For complete nutritional information on this and other *Cooking Light* recipes, please turn to the appendix on pages 280–283.

from all*you

Pesto Pasta Salad

Pesto:
3 cups packed fresh basil leaves
1 cup packed fresh parsley leaves
3 garlic cloves, chopped
1 tablespoon lemon juice
½ teaspoon salt
¼ teaspoon black pepper

⅓ cup pine nuts, toasted
½ cup olive oil
½ cup grated Parmesan
Salad:
1 pound gemelli or other short pasta
1 cup plain 2% Greek yogurt
2 pints cherry or grape tomatoes, halved

1. Make pesto: In a food processor, purée basil, parsley, garlic, lemon juice, salt, pepper, and pine nuts until smooth. With motor running, add oil, and process until a thick paste forms. Add Parmesan, and pulse twice. Season with more salt and pepper, if desired.
2. Make salad: Cook pasta according to package directions until al dente. Drain and run under cold water to stop cooking.
3. In a large bowl, combine pesto and yogurt, and stir until well blended. Add cold pasta, and toss to coat with dressing. Top with tomatoes. Serve salad at room temperature, or cover and refrigerate to serve chilled.

Makes 8 servings ▪ Prep time: 30 minutes ▪ Total time: 30 minutes

For complete nutritional information on this and other *All You* recipes, please turn to the appendix on pages 280–283.

❝ Really delicious! Yum! I made the pesto with walnuts and added some extra walnuts to the finished salad.”

—reneefromboston
★★★★★

30 Minutes or Less

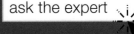
QUICK TIP

Use store-bought pesto to make it even faster.

---

ask the expert

Can I freeze basil leaves?

You absolutely can freeze basil, but you won't end up with beautiful bright green leaves.

To preserve some of the appealing green color when freezing whole leaves, steam them, pat dry, and freeze in a single layer on a baking sheet. Transfer frozen leaves to a zip-top plastic freezer bag and store in the freezer for up to 6 months.

Another method for freezing garden-fresh basil is this: Puree it in the food processor with a little extra-virgin olive oil (about 2 tablespoons per 1 to 1½ cups basil). Spoon the puree into ice cube trays to freeze. Transfer frozen cubes to a zip-top plastic freezer bag and freeze up to 1 year.

SCAN THIS BOX for more cooking know-how from our experts.

30 Minutes or Less   Gluten-Free   Low-Calorie

QUICK TIP

Use maple-cured bacon for more maple flavor, but steer clear of any made with imitation maple flavoring, which can taste artificial.

" This was delicious! Excellent dressing. I used turkey bacon instead of pork and made the dressing ahead of time to let the flavors blend."

—kathleenk

★★★★★

from CookingLight

Spinach Salad with Maple-Dijon Vinaigrette

¼ cup maple syrup
3 tablespoons minced shallots (about 1 medium)
2 tablespoons red wine vinegar
1 tablespoon canola oil
1 tablespoon country-style Dijon mustard
¼ teaspoon salt

¼ teaspoon freshly ground black pepper
1 garlic clove, minced
1 cup sliced mushrooms
½ cup vertically sliced red onion
½ cup chopped Braeburn apple
4 bacon slices, cooked and crumbled
1 (10-ounce) package fresh spinach

Combine first 8 ingredients in a large bowl, stirring with a whisk. Add mushrooms and remaining ingredients; toss well to coat.

Makes 8 servings ▪ Prep time: 10 minutes ▪ Total time: 10 minutes

For complete nutritional information on this and other *Cooking Light* recipes, please turn to the appendix on pages 280–283.

Gluten-Free

from **REAL**SIMPLE

Cabbage and Apple Slaw

2 cups shredded green cabbage
2 cups shredded red cabbage
½ cup mayonnaise
¼ cup sour cream
2 tablespoons cider vinegar
½ teaspoon celery seed

½ teaspoon kosher salt
⅛ teaspoon black pepper
1 large unpeeled Fuji apple, cored, quartered, and thinly sliced
2 tablespoons finely chopped fresh flat-leaf parsley (optional)

1. In a large bowl, combine green and red cabbages; set aside.
2. In a medium bowl, whisk together mayonnaise, sour cream, vinegar, celery seed, salt, and pepper. Add apple slices. Pour over cabbage and toss gently until coated. Cover and chill 1 hour or longer.
3. To serve, spoon into salad bowls and sprinkle with the parsley (if desired).

Makes 4 servings ▪ Prep time: 10 minutes ▪ Total time: 1 hour, 10 minutes

For complete nutritional information on this and other *Real Simple* recipes, please turn to the appendix on pages 280–283.

> **"** I used a bag of coleslaw so I didn't have to chop, and it was fabulous!"
> —klove10381
> ★★★★★

SCAN THIS PHOTO for video on how to slice cabbage.

Kid-Friendly

Grill It!

> " This is, hands
> down, the best
> potato salad that I
> have ever made."
>
> —Schredder
>
>

from Southern Living

Grilled Potato Salad

8 bacon slices
4 medium-size red potatoes, cut into ¾-inch cubes (about 5 cups cubed)
1 large white onion, cut into ½-inch-thick strips

Potato Salad Dry Rub
Potato Salad Dressing
Garnish: chopped fresh parsley

1. Preheat grill to 350° to 400° (medium-high) heat. Cook bacon, in batches, in a large skillet over medium-high heat 8 to 10 minutes or until crisp; remove bacon, and drain on paper towels, reserving drippings in skillet. Crumble bacon.
2. Add potatoes, onion, and Potato Salad Dry Rub to hot drippings in skillet, tossing to coat. Remove potato mixture with a slotted spoon.
3. Grill potato mixture, covered with grill lid, in a grill wok or metal basket 30 minutes or until tender, stirring every 5 minutes.
4. Transfer mixture to a large bowl. Add Potato Salad Dressing, and toss to coat. Stir in bacon. Garnish with parsley, if desired. Serve warm.

Makes 4 to 5 servings ■ Prep time: 20 minutes ■ Total time: 50 minutes

Potato Salad Dry Rub

2 teaspoons salt
1¼ teaspoons black pepper
1 teaspoon paprika
1 teaspoon garlic powder

¼ teaspoon dried thyme
¼ teaspoon crushed dried rosemary
⅛ teaspoon celery seeds

Stir together all ingredients. Store in an airtight container up to 1 month.

Makes about ⅓ cup ■ Prep time: 5 minutes ■ Total time: 5 minutes

Potato Salad Dressing

5½ tablespoons mayonnaise
2 tablespoons Dijon mustard

2 teaspoons Worcestershire sauce

Stir together all ingredients. Store in an airtight container in refrigerator up to 2 weeks.

Makes about 1 cup ■ Prep time: 5 minutes ■ Total time: 5 minutes

SCAN THIS PHOTO for more of our favorite potato salad recipes.

from CookingLight.

Bulgur Salad with Edamame and Cherry Tomatoes

QUICK TIP

Substitute fresh favas for the edamame, if you like.

❝ What an easy, refreshing, filling, and healthy salad! I kept adding more tomatoes as I ate it for meals throughout the week. A spritz of lemon juice helped freshen it up on subsequent days. Delish!"

—LisaMK

★★★★

1 cup uncooked bulgur
1 cup boiling water
1 cup frozen shelled edamame (green soybeans)
1 pound yellow and red cherry tomatoes, halved
1 cup finely chopped fresh flat-leaf parsley

⅓ cup finely chopped fresh mint
2 tablespoons chopped fresh dill
1 cup chopped green onions
¼ cup fresh lemon juice
¼ cup extra-virgin olive oil
1 teaspoon kosher salt
½ teaspoon freshly ground black pepper

1. Combine bulgur and boiling water in a large bowl. Cover and let stand 1 hour or until bulgur is tender.

2. Cook edamame in boiling water 3 minutes or until crisp-tender. Drain. Add edamame, tomatoes, and remaining ingredients to bulgur; toss well. Let stand at room temperature 1 hour before serving.

Makes 6 servings ■ Prep time: 10 minutes ■ Total time: 2 hours, 10 minutes

For complete nutritional information on this and other *Cooking Light* recipes, please turn to the appendix on pages 280–283.

Gluten-
Free

> I've been looking
> for ways to
> make quinoa since it's
> so good for you, and
> this recipe is excellent.
> The mint, onions,
> and lemon are not
> overpowering, and
> the combination is
> really fresh-tasting."

—RobinAutry

★★★★★

from COASTAL LIVING

Quinoa, Corn, and Mint Salad

2 cups quinoa
4 cups water
Kosher salt
3 cups fresh corn kernels (6 ears)
1 bunch green onions, finely chopped
   (about 1 cup)

¾ cup chopped fresh mint
1 tablespoon grated lemon zest
¼ cup fresh lemon juice
¼ cup extra-virgin olive oil
½ teaspoon freshly ground pepper

1. Rinse quinoa in large sieve under cold running water. In a medium saucepan, bring water to a boil. Add 2 teaspoons salt and quinoa, and cook 10 to 15 minutes or until almost tender. Drain; spread quinoa onto a large sheet pan, and cool 15 minutes.
2. Combine quinoa and remaining ingredients; mix well. Season with salt.

Makes 8½ cups ■ Prep time: 10 minutes ■ Total time: 35 minutes

from

30 Minutes or Less Gluten-Free Low-Calorie

Crab, Corn, and Tomato Salad with Lemon-Basil Dressing

1 tablespoon grated lemon rind
5 tablespoons fresh lemon juice, divided
1 tablespoon extra-virgin olive oil
1 teaspoon honey
½ teaspoon Dijon mustard
¼ teaspoon salt
⅛ teaspoon freshly ground black pepper
1 cup fresh corn kernels (about 2 ears)

¼ cup thinly sliced fresh basil leaves
¼ cup chopped red bell pepper
2 tablespoons finely chopped red onion
1 pound lump crabmeat, shell pieces removed
8 (¼-inch-thick) slices ripe beefsteak tomato
2 cups cherry tomatoes, halved

1. Combine lemon rind, 3 tablespoons lemon juice, and next 5 ingredients in a large bowl, stirring well with a whisk. Reserve 1½ tablespoons juice mixture. Add remaining 2 tablespoons juice, corn, and next 4 ingredients to remaining juice mixture; toss gently to coat.
2. Arrange 2 tomato slices and ½ cup cherry tomatoes on each of 4 plates. Drizzle about 1 teaspoon reserved juice mixture over each serving. Top each serving with 1 cup corn and crab mixture.

Makes 4 servings ■ Prep time: 15 minutes ■ Total time: 15 minutes

For complete nutritional information on this and other *Cooking Light* recipes, please turn to the appendix on pages 280–283.

" This is one of the most delicious summer salad recipes I have ever had! I used a half-pound of crab, and it was plenty for two. I would definitely make it again."

—allykrue
★★★★★

myrecipes users suggest:
• doubling the dressing and serving on a bed of baby arugula
• using a combination of fresh shrimp and imitation crab instead of the fresh lump crabmeat
• adding chopped-up steamed shrimp and avocado

desserts |

When it comes to sweets, MyRecipes.com users crave cookies, and that crave-worthy dessert is well represented here. We've folded 4- and 5-star recipes for chocolate chip and peanut butter cookies into the mix—along with recipes for delectable bars, cupcakes, cakes, cheesecakes, and pies.

To use the exclusive **Scan-It/Cook-It**™ features in this chapter, look for the smartphone symbol (shown at left). For detailed instructions, please see page 7.

OATMEAL CREAM PIES
page 233

desserts

from **Southern Living**

Kid-
Friendly

All-Time Favorite Chocolate Chip Cookies

¾ cup butter, softened
¾ cup granulated sugar
¾ cup firmly packed dark brown sugar
2 large eggs
1½ teaspoons vanilla extract
2¼ cups plus 2 tablespoons all-purpose flour

1 teaspoon baking soda
¾ teaspoon salt
1½ (12-ounce) packages semisweet
    chocolate morsels
Parchment paper

🔊 **QUICK TIP**

For chewier cookies,
bake them 10 minutes. For
crisper cookies, bake them
up to 14 minutes.

1. Preheat oven to 350°. Beat butter and sugars at medium speed with a heavy-duty electric stand mixer until creamy. Add eggs and vanilla, beating until blended.
2. Combine flour, baking soda, and salt in a small bowl; gradually add to butter mixture, beating just until blended. Beat in morsels just until combined. Drop by tablespoonfuls onto parchment paper–lined baking sheets.
3. Bake at 350° for 10 to 14 minutes or until desired degree of doneness. Remove to wire racks, and cool completely (about 15 minutes).

Note: Try one of the following variations for a different flavor:
• Beat in 2 cups coarsely crushed pretzel sticks or 1 (7-ounce) bag white chocolate–covered mini pretzel twists, coarsely crushed, with the chocolate morsels.
• Substitute 1 (12-ounce) package white chocolate morsels, 1 (6-ounce) package sweetened dried cranberries, and 1 cup pistachios for the chocolate morsels.
• Substitute 6 (1.4-ounce) chopped chocolate-covered toffee candy bars and 1½ cups toasted slivered almonds for the chocolate morsels.
• Substitute 1 (7-ounce) package milk chocolate-caramel-pecan clusters, coarsely chopped, and 1 (12-ounce) package dark chocolate morsels for the semisweet morsels.

Makes about 5 dozen ■ Prep time: 15 minutes ■ Total time: 40 minutes

 These chocolate
chip cookies
are the best thing.
They bake up perfectly
and don't spread
like break-and-bake
cookie dough."

—aj2005
★★★★★

Kid-Friendly

> **The butterscotch really adds flavor. Whether 5 or 50 years old, all the boys in our family loved them!"**
>
> —Princess222
>
> ★★★★★

 from **all you**

Peanut Butter Cookies with Butterscotch Bits

1⅓ cups all-purpose flour
½ teaspoon baking soda
½ teaspoon salt
½ cup unsalted butter, at room temperature
1½ cups chunky peanut butter (not "all natural")

1 cup sugar
1 large egg
1 teaspoon vanilla extract
1 (11-ounce) package butterscotch morsels
Parchment paper

1. In a large bowl, mix flour, baking soda, and salt.
2. Beat butter and peanut butter until smooth. Gradually add sugar, beating to blend. Beat in egg and vanilla. Stir in flour mixture and butterscotch morsels. Form into a large disk and wrap in plastic. Chill for 2 hours or overnight.
3. Preheat oven to 375°; line 2 baking sheets with parchment paper. Use hands to form dough into 1½-inch balls. Place balls about 2 inches apart on cookie sheets. Using a fork, press balls flat, then press again to form a crisscross pattern. Bake cookies at 375° until lightly browned, about 15 minutes. Cool on sheets for 10 minutes, then transfer to racks to cool completely. Repeat with remaining dough.

Makes about 2 dozen ■ Prep time: 20 minutes ■ Total time: 2 hours, 45 minutes

For complete nutritional information on this and other *All You* recipes, please turn to the appendix on pages 280–283.

SCAN THIS PHOTO for video on peanut-butter measuring.

Oatmeal Cream Pies (pictured on page 229)

1¼ cups butter, softened
1 cup firmly packed brown sugar
½ cup granulated sugar
1 large egg
2 teaspoons vanilla extract
1½ cups all-purpose flour

1 teaspoon baking soda
½ teaspoon salt
¼ teaspoon ground cinnamon
3 cups uncooked quick-cooking oats
Cream Filling
Parchment paper

1. Preheat oven to 375°.
2. Beat butter and sugars at medium speed with an electric mixer until creamy. Add egg and vanilla, beating well.
3. Lightly spoon flour into dry measuring cups, and level with a knife. Combine flour and next 3 ingredients in a bowl, stirring well. Add oats; stir well. Add to butter mixture; stir until well blended. Drop by rounded tablespoons 2 inches apart onto baking sheets lined with parchment paper. Bake at 375° for 10 minutes. Cool on pan 2 to 3 minutes. Remove cookies from pan; cool on wire racks.
4. Spread 1 tablespoon Cream Filling over bottom side of half of cookies; top with remaining cookies, right side up.

Makes 18 cream pies ■ Prep time: 25 minutes ■ Total time: 45 minutes

Cream Filling

½ cup butter, softened
2 cups powdered sugar

1 to 2 tablespoons whipping cream
1 teaspoon vanilla extract

Combine all ingredients in a medium bowl. Beat with an electric mixer on low speed until combined, scraping bowl. Beat on high until light and fluffy.

Makes about 3 cups ■ Prep time: 5 minutes ■ Total time: 5 minutes

Kid-Friendly

❝ Incredibly amazing and surprisingly easy! Tasty, scrumptious, and delicious. A+.❞

—classycooking
★★★★★

5

5 Ingredients
or Less

Kid-
Friendly

> **"** What a fabulous
> recipe. My
> children love these,
> and they are the
> perfect size for
> munching! These
> will be a welcome
> addition to my
> holiday treats."
>
> —mspeter
>
> ★★★★★

from **Oxmoor House.**

Brownie Buttons

Cooking spray
1 (16.5-ounce) package refrigerated
  brownie dough

1 bag assorted miniature peanut butter cup
  candies and chocolate-coated caramels
  (such as Rolos)

1. Preheat oven to 350°. Spray miniature (1¾-inch) muffin pans with cooking spray,
or line pans with paper liners and spray liners with cooking spray. Spoon brownie
batter evenly into each cup, filling almost full. Bake at 350° for 19 to 20 minutes.
2. Cool in pans 3 to 4 minutes, and then gently press a miniature candy into each
baked brownie until top of candy is level with top of brownie. Cool 10 minutes in
pans. Gently twist each brownie to remove from pan. Cool on a wire rack.

Makes 20 brownies ■ Prep time: 15 minutes ■ Total time: 50 minutes

SCAN THIS PHOTO
for 17 more of our
best brownie recipes.

Kid-
Friendly

from Cooking Light

Salted Caramel Brownies

Brownies:
3.38 ounces all-purpose flour (about ¾ cup)
1 cup granulated sugar
¾ cup unsweetened cocoa
½ cup packed brown sugar
½ teaspoon baking powder
6 tablespoons butter, melted
2 large eggs
1 teaspoon vanilla extract
Cooking spray

Topping:
¼ cup butter
¼ cup packed brown sugar
3½ tablespoons evaporated fat-free milk, divided
¼ teaspoon vanilla extract
½ cup powdered sugar
1 ounce bittersweet chocolate, coarsely chopped
⅛ teaspoon coarse sea salt

1. Preheat oven to 350°.
2. To prepare brownies, weigh or lightly spoon flour into dry measuring cups; level with a knife. Combine flour and next 4 ingredients in a large bowl, stirring well with a whisk. Combine 6 tablespoons melted butter, eggs, and 1 teaspoon vanilla. Add butter mixture to flour mixture; stir to combine. Scrape batter into a 9-inch square metal baking pan lightly coated with cooking spray. Bake at 350° for 19 minutes or until a wooden pick inserted in center comes out with moist crumbs clinging. Cool in pan on a wire rack.
3. To prepare topping, melt ¼ cup butter in a saucepan over medium heat. Add ¼ cup brown sugar and 1½ tablespoons evaporated milk; cook 2 minutes. Remove from heat. Add vanilla and powdered sugar; stir with a whisk until smooth. Spread mixture evenly over cooled brownies. Let stand 20 minutes or until set.
4. Combine remaining 2 tablespoons evaporated milk and chocolate in a microwave-safe bowl; microwave at HIGH for 45 seconds or until melted, stirring after 20 seconds. Stir just until smooth; drizzle over caramel. Sprinkle with sea salt; let stand until set. Cut into squares.

Makes 20 servings ■ Prep time: 30 minutes ■ Total time: 1 hour, 5 minutes

For complete nutritional information on this and other *Cooking Light* recipes, please turn to the appendix on pages 280–283.

ask the expert

How do I adjust a recipe for high-altitude cooking?

Most foods take longer to cook and dry out more easily at more than 3,000 feet above sea level. Plan for extra time, and add anywhere from 25 percent to 50 percent more liquid to braised dishes.

Baking at high altitude requires more-complicated adjustments. Finding what works best in your area is largely a process of trial and error, but here are a few suggestions:

• *at 3,000 feet:* Reduce baking powder by ⅛ teaspoon, reduce sugar by as much as 1 tablespoon, and increase the liquid in the recipe 1 to 2 tablespoons for each cup.

• *at 5,000 feet :* Reduce baking powder by ⅛ to ¼ teaspoon, reduce sugar by as much as 2 tablespoons, and increase the liquid in the recipe 2 to 4 tablespoons for each cup.

• *at 7,000 feet:* Reduce baking powder by ¼ teaspoon, reduce sugar by as much as 3 tablespoons, and increase the liquid in the recipe 3 to 4 tablespoons for each cup.

SCAN THIS BOX for more cooking know-how from our experts.

QUICK TIP

To line the pan with foil, trim two long foil pieces to a 9-inch width. Fit the strips, crossing each other, in the pan.

myrecipes users suggest:
- using the recipe to make brownie cake pops
- cooling the baked brownies, reserving and crumbling one of them, and sprinkling the crumbs over the frosted brownies as a garnish

❝ Great recipe! It's very easy and only requires one bowl, which is nice."

—pindseylou

★★★★★

from Southern Living

Red Velvet Brownies

1 (4-ounce) bittersweet chocolate baking bar, chopped
¾ cup butter
2 cups sugar
4 large eggs
1½ cups all-purpose flour
1 (1-ounce) bottle red liquid food coloring
1½ teaspoons baking powder
1 teaspoon vanilla extract
⅛ teaspoon salt
Small-Batch Cream Cheese Frosting
Garnish: white chocolate curls

1. Preheat oven to 350°. Line bottom and sides of a 9-inch square pan with aluminum foil, allowing 2 to 3 inches to extend over sides; lightly grease foil.
2. Microwave chocolate and butter in a large microwave-safe bowl at HIGH 1½ to 2 minutes or until melted and smooth, stirring at 30-second intervals. Whisk in sugar. Add eggs, 1 at a time, whisking just until blended after each addition. Gently stir in flour and next 4 ingredients. Pour mixture into prepared pan.
3. Bake at 350° for 44 to 48 minutes or until a wooden pick inserted in center comes out with a few moist crumbs. Cool completely on a wire rack (about 2 hours).
4. Lift brownies from pan, using foil sides as handles; gently remove foil. Spread Small-Batch Cream Cheese Frosting on top of brownies, and cut into 16 squares. Garnish, if desired.

Makes 16 servings ■ Prep time: 10 minutes ■ Total time: 3 hours

Small-Batch Cream Cheese Frosting

1 (8-ounce) package cream cheese, softened
3 tablespoons butter, softened
1½ cups powdered sugar
⅛ teaspoon salt
1 teaspoon vanilla extract

Beat cream cheese and butter at medium speed with an electric mixer until creamy. Gradually add powdered sugar and salt, beating until blended. Stir in vanilla.

Makes about 1⅔ cups ■ Prep time: 10 minutes ■ Total time: 10 minutes

SCAN THIS PHOTO for video on how to soften butter.

Kid-Friendly

from

Pumpkin Cheesecake Bars

Crust:
Cooking spray
20 crème-filled chocolate sandwich cookies
2½ tablespoons unsalted butter, melted
Filling:
2 (8-ounce) packages cream cheese, at room temperature
1 cup sugar

1 cup canned pumpkin puree
3 large eggs, at room temperature
1 teaspoon vanilla extract
3 tablespoons all-purpose flour
1 teaspoon pumpkin pie spice
¼ teaspoon salt
Garnish: whipped cream ghosts

1. Preheat oven to 350°. Line an 8-inch square pan with foil so that foil overhangs sides. Mist with cooking spray.
2. Make crust: Process cookies in food processor until ground. Pulse in butter. Press evenly into pan. Bake until firm, 10 to 12 minutes. Cool slightly.
3. Make filling: With an electric mixer on medium speed, beat cream cheese and sugar until smooth, about 2 minutes. Beat in pumpkin, then eggs, 1 at a time. Beat in vanilla, flour, spice, and salt until just combined.
4. Pour mixture into pan. Put pan on a large rimmed baking sheet; place in oven. Pour hot water into baking sheet until nearly filled. Bake at 350° until cheesecake is set around edges but jiggles slightly in center, 40 to 45 minutes. Remove pan from sheet; cool completely on rack. Cover with plastic wrap. Chill until firm, at least 3 hours. Garnish, if desired.

Makes 12 bars ■ Prep time: 15 minutes ■ Total time: 4 hours, 5 minutes

For complete nutritional information on this and other *All You* recipes, please turn to the appendix on pages 280–283.

QUICK TIP

To garnish these bars, pipe whipped cream in a circular, upward motion atop each bar. Use mini chocolate chips or chocolate cookie pieces for eyes.

ask the expert

How do I adjust cooking time or temperature when I use the convection setting on my oven?

Convection cooking is often faster and always at a lower temperature than regular oven cooking. Set your convection oven 25° lower than the recipe calls for, and feel free to crowd your oven: Even with food on every rack, convection keeps the air circulating so the food cooks evenly. (That makes life easier when you're entertaining!)

A whole roast—be it a whole turkey, leg of lamb, pork roast, or crown roast—may cook in 25 percent less time (using the "convection roast" setting), while several trays of cookies may bake (again, at a 25° lower temperature) in just a little less time than the recipe calls for.

SCAN THIS BOX for more cooking know-how from our experts.

❝ Wow! These are amazing. Follow the recipe exactly, and you can't go wrong. Best cupcakes ever. The icing is amazing, too!"

— KellyAF

from CookingLight

Coconut Cupcakes with Lime Buttercream Frosting

Cupcakes:
Cooking spray
4.5 ounces all-purpose flour (about 1 cup)
3 tablespoons potato starch
1 teaspoon baking powder
½ teaspoon salt
¾ cup sugar
2 tablespoons butter, softened
1 large egg
1 large egg white
⅔ cup fat-free milk

2 tablespoons flaked sweetened coconut
½ teaspoon vanilla extract
Frosting:
3 tablespoons butter, softened
1 teaspoon half-and-half
½ teaspoon grated lime rind
1 tablespoon fresh lime juice
4.75 ounces powdered sugar, sifted
   (about 1⅓ cups)
Toasted coconut flakes (optional)

1. Preheat oven to 350°.
2. To prepare cupcakes, place 2 muffin cup liners in each of 12 muffin cups; coat liners with cooking spray.
3. Weigh or lightly spoon flour into a dry measuring cup; level with a knife. Combine flour and next 3 ingredients in a small bowl; stir with a whisk.
4. Combine sugar and 2 tablespoons butter in a large bowl; beat with a mixer at medium speed until blended (mixture will be the consistency of damp sand). Add egg and egg white, one at a time, beating well after each addition. Add flour mixture and milk alternately to egg mixture, beginning and ending with flour mixture. Fold in coconut and vanilla.
5. Spoon batter evenly into prepared muffin cups. Bake at 350° for 18 minutes or until cupcakes spring back when touched lightly in the center. Cool in pan 2 minutes; remove from pan. Cool completely on wire rack.
6. To prepare frosting, combine 3 tablespoons butter and next 3 ingredients in a medium bowl; beat with a mixer at medium speed until smooth. Gradually add powdered sugar, beating just until smooth. Spread about 2½ teaspoons frosting onto each cupcake. Garnish with toasted coconut, if desired.

Makes 12 servings ■ Prep time: 30 minutes ■ Total time: 50 minutes

For complete nutritional information on this and other *Cooking Light* recipes, please turn to the appendix on pages 280–283.

SCAN THIS PHOTO for dozens more cupcake recipes.

Kid-Friendly   Low-Calorie   Make-Ahead

I love this recipe! It was super easy to make and really tasty. My teenage niece and her best friend even liked it."

—guerita21

★★★★★

SCAN THIS PHOTO for video on how to measure liquids.

from *Sunset*

Raspberry Lemon Pudding Cakes

2 large eggs, separated
½ cup granulated sugar
3 tablespoons flour
2 tablespoons butter, melted
Finely shredded zest of 1 lemon

3 tablespoons fresh lemon juice
1 cup low-fat (1%) milk
⅛ teaspoon cream of tartar
2⅔ cups (12 ounces) raspberries, divided
Powdered sugar

1. Preheat oven to 350°. Set 6 (⅔-cup) ramekins in a 13 x 9–inch baking pan.
2. In a medium bowl, whisk together egg yolks and granulated sugar until thick and creamy. Whisk in flour, butter, lemon zest and juice, and milk until blended.
3. In a deep bowl with an electric mixer on high speed, beat egg whites and cream of tartar until whites hold stiff, moist peaks when beater is lifted. Stir one-quarter of whites into yolk mixture until blended, then gently fold in remaining whites. Gently fold in half of raspberries.
4. Spoon batter into ramekins. Pour enough hot tap water into baking pan to come 1 inch up sides of ramekins.
5. Bake at 350° until cake layers are set and tops are golden, 30 to 35 minutes. Remove ramekins from water; let cool at least 30 minutes. Serve with more berries on top and a dusting of powdered sugar.

Note: To make ahead, prepare as directed. Chill cakes in an airtight container up to 1 day; pudding layer will become more distinct.

Makes 6 servings ■ Prep time: 20 minutes ■ Total time: 1 hour, 20 minutes

For complete nutritional information on this and other *Sunset* recipes, please turn to the appendix on pages 280–283.

from Oxmoor House.

Slow Cooker

Mocha Pudding Cake

1⅓ cups sugar
1 cup all-purpose flour
½ cup butter, melted
4 large eggs, lightly beaten
⅓ cup unsweetened cocoa
¼ cup chopped pecans, toasted

2 teaspoons instant coffee granules
½ teaspoon ground cinnamon
¼ teaspoon salt
2 teaspoons vanilla extract
Vanilla ice cream (optional)

1. Stir together all ingredients except ice cream in a large bowl. Pour into a lightly greased 3-quart slow cooker.
2. Cover and cook on LOW 2 to 2½ hours or until set around edges but still soft in center. Let stand, covered, 30 minutes. Serve warm with ice cream, if desired.

Makes 6 to 8 servings ▪ Prep time: 10 minutes ▪ Total time: 2 hours, 40 minutes

> " I made this on one of our snow days. It was a hit—easy to make and had great flavor!"
>
> —TanyaEll
> ★★★★★

30 Minutes or Less **Kid-Friendly** **LC Low-Calorie**

" This is an excellent dessert—delicious alone or with vanilla ice cream, surprisingly good given how simple it is to make, and impressive coming out of the oven."

—afoxcaintx

SCAN THIS PHOTO for more low-calorie cake recipes.

from *Sunset*

Apple Oven Cake

3 tablespoons butter
¼ cup packed light brown sugar
⅛ teaspoon ground cinnamon
1 sweet apple such as Fuji, peeled, cored, and sliced
3 large eggs

¼ teaspoon salt
½ cup flour
½ cup milk
1 tablespoon fresh lemon juice
1 tablespoon powdered sugar

1. Preheat oven to 425°. Melt butter in a 12-inch ovenproof frying pan over high heat. Add brown sugar and cinnamon, swirling to combine. Add apple, and cook until just starting to soften, about 3 minutes.
2. Meanwhile, in a blender, whirl together eggs, salt, flour, and milk. Pour egg mixture into pan and bake at 425° until puffed and brown, about 15 minutes. Sprinkle with lemon juice and powdered sugar.

Makes 6 servings ■ Prep time: 15 minutes ■ Total time: 30 minutes

For complete nutritional information on this and other *Sunset* recipes, please turn to the appendix on pages 280–283.

from **Southern Living**

Key Lime Pound Cake

1 cup butter, softened
½ cup shortening
3 cups sugar
6 large eggs
3 cups all-purpose flour
½ teaspoon baking powder
⅛ teaspoon salt

1 cup milk
1 teaspoon vanilla extract
1 teaspoon grated lime zest
¼ cup fresh Key lime juice
Key Lime Glaze
Garnishes: whipped cream and lime slices

1. Preheat oven to 325°. Beat butter and shortening at medium speed with a heavy-duty electric stand mixer until creamy. Gradually add sugar, beating at medium speed until light and fluffy. Add eggs, 1 at a time, beating just until blended after each addition.
2. Stir together flour, baking powder, and salt. Add to butter mixture alternately with milk, beginning and ending with flour mixture. Beat at low speed just until blended after each addition. Stir in vanilla, lime zest, and lime juice. Pour batter into a greased and floured 10-inch (12-cup) tube pan.
3. Bake at 325° for 1 hour and 15 minutes to 1 hour and 20 minutes or until a long wooden pick inserted in center comes out clean. Cool in pan on a wire rack 10 to 15 minutes; remove from pan to wire rack.
4. Brush Key Lime Glaze over top and sides of cake. Cool completely (about 1 hour). Garnish, if desired.

Makes 12 servings ■ Prep time: 25 minutes ■ Total time: 2 hours, 50 minutes

Key Lime Glaze

1 cup powdered sugar
2 tablespoons fresh Key lime juice

½ teaspoon vanilla extract

Whisk together powdered sugar, lime juice, and vanilla until smooth.

Makes about 1 cup ■ Prep time: 5 minutes ■ Total time: 5 minutes

> ❝ I've made this cake three times. It turned out fantastic all three times. My daughter and her fiancé would like this as their wedding cake when they get married in Florida next year."
>
> — 1kymom
> ★★★★★

SCAN THIS PHOTO for video on how to frost a layer cake.

from Oxmoor House®

Chocolate Turtle Cake

Unsweetened cocoa
1 (18.25-ounce) package devil's food cake mix
1 (3.9-ounce) package chocolate instant pudding mix
3 large eggs
1¼ cups milk
1 cup canola oil
2 teaspoons vanilla extract
1 teaspoon chocolate extract
1 teaspoon instant coffee granules
1 (6-ounce) package semisweet chocolate morsels

1 cup chopped pecans
1 (16-ounce) can ready-to-spread cream cheese frosting
½ cup canned dulce de leche
2 (7-ounce) packages turtle candies
1 (16-ounce) can ready-to-spread chocolate fudge frosting
1 (12-ounce) jar dulce de leche ice cream topping
¼ cup pecan halves, toasted

1. Preheat oven to 350°. Grease 2 (9-inch) round cake pans, and dust with cocoa. Set aside.
2. Beat cake mix and next 7 ingredients at low speed with an electric mixer 1 minute; beat at medium speed 2 minutes. Fold in chocolate morsels and chopped pecans. Pour batter into prepared pans.
3. Bake at 350° for 30 to 32 minutes or until a wooden pick inserted in center comes out clean. Cool in pans on wire racks 10 minutes. Remove from pans to wire racks, and cool completely. Wrap and chill cake layers at least 1 hour.
4. Whisk together cream cheese frosting and canned dulce de leche in a small bowl until well blended. Set aside. Cut 6 turtle candies in half, and set aside for garnish. Dice remaining turtle candies.
5. Using a serrated knife, slice cake layers in half horizontally to make 4 layers. Place 1 layer, cut side up, on cake plate. Spread with ½ cup cream cheese frosting mixture; sprinkle with one-third diced turtle candies. Repeat procedure twice. Place final cake layer on top of cake, cut side down. Spread chocolate fudge frosting on top and sides of cake. Cover and chill in refrigerator until ready to serve. Just before serving, drizzle dulce de leche ice cream topping over top of cake. Garnish with remaining halved turtle candies and pecan halves. Store in refrigerator.

Makes 12 servings ■ Prep time: 40 minutes ■ Total time: 2 hours, 20 minutes

 QUICK TIP

Canned dulce de leche is available in a 14-ounce can. Look for it near the Mexican ingredients in your grocery store. Jarred dulce de leche is thinner and typically found near the other ice-cream toppings.

❝ I really think the only way to describe the flavor of this cake is total silence and soft groans, or just a low murmur of wow. Great cake.❞

—countrygramma
★★★★★

> **❝** I served this cake last month, and my dinner guests are still talking about it! It feels almost like cheating that something so fabulous should take so little effort."
>
> —SharonAE
> ★★★★★

from COASTAL LIVING

Chocolate-Bourbon Cake

Parchment paper
½ cup bourbon
1⅓ cups sugar
12 ounces bittersweet chocolate, coarsely chopped
1 cup butter, cut into pieces

5 large eggs
1½ tablespoons all-purpose flour
2½ tablespoons cocoa powder, divided
Hot water
Coffee Bourbon Syrup
Hazelnuts

1. Preheat oven to 375°. Grease a 9 x 2–inch cake pan, line bottom with parchment paper, and set aside.
2. Combine bourbon and sugar in a large saucepan; bring mixture to a boil. Remove from heat, and add chocolate and butter, stirring until smooth. Set aside, and let cool to room temperature.
3. Beat in eggs, one at a time, until very well blended. Fold in flour and 1½ tablespoons cocoa powder. Pour batter into prepared cake pan. Set pan in a large roasting pan filled to depth of 1 inch with hot water.
4. Bake at 375° for 1 hour and 15 minutes, basting with Coffee-Bourbon Syrup every 15 minutes after a crust has developed on cake's surface.
5. Cool cake; cover and refrigerate 6 hours or overnight. Transfer cake onto a serving plate, and dust with remaining 1 tablespoon cocoa powder. Top with hazelnuts.

Makes 16 servings ▪ Prep time: 30 minutes ▪ Total time: 10 hours

Coffee-Bourbon Syrup

½ cup sugar
½ cup water

¼ cup strong brewed coffee
1 tablespoon bourbon

Bring sugar, water, and coffee to a boil in a medium saucepan over medium-high heat. Cook 5 minutes. Remove from heat; stir in bourbon.

Makes about 1 cup ▪ Prep time: 5 minutes ▪ Total time: 10 minutes

SCAN THIS PHOTO for video on how to prepare a cake pan.

from **all you**

"Almond Joy" Cheesecake

Crust:
1¼ cups chocolate graham cracker crumbs
½ cup sliced almonds
¼ teaspoon salt
¼ cup unsalted butter, melted

Filling:
2 (8-ounce) packages cream cheese, at room temperature
½ cup sugar

3 large eggs, at room temperature
½ teaspoon vanilla extract
1 cup canned cream of coconut
½ teaspoon salt

Topping (optional):
½ cup canned cream of coconut
½ cup heavy cream
12 ounces semisweet chocolate, chopped
Toasted coconut and sliced almonds

1. Preheat oven to 350°. Make crust: Mix graham cracker crumbs, almonds, and salt. Stir in melted butter until dry ingredients are lightly moistened. Press mixture into bottom of a 9-inch springform pan. Wrap outside of pan tightly with two layers of aluminum foil. Bake at 350° 10 minutes. Cool on a wire rack. Leave foil on.
2. Make filling: With a mixer on medium speed, beat cream cheese and sugar until well combined and light, about 2 minutes. Scrape sides and bottom of bowl; beat again until smooth. Add eggs, one at a time, beating well after each. Scrape bowl. Beat in vanilla, cream of coconut, and salt. (Pour remaining cream of coconut into a small bowl, cover and refrigerate to use later in topping.) Pour filling onto crust. Transfer springform pan to a roasting pan; fill roasting pan with hot tap water until it reaches 1 inch up side of springform pan.
3. Bake at 350° 1 hour, until filling is set but still jiggly in center (it will firm as it cools). Take springform pan out of roasting pan; remove foil. Cool on a wire rack 1 hour. Lightly cover with plastic and refrigerate until cold and firm, at least 6 hours.
4. Make topping: Warm cream of coconut and heavy cream in a saucepan over medium-low heat until just simmering. In a bowl, pour mixture over chocolate and whisk until melted and mixture is smooth. Let cool. Pour ½ cup to 1 cup over cheesecake, spreading with an offset spatula. Garnish with toasted coconut and sliced almonds, if desired. Chill until chocolate mixture has set, about 10 minutes. Run a sharp paring knife around inside of pan; release sides. Slice and serve.

Makes 10 servings ■ Prep time: 40 minutes ■ Total time: 9 hours

For complete nutritional information on this and other *All You* recipes, please turn to the appendix on pages 280–283.

---

ask the expert

Why does my cheesecake get cracks in the top?

There are several reasons your cheesecakes may crack, and there are also ways to prevent it.

Overmixing the ingredients incorporates too much air, which makes the cheesecake rise during baking (the way a soufflé does), then collapse as it cools. Make sure you mix only as much as it takes to make the batter smooth.

As cheesecake cools, it contracts; and, if the edges remain stuck to the pan, cracks form. As soon as you take the cheesecake out of the oven, run a knife along the edge to prevent it from sticking to the sides of the pan.

Cracks also form when cheesecake is overbaked: Take out of the oven when still a little jiggly in the center.

If you do get a couple of cracks in your cheesecake, top it with berries, chocolate shavings, or whipped cream. Unless it is very overbaked, it will taste just as good.

 SCAN THIS BOX for more cooking know-how from our experts.

Kid-
Friendly

 The ginger and cinnamon in the whipped topping added so much to the flavor. A 5-year-old who said he didn't like pumpkin pie gobbled it down after one bite. This one is a keeper."

—Darlene490

★★★★★

from Southern Living

Pumpkin Pie Spectacular

½ (15-ounce) package refrigerated piecrusts
2 cups crushed gingersnaps (about 40 gingersnaps)
1 cup pecans, finely chopped
½ cup powdered sugar
¼ cup butter, melted
1 (15-ounce) can pumpkin puree
1 (14-ounce) can sweetened condensed milk
2 large eggs, beaten
½ cup sour cream
1 teaspoon ground cinnamon
½ teaspoon vanilla extract
¼ teaspoon ground ginger
Pecan Streusel
7 thin ginger cookies, halved
Ginger-Spice Topping
Ground cinnamon

1. Preheat oven to 350°. Fit piecrust into a 9-inch deep-dish pie plate according to package directions; fold edges under, and crimp.
2. Stir together crushed gingersnaps and next 3 ingredients. Press mixture on bottom and ½ inch up side of piecrust.
3. Bake at 350° 10 minutes. Let cool completely on a wire rack (about 30 minutes).
4. Stir together pumpkin and next 6 ingredients until well blended. Pour into prepared crust. Place pie on an aluminum foil–lined baking sheet.
5. Bake at 350° 30 minutes. Sprinkle Pecan Streusel around edges, and continue baking 40 to 45 minutes or until set, shielding edges with aluminum foil during last 25 to 30 minutes, if necessary. Insert ginger cookies around edge of crust. Let cool completely on a wire rack (about 1 hour). Dollop with Ginger-Spice Topping; dust with cinnamon.

Makes 8 servings ■ Prep time: 10 minutes ■ Total time: 3 hours

Pecan Streusel

¼ cup all-purpose flour
¼ cup firmly packed dark brown sugar
2 tablespoons butter, melted
¾ cup coarsely chopped pecans

Stir together flour, brown sugar, melted butter, and pecans.

Makes about 1⅓ cups ■ Prep time: 5 minutes ■ Total time: 5 minutes

Ginger-Spice Topping

1 (8-ounce) container frozen whipped topping, thawed
¼ teaspoon ground cinnamon
¼ teaspoon ground ginger

Stir together thawed whipped topping, cinnamon, and ginger.

Makes about 2 cups ■ Prep time: 5 minutes ■ Total time: 5 minutes

SCAN THIS PHOTO for video on making piecrust garnishes.

from Southern Living

Pecan Cheesecake Pie

½ (15-ounce) package refrigerated piecrusts
1 (8-ounce) package cream cheese, softened
4 large eggs, divided
¾ cup sugar, divided
2 teaspoons vanilla extract, divided

¼ teaspoon salt
1¼ cups chopped pecans
1 cup light corn syrup
Whipped cream and fresh mint leaves
   (optional)

1. Preheat oven to 350°. Fit piecrust into a 9-inch pie plate. Fold edges under, and crimp.
2. Beat cream cheese, 1 egg, ½ cup sugar, 1 teaspoon vanilla, and salt at medium speed with an electric mixer until smooth. Pour cream cheese mixture into piecrust; sprinkle evenly with pecans.
3. Whisk together corn syrup and remaining 3 eggs, ¼ cup sugar, and 1 teaspoon vanilla; pour mixture over pecans. Place pie on a baking sheet.
4. Bake at 350° on lowest oven rack 50 to 55 minutes or until pie is set. Cool on a wire rack 1 hour or until completely cool. Serve immediately, or cover and chill up to 2 days. Garnish, if desired.

Makes 8 servings ■ Prep time: 15 minutes ■ Total time: 2 hours, 5 minutes

Kid-Friendly   **Make-Ahead**   **Slow Cooker**

Triple Chocolate–Covered Peanut Clusters

1 (16-ounce) jar dry-roasted peanuts
1 (16-ounce) jar unsalted dry-roasted peanuts
18 (2-ounce) chocolate bark coating squares, cut in half
2 cups (12-ounce package) semisweet chocolate morsels
1 (4-ounce) package German chocolate baking squares, broken into pieces
1 (9.75-ounce) can salted whole cashews
1 teaspoon vanilla extract
Wax paper

1. Combine first 5 ingredients in a 3½- or 4-quart slow cooker.
2. Cover and cook on LOW 2 hours or until melted. Stir chocolate mixture. Add cashews and vanilla, stirring well to coat cashews.
3. Drop nut mixture by heaping tablespoonfuls onto wax paper. Let stand until firm. Store in an airtight container.

Note: To make ahead, prepare as directed. Store in an airtight container for up to 1 month.

Makes about 60 clusters ▪ Prep time: 15 minutes ▪ Total time: 2 hours, 15 minutes

> " This was so easy and tasty, and it makes plenty for sharing. I dropped the mixture into individual paper candy cups, and that worked out great."
>
> —nellenana
> ★★★★★

SCAN THIS PHOTO
for more homemade
candy gift recipes.

Kid-
Friendly

❝ It's just me
and my hubby,
so I cut the recipe in
half and put it in an
8 x 8–inch dish. It
turned out great. No
ice cream needed."

—seattlekh

from CookingLight

Blueberry-Peach Cobbler

5 pounds peaches, peeled, pitted, and sliced
2 tablespoons fresh lemon juice
1 cup granulated sugar, divided
⅜ teaspoon salt, divided
6.75 ounces (about 1½ cups) plus 2
    tablespoons all-purpose flour, divided
Cooking spray

1 teaspoon baking powder
½ cup butter, softened
2 large eggs
1 teaspoon vanilla extract
¾ cup buttermilk
2 cups fresh blueberries
2 tablespoons turbinado sugar

1. Preheat oven to 375°.
2. Place peaches in a large bowl. Drizzle with lemon juice; toss. Add ¾ cup granulated sugar, ⅛ teaspoon salt, and 2 tablespoons flour to peach mixture; toss to
combine. Arrange peach mixture evenly in a 13 x 9–inch glass or ceramic baking
dish coated with cooking spray.
3. Weigh or lightly spoon 6.75 ounces flour into dry measuring cups; level with
a knife. Combine with remaining ¼ teaspoon salt, and baking powder in a bowl,
stirring well with a whisk. Place the remaining ¼ cup granulated sugar and
butter in a medium bowl, and beat with an electric mixer at medium speed until
light and fluffy (about 2 minutes). Add eggs, 1 at a time, beating well after each
addition. Stir in vanilla. Add flour mixture and buttermilk alternately to butter
mixture, beginning and ending with flour mixture, beating just until combined.
Stir in blueberries.
4. Spread batter evenly over peach mixture; sprinkle with turbinado sugar.
Place baking dish on a foil-lined baking sheet. Bake for at 375° 1 hour or until
topping is golden and filling is bubbly.

Makes 12 servings ■ Prep time: 30 minutes ■ Total time: 1 hour, 30 minutes

For complete nutritional information on this and other *Cooking Light* recipes, please turn to the appendix on pages
280–283.

SCAN THIS PHOTO
for video on how to
skin a peach.

breakfast & brunch

Whether for weekend brunches or breakfast-for-supper weeknight meals, eggy casseroles are popular picks on MyRecipes.com. You'll find a tasty selection of users' top-rated choices here, as well as scrumptious twists on pancakes, muffins, and other breakfast-anytime favorites.

 To use the exclusive **Scan-It/Cook-It**™ features in this chapter, look for the smartphone symbol (shown at left). For detailed instructions, please see page 7.

**BRIE-AND-SAUSAGE
BREAKFAST CASSEROLE**
page 276

Kid-
Friendly

Make-
Ahead

> This recipe is easy, fast, and tastes great! It is a wholesome snack for kids and will keep them filled up for a while. I keep the granola in the freezer and pull it out for snacks or crumble it in plain yogurt."

—LisaB09

★★★★★

from Cooking Light.

Molasses-Almond Granola

2 cups regular oats
½ cup sliced almonds
2 tablespoons wheat germ
½ teaspoon sea salt
¼ teaspoon ground cinnamon
⅓ cup dried currants
Parchment paper

Cooking spray
¼ cup dried cranberries
2 tablespoons sugar
5 tablespoons molasses
3 tablespoons canola oil
1¼ teaspoons vanilla extract

1. Preheat oven to 325°.
2. Combine first 3 ingredients in a food processor; pulse 10 times or until coarsely chopped. Combine oat mixture, salt, and cinnamon in a medium bowl; toss well. Spread oat mixture on a baking sheet; bake at 325° for 20 minutes or until lightly browned, stirring occasionally. Remove mixture from baking sheet; stir in currants.
3. Cover a baking sheet with parchment paper; coat paper with cooking spray. Combine cranberries, sugar, molasses, oil, and vanilla in a small saucepan over medium heat. Cook 4 minutes or until sugar dissolves, stirring frequently. Pour cranberry mixture over oat mixture, tossing to coat. Spread granola evenly on prepared baking sheet. Bake at 325° for 15 minutes or until the mixture is lightly browned. Remove granola from oven, and cool completely. Break into small pieces.

Note: To make ahead, prepare as directed and store, refrigerated, in an airtight container up to 2 weeks. You can subdivide the batch into individual servings so it's ready when you are.

Makes 3 cups ■ Prep time: 25 minutes ■ Total time: 55 minutes

For complete nutritional information on this and other *Cooking Light* recipes, please turn to the appendix on pages 280–283.

SCAN THIS PHOTO
for 5 more kid-friendly
breakfast recipes.

myrecipes users suggest:
- substituting old-fashioned oats for quick-cooking, and increasing bake time another 8 to 10 minutes
- using a combination of vanilla almond milk and skim milk
- substituting pumpkin puree for the apple-sauce and adding a little cinnamon and/or nutmeg

" I absolutely love this recipe. I stir all ingredients together the night before, let them soak in the fridge overnight, then simply bake it in the morning."

—PulpFiction

★★★★★

from Cooking Light

Baked Oatmeal

2 cups uncooked quick-cooking oats
½ cup packed brown sugar
⅓ cup raisins, plus more for garnish
1 tablespoon chopped walnuts, plus more for garnish
1 teaspoon baking powder

1½ cups fat-free milk
½ cup applesauce
2 tablespoons butter, melted
1 large egg, beaten
Cooking spray

1. Preheat oven to 375°.
2. Combine first 5 ingredients in a medium bowl. Combine milk, applesauce, butter, and egg. Add milk mixture to oat mixture; stir well. Pour oat mixture into an 8-inch square baking dish coated with cooking spray. Bake at 375° for 20 minutes. Serve warm with additional walnuts and raisins, if desired.

Makes 5 servings ■ Prep time: 10 minutes ■ Total time: 30 minutes

For complete nutritional information on this and other *Cooking Light* recipes, please turn to the appendix on pages 280–283.

from Cooking Light

Cinnamon Rolls

Rolls:
1 cup warm fat-free milk (100° to 110°)
6 tablespoons melted butter, divided
⅓ cup granulated sugar, divided
1 package quick-rise yeast
16.9 ounces all-purpose flour (about 3¾ cups)
1 large egg, lightly beaten
¼ teaspoon salt

Cooking spray
⅔ cup packed brown sugar
1½ tablespoons ground cinnamon
Icing:
3 tablespoons butter, softened
2 tablespoons heavy cream
½ teaspoon vanilla extract
1 cup powdered sugar

1. To prepare rolls, combine milk, 3 tablespoons melted butter, 1 tablespoon granulated sugar, and yeast in a large bowl; let stand 5 minutes. Weigh or lightly spoon flour into dry measuring cups. Add egg and remaining granulated sugar to bowl. Stir in 4.5 ounces (1 cup) flour; let stand 10 minutes.
2. Add 11.25 ounces (about 2½ cups) flour and salt to milk mixture; stir until a soft dough forms (dough will be sticky). Turn out onto a lightly floured surface. Knead until smooth and elastic (about 6 minutes); add enough of remaining flour, 1 tablespoon at a time, to prevent dough from sticking to hands. Place dough in a large bowl coated with cooking spray; turn to coat top. Cover and let rise in a warm place (85°), free from drafts, 35 minutes or until doubled in size. (Gently press two fingers into dough. If indentation remains, dough has risen enough.) Punch dough down; cover and let rise 35 minutes or until doubled in size. Punch dough down; cover and let rest 5 minutes.
3. Combine brown sugar and cinnamon. Turn dough out onto a lightly floured surface; roll dough into an 18 x 11–inch rectangle. Brush remaining 3 table-spoons melted butter over dough; sprinkle evenly with brown sugar mixture. Beginning at one long side, roll up dough tightly, jelly-roll fashion; pinch seam to seal (do not seal ends of roll). Cut dough into 18 (1-inch-thick) slices. Arrange 9 slices, cut sides up, in each of 2 (8-inch) square baking dishes coated with cooking spray. Cover and let rise 35 minutes or until doubled in size.
4. Preheat oven to 350°.
5. Uncover rolls. Bake at 350° for 22 minutes or until lightly browned. Cool 10 minutes in dishes on a wire rack. Turn rolls out onto wire rack; cool 5 minutes. Turn rolls over.
6. To prepare icing, combine softened butter and cream; stir with a whisk. Stir in vanilla. Gradually add powdered sugar; stir until blended. Spread icing over rolls; serve warm.

Makes 18 servings ■ Prep time: 35 minutes ■ Total time: 3 hours, 15 minutes

For complete nutritional information on this and other *Cooking Light* recipes, please turn to the appendix on pages 280–283.

> **"** I have tried countless cinnamon roll recipes, only to have them come out rock-hard. This recipe was perfect. The dough is very sticky to work with, but that is what keeps the rolls from becoming too hard in the oven."
>
> —Healthyatbest
> ★★★★★

Kid-Friendly

QUICK TIP

Make it a quick bread:
Omit butter, brown sugar, and corn syrup, and skip Step 2. Chop the toasted pecans, and stir them into the batter. Spoon batter into 2 greased and floured 9 x 5–inch loaf pans. Bake at 350° for about 1 hour or until a wooden pick inserted in center comes out clean. Cool 10 minutes. Remove from pans to a wire rack, and cool completely (about 1 hour).

from *Southern Living*

Sticky-Bun Pumpkin Muffins

2 cups pecan halves and pieces
½ cup butter, melted
½ cup firmly packed light brown sugar
2 tablespoons light corn syrup
3½ cups all-purpose flour
3 cups granulated sugar
1 tablespoon pumpkin pie spice

1 teaspoon baking soda
1 teaspoon salt
1 (15-ounce) can pumpkin puree
1 cup canola oil
4 large eggs
⅔ cup water

1. Preheat oven to 350°. Bake pecans in a single layer in a shallow pan 8 to 10 minutes or until toasted and fragrant, stirring halfway through.
2. Stir together melted butter and next 2 ingredients. Spoon 1 rounded tea-spoonful butter mixture into each cup of 2 lightly greased 12-cup muffin pans, and top each with 1 rounded tablespoonful pecans.
3. Stir together flour and next 4 ingredients in a large bowl, and make a well in center of mixture. Whisk together pumpkin and next 3 ingredients; add to dry ingredients, stirring just until moistened.
4. Spoon batter into prepared muffin pans, filling three-fourths full.
5. Bake at 350° on middle oven rack for 25 to 30 minutes or until a wooden pick inserted in center comes out clean. Invert pan immediately to remove muffins, and arrange muffins on a wire rack. Spoon any topping remaining in muffin cups over muffins. Let cool 5 minutes.

Makes 2 dozen ■ Prep time: 20 minutes ■ Total time: 1 hour

from

Lemon-Ricotta Pancakes

1½ cups all-purpose flour
2 tablespoons sugar
1 teaspoon baking soda
½ teaspoon salt
1½ cups buttermilk
2 large eggs, separated

1 tablespoon grated lemon rind
⅓ cup part-skim ricotta cheese
Salad oil
Banana slices, lemon zest, maple syrup
   (optional)

1. In a large bowl, mix flour, sugar, baking soda, and salt. In a medium bowl, whisk buttermilk, egg yolks, and lemon rind to blend. Stir buttermilk mixture into flour mixture just until evenly moistened. Gently stir in ricotta cheese.
2. In a bowl, with an electric mixer on high speed, beat egg whites until soft peaks form. With a flexible spatula, gently fold whites into batter just until they are incorporated.
3. Place a nonstick griddle or a 12-inch nonstick frying pan over medium heat (350°); when hot, coat lightly with oil and adjust heat to maintain temperature. Drop batter in ½-cup portions onto griddle and cook until pancakes are browned on bottom and edges begin to look dry, about 2 minutes; turn cakes with a wide spatula and brown other sides, 1½ to 2 minutes longer. Coat pan with more oil as necessary to cook remaining pancakes.
4. Serve pancakes as cooked, or keep warm in a single layer on baking sheets in a 200° oven for up to 15 minutes. Garnish with banana slices, lemon zest, and maple syrup, if desired.

Makes 4 servings ▪ Prep time: 25 minutes ▪ Total time: 25 minutes

For complete nutritional information on this and other *Sunset* recipes, please turn to the appendix on pages 280–283.

> I made these pancakes for myself and my husband this morning, and we're still ooooh-ing and ahhhh-ing! These are, without a doubt, the fluffiest, tastiest, and most satisfying pancakes we've ever eaten. I followed the recipe to a T."

—jancancook
★★★★★

SCAN THIS PHOTO
for video on how to
beat egg whites.

30 Minutes or Less **Kid-Friendly**

" I made a double batch of these so we could have leftovers—no such luck! My two toddlers were eating them as quickly as I could cook them."

—ReneePech

★★★★★

from CookingLight

Oatmeal Pancakes

1.1 ounces all-purpose flour (¼ cup)
1 cup quick-cooking oats
1 tablespoon sugar
½ teaspoon baking powder
½ teaspoon baking soda
¼ teaspoon ground cinnamon

⅛ teaspoon salt
1 cup nonfat buttermilk
2 tablespoons butter, melted
1 large egg
Cooking spray
Syrup, butter, fruit (optional)

1. Weigh or lightly spoon flour into a dry measuring cup; level with a knife. Combine flour and next 6 ingredients in a medium bowl, stirring with a whisk.
2. Combine buttermilk, butter, and egg in a small bowl. Add to flour mixture, stirring just until moist.
3. Heat a nonstick griddle over medium heat. Coat pan with cooking spray. Spoon about 2½ tablespoons batter per pancake onto griddle. Turn pancakes over when tops are covered with bubbles; cook until bottoms are lightly browned. Serve with syrup, butter, and fruit, if desired.

Makes 3 servings ■ Prep time: 20 minutes ■ Total time: 20 minutes

For complete nutritional information on this and other *Cooking Light* recipes, please turn to the appendix on pages 280–283.

30 Minutes or Less

Kid-Friendly

SCAN THIS PHOTO
for video on how to measure honey.

> These might be the best pancakes I've ever had. Get your griddles out this minute because you won't regret it."

—Carlynarr

★★★★★

from *Cooking Light*

Carrot Cake Pancakes

5.6 ounces all-purpose flour (about 1¼ cups)
¼ cup chopped walnuts, toasted
2 teaspoons baking powder
1 teaspoon ground cinnamon
¼ teaspoon salt
⅛ teaspoon freshly grated nutmeg
Dash of ground cloves
Dash of ground ginger
¼ cup packed brown sugar

¾ cup low-fat buttermilk
1 tablespoon canola oil
1½ teaspoons vanilla extract
2 large eggs, lightly beaten
2 cups finely grated carrots
   (about 1 pound)
Cooking spray
3 tablespoons butter, softened
2 tablespoons honey

1. Weigh or lightly spoon flour into dry measuring cups, and level with a knife. Combine flour and next 7 ingredients in a large bowl, stirring with a whisk. Combine brown sugar and next 4 ingredients; add sugar mixture to flour mixture, stirring just until moist. Fold in carrots.
2. Heat a large nonstick skillet over medium heat. Coat pan with cooking spray. Spoon 4 (¼-cup) batter mounds onto pan, spreading with a spatula. Cook for 2 minutes or until tops are covered with bubbles and edges look cooked. Carefully turn pancakes over; cook 1 minute or until bottoms are lightly browned. Repeat procedure twice with remaining batter. Combine butter and honey in a small bowl; serve with pancakes.

Makes 6 servings ■ Prep time: 20 minutes ■ Total time: 20 minutes

For complete nutritional information on this and other *Cooking Light* recipes, please turn to the appendix on pages 280–283.

Kid-Friendly

from *Cooking Light*

Blueberry Coffee Cake

6.75 ounces all-purpose flour (about 1½ cups)
1 teaspoon baking powder
¼ teaspoon baking soda
¼ teaspoon salt
¾ cup granulated sugar
6 tablespoons butter, softened
1 teaspoon vanilla extract

1 large egg
1 large egg white
1⅓ cups low-fat buttermilk
Cooking spray
2 cups fresh blueberries
1 tablespoon turbinado sugar

1. Preheat oven to 350°.
2. Lightly spoon flour into dry measuring cups; level with a knife. Combine flour, baking powder, baking soda, and salt, stirring with a whisk.
3. Place granulated sugar and butter in a large bowl; beat with an electric mixer at medium speed until well blended (about 2 minutes). Add vanilla, egg, and egg white; beat well. Add flour mixture and buttermilk alternately to sugar mixture, beginning and ending with flour mixture; mix after each addition.
4. Spoon half of batter into a 9-inch round baking pan coated with cooking spray. Sprinkle evenly with 1 cup blueberries. Spoon remaining batter over blueberries; sprinkle evenly with remaining 1 cup blueberries. Sprinkle top evenly with turbinado sugar. Bake at 350° for 50 minutes or until a wooden pick inserted in center comes out clean. Cool in pan 10 minutes on a wire rack; remove from pan. Cool completely on wire rack.

Makes 8 servings ■ Prep time: 20 minutes ■ Total time: 1 hour, 20 minutes

For complete nutritional information on this and other *Cooking Light* recipes, please turn to the appendix on pages 280–283.

from all you

Pumpkin Crumb Coffee Cake

Topping:
1 cup all-purpose flour
½ cup packed dark brown sugar
Pinch of salt
1½ teaspoons ground cinnamon
6 tablespoons cold unsalted butter, cut
    into pieces
Cake:
2 cups all-purpose flour
1½ teaspoons baking powder
½ teaspoon baking soda
½ teaspoon salt

1 tablespoon ground cinnamon
2 teaspoons ground ginger
½ teaspoon ground nutmeg
⅓ cup vegetable oil
¾ cup unsweetened applesauce
1 (15-ounce) can pumpkin puree
1 teaspoon vanilla extract
1½ cups granulated sugar
½ cup packed dark brown sugar
2 large eggs, at room temperature,
    lightly beaten

1. Make topping: In a bowl, stir together flour, brown sugar, salt, and cinnamon. Add butter and combine with fingertips until mixture is crumbly. Refrigerate while making batter.
2. Make cake: Preheat oven to 350°. Butter and flour a 13 x 9–inch cake pan. In a small bowl, combine flour, baking powder, baking soda, salt, and spices. In a large bowl, whisk together oil, applesauce, pumpkin, vanilla, and both sugars until well mixed. Whisk in eggs. Add flour mixture to pumpkin mixture and stir until just combined; do not overmix. Pour batter into cake pan and spread evenly. Sprinkle with reserved topping.
3. Bake at 350° until a toothpick inserted into center comes out clean, 45 to 50 minutes. Allow to cool in pan on a wire rack at least 20 minutes.

Makes 12 servings ■ Prep time: 20 minutes ■ Total time: 1 hour, 25 minutes

For complete nutritional information on this and other *All You* recipes, please turn to the appendix on pages 280–283.

> I've made this coffee cake three times; it's fantastic! It also freezes very well, so half of it goes into the freezer for another weekend."
>
> —irishmaiden222
>
> ★★★★★

30 Minutes
or Less

from *Southern Living*

BLT Benedicts with Avocado-Tomato Relish

1 cup halved grape tomatoes
1 avocado, peeled and diced
1 tablespoon chopped fresh basil
1 garlic clove, minced
2 tablespoons extra virgin olive oil
Salt and black pepper to taste

1 tablespoon red wine vinegar, divided
6 large eggs
¼ cup mayonnaise
6 (¾-inch-thick) bakery bread slices, toasted
3 cups firmly packed arugula
12 thick bacon slices, cooked

1. Combine tomatoes and next 4 ingredients with salt, pepper, and 2½ teaspoons vinegar in a small bowl.
2. Add water to depth of 3 inches in a large saucepan. Bring to a boil; reduce heat, and maintain at a light simmer. Add remaining ½ teaspoon vinegar. Break eggs, and slip into water, 1 at a time, as close as possible to surface. Simmer 3 to 5 minutes or to desired degree of doneness. Remove with a slotted spoon. Trim edges, if desired.
3. Spread mayonnaise on 1 side of each bread slice. Layer each with ½ cup arugula, 2 bacon slices, and 1 egg. Top with tomato mixture.

Makes 6 servings ▪ Prep time: 25 minutes ▪ Total time: 25 minutes

SCAN THIS PHOTO for video on how to poach eggs.

30 Minutes or Less

LC
Low-Calorie

myrecipes users suggest:
- using canned tomatoes with habaneros
- substituting feta or goat cheese for the queso fresco
- preparing the eggs scrambled instead of sunny-side up
- serving with seasoned black beans instead of pintos

❝ Great-tasting and quick."

—JimMarltonNJ

★★★★★

from *Cooking Light*

Huevos Rancheros with Queso Fresco

1 (10-ounce) can diced tomatoes and green chiles, undrained
1 (10-ounce) can red enchilada sauce
⅓ cup chopped fresh cilantro
1 tablespoon fresh lime juice
2 tablespoons water
1 (16-ounce) can pinto beans, rinsed and drained
Cooking spray
4 large eggs
4 (8-inch) fat-free flour tortillas
1 cup (4 ounces) crumbled queso fresco cheese

1. Combine tomatoes and enchilada sauce in a medium saucepan; bring to a boil. Reduce heat; simmer 5 minutes or until slightly thick. Remove from heat; stir in cilantro and lime juice. Set aside.
2. Place water and beans in a microwave-safe bowl, and partially mash with a fork. Cover and microwave at HIGH 2 minutes or until hot.
3. Heat a large nonstick skillet coated with cooking spray over medium-high heat. Add eggs; cook 1 minute on each side or until desired degree of doneness.
4. Warm tortillas according to package directions. Spread about ⅓ cup beans over each tortilla; top each tortilla with 1 egg. Spoon ½ cup sauce around each egg; sprinkle each serving with ¼ cup cheese.

Makes 4 servings ▪ Prep time: 20 minutes ▪ Total time: 20 minutes

For complete nutritional information on this and other *Cooking Light* recipes, please turn to the appendix on pages 280–283.

Make-Ahead

from **Southern Living**

Breakfast Enchiladas

⊙ **QUICK TIP**

Make the cheese sauce before scrambling the eggs so the sauce will be ready to add at the proper time.

❝ I made this over the holidays and, wow, what a hit. It only got better after the first day, and it freezes like a dream. I'm always looking for yummy make-ahead dishes, and this fits the bill."

—lilypadgirl

1 (1-pound) package hot ground pork sausage
2 tablespoons butter or margarine
4 green onions, thinly sliced
2 tablespoons chopped fresh cilantro
14 large eggs, beaten
¾ teaspoon salt
½ teaspoon black pepper
Cheese Sauce
8 (8-inch) flour tortillas
1 cup (4 ounces) shredded Monterey Jack cheese with jalapeños
Toppings: halved grape tomatoes, sliced green onions, chopped fresh cilantro

1. Preheat oven to 350°. Cook sausage in a large nonstick skillet over medium-high heat, stirring until sausage crumbles and is no longer pink. Remove from pan; drain well, pressing between paper towels.
2. Melt butter in a large nonstick skillet over medium heat. Add green onions and cilantro, and sauté 1 minute. Add eggs, salt, and pepper, and cook, without stirring, until eggs begin to set on bottom. Draw a spatula across bottom of pan to form large curds. Continue to cook until eggs are thickened but still moist; do not stir constantly. Remove from heat, and gently fold in 1½ cups Cheese Sauce and sausage.
3. Spoon about ⅓ cup egg mixture down the center of each flour tortilla; roll up. Place, seam side down, in a lightly greased 13 x 9–inch baking dish. Pour remaining Cheese Sauce evenly over tortillas; sprinkle evenly with Monterey Jack cheese.
4. Bake at 350° for 30 minutes or until sauce is bubbly. Serve with desired toppings.

Note: To make ahead, prepare the recipe without baking, and refrigerate overnight. Let stand at room temperature for 30 minutes; bake as directed.

Makes 6 to 8 servings ■ Prep time: 30 minutes ■ Total time: 1 hour, 10 minutes

Cheese Sauce

⅓ cup butter
⅓ cup flour
3 cups milk
2 cups (8 ounces) shredded Cheddar cheese
1 (4.5-ounce) can chopped green chiles, undrained
¾ teaspoon salt

Melt butter in a heavy saucepan over medium-low heat; whisk in flour until smooth. Cook, whisking constantly, 1 minute. Gradually whisk in milk; cook over medium heat, whisking constantly, 5 minutes or until thickened. Remove from heat, and whisk in remaining ingredients.

Makes about 4 cups ■ Prep time: 10 minutes ■ Total time: 10 minutes

SCAN THIS PHOTO for video on how to scramble eggs.

LC
Low-Calorie

from Cooking Light

Rösti Casserole with Baked Eggs

1¼ cups plain fat-free Greek-style yogurt
2 tablespoons all-purpose flour
1½ cups grated peeled turnip (about 8 ounces, 2 small)
1¼ cups (5 ounces) shredded Gruyère cheese
⅓ cup butter, melted
¼ cup chopped fresh chives
1¼ teaspoons salt

½ teaspoon freshly ground black pepper
¼ teaspoon grated nutmeg
1 (30-ounce) package frozen shredded hash brown potatoes, thawed
Cooking spray
8 large eggs
Chopped fresh chives (optional)
Freshly ground black pepper (optional)

1. Preheat oven to 400°.
2. Combine yogurt and flour in a large bowl, stirring well. Add turnip and next 7 ingredients to yogurt mixture. Spread potato mixture evenly in a 13 x 9–inch baking dish coated with cooking spray. Bake at 400° for 30 minutes or until bubbly. Remove from oven.
3. With back of a spoon, make 8 indentations in top of potato mixture. Crack 1 egg into each of 8 indentations. Return dish to oven. Bake for 8 minutes or until egg whites are firm and yolks barely move when pan is touched. Cut into 8 pieces. Garnish with additional chives and black pepper, if desired. Serve immediately.

Makes 8 servings ■ Prep time: 15 minutes ■ Total time: 55 minutes

For complete nutritional information on this and other *Cooking Light* recipes, please turn to the appendix on pages 280–283.

" I made this for dinner last night, and it was a huge hit with my husband and even teenagers. A keeper!"

—TerriS2
★★★★★

Low-Calorie

" This is very easy and doesn't require any unusual ingredients."

—goodrecipehound

★★★★★

 users suggest:
- using fat-free half-and-half to cut the fat
- using mozzarella in place of Swiss
- adding chopped onion or a pinch of nutmeg for added flavor

from all you

Ham, Swiss, and Spinach Quiche

Cooking spray
3 cups packed baby spinach, chopped
6 large eggs, lightly beaten
1½ cups half-and-half
½ teaspoon salt
1 (9-inch) frozen piecrust
¼ pound sliced ham, chopped
1½ cups shredded Swiss cheese

1. Line a rimmed baking sheet with foil, place it in oven, and preheat to 375°. Mist a medium skillet with cooking spray, and warm it over medium heat. Cook spinach, stirring often, until wilted. Remove spinach to a paper towel–lined plate, and pat dry.
2. Combine eggs, half-and-half, and salt in a large bowl, and whisk until well mixed. Arrange spinach on bottom of piecrust. Scatter ham over spinach. Sprinkle cheese over ham. Pour egg mixture into shell.
3. Place quiche on baking sheet, and bake at 375° until filling is set and crust is golden, about 40 minutes. Let stand 10 minutes, slice into wedges, and serve hot.

Makes 8 servings ■ Prep time: 15 minutes ■ Total time: 1 hour, 5 minutes

For complete nutritional information on this and other *All You* recipes, please turn to the appendix on pages 280–283.

Make-Ahead

⊙ QUICK TIP

Use shredded Swiss (2 cups or 8 ounces) instead of the Brie, if desired.

 I have made this at least 20 times in the past few years, and I've never had it turn out soggy or runny. It's not a quick recipe, but the flavor is incredible. It's my go-to recipe for brunches and showers."

—Laura1980

★★★★★

 SCAN THIS PHOTO for 5 more breakfast casserole recipes.

from *Southern Living*

Brie-and-Sausage Breakfast Casserole

1 (8-ounce) round Brie
1 pound ground hot pork sausage
6 white sandwich bread slices
1 cup grated Parmesan cheese
7 large eggs, divided
3 cups whipping cream, divided

2 cups fat-free milk
1 tablespoon chopped fresh sage or
    1 teaspoon dried rubbed sage
1 teaspoon seasoned salt
1 teaspoon dry mustard

1. Trim rind from Brie, and discard; cut cheese into cubes, and set aside.
2. Cook sausage in a large skillet over medium-high heat, stirring until it crumbles and is no longer pink; drain well.
3. Cut crusts from bread slices, and place crusts evenly in bottom of a lightly greased 13 x 9–inch baking dish. Layer evenly with bread slices, sausage, Brie, and Parmesan cheese.
4. Whisk together 5 eggs, 2 cups whipping cream, and next 4 ingredients; pour evenly over cheeses. Cover and chill mixture for 8 hours.
5. Preheat oven to 350°. Whisk together remaining 2 eggs and remaining 1 cup whipping cream; pour evenly over chilled mixture.
6. Bake at 350° for 1 hour or until casserole is set.

Makes 8 to 10 servings ■ Prep time: 25 minutes ■ Total time: 9 hours, 25 minutes

" This is so simple, easy, and delicious—always a hit in our house and with guests!"

—hopebarrgirl

QUICK TIP

Use firm white bread for the best texture in this breakfast casserole.

myrecipes users suggest:

- trying pecan-cranberry sourdough or whole-wheat cinnamon raisin bread instead of white bread
- substituting yogurt for the cream cheese and milk for the half-and-half
- using egg substitute for all or some of the eggs

from *Cooking Light*

French Toast Soufflé

10 cups (1-inch) cubed sturdy white bread (such as Pepperidge Farm Hearty White, about 16 [1-ounce] slices)
Cooking spray
1 (8-ounce) package ⅓-less-fat cream cheese, softened
8 large eggs

1½ cups 2% milk
⅔ cup half-and-half
½ cup maple syrup
½ teaspoon vanilla extract
2 tablespoons powdered sugar
¾ cup maple syrup

1. Place bread cubes in a 13 x 9–inch baking dish coated with cooking spray. Beat cream cheese at medium speed with an electric mixer until smooth. Add eggs, 1 at a time, mixing well after each addition. Add milk, half-and-half, maple syrup, and vanilla, and mix until smooth. Pour cream cheese mixture over top of bread; cover and refrigerate 8 hours or overnight.
2. Preheat oven to 375°.
3. Remove bread mixture from refrigerator; let stand on counter for 30 minutes. Bake at 375° for 50 minutes or until set. Sprinkle soufflé with powdered sugar, and serve with maple syrup.

Makes 12 servings ■ Prep time: 15 minutes ■ Total time: 9 hours, 35 minutes

For complete nutritional information on this and other *Cooking Light* recipes, please turn to the appendix on pages 280–283.

Kid-Friendly   Make-Ahead

from Southern Living

One-Dish Blackberry French Toast

1 cup blackberry jam
1 (12-ounce) French bread loaf, cut into
   1½-inch cubes
1 (8-ounce) package ⅓-less-fat cream
   cheese, cut into 1-inch cubes
4 large eggs

2 cups half-and-half
1 teaspoon ground cinnamon
1 teaspoon vanilla extract
½ cup firmly packed brown sugar
Toppings: maple syrup, whipped cream

1. Cook jam in a small saucepan over medium heat 1 to 2 minutes or until melted and smooth, stirring once.
2. Place half of bread cubes in bottom of a lightly greased 13 x 9–inch baking dish. Top with cream cheese cubes, and drizzle with melted jam. Top with remaining bread cubes.
3. Whisk together eggs and next 3 ingredients. Pour over bread mixture. Sprinkle with brown sugar. Cover tightly, and chill 8 to 24 hours.
4. Preheat oven to 325°. Bake, covered, 20 minutes. Uncover and bake 10 to 15 minutes or until bread is golden brown and mixture is set. Serve with desired toppings.

Makes 8 to 10 servings ■ Prep time: 20 minutes ■ Total time: 8 hours, 50 minutes

> " I made this with strawberry preserves, and it was amazing! The entire family loved it."
>
> —kgonzo
> ★★★★★

all you

"Almond Joy" Cheesecake, page 249 Amount per serving (1/10 of cheesecake): Calories: 677; Fat: 53g; Saturated fat: 34g; Protein: 11g; Carbohydrate: 49g; Fiber: 5g; Cholesterol: 142mg; Sodium: 470mg

Beef and Broccoli Stir-Fry, page 93 Amount per serving (1/4 of mixture): Calories: 266; Fat: 11g; Saturated fat: 2g; Protein: 32g; Carbohydrate: 12g; Fiber: 4g; Cholesterol: 65mg; Sodium: 859mg

Beef Stroganoff, page 100 Amount per serving (1/4 of stroganoff): Calories: 492; Fat: 34g; Saturated fat: 14g; Protein: 37g; Carbohydrate: 6g; Fiber: 1g; Cholesterol: 129mg; Sodium: 1001mg

Black Bean Burgers, page 152 Amount per serving (1 burger): Calories: 215; Fat: 9g; Saturated fat: 1g; Protein: 8g; Carbohydrate: 28g; Fiber: 7g; Cholesterol: 53mg; Sodium: 821mg

Broccoli Casserole, page 202 Amount per serving (1/10 of casserole): Calories: 397; Fat: 36g; Saturated fat: 13g; Protein: 8g; Carbohydrate: 10g; Fiber: 2g; Cholesterol: 95mg; Sodium: 550mg

Buttermilk Chicken Tenders, page 64 Amount per serving (1/6 of chicken tenders): Calories: 409; Fat: 14g; Saturated fat: 2.4g; Protein: 32g; Carbohydrate: 39g; Fiber: 2g; Cholesterol: 133mg; Sodium: 997mg

Butternut Squash Ravioli with Sage, page 174 Amount per serving (1/8 of ravioli): Calories: 374; Fat: 21g; Saturated fat: 11g; Protein: 11g; Carbohydrate: 36g; Fiber: 2g; Cholesterol: 60mg; Sodium: 790mg

Chicken Fried Rice with Vegetables, page 62 Amount per serving (1/4 of mixture): Calories: 516; Fat: 23g; Saturated fat: 4g; Protein: 31g; Carbohydrate: 49g; Fiber: 2g; Cholesterol: 211mg; Sodium: 593mg

Coconut-Curry Beef, page 97 Amount per serving (1/6 of beef): Calories: 427; Fat: 30g; Saturated fat: 13g; Protein: 30g; Carbohydrate: 11g; Fiber: 1g; Cholesterol: 95mg; Sodium: 306mg

Ham, Swiss, and Spinach Quiche, page 274 Amount per serving (1/8 of quiche): Calories: 298; Fat: 21g; Saturated fat: 10g; Protein: 15g; Carbohydrate: 12g; Fiber: 0g; Cholesterol: 202mg; Sodium: 562mg

Mexican Slow-Cooker Chicken, page 59 Amount per serving (1 chicken breast half): Calories: 427; Fat: 13g; Saturated fat: 8g; Protein: 53g; Carbohydrate: 21g; Fiber: 5g; Cholesterol: 144mg; Sodium: 610mg

Peanut Butter Cookies with Butterscotch Bits, page 232 Amount per serving (1 cookie): Calories: 241; Fat: 13g; Saturated fat: 4g; Protein: 5g; Carbohydrate: 29g; Fiber: 1g; Cholesterol: 20mg; Sodium: 207mg

Pesto Pasta Salad, page 219 Amount per serving (1/8 of salad): Calories: 464; Fat: 24g; Saturated fat: 5g; Protein: 15g; Carbohydrate: 49g; Fiber: 7g; Cholesterol: 10mg; Sodium: 414mg

Pork Chops with Apricot Sauce, page 105 Amount per serving (1 pork chop): Calories: 310; Fat: 13g; Saturated fat: 2g; Protein: 21g; Carbohydrate: 28g; Fiber: 0g; Cholesterol: 60mg; Sodium: 577mg

Pumpkin Cheesecake Bars, page 239 Amount per serving (1 bar): Calories: 340; Fat: 21g; Saturated fat: 11g; Protein: 6g; Carbohydrate: 35g; Fiber: 2g; Cholesterol: 101mg; Sodium: 285mg

Pumpkin Crumb Coffee Cake, page 267 Amount per serving (1/12 of cake): Calories: 421; Fat: 13g; Saturated fat: 4g; Protein: 5g; Carbohydrate: 72g; Fiber: 3g; Cholesterol: 51mg; Sodium: 221mg

Spicy Chicken Stew, page 66 Amount per serving (1/6 of stew): Calories: 355; Fat: 6g; Saturated fat: 1g; Protein: 34g; Carbohydrate: 42g; Fiber: 6g; Cholesterol: 85mg; Sodium: 1101mg

Tangy Asian Meatballs, page 103 Amount per serving (1/4 of meatballs): Calories: 419; Fat: 26g; Saturated fat: 9g; Protein: 23g; Carbohydrate: 21g; Fiber: 1g; Cholesterol: 135mg; Sodium: 803mg

Tomato Soup with White Beans and Pasta, page 33 Amount per serving (1/4 of soup): Calories: 286; Fat: 8.6g; Saturated fat: 1.5g; Protein: 14g; Carbohydrate: 40g; Fiber: 7g; Cholesterol: 0mg; Sodium: 854mg

White Bean and Chicken Chili, page 67 Amount per serving (1/6 of chili): Calories: 394; Fat: 6g; Saturated fat: 1.1g; Protein: 55g; Carbohydrate: 30g; Fiber: 8g; Cholesterol: 105mg; Sodium: 597mg

Cooking Light

Apple, Goat Cheese, and Pecan Pizza, page 194 Amount per serving (1 wedge): Calories: 316; Fat: 11.2g; Saturated fat: 4.4g; Monounsaturated fat: 4.3g; Polyunsaturated fat: 1.1g; Protein: 11.3g; Carbohydrate: 43.2g; Fiber: 3g; Cholesterol: 15mg; Iron: 0.7mg; Sodium: 419mg; Calcium: 77mg

Artichoke and Goat Cheese Strata, page 162 Amount per serving (1/6 of strata): Calories: 286; Fat: 10.7g; Saturated fat: 5.1g; Monounsaturated fat: 3.4g; Polyunsaturated fat: 0.9g; Protein: 16.8g; Carbohydrate: 31.1g; Fiber: 2.7g; Cholesterol: 139mg; Iron: 2.5mg; Sodium: 561mg; Calcium: 272mg

Bacon-Corn Chowder with Shrimp, page 45 Amount per serving (1/4 of chowder): Calories: 294; Fat: 7g; Saturated fat: 2.7g; Monounsaturated fat: 1.3g; Polyunsaturated fat: 1.2g; Protein: 26.8g; Carbohydrate: 34.8g; Fiber: 4.3g; Cholesterol: 144mg; Iron: 3.1mg; Sodium: 547mg; Calcium: 94mg

Baked Oatmeal, page 259 Amount per serving (2/3 cup): Calories: 281; Calories from fat: 24%; Fat: 7.6g; Saturated fat: 2.8g; Monounsaturated fat: 1.5g; Polyunsaturated fat: 0.9g; Protein: 7g; Carbohydrate: 48.8g; Fiber: 3.4g; Cholesterol: 47mg; Iron: 0.8mg; Sodium: 171mg; Calcium: 148mg

Beef-Barley Soup, page 43 Amount per serving (1/4 of soup): Calories: 341; Fat: 11.4g; Saturated fat: 4.3g; Monounsaturated fat: 4.6g; Polyunsaturated fat: 0.8g; Protein: 24.1g; Carbohydrate: 36.2g; Fiber: 8.2g; Cholesterol: 53mg; Iron: 2.8mg; Sodium: 837mg; Calcium: 61mg

Beef, Cheese, and Noodle Bake, page 181 Amount per serving (about 1 cup): Calories: 283; Calories from fat: 24%; Fat: 7.7g; Saturated fat: 4.2g; Monounsaturated fat: 2.4g; Polyunsaturated fat: 0.7g; Protein: 22.3g; Carbohydrate: 30.1g; Fiber: 2.1g; Cholesterol: 46mg; Iron: 3.1mg; Sodium: 622mg; Calcium: 209mg

Beef Tagine with Butternut Squash, page 99 Amount per serving (1 1/2 cups): Calories: 283; Fat: 9.5g; Saturated fat: 2g; Monounsaturated fat: 4.8g; Polyunsaturated fat: 0.5g; Protein: 25.6g; Carbohydrate: 25.7g; Fiber: 4.8g; Cholesterol: 67mg; Iron: 4.6mg; Sodium: 617mg; Calcium: 103mg

Black Bean Burrito Bake, page 144 Amount per serving (1 burrito): Calories: 365; Calories from fat: 29%; Fat: 11.7g; Saturated fat: 5.8g; Monounsaturated fat: 2.8g; Polyunsaturated fat: 0.8g; Protein: 15.7g; Carbohydrate: 55.3g; Fiber: 7.2g; Cholesterol: 28mg; Iron: 3.5mg; Sodium: 893mg; Calcium: 311mg

Black Bean, Corn, and Zucchini Enchiladas, page 150 Amount per serving (1 enchilada with 1/3 cup sauce): Calories: 348; Calories from fat: 27%; Fat: 4.2g; Saturated fat: 1.8g; Monounsaturated fat: 1.5g; Polyunsaturated fat: 1.5g; Protein: 16g; Carbohydrate: 47.2g; Fiber: 7g; Cholesterol: 20mg; Iron: 3.3mg; Sodium: 878mg; Calcium: 260mg

Black Pepper and Molasses Pulled Chicken Sandwiches, page 49 Amount per serving (1 sandwich): Calories: 294; Fat: 6.5g; Saturated fat: 1.5g; Monounsaturated fat: 2.6g; Polyunsaturated fat: 1.4g; Protein: 22g; Carbohydrate: 35.6g; Fiber: 1.8g; Cholesterol: 71mg; Iron: 3.1mg; Sodium: 698mg; Calcium: 105mg

Blackberry Limeade, page 21 Amount per serving: (1/8 of limeade): Calories: 125; Calories from fat: 2%; Fat: 0.3g; Saturated fat: 0.0g; Monounsaturated fat: 0.0g; Polyunsaturated fat: 0.2g; Protein: 0.8g; Carbohydrate: 31.9g; Fiber: 0.7g; Cholesterol: 0.0mg; Iron: 0.4mg; Sodium: 5mg; Calcium: 22mg

Blueberry Coffee Cake, page 266 Amount per serving (1 wedge): Calories: 287; Calories from fat: 31%; Fat: 9.9g; Saturated fat: 5.9g; Monounsaturated fat: 2.6g; Polyunsaturated fat: 0.6g; Protein: 5.4g; Carbohydrate: 45.4g; Fiber: 1.5g; Cholesterol: 51mg; Iron: 1.4mg; Sodium: 294mg; Calcium: 93mg

Blueberry-Peach Cobbler, page 254 Amount per serving (about 3/4 cup): Calories: 303; Fat: 9.6g; Saturated fat: 5.4g; Monounsaturated fat: 2.4g; Polyunsaturated fat: 0.7g; Protein: 5.1g; Carbohydrate: 52.2g; Fiber: 3.5g; Cholesterol: 58mg; Iron: 1.5mg; Sodium: 189mg; Calcium: 51mg

Broccoli and Cheese Soup, page 31 Amount per serving (1/6 of soup): Calories: 203; Calories from fat: 28%; Fat: 6.3g; Saturated fat: 4g; Monounsaturated fat: 1.8g; Polyunsaturated fat: 0.4g; Protein: 15.6g; Carbohydrate: 21.7g; Fiber: 2.9g; Cholesterol: 24mg; Iron: 1.2mg; Sodium: 897mg; Calcium: 385mg

Broccoli-Beef Lo Mein, page 182 Amount per serving (1 1/3 cups): Calories: 327; Calories from fat: 26%; Fat: 9.3g; Saturated fat: 3g; Monounsaturated fat: 3.6g; Polyunsaturated fat: 1.6g; Protein: 21.7g; Carbohydrate: 39.1g; Fiber: 2.9g; Cholesterol: 36mg; Iron: 3.6mg; Sodium: 382mg; Calcium: 47mg

Broccoli-Tofu Stir-Fry, page 167 Amount per serving (1 cup stir-fry and 1/2 cup rice): Calories: 451; Calories from fat: 17%; Fat: 8.3g; Saturated fat: 1.4g; Monounsaturated fat: 2.6g; Polyunsaturated fat: 3.8g; Protein: 16.2g; Carbohydrate: 78g; Fiber: 4.4g; Cholesterol: 0.0mg; Iron: 2.8mg; Sodium: 581mg; Calcium: 87mg

Broiled Salmon with Marmalade-Dijon Glaze, page 128 Amount per serving (1 fillet): Calories: 377; Calories from fat: 32%; Fat: 13.4g; Saturated fat: 3.1g; Monounsaturated fat: 5.8g; Polyunsaturated fat: 3.3g; Protein: 36.6g; Carbohydrate: 27.3g; Fiber: 0.4g; Cholesterol: 87mg; Iron: 0.8mg; Sodium: 488mg; Calcium: 42mg

Bulgur Salad with Edamame and Cherry Tomatoes, page 224 Amount per serving (1 1/4 cups): Calories: 208; Fat: 10.5g; Saturated fat: 1.3g; Monounsaturated fat: 6.7g; Polyunsaturated fat: 1.2g; Protein: 6.3g; Carbohydrate: 25.4g; Fiber: 7.1g; Cholesterol: 0mg; Iron: 2.2mg; Sodium: 332mg; Calcium: 59mg

Carrot Cake Pancakes, page 265 Amount per serving (2 pancakes and about 2 teaspoons honey butter): Calories: 315; Fat: 13.3g; Saturated fat: 4.8g; Monounsaturated fat: 4.4g; Polyunsaturated fat: 3.3g; Protein: 7.8g; Carbohydrate: 41.6g; Fiber: 2.2g; Cholesterol: 78mg; Iron: 2.3mg; Sodium: 381mg; Calcium: 177mg

Cheddar Burgers with Red Onion Jam, page 89 Amount per serving (1 burger): Calories: 395; Fat: 13.9g; Saturated fat: 5.7g; Monounsaturated fat: 5.2g; Polyunsaturated fat: 1.6g; Protein: 33.8g; Carbohydrate: 36.1g; Fiber: 3g; Cholesterol: 75mg; Iron: 3.3mg; Sodium: 696mg; Calcium: 190mg

Chicago Deep-Dish Pizza, page 197 Amount per serving (1 piece): Calories: 330; Fat: 9.2g; Saturated fat: 4.6g; Monounsaturated fat: 3.2g; Polyunsaturated fat: 1g; Protein: 17.8g; Carbohydrate: 44g; Fiber: 3.2g; Cholesterol: 31mg; Iron: 3.9mg; Sodium: 365mg; Calcium: 244mg

Chicken Tamale Casserole, page 75 Amount per serving (1/8 of casserole): Calories: 354; Calories from fat: 36%; Fat: 14.1g; Saturated fat: 7.1g; Monounsaturated fat: 3.3g; Polyunsaturated fat: 1.2g; Protein: 18.9g; Carbohydrate: 36.3g; Fiber: 2.5g; Cholesterol: 58mg; Iron: 1.7mg; Sodium: 620mg; Calcium: 179mg

Chicken Tetrazzini, page 185 Amount per serving (1/6 of 1 casserole): Calories: 380; Calories from fat: 29%; Fat: 12.2g; Saturated fat: 6.6g; Monounsaturated fat: 3.4g; Polyunsaturated fat: 0.7g; Protein: 33g; Carbohydrate: 32.7g; Fiber: 2g; Cholesterol: 66mg; Iron: 2.8mg; Sodium: 964mg; Calcium: 319mg

Chipotle Barbecue Burgers with Slaw, page 88 Amount per serving (1 burger): Calories: 358; Calories from fat: 23%; Fat: 9.1g; Saturated fat: 3g; Monounsaturated fat: 2.7g; Polyunsaturated fat: 1.9g; Protein: 32.1g; Carbohydrate: 36.3g; Fiber: 2.6g; Cholesterol: 115mg; Iron: 4.3mg; Sodium: 609mg; Calcium: 112mg

Chipotle Sloppy Joes, page 53 Amount per serving (1 sandwich): Calories: 273; Fat: 6.1g; Saturated fat: 2.1g; Monounsaturated fat: 2.1g; Polyunsaturated fat: 1.3g; Protein: 23.3g; Carbohydrate: 32.1g; Fiber: 3.4g; Cholesterol: 48mg; Iron: 3.7mg; Sodium: 724mg; Calcium: 84mg

Cincinnati Turkey Chili, page 83 Amount per serving (¼ of chili): Calories: 408; Fat: 13.8g; Saturated fat: 6.6g; Monounsaturated fat: 4.3g; Polyunsaturated fat: 1.7g; Protein: 24.5g; Carbohydrate: 47.4g; Fiber: 7.9g; Cholesterol: 67mg; Iron: 3.7mg; Sodium: 765mg; Calcium: 237mg

Cinnamon Rolls, page 261 Amount per serving (1 roll): Calories: 234; Fat: 6.8g; Saturated fat: 4.1g; Monounsaturated fat: 1.8g; Polyunsaturated fat: 0.4g; Protein: 3.8g; Carbohydrate: 39.6g; Fiber: 1.1g; Cholesterol: 28mg; Iron: 1.7mg; Sodium: 87mg; Calcium: 40mg

Coconut Cupcakes with Lime Buttercream Frosting, page 240 Amount per serving (1 cupcake): Calories: 196; Fat: 5.6g; Saturated fat: 3.4g; Monounsaturated fat: 1.4g; Polyunsaturated fat: 0.3g; Protein: 2.5g; Carbohydrate: 34.8g; Fiber: 0.3g; Cholesterol: 31mg; Iron: 0.7mg; Sodium: 179mg; Calcium: 52mg

Corn and Summer Vegetable Sauté, page 208 Amount per serving (⅔ cup): Calories: 90; Calories from fat: 27%; Fat: 2.7g; Saturated fat: 0.2g; Monounsaturated fat: 1.5g; Polyunsaturated fat: 0.9g; Protein: 3.7g; Carbohydrate: 15.9g; Fiber: 4.8g; Cholesterol: 0mg; Iron: 1.2mg; Sodium: 232mg; Calcium: 43mg

Crab Cakes with Spicy Rémoulade, page 132 Amount per serving (2 crab cakes and 1½ tablespoons rémoulade): Calories: 292; Fat: 22g; Saturated fat: 1.6g; Monounsaturated fat: 7.8g; Polyunsaturated fat: 10.2g; Protein: 18.7g; Carbohydrate: 5g; Fiber: 0.5g; Cholesterol: 161mg; Iron: 1.2mg; Sodium: 571mg; Calcium: 53mg

Crab, Corn, and Tomato Salad with Lemon-Basil Dressing, page 227 Amount per serving (¼ of salad): Calories: 242; Calories from fat: 21%; Fat: 5.6g; Saturated fat: 0.6g; Monounsaturated fat: 2.7g; Polyunsaturated fat: 0.7g; Protein: 30g; Carbohydrate: 17.7g; Fiber: 3.6g; Cholesterol: 128mg; Iron: 1.8mg; Sodium: 613mg; Calcium: 161mg

Cuban Black Bean Patties with Pineapple Rice, page 146 Amount per serving (1 patty, 1 tablespoon sour cream, ½ cup rice): Calories: 294; Calories from fat: 27%; Fat: 8.7g; Saturated fat: 5.4g; Monounsaturated fat: 1.7g; Polyunsaturated fat: 0.2g; Protein: 10.2g; Carbohydrate: 45g; Fiber: 3.5g; Cholesterol: 28mg; Iron: 2mg; Sodium: 532mg; Calcium: 155mg

Duck and Black-Eyed Pea Cassoulet, page 85 Amount per serving (⅛ of cassoulet): Calories: 307; Calories from fat: 32%; Fat: 10.9g; Saturated fat: 3.5g; Monounsaturated fat: 4.7g; Polyunsaturated fat: 1.5g; Protein: 24.4g; Carbohydrate: 27g; Fiber: 7.6g; Cholesterol: 69mg; Iron: 3.4mg; Sodium: 795mg; Calcium: 185mg

Easy Baked Fish Fillets, page 116 Amount per serving (5 ounces fish): Calories: 223; Calories from fat: 30%; Fat: 7.5g; Saturated fat: 2.7g; Monounsaturated fat: 2g; Polyunsaturated fat: 1.3g; Protein: 33.6g; Carbohydrate: 5.3g; Fiber: 0.2g; Cholesterol: 84mg; Iron: 1.8mg; Sodium: 223mg; Calcium: 56mg

Eggplant Parmesan, page 163 Amount per serving (⅛ of eggplant parmesan): Calories: 298; Calories from fat: 26%; Fat: 8.5g; Saturated fat: 5g; Monounsaturated fat: 2.2g; Polyunsaturated fat: 0.4g; Protein: 19.2g; Carbohydrate: 38.8g; Fiber: 2.6g; Cholesterol: 27mg; Iron: 2.8mg; Sodium: 818mg; Calcium: 422mg

Farfalle with Tomatoes, Onions, and Spinach, page 171 Amount per serving (about 1½ cups pasta mixture and 3 tablespoons feta): Calories: 374; Fat: 13.3g; Saturated fat: 5g; Monounsaturated fat: 6.2g; Polyunsaturated fat: 0.9g; Protein: 13.7g; Carbohydrate: 51.1g; Fiber: 3.8g; Cholesterol: 22mg; Iron: 2.6mg; Sodium: 632mg; Calcium: 212mg

Fettuccine Alfredo with Bacon, page 178 Amount per serving (about 1 cup): Calories: 339; Fat: 11.7g; Saturated fat: 5g; Monounsaturated fat: 3.8g; Polyunsaturated fat: 0.7g; Protein: 17.3g; Carbohydrate: 38.4g; Fiber: 2g; Cholesterol: 22mg; Iron: 0.5mg; Sodium: 833mg; Calcium: 291mg

Fish Tacos with Lime-Cilantro Crema, page 117 Amount per serving (2 tacos): Calories: 394; Calories from fat: 14%; Fat: 6.3g; Saturated fat: 1.5g; Monounsaturated fat: 1.5g; Polyunsaturated fat: 1.5g; Protein: 40.3g; Carbohydrate: 40.1g; Fiber: 5.5g; Cholesterol: 70mg; Iron: 3.5mg; Sodium: 857mg; Calcium: 233mg

French Toast Soufflé, page 277 Amount per serving (1 slice of soufflé and 1 tablespoon maple syrup): Calories: 346; Calories from fat: 30%; Fat: 11.5g; Saturated fat: 5.5g; Monounsaturated fat: 3.8g; Polyunsaturated fat: 1g; Protein: 11.6g; Carbohydrate: 51.7g; Fiber: 2.7g; Cholesterol: 169mg; Iron: 1.9mg; Sodium: 396mg; Calcium: 131mg

Fresh Salmon-Cilantro Burgers, page 131 Amount per serving (1 burger): Calories: 341; Fat: 11.5g; Saturated fat: 2g; Monounsaturated fat: 2.9g; Polyunsaturated fat: 4.9g; Protein: 31.6g; Carbohydrate: 30.9g; Fiber: 1.8g; Cholesterol: 66mg; Iron: 2.2mg; Sodium: 816mg; Calcium: 67mg

Fresh Tomato, Sausage, and Pecorino Pasta, page 180 Amount per serving (about 2 cups pasta mixture, 1 tablespoon cheese, and 1 tablespoon basil): Calories: 389; Fat: 10.7g; Saturated fat: 4g; Monounsaturated fat: 4.5g; Polyunsaturated fat: 2g; Protein: 21.6g; Carbohydrate: 53.5g; Fiber: 4.5g; Cholesterol: 27mg; Iron: 3.3mg; Sodium: 595mg; Calcium: 159mg

Garden-Style Lasagna, page 176 Amount per serving (1/12 of lasagna): Calories: 272; Calories from fat: 27%; Fat: 8.3g; Saturated fat: 4.4g; Monounsaturated fat: 2.5g; Polyunsaturated fat: 0.5g; Protein: 18.5g; Carbohydrate: 31.2g; Fiber: 3.6g; Cholesterol: 20mg; Iron: 1.4mg; Sodium: 589mg; Calcium: 456mg

Gratin of Cauliflower with Gruyère, page 204 Amount per serving (⅔ cup): Calories: 161; Calories from fat: 34%; Fat: 6g; Saturated fat: 3.6g; Monounsaturated fat: 1.7g; Polyunsaturated fat: 0.3g; Protein: 9.7g; Carbohydrate: 18g; Fiber: 3.6g; Cholesterol: 20mg; Iron: 1mg; Sodium: 295mg; Calcium: 233mg

Grilled Balsamic Skirt Steak, page 90 Amount per serving (3 ounces): Calories: 201; Fat: 10.3g; Saturated fat: 4g; Monounsaturated fat: 5.2g; Polyunsaturated fat: 0.4g; Protein: 22.3g; Carbohydrate: 3.1g; Fiber: 0.0g; Cholesterol: 51mg; Iron: 2.6mg; Sodium: 323mg; Calcium: 16mg

Grilled Orange-and-Bourbon Salmon, page 129 Amount per serving (1 fillet): Calories: 365; Calories from fat: 35%; Fat: 14.1g; Saturated fat: 2.5g; Monounsaturated fat: 6.8g; Polyunsaturated fat: 3.1g; Protein: 36g; Carbohydrate: 18g; Fiber: 0.3g; Cholesterol: 111mg; Iron: 1.4mg; Sodium: 575mg; Calcium: 34mg

Grilled Stuffed Jalapeños, page 16 Amount per serving (2 stuffed jalapeño halves): Calories: 56; Fat: 4.1g; Saturated fat: 2.2g; Monounsaturated fat: 1.1g; Polyunsaturated fat: 0.2g; Protein: 2.9g; Carbohydrate: 2.1g; Fiber: 0.5g; Cholesterol: 13mg; Iron: 0.2mg; Sodium: 157mg; Calcium: 55mg

Grown-Up Grilled Cheese Sandwiches, page 48 Amount per serving (1 sandwich): Calories: 376; Fat: 11g; Saturated fat: 5.3g; Monounsaturated fat: 4.8g; Polyunsaturated fat: 0.6g; Protein: 20.2g; Carbohydrate: 50.3g; Fiber: 3.3g; Cholesterol: 24mg; Iron: 2.9mg; Sodium: 876mg; Calcium: 308mg

Guinness Lamb Stew, page 113 Amount per serving (about 1 cup): Calories: 430; Fat: 22.9g; Saturated fat: 8.3g; Monounsaturated fat: 11g; Polyunsaturated fat: 2g; Protein: 26.3g; Carbohydrate: 24.2g; Fiber: 3.4g; Cholesterol: 83mg; Iron: 3.3mg; Sodium: 702mg; Calcium: 50mg

Halibut with Coconut-Red Curry Sauce, page 121 Amount per serving (1 fillet and about ⅓ cup sauce): Calories: 278; Fat: 9.3g; Saturated fat: 3.6g; Monounsaturated fat: 2.7g; Polyunsaturated fat: 2g; Protein: 37.1g; Carbohydrate: 10.9g; Fiber: 1.1g; Cholesterol: 54mg; Iron: 2mg; Sodium: 475mg; Calcium: 102mg

Hot Crab Dip, page 13 Amount per serving: Calories: 63; Calories from fat: 53%; Fat: 3.1g; Saturated fat: 1.8g; Monounsaturated fat: 0.1g; Polyunsaturated fat: 0.0g; Protein: 6.8g; Carbohydrate: 1.9g; Fiber: 0.1g; Cholesterol: 30mg; Iron: 0.3mg; Sodium: 264mg; Calcium: 29mg

Huevos Rancheros with Queso Fresco, page 269 Amount per serving (1 topped tortilla): Calories: 340; Calories from fat: 26%; Fat: 9.8g; Saturated fat: 3.2g; Monounsaturated fat: 2.7g; Polyunsaturated fat: 1g; Protein: 15.7g; Carbohydrate: 37.8g; Fiber: 6.1g; Cholesterol: 222mg; Iron: 2.1mg; Sodium: 970mg; Calcium: 153mg

Jamaica Margaritas, page 26 Amount per serving (⅛ of mixture): Calories: 205; Calories from fat: 0.0%; Fat: 0.0g; Protein: 0.1g; Carbohydrate: 24.7g; Fiber: 0.1g; Cholesterol: 0mg; Iron: 0.0mg; Sodium: 3mg; Calcium: 4mg

Jambalaya with Shrimp and Andouille Sausage, page 138 Amount per serving (1½ cups): Calories: 426; Calories from fat: 27%; Fat: 12.7g; Saturated fat: 3.9g; Monounsaturated fat: 2.8g; Polyunsaturated fat: 1g; Protein: 25g; Carbohydrate: 52.7g; Fiber: 4.9g; Cholesterol: 117mg; Iron: 5.1mg; Sodium: 763mg; Calcium: 99mg

Jane's Vegetarian Chili, page 154 Amount per serving (1½ cups): Calories: 276; Calories from fat: 11%; Fat: 3.5g; Saturated fat: 0.3g; Monounsaturated fat: 1.3g; Polyunsaturated fat: 1g; Protein: 12.7g; Carbohydrate: 49.7g; Fiber: 14.7g; Cholesterol: 0.0mg; Iron: 4.2mg; Sodium: 587mg; Calcium: 107mg

Macaroni Salad with Bacon, Peas, and Creamy Dijon Dressing, page 217 Amount per serving (1 cup salad and about 1 teaspoon bacon): Calories: 208; Calories from fat: 30%; Fat: 7g; Saturated fat: 3.2g; Monounsaturated fat: 2.2g; Polyunsaturated fat: 1.4g; Protein: 8.6g; Carbohydrate: 29.1g; Fiber: 2.3g; Cholesterol: 16mg; Iron: 1.5mg; Sodium: 454mg; Calcium: 44mg

Molasses-Almond Granola, page 258 Amount per serving (⅓ cup): Calories: 214; Fat: 8.8g; Saturated fat: 0.8g; Monounsaturated fat: 4.8g; Polyunsaturated fat: 2.4g; Protein: 4.5g; Carbohydrate: 31.4g; Fiber: 2.9g; Cholesterol: 0.0mg; Iron: 1.7mg; Sodium: 133mg; Calcium: 53mg

Mongolian Beef, page 91 Amount per serving (1 cup): Calories: 237; Fat: 10.5g; Saturated fat: 3.5g; Monounsaturated fat: 4.3g; Polyunsaturated fat: 1.1g; Protein: 26g; Carbohydrate: 9.1g; Fiber: 1.7g; Cholesterol: 60mg; Iron: 2.7mg; Sodium: 517mg; Calcium: 67mg

Moroccan Chickpea Chili, page 155 Amount per serving (1½ cups): Calories: 215; Calories from fat: 23%; Fat: 5.5g; Saturated fat: 0.4g; Monounsaturated fat: 2.9g; Polyunsaturated fat: 1.9g; Protein: 7.7g; Carbohydrate: 36.3g; Fiber: 9.8g; Cholesterol: 0.0mg; Iron: 3.4mg; Sodium: 534mg; Calcium: 102mg

Oatmeal Pancakes, page 264 Amount per serving (4 pancakes): Calories: 273; Fat: 11.2g; Saturated fat: 5.7g; Monounsaturated fat: 3.3g; Polyunsaturated fat: 1.3g; Protein: 10g; Carbohydrate: 34.7g; Fiber: 2.8g; Cholesterol: 91mg; Iron: 2.1mg; Sodium: 526mg; Calcium: 184mg

Pasta with Asparagus, Pancetta, and Pine Nuts, page 179 Amount per serving (about 2 cups): Calories: 385; Fat: 14.3g; Saturated fat: 3.9g; Monounsaturated fat: 5.2g; Polyunsaturated fat: 2.8g; Protein: 14.9g; Carbohydrate: 47.2g; Fiber: 3.6g; Cholesterol: 15mg; Iron: 3.6mg; Sodium: 584mg; Calcium: 113mg

Pasta with Zucchini and Toasted Almonds, page 170 Amount per serving (¼ of pasta): Calories: 344; Fat: 12.7g; Saturated fat: 3.1g; Monounsaturated fat: 6.6g; Polyunsaturated fat: 2g; Protein: 14g; Carbohydrate: 45.5g; Fiber: 5.3g; Cholesterol: 58mg; Iron: 3.4mg; Sodium: 601mg; Calcium: 163mg

Peach and Brie Quesadillas with Lime-Honey Dipping Sauce, page 17 Amount per serving (2 wedges): Calories: 157; Calories from fat: 23%; Fat: 4g; Saturated fat: 2.5g; Monounsaturated fat: 1.2g; Polyunsaturated fat: 0.1g; Protein: 5.3g; Carbohydrate: 25.5g; Fiber: 0.7g; Cholesterol: 14mg; Iron: 0.9mg; Sodium: 316mg; Calcium: 30mg

Peach and Gorgonzola Chicken Pizza, page 195 Amount per serving (2 pizza wedges and 1½ teaspoons balsamic reduction): Calories: 384; Fat: 12.5g; Saturated fat: 4.9g; Monounsaturated fat: 2.1g; Polyunsaturated fat: 0.5g; Protein: 24.3g; Carbohydrate: 42.5g; Fiber: 2.1g; Cholesterol: 46mg; Iron: 2.9mg; Sodium: 643mg; Calcium: 264mg
Pecan-Crusted Trout, page 124 Amount per serving (2 fillet halves): Calories: 267; Fat: 15.3g; Saturated fat: 2.9g; Monounsaturated fat: 7.2g; Polyunsaturated fat: 4.1g; Protein: 27.8g; Carbohydrate: 3.5g; Fiber: 0.8g; Cholesterol: 75mg; Iron: 0.6mg; Sodium: 203mg; Calcium: 91mg
Pork Chops with Country Gravy, page 104 Amount per serving (1 chop and ½ cup gravy): Calories: 252; Calories from fat: 34%; Fat: 9.6g; Saturated fat: 4.4g; Monounsaturated fat: 3.6g; Polyunsaturated fat: 0.8g; Protein: 28.9g; Carbohydrate: 10.6g; Fiber: 0.3g; Cholesterol: 83mg; Iron: 1.5mg; Sodium: 584mg; Calcium: 142mg
Prosciutto, Fresh Fig, and Manchego Sandwiches, page 47 Amount per serving (1 sandwich): Calories: 295; Fat: 5.3g; Saturated fat: 2.6g; Monounsaturated fat: 2.1g; Polyunsaturated fat: 0.6g; Protein: 11.5g; Carbohydrate: 52.3g; Fiber: 4.2g; Cholesterol: 18mg; Iron: 1.8mg; Sodium: 805mg; Calcium: 114mg
Quick Lamb Kofta with Harissa Yogurt Sauce, page 112 Amount per serving (3 patties, ¼ cup sauce, and ⅓ cup rice): Calories: 344; Fat: 16.3g; Saturated fat: 6.9g; Monounsaturated fat: 6.4g; Polyunsaturated fat: 1.1g; Protein: 24.8g; Carbohydrate: 24.4g; Fiber: 0.8g; Cholesterol: 77mg; Iron: 2.9mg; Sodium: 563mg; Calcium: 72mg
Quinoa-Stuffed Poblano Chiles, page 161 Amount per serving (2 stuffed chile halves): Calories: 329; Calories from fat: 26%; Fat: 9.6g; Saturated fat: 4.3g; Monounsaturated fat: 2.5g; Polyunsaturated fat: 2.2g; Protein: 20.4g; Carbohydrate: 47.9g; Fiber: 7g; Cholesterol: 19mg; Iron: 7.4mg; Sodium: 787mg; Calcium: 347mg
Red Lentil-Rice Cakes with Simple Tomato Salsa, page 157 Amount per serving (2 cakes and ½ cup salsa): Calories: 279; Calories from fat: 28%; Fat: 8.7g; Saturated fat: 2.5g; Monounsaturated fat: 4.2g; Polyunsaturated fat: 0.8g; Protein: 15.9g; Carbohydrate: 35.8g; Fiber: 6.6g; Cholesterol: 8mg; Iron: 2.8mg; Sodium: 660mg; Calcium: 142mg
Roast Chicken with Balsamic Bell Peppers, page 57 Amount per serving (1 chicken breast with ¼ of bell pepper mixture): Calories: 282; Fat: 11g; Saturated fat: 2.1g; Monounsaturated fat: 6.4g; Polyunsaturated fat: 1.7g; Protein: 35.9g; Carbohydrate: 8.8g; Fiber: 1.9g; Cholesterol: 94mg; Iron: 2mg; Sodium: 644mg; Calcium: 38mg
Roasted Cauliflower, Chickpeas, and Olives, page 206 Amount per serving (about ⅔ cup): Calories: 176; Fat: 10.1g; Saturated fat: 1g; Monounsaturated fat: 6.4g; Polyunsaturated fat: 2.4g: Protein: 4.2g; Carbohydrate: 17.6g; Fiber: 4.2g; Cholesterol: 0mg; Iron: 1.2mg; Sodium: 585mg; Calcium: 42mg
Rösti Casserole with Baked Eggs, page 273 Amount per serving (1 piece): Calories: 347; Fat: 17.4g; Saturated fat: 9.3g; Monounsaturated fat: 5.7g; Polyunsaturated fat: 1.4g; Protein: 18.1g; Carbohydrate: 27.3g; Fiber: 2.1g; Cholesterol: 220mg; Iron: 1.2mg; Sodium: 605mg; Calcium: 242mg
Salted Caramel Brownies, page 235 Amount per serving (1 brownie): Calories: 180; Fat: 7.2g; Saturated fat: 4.1g; Monounsaturated fat: 1.7g; Polyunsaturated fat: 0.3g; Protein: 2.1g; Carbohydrate: 27.8g; Fiber: 0.8g; Cholesterol: 37mg; Iron: 0.9mg; Sodium: 76mg; Calcium: 26mg
Sautéed Tilapia with Lemon-Peppercorn Pan Sauce, page 122 Amount per serving (1 fillet and 2 tablespoons sauce): Calories: 282; Calories from fat: 26%; Fat: 8.3g; Saturated fat: 3.2g; Monounsaturated fat: 2g; Polyunsaturated fat: 2.1g; Protein: 35g; Carbohydrate: 15.3g; Fiber: 0.8g; Cholesterol: 92mg; Iron: 1.5mg; Sodium: 739mg; Calcium: 43mg
Seared Scallops with Warm Tuscan Beans, page 134 Amount per serving (about 4 ounces scallops and ¾ cup bean mixture): Calories: 314; Fat: 8.7g; Saturated fat: 1.2g; Monounsaturated fat: 5.1g; Polyunsaturated fat: 1.8g; Protein: 33.7g; Carbohydrate: 24.8g; Fiber: 6.1g; Cholesterol: 56mg; Iron: 3.2mg; Sodium: 781mg; Calcium: 112mg
Shrimp Pad Thai, page 189 Amount per serving (¼ of noodles): Calories: 462; Fat: 16.1g; Saturated fat: 1.6g; Monounsaturated fat: 9.1g; Polyunsaturated fat: 4.8g; Protein: 15.8g; Carbohydrate: 64.3g; Fiber: 2.6g; Cholesterol: 86mg; Iron: 3.7mg; Sodium: 779mg; Calcium: 90mg
Slow-Cooker Char Siu Pork Roast, page 110 Amount per serving (3 ounces pork and ¼ cup sauce): Calories: 227; Calories from fat: 38%; Fat: 9.5g; Saturated fat: 3.1g; Monounsaturated fat: 3.9g; Polyunsaturated fat: 1.1g; Protein: 21.6g; Carbohydrate: 12.7g; Fiber: 0.4g; Cholesterol: 73mg; Iron: 1.7mg; Sodium: 561mg; Calcium: 30mg
Snapper with Grilled Mango Salsa, page 123 Amount per serving (1 fillet and ⅓ cup salsa): Calories: 246; Fat: 6.1g; Saturated fat: 1g; Monounsaturated fat: 3g; Polyunsaturated fat: 1.2g; Protein: 35.8g; Carbohydrate: 11.2g; Fiber: 1.6g; Cholesterol: 63mg; Iron: 0.6mg; Sodium: 402mg; Calcium: 67mg
Spice-Rubbed Pork Tenderloin with Mustard Barbecue Sauce, page 106 Amount per serving (3 ounces pork and about 2½ tablespoons sauce): Calories: 235; Calories from fat: 25%; Fat: 6.5g; Saturated fat: 2.1g; Monounsaturated fat: 2.8g; Polyunsaturated fat: 0.7g; Protein: 26.2g; Carbohydrate: 17.6g; Fiber: 1.3g; Cholesterol: 77mg; Iron: 1.8mg; Sodium: 569mg; Calcium: 26mg
Spicy Black Bean Hummus, page 12 Amount per serving: Calories: 148; Fat: 6.2g; Saturated fat: 0.7g; Monounsaturated fat: 1.2g; Polyunsaturated fat: 0.6g; Protein: 4.5g; Carbohydrate: 20.6g; Fiber: 3.5g; Cholesterol: 0.0mg; Iron: 1.7mg; Sodium: 381mg; Calcium: 16mg
Spicy Chicken Sandwiches with Cilantro-Lime Mayo, page 51 Amount per serving (1 sandwich): Calories: 419; Fat: 13.2g; Saturated fat: 1.7g; Monounsaturated fat: 6.1g; Polyunsaturated fat: 3.4g; Protein: 28.1g; Carbohydrate: 46.8g; Fiber: 2.6g; Cholesterol: 49mg; Iron: 3.2mg; Sodium: 759mg; Calcium: 101mg
Spicy Honey-Brushed Chicken Thighs, page 70 Amount per serving (2 thighs): Calories: 321; Calories from fat: 31%; Fat: 11g; Saturated fat: 3g; Monounsaturated fat: 4.1g; Polyunsaturated fat: 2.5g; Protein: 28g; Carbohydrate: 27.9g; Fiber: 0.6g; Cholesterol: 99mg; Iron: 2.1mg; Sodium: 676mg; Calcium: 21mg
Spinach Calzones with Blue Cheese, page 199 Amount per serving (1 calzone): Calories: 297; Calories from fat: 28%; Fat: 9.1g; Saturated fat: 4g; Monounsaturated fat: 3.2g; Polyunsaturated fat: 1g; Protein: 13.4g; Carbohydrate: 40.7g; Fiber: 5.1g; Cholesterol: 16mg; Iron: 3.8mg; Sodium: 818mg; Calcium: 180mg
Spinach Salad with Maple-Dijon Vinaigrette, page 220 Amount per serving (about 1½ cups): Calories: 80; Calories from fat: 37%; Fat: 3.3g; Saturated fat: 0.6g; Monounsaturated fat: 1.6g; Polyunsaturated fat: 0.7g; Protein: 2.6g; Carbohydrate: 11.1g; Fiber: 1.2g; Cholesterol: 3mg; Iron: 1.2mg; Sodium: 219mg; Calcium: 43mg
Spinach-and-Artichoke Dip, page 10 Amount per serving: Calories: 148; Calories from fat: 30%; Fat: 5g; Saturated fat: 2.9g; Monounsaturated fat: 1.5g; Polyunsaturated fat: 0.5g; Protein: 7.7g; Carbohydrate: 18.3g; Fiber: 1.5g; Cholesterol: 17mg; Iron: 0.6mg; Sodium: 318mg; Calcium: 164mg
Steak Tips with Peppered Mushroom Gravy, page 92 Amount per serving (about ¾ cup beef mixture and ⅔ cup noodles): Calories: 344; Fat: 12.5g; Saturated fat: 5.3g; Monounsaturated fat: 4.2g; Polyunsaturated fat: 1.2g; Protein: 27.3g; Carbohydrate: 28.7g; Fiber: 1.7g; Cholesterol: 95mg; Iron: 4.3mg; Sodium: 538mg; Calcium: 28mg
Summer Lemon-Vegetable Risotto, page 159 Amount per serving (1½ cups): Calories: 395; Fat: 12.3g; Saturated fat: 4.7g; Monounsaturated fat: 4.9g; Polyunsaturated fat: 0.8g; Protein: 10.6g; Carbohydrate: 56.2g; Fiber: 7.1g; Cholesterol: 18mg; Iron: 3.1mg; Sodium: 512mg; Calcium: 191mg
Summer Squash and Corn Chowder, page 32 Amount per serving (1½ cups): Calories: 285; Fat: 9.4g; Saturated fat: 3.9g; Monounsaturated fat: 3.4g; Polyunsaturated fat: 1.2g; Protein: 13.3g; Carbohydrate: 37.8g; Fiber: 5.4g; Cholesterol: 20mg; Iron: 1.3mg; Sodium: 605mg; Calcium: 260mg
Swiss Chard Spanakopita Casserole, page 213 Amount per serving (1⁄12 of casserole): Calories: 121; Calories from fat: 35%; Fat: 4.7g; Saturated fat: 2.8g; Monounsaturated fat: 1.4g; Polyunsaturated fat: 0.3g; Protein: 6.1g; Carbohydrate: 13.6g; Fiber: 1.6g; Cholesterol: 14mg; Iron: 1.3mg; Sodium: 449mg; Calcium: 134mg
Szechuan-Style Tofu with Peanuts, page 166 Amount per serving (¾ cup rice, about ¾ cup tofu mixture, and 1 tablespoon peanuts): Calories: 377; Fat: 13.6; Saturated fat: 1.6g; Monounsaturated fat: 6g; Polyunsaturated fat: 4.9g; Protein: 16.6g; Carbohydrate: 50g; Fiber: 2.5g; Cholesterol: 0mg; Iron: 4mg; Sodium: 641.9mg; Calcium: 208.2mg
Tex-Mex Calzones, page 198 Amount per serving (1 calzone and 1 tablespoon sour cream): Calories: 416; Fat: 14.1g; Saturated fat: 6.1g; Monounsaturated fat: 4.9g; Polyunsaturated fat: 1.6g; Protein: 25.7g; Carbohydrate: 46.2g; Fiber: 2.5g; Cholesterol: 44mg; Iron: 2.5mg; Sodium: 771mg; Calcium: 195mg
Three-Cheese Chicken Penne Florentine, page 183 Amount per serving (about 1 cup): Calories: 345; Calories from fat: 25%; Fat: 9.7g; Saturated fat: 5.1g; Monounsaturated fat: 3.1g; Polyunsaturated fat: 1g; Protein: 31.7g; Carbohydrate: 32.9g; Fiber: 2.1g; Cholesterol: 56mg; Iron: 2mg; Sodium: 532mg; Calcium: 275mg
Tofu Fried Rice, page 164 Amount per serving (1½ cups): Calories: 376; Calories from fat: 26%; Fat: 11g; Saturated fat: 2g; Monounsaturated fat: 3g; Polyunsaturated fat: 5.1g; Protein: 15.8g; Carbohydrate: 50.6g; Fiber: 3.2g; Cholesterol: 106mg; Iron: 3.8mg; Sodium: 629mg; Calcium: 79mg
Tofu Steaks with Red Pepper–Walnut Sauce, page 165 Amount per serving (1 tofu piece and about ⅓ cup sauce): Calories: 291; Calories from fat: 47%; Fat: 15.1g; Saturated fat: 1.3g; Monounsaturated fat: 6.4g; Polyunsaturated fat: 5.9g; Protein: 15.9g; Carbohydrate: 23g; Fiber: 3.5g; Cholesterol: 0.0mg; Iron: 2.8mg; Sodium: 661mg; Calcium: 74mg
Tuna Noodle Casserole, page191 Amount per serving (1⅓ cups): Calories: 422; Fat: 16.5g; Saturated fat: 7.1g; Monounsaturated fat: 6.3g; Polyunsaturated fat: 1.8g; Protein: 27.4g; Carbohydrate: 40.6g; Fiber: 3g; Cholesterol: 88mg; Iron: 2.4mg; Sodium: 756mg; Calcium: 293mg
Turkey Reuben Sandwiches, page 52 Amount per serving (1 sandwich): Calories: 255; Calories from fat: 38%; Fat: 10.7g; Saturated fat: 4.8g; Monounsaturated fat: 3.9g; Polyunsaturated fat: 1.5g; Protein: 19.6g; Carbohydrate: 18.9g; Fiber: 3.4g; Cholesterol: 44mg; Iron: 0.7mg; Sodium: 865mg; Calcium: 311mg
Two-Bean Soup with Kale, page 35 Amount per serving: Calories: 250; Fat: 10.4g; Saturated fat: 1.4g; Monounsaturated fat: 5.5g; Polyunsaturated fat: 2.2g; Protein: 11.8g; Carbohydrate: 30.5g; Fiber: 9.2g; Cholesterol: 0mg; Iron: 3.8mg; Sodium: 593mg; Calcium: 189mg
Vegetable and Chickpea Curry, page 145 Amount per serving (1⅓ cups vegetable mixture and 1 lemon wedge): Calories: 276; Calories from fat: 23%; Fat: 7.2g; Saturated fat: 1.9g; Monounsaturated fat: 2.3g; Polyunsaturated fat: 1.3g; Protein: 10.9g; Carbohydrate: 44.7g; Fiber: 10.6g; Cholesterol: 0.0mg; Iron: 4.3mg; Sodium: 623mg; Calcium: 107mg
Watermelon Margaritas, page 27 Amount per serving (½ cup): Calories: 105; Fat: 0.2g; Saturated fat: 0.0g; Monounsaturated fat: 0.0g; Polyunsaturated fat: 0.1g; Protein: 0.6g; Carbohydrate: 14.1g; Fiber: 0.4g; Cholesterol: 0.0mg; Iron: 0.2mg; Sodium: 1mg; Calcium: 7mg

White Pizza, page 192 Amount per serving (1 slice); Calories: 339; Calories from fat: 27%; Fat: 10.2g; Saturated fat: 4.6g; Monounsaturated fat: 2.1g; Polyunsaturated fat: 0.3g; Protein: 18g; Carbohydrate: 43g; Fiber: 2g; Cholesterol: 26mg; Iron: 3mg; Sodium: 712mg; Calcium: 303mg
Zucchini Oven Chips, page 211 Amount per serving (about ¾ cup): Calories: 61; Calories from fat: 28%; Fat: 1.9g; Saturated fat: 1g; Monounsaturated fat: 0.5g; Polyunsaturated fat: 0.2g; Protein: 3.8g; Carbohydrate: 7.6g; Fiber: 1g; Cholesterol: 5mg; Iron: 0.6mg; Sodium: 231mg; Calcium: 87mg

Health

Butternut Squash and Apple Soup, page 30 Amount per serving (½ cup): Calories: 103; Fat: 4g; Saturated fat: 2g; Monounsaturated fat: 1g; Polyunsaturated fat: 0g; Protein: 4g; Carbohydrate: 15g; Fiber: 3g; Cholesterol: 9mg; Iron: 1mg; Sodium: 115mg; Calcium: 84mg
Vegetarian Stuffed Mushrooms, page 160 Amount per serving (2 mushrooms): Calories: 378; Fat: 22g; Saturated fat: 6g; Monounsaturated fat: 12g; Polyunsaturated fat: 2g; Protein: 16g; Carbohydrate: 32g; Fiber: 6g; Cholesterol: 32mg; Iron: 4mg; Sodium: 914mg; Calcium: 222mg

Oxmoor House

Apricot-Lemon Chicken, page 56 Amount per serving (1 chicken breast half): Calories: 245; Calories from fat: 8%; Fat: 2g; Saturated fat: 0.6g; Monounsaturated fat: 0.5g; Polyunsaturated fat: 0.5g; Protein: 39.4g; Carbohydrate: 14.5g; Fiber: 0.3g; Cholesterol: 99mg; Iron: 1.4mg; Sodium: 402mg; Calcium: 24mg
Beer-Braised Beef, page 96 Amount per serving (1 cup): Calories: 265; Calories from fat: 28%; Fat: 8g; Saturated fat: 3.1g; Monounsaturated fat: 3.4g; Polyunsaturated fat: 0.3g; Protein: 25.5g; Carbohydrate: 20.4g; Fiber: 1.5g; Cholesterol: 64mg; Iron: 3.7mg; Sodium: 514mg; Calcium: 64mg
Cheesy Chicken Spaghetti, page 188 Amount per serving (1⅓ cups): Calories: 395; Calories from fat: 19%; Fat: 8.5g; Saturated fat: 4.9g; Monounsaturated fat: 0.1g; Polyunsaturated fat: 0.4g; Protein: 36g; Carbohydrate: 45.3g; Fiber: 3.1g; Cholesterol: 65mg; Iron: 1.9mg; Sodium: 934mg; Calcium: 417mg
Chicken and Shiitake Marsala, page 58 Amount per serving (1 chicken breast half with ¼ of sauce and onions): Calories: 291; Calories from fat: 24%; Fat: 8g; Saturated fat: 4.2g; Monounsaturated fat: 2g; Polyunsaturated fat: 0.7g; Protein: 40.9g; Carbohydrate: 6.2g; Fiber: 0.6g; Cholesterol: 114mg; Iron: 1.6mg; Sodium: 303mg; Calcium: 40mg
Creamy Butternut Squash Risotto, page 158 Amount per serving (1¼ cups): Calories: 326; Calories from fat: 20%; Fat: 7g; Saturated fat: 2g; Monounsaturated fat: 2.3g; Polyunsaturated fat: 0.4g; Protein: 10.5g; Carbohydrate: 55.9g; Fiber: 3.3g; Cholesterol: 7mg; Iron: 0.8mg; Sodium: 814mg; Calcium: 98mg
Maple-Glazed Salmon, page 130 Amount per serving (1 fillet): Calories: 320; Calories from fat: 38%; Fat: 13.6g; Saturated fat: 3.2g; Monounsaturated fat: 5.8g; Polyunsaturated fat: 3.4g; Protein: 36.6g; Carbohydrate: 10.7g; Fiber: 0.3g; Cholesterol: 87mg; Iron: 0.9mg; Sodium: 273mg; Calcium: 34mg
Mushroom-Herb Chicken, page 63 Amount per serving (1 chicken breast half with ¼ of mushroom mixture): Calories: 226; Calories from fat: 10%; Fat: 3g; Saturated fat: 0.6g; Monounsaturated fat: 0.5g; Polyunsaturated fat: 0.6g; Protein: 41.6g; Carbohydrate: 5g; Fiber: 1g; Cholesterol: 99mg; Iron: 1.9mg; Sodium: 262mg; Calcium: 33mg
Smoked Turkey-Lentil Soup, page 42 Amount per serving: Calories: 159; Calories from fat: 16%; Fat: 3g; Saturated fat: 0.6g; Monounsaturated fat: 0.7g; Polyunsaturated fat: 0.5g; Protein: 12.7g; Carbohydrate: 21.3g; Fiber: 5g; Cholesterol: 17mg; Iron: 2.2mg; Sodium: 648mg; Calcium: 26mg
Refried Bean Poblanos with Cheese, page 148 Amount per serving (2 stuffed chile halves): Calories: 303; Calories from fat: 19%; Fat: 6g; Saturated fat: 3.1g; Monounsaturated fat: 0.0g; Polyunsaturated fat: 0.1; Protein: 17g; Carbohydrate: 45.4g; Fiber: 7.7g; Cholesterol: 10mg; Iron: 0.7mg; Sodium: 960mg; Calcium: 232mg
Sweet Potato, Leek, and Ham Soup, page 44 Amount per serving (¼ of soup): Calories: 193; Calories from fat: 7%; Fat: 1g; Saturated fat: 0.2g; Monounsaturated fat: 0g; Polyunsaturated fat: 0.1g; Protein: 15.5g; Carbohydrate: 29.2g; Fiber: 3.6g; Cholesterol: 26mg; Iron: 2mg; Sodium: 625mg; Calcium: 153mg

REAL SIMPLE

Cabbage and Apple Slaw, page 221 Amount per serving (¼ of slaw): Calories: 278; Calories from fat: 82%; Carbohydrate: 14g; Cholesterol: 23mg; Fat: 25g; Fiber: 3g; Iron: 1mg; Protein: 2mg; Saturated fat: 4g; Sodium: 469mg; Calcium: 62mg
Cedar-Plank Salmon, page 126 Amount per serving (1 fillet): Calories: 550; Calories from fat: 52%; Carbohydrate: 19g; Cholesterol: 134mg; Fat: 32g; Fiber: 1g; Iron: 3mg; Protein: 45mg; Saturated fat: 5g; Sodium: 142mg; Calcium: 63mg
Chicken Cacciatore, page 73 Amount per serving (¼ of cacciatore): Calories: 701; Calories from fat: 25%; Fat: 19.5g; Saturated fat: 3.5g; Cholesterol: 247mg; Sodium: 332mg; Fiber: 3.3g; Sugars: 7.3g; Protein: 102g
Chili-Roasted Cod, page 125 Amount per serving (1 fillet): Calories: 151; Fat: 4g; Saturated fat: 2g; Cholesterol: 72mg; Fiber: 0g; Carbohydrate: 1g; Iron: 1mg; Protein: 27mg; Sodium: 241mg; Calcium: 21mg
Classic Beef Stew, page 94 Amount per serving (⅛ to ⅒ of stew): Calories: 520; Fat: 20g; Saturated fat: 5g; Cholesterol: 127mg; Sodium: 1061mg; Fiber: 4g; Carbohydrate: 31g; Iron: 6mg; Calcium: 54mg; Protein: 48mg
Roasted Brussels Sprouts with Pecans, page 203 Amount per serving (⅛ of Brussels sprouts): Calories: 168; Calories from fat: 72%; Protein: 5g; Carbohydrate: 11g; Sugars: 3g; Fiber: 5g; Fat: 13g; Saturated fat: 1g; Sodium: 146mg; Cholesterol: 0mg
Southwestern Chicken Soup, page 40 Amount per serving (¼ of soup): Calories: 381; Carbohydrate: 27g; Cholesterol: 91mg; Fat: 13g; Saturated fat: 6g; Fiber: 5g; Iron: 4mg; Protein: 35mg; Sodium: 668mg; Calcium: 124mg
Turkey and Roasted Red Pepper Meat Loaf, page 82 Amount per serving (¼ of meat loaf): Calories: 610; Calories from fat: 50%; Fat: 34g; Saturated fat: 6g; Cholesterol: 83mg; Sodium: 1089mg; Carbohydrate: 21g; Fiber: 3g; Sugars: 3g; Protein: 47g
Turkey Burgers with Grated Zucchini and Carrot, page 84 Amount per serving (1 burger): Calories: 303; Calories from fat: 42%; Fat: 14g; Saturated fat: 1g; Cholesterol: 94mg; Sodium: 633mg; Carbohydrate: 20g; Fiber: 2g; Sugars: 2g; Protein: 26g

Sunset

Apple Oven Cake, page 244 Amount per serving (⅙ of cake): Calories: 189; Calories from fat: 43%; Protein: 5g; Fat: 9g; Saturated fat: 4.8g; Carbohydrate: 23g; Fiber: 0.7g; Sodium: 203mg; Cholesterol: 124mg
Brandied Cranberry Short-Rib Stew, page 101 Amount per serving (⅛ of stew): Calories: 982; Calories from fat: 70%; Protein: 41g; Fat: 77g; Saturated fat: 31g; Carbohydrate: 31g; Fiber: 4.2g; Sodium: 748mg; Cholesterol: 160mg
Grilled Buttermilk Chicken, page 74 Amount per serving (2 pieces of chicken): Calories: 518; Calories from fat: 31%; Protein: 70.5g; Fat: 17.5g; Saturated fat: 6.4g; Carbohydrate: 16g; Fiber: 0.5g; Sodium: 396mg; Cholesterol: 282mg
Grilled Cilantro Chicken with Pickled Tomato and Avocado Salsa, page 68 Amount per serving (1 chicken breast half with ¼ of salsa): Calories: 746; Calories from fat: 64%; Protein: 50g; Fat: 53g; Saturated fat: 9.2g; Carbohydrate: 23g; Fiber: 4.9g; Sodium: 591mg; Cholesterol: 129mg
Italian Chard Dressing, page 214 Amount per serving (¾ cup): Calories: 318; Calories from fat: 59%; Protein: 15g; Fat: 21g; Saturated fat: 8.3g; Carbohydrate: 16g; Fiber: 1.6g; Sodium: 815mg; Cholesterol: 51mg
Lemon-Ricotta Pancakes, page 263 Amount per serving (about 2 pancakes): Calories: 318; Calories from fat: 21%; Protein: 13g; Fat: 7.6g; Saturated fat: 2.6g; Carbohydrate: 48g; Fiber: 1.4g; Sodium: 759mg; Cholesterol: 116mg
Mojito Shrimp, page 137 Amount per serving (¼ to ⅙ of shrimp): Calories: 150; Calories from fat: 17%; Protein: 19g; Fat: 2.8g; Saturated fat: 0.5g; Carbohydrate: 7.6g; Fiber: 0.1g; Sodium: 301mg; Cholesterol: 144mg
Moroccan Vegetable Stew, page 147 Amount per serving (⅙ to ⅛ of stew): Calories: 292; Calories from fat: 43%; Protein: 10g; Fat: 14g; Saturated fat: 1.4g; Carbohydrate: 36g; Fiber: 8g; Sodium: 741mg; Cholesterol: 2.3mg
Raspberry Lemon Pudding Cakes, page 242 Amount per serving (1 cake): Calories: 189; Calories from fat: 30%; Protein: 4.4g; Fat: 6.3g; Saturated fat: 3.2g; Carbohydrate: 30g; Fiber: 2.9g; Sodium: 83mg; Cholesterol: 82mg
Salsa Verde Braised Pork, page 111 Amount per serving (⅙ of pork): Calories: 571; Calories from fat: 63%; Protein: 36g; Fat: 40g; Saturated fat: 14g; Carbohydrate: 16g; Fiber: 0.8g; Sodium: 1,101mg; Cholesterol: 147mg
Salt-and-Pepper Cheese Puffs, page 15 Amount per puff: Calories: 53; Calories from fat: 61%; Protein: 1.9g; Fat: 3.6g; Saturated fat: 2g; Carbohydrate: 3.1g; Fiber: 0.1g; Sodium: 87mg; Cholesterol: 35mg
Spaghetti Squash with Jalapeño Cream, page 209 Amount per serving (⅙ of squash): Calories: 168; Calories from fat: 53%; Protein: 6.7g; Fat: 9.9g; Saturated fat: 5.7g; Carbohydrate: 14g; Fiber: 2g; Sodium: 447mg; Cholesterol: 31mg
Ultimate Mac 'n' Cheese, page 172 Amount per serving (⅙ of pasta): Calories: 586; Calories from fat: 49%; Protein: 21g; Fat: 32g; Saturated fat: 19g; Carbohydrate: 44g; Fiber: 1.6g; Sodium: 739mg; Cholesterol: 107mg
White Wine Coq au Vin, page 71 Amount per serving (¼ of mixture): Calories: 482; Calories from fat: 44%; Protein: 46g; Fat: 33g; Saturated fat: 7.5g; Carbohydrate: 17g; Fiber: 2.6g; Sodium: 423mg; Cholesterol: 177mg

METRIC EQUIVALENTS

The recipes that appear in this cookbook use the standard U.S. method for measuring liquid and dry or solid ingredients (teaspoons, tablespoons, and cups). The information in the following charts is provided to help cooks outside the United States successfully use these recipes. All equivalents are approximate.

Metric Equivalents for Different Types of Ingredients

A standard cup measure of a dry or solid ingredient will vary in weight depending on the type of ingredient. A standard cup of liquid is the same volume for any type of liquid. Use the following chart when converting standard cup measures to grams (weight) or milliliters (volume).

Standard Cup	Fine Powder (ex. flour)	Grain (ex. rice)	Granular (ex. sugar)	Liquid Solids (ex. butter)	Liquid (ex. milk)
1	140 g	150 g	190 g	200 g	240 ml
¾	105 g	113 g	143 g	150 g	180 ml
⅔	93 g	100 g	125 g	133 g	160 ml
½	70 g	75 g	95 g	100 g	120 ml
⅓	47 g	50 g	63 g	67 g	80 ml
¼	35 g	38 g	48 g	50 g	60 ml
⅛	18 g	19 g	24 g	25 g	30 ml

Useful Equivalents for Dry Ingredients by Weight

(To convert ounces to grams, multiply the number of ounces by 30.)

1 oz	=	¹⁄₁₆ lb	=	30 g
4 oz	=	¼ lb	=	120 g
8 oz	=	½ lb	=	240 g
12 oz	=	¾ lb	=	360 g
16 oz	=	1 lb	=	480 g

Useful Equivalents for Length

(To convert inches to centimeters, multiply the number of inches by 2.5.)

1 in				=	2.5 cm	
6 in	=	½ ft		=	15 cm	
12 in	=	1 ft		=	30 cm	
36 in	=	3 ft	= 1 yd	=	90 cm	
40 in				=	100 cm	= 1 m

Useful Equivalents for Liquid Ingredients by Volume

¼ tsp					=	1 ml	
½ tsp					=	2 ml	
1 tsp					=	5 ml	
3 tsp	=	1 Tbsp		= ½ fl oz	=	15 ml	
		2 Tbsp	= ⅛ cup	= 1 fl oz	=	30 ml	
		4 Tbsp	= ¼ cup	= 2 fl oz	=	60 ml	
		5⅓ Tbsp	= ⅓ cup	= 3 fl oz	=	80 ml	
		8 Tbsp	= ½ cup	= 4 fl oz	=	120 ml	
		10⅔ Tbsp	= ⅔ cup	= 5 fl oz	=	160 ml	
		12 Tbsp	= ¾ cup	= 6 fl oz	=	180 ml	
		16 Tbsp	= 1 cup	= 8 fl oz	=	240 ml	
		1 pt	= 2 cups	= 16 fl oz	=	480 ml	
		1 qt	= 4 cups	= 32 fl oz	=	960 ml	
				33 fl oz	=	1000 ml	= 1 l

Useful Equivalents for Cooking/Oven Temperatures

	Fahrenheit	Celsius	Gas Mark
Freeze water	32° F	0° C	
Room temperature	68° F	20° C	
Boil water	212° F	100° C	
Bake	325° F	160° C	3
	350° F	180° C	4
	375° F	190° C	5
	400° F	200° C	6
	425° F	220° C	7
	450° F	230° C	8
Broil			Grill

INDEX

ACKNOWLEDGMENTS

PHOTOGRAPHY: Melanie Acevedo, 225; **Antonis Achilleos,** 239, 267; **Johnny Autry,** 13, 23, 29, 37, 41, 60, 72, 95, 109, 119, 122, 133, 139, 146, 154, 160, 169, 181, 186, 190, 193, 207, 241, 242, 248, 257, 262, 271, 275, 276 **Quentin Bacon,** 84; **Iain Bagwell,** 101; **James Baigrie,** 127; **Leigh Beisch,** 71, 111, 201, 209, 215; **Ryan Benyi,** 153; **Annabelle Breakey,** cover, 69; **Levi Brown,** 189; **Monica Buck,** 81; **Beatriz Da Costa,** 221; **Jennifer Davick,** 22, 25, 141, 237, 245, 251, 252, 268; **William Dickey,** 76; **Beth Dreiling Hontzas,** 55, 78, 223, 230, 278; **Jim Franco,** 172; **Leo Gong,** 244; **John Kernick,** 203; **John Montana,** 232; **Kana Okada,** 82; **Howard L. Puckett,** 19, 216; **Mark Russell,** 249; **Charles Schiller,** 175; **Kate Sears,** 33, 97; **Karen Steffens,** 147; **Jonny Valiant,** 11; **Dasha Wright Ewing,** 125.

RECIPES: Kathleen Blackman, 245; **Chris Bryant,** 207; **Vivian Chateau,** 250; **Diana Coppernoll,** 24; **Jane Doerfer,** 116; **Carrie Hannah,** 216; **Elaine Jeansonne,** 135; **Jeff Jackson,** 248; **Kathy Kingsley,** 160; **Rebecca Kracke Gordon,** 231; **Chris Lilly,** 222; **Beth Lipton,** 249; **Jessica McKinney,** 278; **Jan Moon,** 233; **Catherine O'Brien Sturgis,** 276; **Natalie Pritchard,** 61; **Denise Vivaldo,** 118; **Laura Zapalowski,** 30.

"Almond Joy" Cheesecake recipe and photo on page 249 reprinted with permission from *You Made That Dessert?* (©2009 Globe Pequot Press) by **Beth Lipton** and photographer **Mark Russell.** All other photos and recipes reprinted courtesy of *All You, Coastal Living, Cooking Light, Health,* MyRecipes.com, Oxmoor House, *Real Simple, Southern Living,* and *Sunset.*

Ask the Expert content excerpted and adapted from MyRecipes.com cooking expert **Marge Perry.**